雅思写作题库全攻略

Ideas and Examples for IELTS Writing

雅思写作官方真题

216题万能思路与高分范文
10年题库　A&G类尽收其中
10大类题材　横扫考前预测

蒋晓刚 / 编著

雅思写作百科全书

○核心技巧 ○万能思路
○高分结构 ○高频词汇

雅思教父刘洪波倾情作序

无忧雅思网鼎力推荐 TOP RECOMMENDATION FROM 51ielts.com

考生备考高分指南　教师备课完美助手

石油工業出版社

图书在版编目（CIP）数据

雅思写作题库全攻略 / 蒋晓刚编著.
北京：石油工业出版社，2016.10
ISBN 978-7-5183-1386-0

Ⅰ. 雅…
Ⅱ. 蒋…
Ⅲ. IELTS —写作—自学参考资料
Ⅳ. H315

中国版本图书馆 CIP 数据核字（2016）第 178242 号

雅思写作题库全攻略
蒋晓刚　编著

出版发行：石油工业出版社有限公司
（北京安定门外安华里 2 区 1 号　100011）
网　　址：www.petropub.com
编 辑 部：（010）64250213　　图书营销中心：（010）64523633
经　　销：全国新华书店
印　　刷：北京晨旭印刷厂

2016 年 10 月第 1 版　2016 年 10 月第 1 次印刷
787 毫米 × 1092 毫米　开本：1/16　印张：24
字数：450 千字

定价：48.00 元

编委会

编著：蒋晓刚

IELTS
IELTS
IELTS
IELTS
IELTS
IELTS
IELTS
IELTS
IELTS
IELTS
IELTS
IELTS
IELTS
IELTS
IELTS
IELTS
IELTS

推荐序 1

FOREWORD

我非常欣赏蒋晓刚老师（John）的这本《雅思写作题库全攻略》。

我曾经在澳洲参加过11次雅思考试。不论是作为考生，还是后来作为校长，我都鼓励学生、鼓励老师们研究评分标准。因为评分标准是考试的指挥棒，也是考生提高自己写作水平和写作分数的必要工具。

这本书不仅深入研究了雅思写作评分标准，而且对考试细节也做了深入阐述。这是所有考生都必须注意的内容。

更令人印象深刻的是作者对于雅思写作题库的了解与写作思路的透彻分析。与传统意义上的单独就某题进行讲解分析不同，本书根据写作真题之间的内部逻辑，归纳出万能思路，举一反三，使得考生得以事半功倍地备考雅思写作。

本书的讲解非常全面而且具体。通过研究考官范文，深入展示各种写作技巧，以及对写作评分标准的深入理解和灵活运用。各种技法的讲解如庖丁解牛，要言不烦。

蒋晓刚老师在这本书里，不仅展示了出色的英文水平，而且中文表述也形象生动。从某种意义上来说，中英文写作水平是互通的。

跟蒋晓刚老师多年前有过交集，因为对学术的热爱，颇有共鸣，希望本书能够为考生们带来更多帮助。

劉洪波

推荐序2

FOREWORD

这是一本雅思写作大全，我特别向所有考生推荐。

本书从考试介绍开始，以评分标准为切入点，在这方面得到了刘洪波老师的充分肯定。

在写作技法部分，从议论文开始，逐一破解议论文写作的各种结构。而且，所有这些内容都结合大作文的历年真题。在议论文阶段所积累的词汇、短语、语法和写作技巧，也是小作文的基础。议论文的写作攻略包括审题、开头、正文、结论和检查。考生只要按照这样的程序，就能很快写出符合要求的答案。

第三章到第九章分话题破解雅思写作题库，涵盖雅思大作文的各类题材。通过对不同题材的讨论，有助于拓宽考生视野，积累语言基本知识。这些话题也是目前考试中最高频、最基本的话题。构成了大部分题目的骨干。

第十章讨论的是报告型的大作文，从出题模式、写作方法，到高分范文，完整呈现。

第十一章和第十二章分别针对A类和G类的小作文。在大作文扎实积累的基础上，小作文并不难。按照本书的攻略，避免记流水账式的罗列信息，可以轻松获得高分。

本书的附录也相当煞费苦心。附录1是完整的题库，每位考生在考试之前都应该快速浏览，尝试展开思路，考虑自己是否能够应对。附录2再度强调了雅思评分标准。附录3是雅思写作答题纸。考生们在自我测试的时候，尽量使用答题纸，这样会更加适应考试。

全书的讲解，建立在深入研究写作评分标准、充分熟悉雅思考试、大量积累考生的经验教学以及扎实的英文学术功底基础上。适合每一位参加雅思考试的学生。

成功=汗水+方向。跟随名师，沿着正确的方向，勤奋刻苦，一定会取得好成绩！

江蕾

微信公众号二维码　　微博二维码

IELTS
IELTS
IELTS
IELTS
IELTS
IELTS
IELTS
IELTS
IELTS
IELTS
IELTS
IELTS
IELTS
IELTS
IELTS
IELTS
IELTS

前　言

PREFACE

专职做出国考试培训这些年下来，帮助众多学员圆了出国留学、移民的梦想，于自己也成就了“桃李满天下”的虚名。回顾这些年的教学历程，总觉得应该写点东西给自己一个交代；同时，也期待给广大雅思考生在备考写作时多一个选择，为大家的备考铺一条事半功倍的快捷小道。原本只是想写本通俗易懂的备考手册，结果越写越多，野心也越写越大，心想着干脆写本既可以让所有雅思考生受用又可供同行参考的写作宝典。于是，经过无数个日夜的资料整理、抓头挠耳、码字排版，书本诞生；诚惶诚恐，期待各位的检验。

本书的创作思路大抵是，根据不同题材整理剑桥雅思近十年写作题库，分析各类话题的内部逻辑，力争为考生们还原出一个清晰的出题脉络，并总结出相应的答题思路。因此，本书在编写过程中十分强调逻辑的严谨性。同时，鉴于众多考生在进行英文写作时往往按照中式思维堆砌一通华丽的辞藻，本书在创作过程中尽量将一些好的词汇表达用不同的字体颜色或下划线予以突出，希望读者在阅读和学习的过程中务必关注上下文语境。

在本书创作过程中，笔者的心理是矛盾的。一方面，希望每个字都能是原创，或者至少在引用相关资料时能给出准确的出处；但是，书中的部分章节（尤其是Chapter 11）还是引用了《剑桥雅思考试全真试题集》系列丛书的相关内容，以便为读者解释官方的相关内容。同时，本书中的部分图表（含答题纸样稿）来自互联网，尽管已在注释处给出相应的搜索链接，但无法考证原始出处。

笔者坚持原创。然，在长期的教学过程中阅读了众多国内外同行的资料，故不敢说完全没有受到影响。倘若同行或者读者发现雷同之处，请不吝赐教，笔者将不胜感激。

本书在创作过程中得到朋友们的大力支持。感谢外教帮忙校稿，感谢无忧雅思网的鼎力相助，感谢雅思教父刘洪波慷慨作序，感谢吕蕾女士的协调策划，使得本书最终得以和广大考生见面。

新浪微博：@蒋干会群英

启优教育

2016年10月　福州

目 录

CONTENTS

CHAPTER 1
雅思考试及写作简介

一、雅思考试

（一）考试结构

雅思考试（International English Language Testing System，简称IELTS），包含听力、阅读、写作和口语四个板块。由British Council, IDP: IELTS Australia and Cambridge English Language Assessment共同所有。

根据使用目的不同，雅思考试分为学术类（Academic Module，简称A类）和移民类（General Training Module，简称G类）。前者主要用于留学目的，而后者则适用于国外工作、移民等目的。A类与G类只在阅读和写作两个板块有所区别：A类阅读文章均为学术类题材，如建筑学、社会学研究等，而G类阅读的前两个section主要涉及海外生存英语，如看广告传单、工作/职场相关的文章等；A类写作的task 1是分析图表，而G类则是书信写作，如投诉信、求职信等。

雅思考试的试卷结构如下：

- 听力：40题，30分钟（另有10分钟转移答案）
- 阅读：40题，60分钟（无额外时间转移答案）
- 写作：2篇作文，60分钟
- 口语：3部分，11—14分钟

IELTS Academic

IELTS Academic module measures English language proficiency needed for an academic, higher education environment. The tasks and texts are accessible to all test-takers, irrespective of their subject focus.

Listening* (30 minutes)
- Four recorded monologues and conversations

Reading (60 minutes)
- Three long reading passages with tasks
- Texts range from the descriptive and factual to the discursive and analytical
- Includes non-verbal materials such as diagrams, graphs or illustrations
- Texts are authentic (e.g. taken from books, journals and newspapers)

Writing (60 minutes)
- Writing task of at least 150 words where the candidate must summarise, describe or explain a table, graph, chart or diagram
- Short essay task of at least 250 words

Speaking (11 to 14 minutes)
- Face-to-face interview
- Includes short questions, speaking at length about a familiar topic and a structured discussion

IELTS General Training

IELTS General Training module measures English language proficiency in a practical, everyday context. The tasks and texts reflect both workplace and social situations.

Listening* (30 minutes)
- Four recorded monologues and conversations

Reading (60 minutes)
- Three reading passages with tasks
- Section 1 contains two or three short factual texts
- Section 2 contains two short, work-related, factual texts
- Section 3 contains one longer text on a topic of general interest
- Texts are authentic (e.g. taken from company handbooks, official documents, books and newspapers)

Writing (60 minutes)
- Letter writing task of at least 150 words
- Short essay task of at least 250 words

Speaking (11 to 14 minutes)
- Face-to-face interview
- Includes short questions, speaking at length about a familiar topic and a structured discussion

（资料来源：*the Internet*）

说 明

2015年4月6日起，前往英国的留学生在选择雅思考试时必须确认自己要选择何种雅思考试。大致可以参照下表：

申请课程类别 / 英国院校类别	英语强化课程、语言课程、预科课程及本科以下课程	本科、研究生及以上学位课程
英国高等教育机构/Tier4高度可信担保方	用于英国签证及移民的雅思考试	普通雅思考试（院校特别要求除外）
非英国高等教育机构/Tier 4高度可信担保方	用于英国签证及移民的雅思考试	用于英国签证及移民的雅思考试

（资料来源：https://www.chinaielts.org/about_ielts/what_is_ielts.shtml）

具体信息请登录雅思考试中文官网查阅。

（二）评分系统

雅思考试采用国际认可的9分制评分系统，准确反映考生的语言水平。每个分数级别有对应的描述。总分可以是整数分或半分。十个分数段及其描述如下：

- 9分　专家水平

具有完全的英语运用能力，做到适当、精确、流利并能完全理解语言。

- 8分　优秀水平

能将英语运用自如，只是有零星的错误或用词不当。在不熟悉语境下可能出现误解，可将复杂细节的争论掌握得相当好。

- 7分　良好水平

能有效运用英语，虽然偶尔出现不准确、不适当和误解。大致可将复杂的英语掌握得不错，也能理解详细的推理。

- 6分　合格水平

大致能有效运用英语，虽然有不准确、不适当和误解发生但能使用并理解比较复杂的英语，特别是在熟悉的语境下。

- 5分　基础水平

可部分运用英语，在大多数情况下可明白大致的意思。虽然经常出现错误，但在经常涉及的领域内可应付基本的沟通。

- 4分　有限水平

只限在熟悉的状况下有基本的理解力，在理解与表达上常发生问题，无法使用复杂英语。

- 3分　极有限水平

在极熟悉的情况下也只能进行一般的沟通，频繁发生沟通障碍。

- 2分　初学水平

除非在熟悉的语境下，几乎只能使用孤立单词或短句表达最基本的信息，不能达成有效沟通。难以听懂或者看懂英语。

- 1分　不懂英语

最多能说出个别单词，根本无法用英语沟通。

- 0分　考生缺席

缺乏评分依据。

（资料来源：剑桥大学出版社的《剑桥雅思考试全真试题集》（*Cambridge IELTS*）系列丛书）

▶ 总成绩

考试成绩记录在成绩单上，包括一个总分，及听力、阅读、写作和口语四个单项分，成绩从1分至9分不等，每一项的分数权重相同。总分即是四个部分所得分数经过平均后四舍五入的成绩。

总分会以最接近的整分或半分报告。为了避免疑惑，采用以下取整规定：如果平均成绩的小数位是.25，就四舍五入到下个半分档；如果平均成绩的小数位是.75，就四舍五入到下一整分档。

- 如果一位考生听力成绩是6.5，阅读6.5，写作5.0，口语7.0，那么他的总成绩就是6.5。（25 ÷ 4= 6.25 = 6.5）

- 相应地，如果一位考生听力成绩4.0，阅读3.5，写作4.0，口语4.0，那么他的总成绩就是4.0。（15.5 ÷ 4 = 3.875 = 4.0）

- 而如果一位考生的成绩是：听力6.5，阅读6.0，写作6.0，口语6.0，总成绩将是6.0。（24.5 ÷ 4 = 6.125 = 6.0）

（三）考试流程

▶ 雅思笔试日期前10天

1．请登录教育部考试中心雅思报名网站“我的状态”页面查看您的考号、口试时间、口笔试楼和教室号，并打印准考证。建议提前查阅好考试中心地址，选择合适的交通方式。

2．请在参加考试前仔细阅读《中国地区雅思考生须知》，了解考试相关重要信息。

请注意

- 口语考试可能安排在笔试前一周至笔试后一周的任意一天。口试时间不能按照考生的要求进行预定或更改。

- 口笔试场地和地址有可能不同于考点场地和地址。

- 所有考试安排均以考试当天通知为准，报名网站考试安排信息仅供参考。

▷ 雅思考试当天

笔试部分：

到达考试中心：

1. 请在上午8:00前到达考试中心。请提前安排好早餐，保证体力。
2. 在考场张贴的名单上找到自己的名字，与准考证核对，确认自己的笔试教室号。
3. 出示准考证，听从考试中心工作人员的指引到候考室候考，并将您的个人物品置放在指定的区域。

进入笔试考场：

1. 到达候考室后，工作人员将在8:00 到8:30间安排考生检录进入考场。
2. 请准备好报名时使用的身份证件和一张6个月内护照照片尺寸的彩照，并在照片背面写上姓名与考号（照片为白底，不可佩戴眼镜）。禁止携带任何其他个人物品。
3. 在考试中心工作人员的安排下在笔试教室前按照考号顺序排队等候。请在排队前使用卫生间。
4. 考场检录时，监考人员会核对考生的身份证件和照片，并告知考生座位号。考生有可能被考场工作人员要求在检录时进行非透视式电子扫描。
5. 根据桌卡找到座位后就座，并核对桌卡上的个人信息和考试安排。

注意

- 晚于8:30到达笔试教室的考生将被无法进入考场，无法参加任何考试科目，并不得转考、退考或退费。
- 除个人必需的药品外，考生的其他物品不允许带进考场，如果考生在考场内携带手机等任何违规物品，将被取消考试资格及考试成绩，并不得转考、退考或退费。强烈建议考生不要携带贵重物品前往考场，

笔试前准备：

1. 进入考场后，监考人员将宣读考试注意事项。
2. 考生的身份证会被暂时集中收起进行查验，并在笔试结束前归还。
3. 监考人员发放听力与阅读答题纸，请根据监考人员指示进行填写（考试答题纸为一张，两面分别为听力与阅读，请注意区分）。
4. 请根据监考人员指示测试耳机，如有任何问题请及时举手示意。
5. 监考人员将会现场拆封并分发听力试卷，指示考生填写姓名与考号。

6. 考试正式开始之前，监考人员会提示考生再次测试耳机。
7. 听力考试录音将会提示考生何时可以打开试卷。在此之前，请勿打开。

笔试进行中：

1. 笔试答题大约将在上午9:00到12:00进行。
2. 在整个考试过程中，考生必须遵守考场规则，并独立完成各项考试。
3. 如果您认为您得到的试卷类型有误，需要帮助，或有其他问题，请马上举手向监考人员示意。
4. 听力考试结束后将有10分钟时间供考生将答案誊写到答题纸上。阅读考试没有专门的誊写答案时间，请考生注意及时誊写答案。
5. 请仔细阅读写作试题说明，注意2篇作文的字数限制。每篇作文都有建议时长，方便考生掌握时间。每间考试教室都有挂钟，监考人员也会提供考试全程报时服务。
6. 当监考人员要求停笔时，请考生马上停笔并放下铅笔和橡皮。否则将会被视为违规，情节严重者会被取消考试成绩。
7. 考生只能在阅读和写作考试期间使用洗手间，使用洗手间前须征得监考人员同意。使用洗手间后，考生有可能被考场工作人员要求在考场范围内进行非透视式电子扫描。

笔试结束后：

1. 考生请在座位上保持安静。
2. 按照监考人员指示，按顺序离场。
3. 请带好自己的身份证件和桌卡。
4. 请勿忘记带走置放在考场外的个人物品。
5. 考生如认为考试过程中有任何干扰因素，请及时向监考人员反映。监考人员将带领考生与主考官面谈，如有需要主考官将安排考生填写书面投诉表格。

口试部分：

1. 请在预定的口试时间前30分钟到达考试中心并签到。未能在考试前15分钟到达并签到的考生，将有可能无法进入考场，无法参加任何考试科目，并不得转考、退考或退费。
2. 在签到时请出示身份证件和桌卡（如桌卡丢失，请向工作人员说明），签到后请保持安静，在候考室候考。
3. 工作人员会在考前安排考生现场照相。照相时，请摘下眼镜，露出双耳，表情自然，并直视前方镜头。
4. 现场照相后，工作人员会将考生指引到口试考场。请在考场外椅子上安静等候，不要敲门。

5. 得到考官指示后进入考场，入场前请将所有个人物品放在椅子上，只带身份证件和桌卡进入考场。
6. 口试考试时间大约为11到14分钟。
7. 在完成口试后，请立即离开考场。不要与任何人谈及您的考试情况，否则会被视作违规，情节严重会被取消考试资格。
8. 考生如认为考试过程中有任何干扰因素，请及时向主考官反映，如有需要主考官将安排考生填写书面投诉表格。

声 明

以上信息来自雅思考试中文官网。考生可以登录该网站查看视频解说。

关于雅思考试当天流程调整的通知

（资料来源：https://www.chinaielts.org/whats_new/ielts_news/59215.shtml）

发布时间：

2016-06-14 10:30

为保证考务流程管理的安全性，自2016年6月18日的考试日期起，雅思考试将全面启用现场照相和生物识别技术，包括指纹采集和验证。考生将无需提供个人照片。我们建议考生在考试当天提前到场以完成个人物品放置、身份证件验证、检录入场等一系列重要考前准备工作。

笔试：

请于考试当天07:30前到达考点报到候考，入场截止时间为08:30。

口试：

请于口试时间前30分钟到达考点报到候考，截止入场时间为口试时间前15分钟。

二、雅思写作简介

（一）考试结构

考试时间为60分钟，共2篇作文。具体为：

	A类	G类	备注
Task 1 （20分钟，至少150字）	Line charts曲线图 Bar charts柱状图 Pie charts饼状图 Tables表格题 Maps地图题 Diagrams/Flow/process charts流程图/示意图	Letters （投诉信、求职信、感谢信等）	/
Task 2 （40分钟，至少250字）	a short essay，如：Some people think the government should pay for those who go to university while others believe students should pay themselves. Discuss both these views and give your own opinion.		A类与G类大同小异

（二）评分标准

雅思写作从四个方面进行评分，具体为：

Task 1 Task Achievement Task 2 Task Response		Coherence and Cohesion	Lexical Resource	Grammatical Range and Accuracy
备注	大体是指考生准确和完整地回应题目中的所有信息。	大体是指考生恰当地使用衔接，使得行文流畅。	大体是指考生准确地使用比较好的词汇表达。	大体是指考生准确地使用了多样化的语法结构。

（雅思写作的具体评分标准请参照本书的附录。）

需要指出的是，写作的评分方式并非完全是是四项分数的平均分。例如：

Overall	TR/TA	C&C	LR	GRA
5.0	5.0	5.0	5.0	5.0
	5.0	5.0	5.0	6.0
5.5	5.0	5.0	6.0	6.0
	5.0	6.0	6.0	6.0
6.0	6.0	6.0	6.0	6.0
	6.0	6.0	6.0	7.0
6.5	6.0	6.0	7.0	7.0
	6.0	7.0	7.0	7.0
7.0	7.0	7.0	7.0	7.0
	7.0	7.0	7.0	8.0
7.5	7.0	7.0	8.0	8.0
	7.0	8.0	8.0	8.0

雅思官方公布的信息表明国内考生的写作平均分是在5.5分附近（详见雅思官方），而这就解释了为什么众多考生的雅思写作很难上6分。实际上，6.0的雅思写作其实不难，但对于很多考生来讲这是个很难跨过去的坎。原因当然很多，但是很重要的一个因素是很多考生的作文将评分标准置之脑后，完全按照自己的意愿来安排写作内容和词汇表达，导致立场不明确、回应题目不完整、句子表达怪异（awkward）。因此，对于任何需要雅思写作达到6分的考生来讲，一定要细心。

（三）样题举例

▶ A类写作（《剑桥雅思考试全真试题集7》Test 2）

WRITING TASK 1

You should spend about 20 minutes on this task.

> ***The graph below shows the consumption of fish and some different kinds of meat in a European country between 1979 and 2004.***
>
> ***Summarise the information by selecting and reporting the main features, and make comparisons where relevant.***

Write at least 150 words.

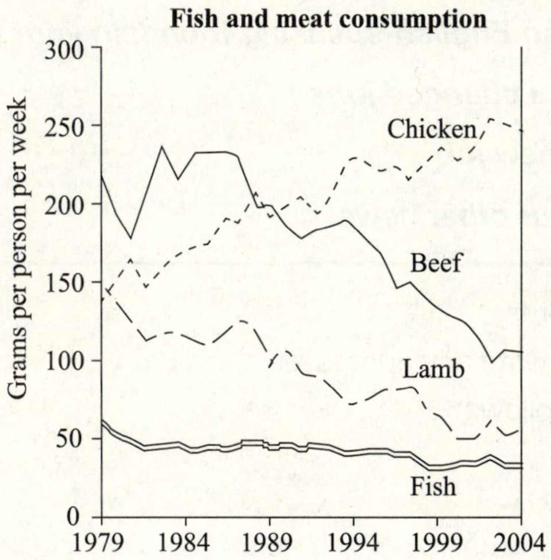

WRITING TASK 2

You should spend about 40 minutes on this task.

Write about the following topic:

Some people believe that there should be fixed punishments for each type of crime. Others, however, argue that the circumstances of an individual crime, and the motivation for committing it, should always be taken into account when deciding on the punishment.

Discuss both these views and give your own opinion.

Give reasons for your answer and include any relevant examples from your own knowledge or experience.
Write at least 250 words.

▶ G类写作

Grneral Training: Reading and Writing

WRITING

WRITING TASK 1

You should spend about 20 minutes on this task.

You have recently started work in a new company.

Write a letter to an English-speaking friend. In your letter

- ***explain why you changed jobs***
- ***describe your new job***
- ***tell him/her your other news***

Write at least 150 words.
You do NOT need to write any addresses.
Begin your letter as follows:

Dear .... ,

WRITING TASK 2

You should spend about 40 minutes on this task.
Write about the following topic:

> ***Some people prefer live in a house, while others feel that there are more advantages living in an apartment.***
>
> ***Are there more advantages than disadvantages of living in a house compared with living in an apartment?***

Give reasons for your answer and include any relevant examples from your own knowledge or experience.

Write at least 250 words.

（四）写作答题纸

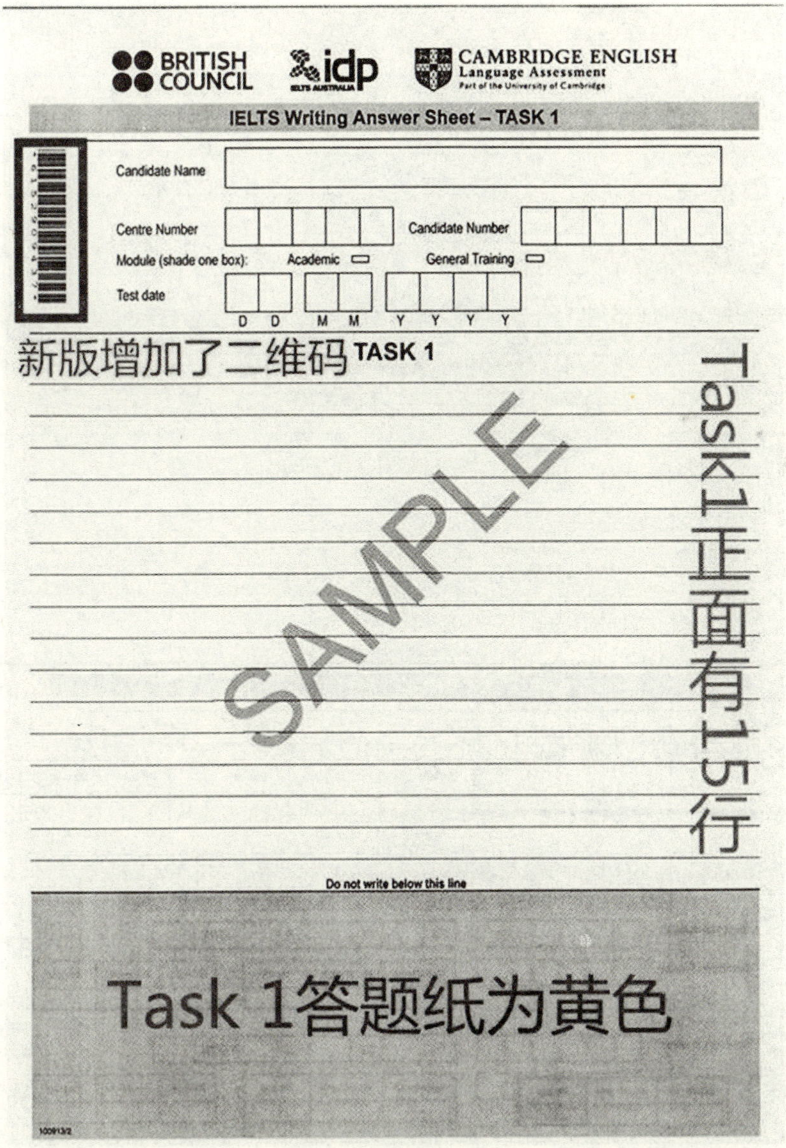
BRITISH COUNCIL idp CAMBRIDGE ENGLISH Language Assessment Part of the University of Cambridge

IELTS Writing Answer Sheet – TASK 1

Candidate Name

Centre Number Candidate Number

Module (shade one box): Academic General Training

Test date D D M M Y Y Y Y

新版增加了二维码 TASK 1

SAMPLE

Task1正面有15行

Do not write below this line

Task 1答题纸为黄色

100913/2

总共有24行，行间距缩小80%至0.8CM

SAMPLE

Do not write below this line

OFFICIAL USE ONLY

Candidate Number:
Examiner 2 Number:

TA | CC | LR | GRA

写作是由两位考官批改，一位打分，一位复核

Underlength | No. of words | Penalty

Off-topic | Memorised | Illegible

Candidate Number:
Examiner 1 Number:

TA | CC | LR | GRA

Underlength | No. of words | Penalty

Off-topic | Memorised | Illegible

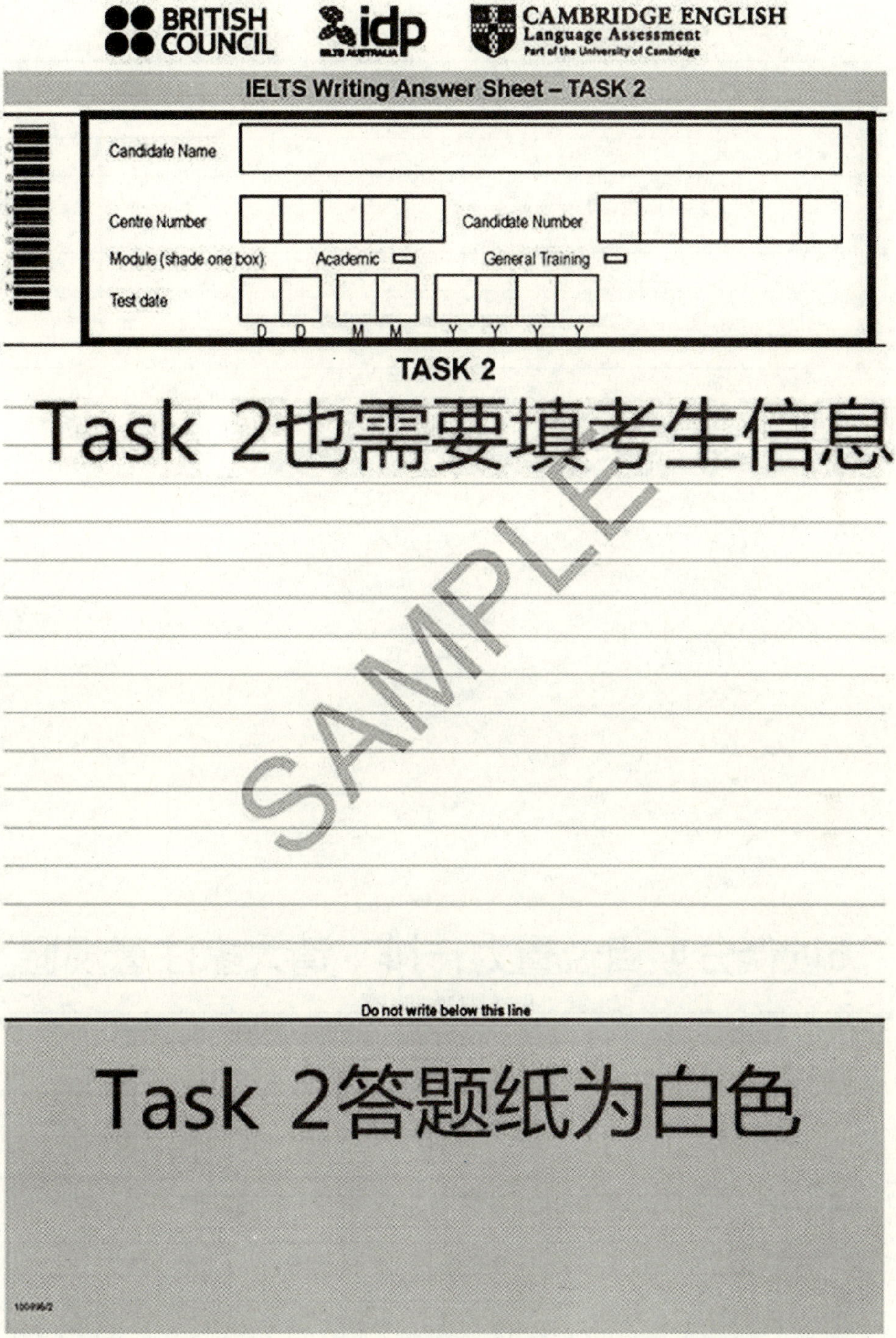

BRITISH COUNCIL

idp IELTS AUSTRALIA

CAMBRIDGE ENGLISH Language Assessment Part of the University of Cambridge

IELTS Writing Answer Sheet – TASK 2

Candidate Name

Centre Number

Candidate Number

Module (shade one box): Academic General Training

Test date D D M M Y Y Y Y

TASK 2

Task 2也需要填考生信息

SAMPLE

Do not write below this line

Task 2答题纸为白色

100896/2

6项低分项目位置为一排，请大家注意规避

Do not write below this line

OFFICIAL USE ONLY

Candidate Number:		TR		CC		LR	GRA
Examiner 2 Number:		Underlength	No. of words	Penalty	Off topic	Memorised	Illegible

Candidate Number:		TR		CC		LR	GRA
Examiner 1 Number:		Underlength	No. of words	Penalty	Off topic	Memorised	Illegible

（资料来源：http://edu.163.com/14/0821/11/A45UHF1L00293L7F.html）

CHAPTER 2
雅思议论文写作攻略

雅思写作task 2（俗称大作文）分成以下几种类型：

- Argumentative essays议论文
- Cause-solution essays原因+对策（有老师管这类叫说明文或者报告）
- Cause-effect essays原因+影响
- Effect-solution essays影响+对策
- Mixed types混合型

本章节我们只分析Argumentative essays议论文，而这是雅思写作中最重要的考题。其他题型将在Chapter 10得到展示。

考生们在拿到一道雅思大作文题目时，往往会显得很迷茫：到底我该用那一种结构呢？是很死板地套用写作模板呢？还是自己标新立异，独创一种写作模式？

其实我认为，雅思写作没有所谓的固定套路。雅思考试考的是考生的英语语言应用能力，只要考生能够很有逻辑地呈现出自己对某事物的看法，在确保语法准确的前提下，官方一定会认可考生的语言能力。实际上，对照《剑桥雅思考试全真试题集》这套书里所收录的官方范文，我们会发现，除非考题很难，否则官方提供的范文一定是用词简练，但逻辑论证十分严谨。在我看来，广大考生在准备雅思写作时，只要按以下几步走，写作目标分唾手可得。

一、审题

我经常跟学生讲，在读懂考题的前提下，审题的好坏与一个人的英文程度毫无关系。审题完全取决于考生的逻辑思维能力，取决于考生的知识面与阅历。纵观雅思写作题库，我们发现考试题材涉及教育、文化、科技、政府、环境、犯罪、工作职场、健康、媒体及社会万象等方方面面。这务必要求考生对整个社会有个基本的认知。而这恰恰是很多考生们所欠缺的。很多考生们一直以来更多的是关注学校象牙塔里的生活，很少接触外界，所以在拿到一道雅思写作题目时往往脑袋一片空白；加上考场上的紧张氛围和压力，最后的雅思写作就难免“杯具”。

带着这些疑问，笔者系统地对比了近10年来的雅思写作真题，发现只要把握好了雅思写作的特点，审题原来也可以易如反掌，势如破竹。笔者通过对雅思题库的研究，发现很多雅思考题本身就可以作为另外一道考题的解题思路。举个很简单的例子：2008年1月12日考了一道题目Some people think the best way of reducing crime is to give longer prison sentences. Others, however, think there are other better ways to reduce crime. Discuss both views and give your own opinion. 这道题目要求考生分析“延长服刑期间”是否真正有助于降低社会的犯罪率。但与此同时，考生还得回应是否有其他方法来帮助降低犯罪率。而2008年9月18日的考题则刚好给出了思路：Putting criminals into prisons is not so effective in dealing with them. Instead, education and job training should be offered to them. To what extent do you agree or disagree? 实际上，这道雅思考题在2005年6月18日也考过。类似的例子充斥着整个雅思写作题库。所以，只要广大考生能够认真回顾历年考题，稍加对比就可以把审题这一块做得很好。

笔者总结出来的审题的另一个高分窍门是，考生先别急着去写自己会怎么看待被辩论的事物。相反，考生应该先设身处地地想一想为什么会出现题目中所呈现的观点。想明白之后，考生再认真去分析一下这些人的看法是否周全，他们的观点是否片面，他们是否忽略了一些事实，并顺着这条思路一直论证下去。如此一来，高分写作自然手到擒来。关于这种写作方法的详细范例，本书“正文的结构与段落的写法”这个板块将予以完整展示。

关于审题，还有一个非常细致的地方是，每一道雅思写作考题中都可能有不止一个信息需要考生去回应。但实际情况是，很多考生通常只瞄准其中的部分信息，然后就飞快地下笔。这样做的后果就是考生在第一个评分标准task response方面失手。要知道，5分的审题是“addresses the task only partially（仅仅部分地回应了话题）”。举个例子：

2015年5月雅思写作考题是：Development in technology causes environmental problems. Some people believe the solution in these problems is everyone accepts a simpler way of life, while others say that technology can solve these problems. Discuss both views and give your own opinion.

本题中，题干有三个重要信息，分别是：Development in technology causes environmental problems, a simpler way of life及technology can solve these problems. 但很多考生在实际写作时只是回应科技是否能解决环境问题。更糟糕的是，

即便如此，有部分考生写的环境问题也没指明是科技导致的。如此审题，写作堪忧。

再比如，2015年2月有一道考题为：Some students take one year off between finishing school and going to university, in order to travel or to work. Do you think advantages outweigh disadvantages? 显然，考题需要考生对比利弊（advantages VS disadvantages）。然而，很多学生往往只写到advantages或者disadvantages；又或者，两方面都有写到，但是没有将两者进行对比。关于这类题目的结构，本章节的“正文的结构与段落的写法”也将予以完整示范。

至此，我建议考生在拿到考题时，务必将题目中的关键信息（key words/phrases）标明，并且先花点时间构思提纲。思路有了，写作就奋笔如飞了。

此外，考生只要再配合读一些优秀的雅思作文及英语新闻，并在阅读的过程中积累一些好的思路和表达方法，则考生在拿到雅思写作时一定文思泉涌。需要指出的是，广大考生们一定要根据自己的目标分数选择适合自己的文章进行阅读，不是每个人都得读8分作文或者考官的完美范文。适合自己的才是最好的！

二、开头段

俗话说，好的开头是成功的一半。英文中也有类似的说法：Well begun is half done. 雅思写作不同于其他英文写作。对于一般的英文写作，我们可以泛泛地将话题的相关背景信息较为详细地改写出来，而雅思作文的开头段需要考生非常简明扼要地对话题信息改写，并明确地表明自己的立场。另外，建议考生在开头段要回应到题目中的所有重要信息/关键词（key words/phrases）。这么做，一方面是答题要求，另一方面则是确保后面的写作不会偏题。

▶ 雅思作文之开头段的写法

雅思作文的开头段一定要具备以下两个要素：①题目中所涉及的相关背景信息，②考生本人的立场。如前文所说，雅思作文的开头段要简洁、切题，同时考生要明确地表明自己的立场。以下为雅思作文开头段的两种常见写法。

方法一：同义词改写。即按照题目所给的内容，用不同的表达方法重新写一遍，千万不能抄袭。注意：改一两个词不算改写，一定要将整个表达方式改掉。

方法二：自己展开。即根据题目所谈的话题内容适当展开。注意：不要谈得太多，更不能偏题，与题目话题毫不相干。同时，考生在写开头段时务必要注意段落内部的逻辑衔接。

例题：Schools should teach children some academic subjects which will be beneficial to their future careers. Therefore, other subjects such as music and sports are not important. To what extent do you agree or disagree with this opinion?

同义词改写：Some people think that subjects that are useful in students' future careers are important and should be included in the school curriculum. Therefore, other subjects like music and sports are of no significance and should be left out. Personally, however, such a claim is quite short-sighted and cannot be sustained.（50 words）

自己展开：Recent years have seen increasing criticism on education in many places, particularly when pragmatism is emphasized in people's life. Pragmatists believe that subjects which are rewarding to young people's future employment should be taught and thus subjects like music and sports are of little significance and should be excluded from the school curriculum. Personally, however, such a claim is quite short-sighted and cannot be justified.（65 words）

再如，《剑桥雅思考试全真试题集6》中收录了一篇7.5分的考生作文，题目为Today the high sales of popular consumer goods reflect the power of advertising and not the real needs of the society in which they are sold. To what extent do you agree with these views? Give reasons for your answer and include any relevant examples from your own knowledge or experience.

这篇文章，考生的开头段摘录为：Nowadays, there are lots of advertisements on television or on the streets. Some people think that the advertising boosts the sales of goods and it encourages people to buy things unnecessarily. This arguments may be true. In my country, many advertising companies produce advertisements with famous and popular actors or singers. People, especially youngsters, buy goods that their favourite singer advertise, although they do not really need the products.

且不说其语法错误，这样的开头段只能算中规中矩。如果考生能够仔细体会题目中的意思，则完全可以写得更好：Nowadays, people's daily life has been bombarded with advertisements of all kinds. Some people even claim that it is the power of advertising that determines the sales of consumer goods. Personally, however, I think advertising is not the only factor that influences individuals' decision making for shopping because people's needs also matter.（52 words）

总之，考生只要能在开头段很简要地切入题目并让自己的立场（thesis statement）被easily recognized and understood，就出色地完成了一个好的开端。正所谓Well begun is half done。有了好的开头，后文的论证自然水到渠成。

笔者补充：

关于是否要在开头段表明立场，有些老师赞同有些老师反对，以至于考生们夹在中间不知所措。其实如果大家去看《剑桥雅思考试全真试题集》系列丛书中收录的高分作文及官方范文，基本都是有明确立场的。并且，从7分写作开始，官方明确表示文章需要present a clear position throughout the response，即通篇文章都要立场明确。所以，别纠结了。Go for it，少年。

三、正文的结构及段落的写法

雅思议论文写作的命题有各种不同的变体。但是泛泛而谈，主要有以下五种出题形式。

题型①	出题形式	某现象/趋势 + Is it a positive or negative development/trend?
	例题	In some countries, some high school students do not go to university directly. Instead, they travel or work for one year first. Is it a positive or negative act?
题型②	出题形式	某现象/趋势 + Do (you think) the advantages outweigh the disadvantages?
	例题	More and more students choose to go to another country to finish their higher education. Do you think the advantages outweigh the disadvantages?
题型③	出题形式	某现象/趋势 + What effects can this bring?
	例题	Nowadays, people perform their everyday tasks, such as banking, shopping as well as business transactions, without the need of meeting other people face to face. What are the possible effects of the phenomenon on the individual and the society as a whole?
题型④	出题形式	某观点 + (To what extent) do you agree or disagree with this opinion?/What's your opinion?
	例题	Many employees may work from home with the modern technology. Some people claim that it cannot benefit the employers. To what extent do you agree or disagree with this opinion?

题型⑤	出题形式	观点A + 观点B. Discuss both these views and give your own opinion.
	例题	Some people say that the best way to a successful career is to work straight after school, while others say that it is better to go to university or college. Discuss both these views and give your own opinion.

理论上，雅思写作考查的是考生的英语语言应用能力。只要考生能够很有逻辑地将自己对题目中所辩论的事物的看法陈述清晰，写作结构本身并不重要。

但事实上，在实际教学过程中我发现很多学生经常用错结构，导致正文中的论证与自己在开头段所提出的立场自相矛盾。因此，我认为有必要来给考生们梳理一下各类议论文写作的方法和结构。

题型①：某现象/趋势 + Is it a positive or negative development/trend?

例题：In some countries, some high school students do not go to university directly. Instead, they travel or work for one year first. Is it a positive or negative act?

说 明

很多考生在写这种题目的时候往往正反两方面都写，原因有两个：一是这么写感觉更全面，公正客观；二是这么写字数很容易写到250字以上。倒不是说不能这么做，而是很多考生在这么写的时候由于过渡衔接和语言没把握好，往往导致自相矛盾。

针对这类题目，我比较建议考生只选一个方面去写，这样可以写得非常有说服力。不用去担心字数的要求，因为只要能够将正文中的要点拓展充分，字数一定可以达到250字。

因此，这类题目的结构可以总结为：

题型①	开头段	改写题目+表明立场	/
	正文	1）1st idea to support your position	Paragraph=topic sentence + supporting sentences + example (+ closing sentence/echo sentence)
		2）2nd idea to support your position	
		3）3rd idea to support your position	
	结论段	总结上文+重申立场	/

具体操作为：

题型①	例题	In some countries, some high school students do not go to university directly. Instead, they travel or work for one year first. Is it a positive or negative act?（gap year，间隔年）
	开头段	It has been noticed that some high school graduates take one year off before starting university. From my perspective, such a practice is positive and can benefit young people remarkably.
	正文	1）First of all, doing a gap year can offer a golden opportunity for young people to develop independence
		2）Meanwhile, young people will get the opportunity to explore the globe and expand their vision.
		3）In addition, students will also have a better understanding about themselves if they take one year off to work or travel, which can greatly help them to better plan their future life and career.
	结论段	In conclusion, I am confident that doing a gap year before starting university is a positive practice for young students because it enables them to see clearer who they are and what the real life is like and helps them develop good qualities to better prepare themselves for future life.

提示：段落的拓展

Paragraph=topic sentence（i.e. the idea）→ supporting sentences（i.e. explain and extend the idea）→ example（i.e. give details or example to support the idea）→（closing sentence/echo sentence, if necessary.）

即，正文段的每个段落可以按照以下结构：段落＝主旨句＋分析拓展＋举例论证（＋视情况而定是否要写总结句将前面的论述扣回到题目上）。

遗憾的是，很多考生都不习惯这种写作模式。多数学生都是娓娓道来，一直前因后果地铺垫各种华丽的辞藻和句法结构，导致段落主旨不突出。而实际上，官方在7分的评分标准中明确指出：present, extend and support main ideas（task response评分标准），present a clear central topic within each paragraph（coherence and cohesion评分标准）。

以上述题目（gap year）为例，第一个要点可以拓展为

First of all, doing a gap year can offer a golden opportunity for young people to develop independence（主旨句）. As is known, when students work or travel to a different place, their parents or guardians will be unable to stay around and get things organized for them. As a consequence, these young people will have to learn to take care of themselves and handle things on their own. All these experiences, I believe, can push them to be independent（分析拓展）. For example, if a British student takes one year off to travel to China, he or she will at least learn to book international flights and overcome culture shock to fit in. it can also be expected that s/he learn to organize time on his or her own（例子）.（126 words）

题型②：某现象/趋势 + Do（you think）the advantages outweigh the disadvantages?

例题：More and more students choose to go to another country to finish their higher education. Do you think the advantages outweigh the disadvantages?

说 明

与题型①不同的是，题型②需要考生对比advantages与disadvantages，因此考生必须两方面回应到。但是，两方面都回应到的前提是立场必须明确。但事实如何呢？

先来看看考生中比较普遍的一种做法：

立场：在我看来，出国留学是利大于弊的。

正文：1）首先，出国留学可以让学生接受更好的教育。中国的教育都是应试教育，而国外的教育则强调实用性。

2）其次，出国留学可以让学生把英语学好。众所周知，学生天天在国外生活，每天都是英语的环境，耳濡目染几年下来，他们的英文能力将得到极大提升。

3）当然与此同时，出国留学也会带来一定的负面影响，我们也不应该对此视而不见。例如，出国留学成本巨大，这可能会给家里造成一定的经济负担。

总结段：总之，尽管出国留学会存在一定的负面之处，但总体上是利大于弊的。blah blah blah……

笔者吐槽：

1. 首先题目没有说是中国学生出国留学，其次也没有说一定是去说英语的国家留学。所以，正文中的两个好处明显是逻辑不够严谨的。而这是很多国内考生的通病。如果考生只要5.5～6分的写作，这也就凑合着过了；但是如果想要更高分数，则务必要逻辑缜密一些。

2. 同时，文章中提到的disadvantage是对于家庭的。我建议最好是围绕留学生这个主体来写。

3. 当然，本文最大的失误在于它并没有有效地论证“利大于弊”这个立场。表面上，文章有提到两点好处，一点坏处，所以部分考生们理所当然地认为2>1。但是认真想想，果真如此吗？我在实际教学过程中，也总有学生跟我辩论说：老师你看，我有在总结段说“尽管有弊端，但总体是利大于弊的”啊。所以，我有证明啊。我的回应是：少年，总结段只负责重申立场，正文段才应该证明立场。而你这样的正文段根本就没能证明出“利大于弊”这个立场。即便是我妥协，让你在总结段证明你的立场，可是你这样的总结段真的有证明出来吗？你凭什么说好处是大于坏处的呢？你这样的总结段其实就跟小孩子耍赖似的：我不管，总之就是好。几年前我看到蒙娜丽莎婚纱摄影的广告，广告词大致是“蒙娜丽莎就是好，范冰冰心中的蒙娜丽莎就是好！”我想说：呵呵～好在哪里？

言归正传，那么问题来了，这类题目究竟该如何写呢？

其实也没有什么标准答案。不过考生可以试着将上述被吐槽的结构做点调整，则问题迎刃而解。

例如：

题型②	开头段	改写题目+表明立场
	正文	1）利① →正面证明你的立场
		2）利② →正面证明你的立场
		3）否定弊端 → 从而突出利>弊
	结论段	总结上文+重申立场

具体操作为：

<table>
<tr><td rowspan="7">题型②</td><td>例题</td><td>More and more students choose to go to another country to finish their higher education. Do you think the advantages outweigh the disadvantages?（出国留学）</td></tr>
<tr><td>开头段</td><td>These days, a growing number of young people further their studies overseas.（From time to time, people fiercely debate over the pros and cons such an act can bring to young people.）The purpose of this essay is to examine that studying abroad can be a very rewarding experience to young people.</td></tr>
<tr><td rowspan="3">正文</td><td>1）The first point to make is that young people can have access to a different yet usually better education when studying abroad.</td></tr>
<tr><td>2）The second important point to make is that students can have a golden opportunity to develop their language skills.</td></tr>
<tr><td>3）As for the potential problems of studying overseas, I would say it is merely because of culture shock and language barrier. Thus, if students can get themselves familiarized with the new culture through the Internet and learn the language from their foreign teachers and friends, they will easily fit into the new life.</td></tr>
<tr><td>结论段</td><td>In conclusion, young people can gain academic advantages and develop critical skills for future career and life if they further their studies overseas. Overall, it is a positive thing for them.</td></tr>
</table>

我个人认为，上述结构中，正文第三段的写法很关键。因为如果考生只是写一个弊端，则只是表面上呈现出利弊2:1的结构，但实际上并未证明利>弊。所以，建议考生在写作时一定要立场明确，并且保证整个文章在逻辑上是前后一致。

题型③：某现象/趋势 + What effects can this bring?

例题：Nowadays, people perform their everyday tasks, such as banking, shopping as well as business transactions, without the need of meeting other people face to face. What are the possible effects of the phenomenon on the individual and the society as a whole?

说 明

由于这类题目并未明确要求考生从正反两方面做出选择，所以考生的可操作性比较大。即，考生既可以用题型①的方式只写一方面，也可以用题型②的方式对比两方面。当然，考生还可以不做任何对比，而是将正反双方都写出来即可。例如：

例题	Nowadays, people perform their everyday tasks, such as banking, shopping as well as business transactions, without the need of meeting other people face to face. What are the possible effects of the phenomenon on the individual and the society as a whole?
开头段	With improved technology, people are now able to get many daily tasks done without leaving home. For example, people can make purchases online, wire money online and even work from home. From my perspective, such a trend can exert both positive and negative effects on individuals and society.
正文	1）On the bright side, both individuals and society can benefit from the convenience and higher productivity it brings. Specifically, ...
	2）Yet there is also the dark side. For society, ...
	3）当然，如果考生愿意，还可以在此对比评论一下利弊谁多谁少。
结论段	In conclusion, ...

题型④：某观点A +（To what extent）do you agree or disagree with this opinion?/ What's your opinion?

例题：Many employees may work from home with modern technology. Some people claim that it cannot benefit the employers. To what extent do you agree or disagree with this opinion?

说 明

针对这种题型，我建议考生选一方写，即要么同意，要么反对。在实际教学过程中，发现有些学生总是说“I partly agree with the opinion.”或者是“I do not completely agree with the opinion.”

我认为，既然题目让考生做出选择，考生最好就给个明确的看法。就好比如果题目问“梁朝伟是个好演员。请问你同意还是反对这个观点？”或者说“刘德华是位帅哥。请问你同意还是反对？”你总不好说“梁朝伟的演技时好时坏”；而“刘德华时帅时不帅”吧。尽管理论上讲，我们可以争辩说“梁朝伟在××电影中演技如神，而在××影片中则演技笨拙”；而“刘德华年轻时很帅，老了则不帅”。问题是，考场上多数考生很难在40分钟内如此理性高效地对正反两方面都做如此深入的分析。所以，我建议考生立场明确些，同意就同意，反对就反对。

需要指出的是，不管考生同意还是反对，思路和结构都应该简洁明了。建议考生参考以下结构写作：

▶ 当考生同意题目中的观点时，可以用题型①的结构。

<table>
<tr><td rowspan="5">题型</td><td>开头段</td><td>改写题目+表明立场</td><td>/</td></tr>
<tr><td rowspan="3">正文</td><td>1）1st idea to support your position</td><td rowspan="3">Paragraph=topic sentence + supporting sentences + example（+ closing sentence/ echo sentence）</td></tr>
<tr><td>2）2nd idea to support your position</td></tr>
<tr><td>3）3rd idea to support your position</td></tr>
<tr><td>结论段</td><td>总结上文+重申立场</td><td>/</td></tr>
</table>

具体操作为：

<table>
<tr><td>例题</td><td>Many employees may work from home with modern technology. Some people claim that it cannot benefit the employers. To what extent do you agree or disagree with this opinion?（在家办公）</td></tr>
<tr><td>开头段</td><td>People say that when employees work from home, the employer can not benefit much from it. Personally, I agree that the employer should be worried because it can bring problems to the business.</td></tr>
<tr><td rowspan="3">正文</td><td>1）First of all, employees' productivity will take a dive.</td></tr>
<tr><td>2）Meanwhile, home office keeps employees away from their colleagues and ruins the team spirit among them.</td></tr>
<tr><td>3）In addition, home office also cut off the emotional connection between employees and the business, which can weaken their loyalty to the employer.</td></tr>
<tr><td>结论段</td><td>In conclusion, ...</td></tr>
</table>

▶ 当考生反对题目中的观点时，也可以用题型①的结构。

<table>
<tr><td rowspan="5">题型</td><td>开头段</td><td>改写题目+表明立场</td><td>/</td></tr>
<tr><td rowspan="3">正文</td><td>1）1st idea to support your position</td><td rowspan="3">Paragraph=topic sentence + supporting sentences + example（+ closing sentence/ echo sentence）</td></tr>
<tr><td>2）2nd idea to support your position</td></tr>
<tr><td>3）3rd idea to support your position</td></tr>
<tr><td>结论段</td><td>总结上文+重申立场</td><td>/</td></tr>
</table>

具体操作为：

例题	Many employees may work from home with modern technology. Some people claim that it cannot benefit the employers. To what extent do you agree or disagree with this opinion?（在家办公）
开头段	The improvement of technology makes it possible for people to get their work done at home. Yet some people say that this new work pattern can hardly benefit the employer. Personally, however, I believe the employer can reap great benefits from it.
正文	1）First of all, home office can save the employer costs.
	2）Meanwhile, with the humanity of this employee-centered management, employees will be more loyal to the corporation.
	3）In addition, home office enables employees to better organize their time to work, and thus there will be a higher productivity among them.
结论段	In conclusion, ...

▶ 当考生反对题目中的观点时，还可以用“反驳型”的写作结构。

反驳型	开头段	改写题目＋表明立场	/
	正文	1）改写题目中的观点→设身处地想一想为什么出现这种看法，即人们究竟是出于什么样的考虑或者忧虑才会提出这种看法（要言简意赅）→指出对方其实忽略了某个/某些事实，从而驳倒对方→最后再次改写/强调你自己的立场	注意：①对方的理由可能很多，挑一个即可；②反驳时一定是针对前面的理由来反驳；③最后再次强调自己的立场是为了上下文的连贯与衔接，放到下一段的段首也行。
		2）1st idea to support your position	也可合并，将所有理由写在同一段。
		3）2nd idea to support your position	
	结论段	总结上文＋重申立场	/

说 明

这个结构其实非常实用。因为它至少有以下几个优势：

1. 立场足够明确。
2. 正反两方面都回应到了。

3. 逻辑非常严谨，得理不饶人。
4. 字数多：在题型①的结构基础上多出了一段反驳的段落。
5. 用这种思路去审题不仅不容易偏题，而且扣题扣得十分好。

按照“反驳型”的结构，“在家办公”一文的具体操作为：

例题	Many employees may work from home with modern technology. Some people claim that it cannot benefit the employers. To what extent do you agree or disagree with this opinion?（在家办公）
开头段	The improvement of technology makes it possible for people to get their work done at home. Yet some people say that this new work pattern can hardly benefit the employer. Personally, however, I believe the employer can reap great benefits from it.
正文	1）People always assume that computer-assisted home office (for employees) benefits employers little because when employees work from home, without the supervision of the employer or superior, chances are the employees would slack off or take this opportunity to take care of personal matters. However, I think these people fail to realize that most employers are result-oriented, and when the employer assigns tasks to his or her subordinates, a deadline will also be attached. In other words, there is no need to be concerned about employees' productivity at home. Employers, unsurprisingly, can also benefit remarkably from such a working style.
	2）For one thing, with the humanity of this employee-centered management, employees will be more loyal to the corporation.
	3）For another, home office enables employees to better organize their time to work, and thus there will be a higher productivity among them.
结论段	In conclusion, ...

前文提到，用这种思路去审题不仅不容易偏题，而且扣题扣得十分好。我们举个例子予以说明：

Schools should teach children some academic subjects which will be beneficial to their future careers. Therefore, other subjects such as music and sports are not important. To what extent do you agree or disagree with this opinion?

读完题目后，考生不妨合上书，想一想自己会怎么回应这道题目。之后再参考本书提供的答题思路。

在实际教学中，我发现绝大多数学生的答题思路是：

立场：我反对题中观点；在我看来，音乐课和体育课非常重要，一定要教。

正文：

1）整天学习会让学生身心疲惫，开设音乐课和体育课可以调节。这样，学生会更好地学习。
2）学生不应该只学某几门学科，应该要德智体美学全面发展。
3）音乐可以让人陶冶情操。
4）体育可以让人锻炼身体，而身体是革命的本钱。

结论段：总之，音乐和体育非常重要。

评论：且不说上述答题思路是否回应到了题目中的所有信息（academic subjects, future careers, other subjects such as music and sports, ），光是上述观点本身能否写得的有说服力就值得商榷，尤其是第三点。情操是什么？为什么陶冶情操很重要？不陶冶可不可以？

接下来我们用“反驳型”的结构来审题：

我们来想一想，为什么人们会认为”other subjects such as music and sports are not important”？原因可能很多，不过题目本身就有提示了，即“Schools should teach children some academic subjects which will be beneficial to their future careers.”题目中的“therefore”起了很关键的作用。原来人们之所以说音乐和体育这类学科不重要是因为它们对年轻人未来的职业没有帮助。

搞清楚了这个逻辑，我们就得去证明其实音乐和体育这样的课程对以后的职业其实是有帮助的，从而来反驳人们的看法。那么，音乐和体育这些课程对以后的职业究竟有何帮助呢？考生们马上会想到：很多人其实很有音乐天分和体育天赋，而且他们将来说不定会从事与音乐和体育相关的行业/职业，所以当然要教这些课程了。

这个思路也对。不过我更希望考生们能够想得再严谨一些，即泛泛而谈，即使一个人不从事相关行业时，音乐和体育这样的课程对其职业是否有帮助。答案是肯定的。试想一下，无论一个人将来从事什么职业，他都需要学会团队合作。体育课（尤其是团队体育）可以让年轻人学会妥协、合作、分享以及承担责任。这些品质对一个人的职业生涯的帮助太大了。至于音乐，尽管它的作用不如体育课这么直接，它可以帮助人们很好地应对职场压力。

至此，我们已经很好地论证了音乐和体育课程对职业的好处。如果在这个基础上，考生能够再进一步证明这些课程在其他方面对于年轻人的利好，则本文势必高分。

那么，音乐和体育这类课程对学生还有什么其他的好处呢？在我看来，音乐会让年轻人学会去欣赏生活中的美好事物，例如亲情、友情、爱情等等。正如歌词里唱的：爱情不是你想买想买就能买（《爱情买卖》）。我们喜欢一首歌，不仅仅是因为它的旋律优美，很多时候还因为它的歌词打动人心，发人深省。此外，如果音乐课教的是民族音乐或者传统音乐，则它还可以让年轻人了解民族文化。至于体育课，就像多数考生所说的，可以让学生强身健体，避免久坐不动的生活。

说到这里，考生们可以回头对比一下之前的答题思路和“反驳型”答题思路的审题哪个做得更好。答案是不言而喻的。

当然，有了上述的答题思路后，考生不是一定要用“反驳型”的结构写作，也可以用正常的结构写，只是记得当你不同意题目中的观点时，你可以用“反驳型”的结构去审题，找观点。

注意事项

- 但在“反驳型”结构的实际应用中，偶尔会碰到一个很尴尬的事实，即考生明显不赞同题目中出现的观点；但是当考生试着去反驳对方时，却又发现对方的理由很有道理，很难驳倒。

举个例子：Nowadays many people enjoy dangerous sports such as mountain climbing or parachuting. Governments should ban these sports to protect the safety of the people. To what extent do you agree or disagree with this opinion?

对于极限运动（extreme sports, X-sports）这项活动，我相信大多数考生都会认为没有必要去禁止。所以，按照我们前面的逻辑结构，我们先不急着去写为什么我们认为要保留极限运动。我们先分析一下为什么有些人认为要禁止极限运动，找到他们的理由后我们再看看他们的逻辑上是否存在漏洞并加以反驳。至于禁止极限运动的理由，题目中已经说得很清楚，即extreme sports are dangerous and the government need to protect the safety of the people. 对于这个理由，考生是否也能够做到像“在家办公”那样很轻松地便将其驳倒？答案是否定的。毕竟，相对而言，极限运动的本质就是危险的。无论采取什么措施，其危险的性质不会改变。

针对这种情况的题目，我建议考生们不用正面去反驳对方，而应该采取妥协的做法。即，承认极限运动在一定程度上讲确实很危险，但是仅仅因为危险并不意味着它应该被禁止掉；实际上，只要能够采取相应措施对其予以规范和约束，非常有必要保留极限运动。然后，考生再顺着这个思路去写为什么要保留极限运动以及应该如何来规范它。有了这个思路，这类题目的解答便游刃有余。请看“极限运动”的完整范文。

极限运动

Nowadays many people enjoy dangerous sports such as mountain climbing or parachuting. Governments should ban these sports to protect the safety of the people. To what extent do you agree or disagree with this opinion?

It is reported that many people lose their lives when doing extreme sports. Thus, some people propose that such activities should be banned for the sake of people's safety. Although I agree that there are dangers associated with extreme sports, I think it is wrong to ban these pursuits.

Some people would say that extreme sports can cause injuries or even death to participants and this is not good to society. For this reason, the government needs to take action to prevent people from doing those activities. Personally, I would not deny the dangers of extreme sports. However, simply because extreme sports are dangerous does not necessarily mean such activities should be banned. As a matter of fact, it is necessary to keep extreme sports as long as actions can be taken to restrict and regulate these pursuits.

It is important to stress that, for some people, extreme sports help them handle the intense pressure from work or life; and it is individuals' basic right to do what they like as long as it is not against the law, nor is it morally wrong. Should these sports be banned, it would be an infringement of people's right.

Yet in the meanwhile, it is important to stress that certain sports should be regulated. For example, if a person decides to go rock-climbing or parachuting, he or she must be required to take some training and obtain a license. The government should also tighten up its regulation on clubs or organizations that run extreme sports service. For instance, stricter rules on certification or license would push those service providers to attach more importance to safety concerns.

In conclusion, I do not see any reason to impose a ban on extreme sports despite the potential risks to participants. As long as both participants' behavior and related associations' business can be regulated, extreme sports should be just left alone.

上面“极限运动”这篇文章便是对反驳型结构的灵活应用——妥协型，即打得过就打，打不过就躲。但是考生们一定要躲的有条不紊，不要太心急，否则就容易成为“逃兵”。类似的情况在“动物实验”（animal experiments）“政府审查影视暴力”（censorship on violence in TV program and movies）等文章中同样适用。

题型⑤：观点A + 观点B. Discuss both these views and give your own opinion.

例题：Some people say that the best way to a successful career is to work straight after school, while others say that it is better to go to university or college. Discuss both these views and give your own opinion.

说 明

这类题目属于比较麻烦的一类，也是很多考生容易出错的一类。先来看看很常见的一种写法。

<table>
<tr><td rowspan="5">题型⑤</td><td>开头段</td><td>Whether working straight after school or studying in university or college is the best way to have a successful career has always been a hot topic. While some people think working straight after school is better, others say that studying in university is better. Before presenting my opinion, it is necessary to look into both sides of the topics. (或 Speaking for myself, I prefer the latter.)</td></tr>
<tr><td rowspan="3">正文</td><td>1) Some people think working straight after school is the best way to have a successful career. Firstly...Meanwhile, ... Besides, ...</td></tr>
<tr><td>2) However, some others say that it is better to go to university or college. Their reasons are as follows. First and foremost, ... Moreover, ... In addition, ...</td></tr>
<tr><td>3) Personally, although both sides have reasons, I prefer the latter, because...</td></tr>
<tr><td>结论段</td><td>In conclusion, I think that if people want to have a successful career, they should go to university or college first.</td></tr>
</table>

注：有些作文也会不写结论段，而是将正文第三段作文结论段。

表面上，上面这个结构很好：有按照题目的要求回应到两方面，而且字数也很容易写到。正因为如此，这个结构深受广大考生喜欢，我在实际教学过程中经常批改到这种模式的作文。我想说，对于广大的6.0分以下的考生来讲，这个结构的确可以借鉴。但若考生想要6.0分甚至更高的分数，则不建议这么写。

让我们来看一下上面这个结构有什么不妥之处。

首先，它的正文并没有按照题目的要求去“discuss both these views”，而只是观点的罗列，就像是列购物清单。请注意，真正的“discuss both these views”应该要体现考生对这些观点的评论。

其次，上述结构中的正文部分并没有体现出考生在开头段及结论段所提出的立场。如果考生真的支持后者，就应该在正文部分去予以论证。

请考生们记住，官方的评分标准里明确表明，高分作文需要一个非常清晰的立场，而且要贯穿全文（present a clear position throughout the response）；高分作文需要每段都有一个明确的主旨句（present a central topic within each paragraph）。不言而喻的是，正文中每段话的主旨句都应该呼应到开头段提出的立场，这样才能让结论段顺理成章地重申这个立场。

那么，如何写好题型⑤这类作文呢？

实际上，要写好题型⑤这类作文，考生需要非常冷静的头脑和淡定的心态来审题。就平常练习而言，我建议考生在拿到题目后，先冷静地只看第一方的观点，看看自己想同意还是反对；然后，再看看另一方的观点，想一想只针对这方观点时自己又有什么评论想发表又或是有什么可以吐槽。此时，考生其实对两方的观点都有了比较明确的态度了；接下来要做的就是用一句话来综合概括一下自己的看法，而这句话其实就可以放在开头段中作为自己的立场。正常情况下，这个立场会有将题目中两方面的信息都涵盖进去，而考生只需按照这个立场去正常写正文就好，因为只要立场明确且涵盖了题目中的所有关键信息，则正文段的论证也势必会回应到所有这些信息。

▶ 举个例子：越来越多的年轻人上大学

Some people say that the country will benefit greatly when a higher percentage of young people go to university, while others say that this will only lead to graduate unemployment. Discuss both these views and give your own opinion.

针对第一方的观点 the country will benefit greatly when a higher percentage of young people go to university，我认为挺有道理的。毕竟，当越来越多的年轻人接受了高等教育，国家就可以储备大量的人才，国家的创新能力就可以得以提升。中国这些年的发展就可以充分证明这一点。

针对第二方的观点 this will only lead to graduate unemployment，我认为它挺偏激的。的确，当大学生多了，就业压力确实会加大，但不能说"只会导致（大学）毕业生失业"。毕竟接受了大学教育，年轻人自身的竞争力会得到提升，而国家也会从中受益嘛。

由此，我的立场可以总结为：我承认会加大年轻人的就业压力，但是如果说它只带来问题则太武断了，因为实际上长远来看年轻人和国家都可以从中受益。

题型⑤	开头段立场	Personally, I think it is ridiculous to say that such a trend would only result in graduate unemployment because in the long term both young people themselves and the country can reap remarkable benefits from it.
	正文	1）I can understand people's concern about the possible unemployment issue that university graduates face when university enrolment expands...
		2）However, I think it is irresponsible for people to say that graduate unemployment is the only effect such a trend brings, because it can actually benefit both the country and young people themselves.
	结论段	In conclusion, it is unfair to say the expansion of university enrolment brings nothing but graduate unemployment. The country, as has been proven, can also benefit from it, and so do young people themselves.

回头来看，我们会发现上面这个模式有按照题目要求discuss both these views，同时它的立场又十分明确，包括正文部分也是如此；因此，它满足了高分作文所要求的present a clear position throughout the response及present a clear central topic within each paragraph。设想一下，如果你是考官，如果你只看开头段、每段的第一句及结论段，你依然可以看到一篇信息完整、立场明确的作文。当然，最后决定分数的，则要看考生的英文表达了。

说 明

针对题型⑤，当考生掌握了以上写作方法去认真审题时，会有以下几种可能：

- 可能性①：考生完全反对A，赞同B；
- 可能性②：考生不否认A，但更倾向B；
- 可能性③：考生既反对A，又反对B；
- 可能性④：考生既赞同A，也赞同B。

有时，同一篇文章同时具备2～3种可能。至于具体选用哪种模式写作，则取决于考生当时的状态。

下面具体来展示一下每种可能性的写作结构，共考生参考。

▶ 针对题型⑤，可能性①：考生完全反对A，赞同B；

例题：Some people say that the best way to a successful career is to work straight after school, while others say that it is better to go to university or college. Discuss both these views and give your own opinion.

可以用“反驳型”结构，具体操作为：

开头段	A successful career is what everyone desires for, yet people hold different opinions about the key to it. While some people say working straight after school is the best route to a successful career, I believe people who attend university or college stand a better chance to have a successful career (than those who only finish high school) .
正文 (180 words)	1) People always assume that working straight after school gives a person more time to accumulate working experience and build his or her professional contacts, which can bring a good chance for promotion and a decent career. However, these people fail to realize that most employers only hire high school graduates to do physically demanding jobs. These young people work long hours and get low pay. They do not have job security and they seldom have the chance to get into the management team. In contrast, people who receive higher education have better career prospects.
	2) Specifically, attending university can get people a degree, which works like a passport in the job market, opening door to opportunity. In most prospective employers' eyes, a university degree equals qualifications. Without such paper qualification, it would be difficult for people to land a decent job. For instance, in many countries, it is almost impossible for a person to be a doctor, a lawyer or a university professor. All these professions are respectable and well-paid, and people in these fields are usually considered to be successful.
结论段	In conclusion, while it may seem that people who work straight after school have more time to build their career, it is better for people to go beyond school level before getting into the workplace.

▶ 针对题型⑤，可能性②：考生不否认A，但更倾向B；

例题：Some people say that the best way to a successful career is to work straight after school, while others say that it is better to go to university or college. Discuss both these views and give your own opinion.

这种写作模式可以操作为：

开头段立场	Although I do not deny that some people do build a successful career when they work straight after school, I would say that people who attend university or college stand a better chance for it.
正文	1) On the one hand, there are examples to show that high school graduates also have the chance to create a successful career...
	2) Yet on the other hand, I still believe it is better for people to receive university education if they want to have a decent career...
结论段	In conclusion, I am confident that people who hold university degrees have distinct advantages over those who only finish high school. To secure a successful career, the former have the upper hand.

▶ 针对题型⑤，可能性③：考生既反对A，也反对B；

例题：Some people prefer to spend their lives doing the same things and avoiding changes. Others, however, think that change is always a good thing. Discuss both these views and give your own opinion.

这种写作模式可以操作为：

开头段立场	Personally, I think it is unwise to resist change, but it does not necessarily mean that change always brings positive outcomes.
正文	1) Those people who believe they have achieved some security by doing the same, familiar things are living in denial...
	2) However, reaching the conclusion that change is inevitable is not the same as assuming that "change is always for the better" ...
结论段	In conclusion, I would say that change can be stimulating and energizing for individuals when they pursue it themselves, but that change, including that which is imposed on people, does not necessarily have good outcomes.

说 明

除开头段外，本文上述要点均摘自《剑桥雅思考试全真试题集6》Test 4所收录的考官作文。

▶ 针对题型⑤，可能性④：考生既赞同A，也赞同B；

例题：Some people say that public museums should be enjoyable places to entertain people, while others say the true function of museums should be education. Discuss both these views and give your own opinion.

这种写作模式可以操作为：

开头段立场	From my perspective, museums should be both entertaining and educational.
正文	1) On the one hand, it can be argued that museums should serve entertaining purposes...
	2) On the other hand, I would also say that public museums should fulfill educational functions.
结论段	In conclusion, museums should provide interesting and educational experience to visitors so that they can have fun and learn something simultaneously.

说 明

“博物馆”这题实际上还可以是可能性①和可能性②，只要考生能够自圆其说即可。此处略去不表。

最后，针对题型⑤再附上两篇官方公布的考官作文。请读者们好好体会一下文章的逻辑。

▶《剑桥雅思考试全真试题集5》Test 4 “nature vs nurture”（280 words）

It is generally believed that some people are born with certain talents, for instance for sport or music, and others are not. However, it is sometimes claimed that any child can be taught to become a good sports person or musician. Discuss both these views and give your own opinion.

The relative importance of natural talent and training is a frequent topic of discussion when people try to explain different levels of ability in, for example, sport, art or music.

Obviously, education systems are based on the belief that all children can effectively be taught to acquire different skills, including those associated with sport, art or music. So from our own school experience, we can find plenty of evidence to support the view that a child can acquire these skills with continued teaching and guided practice.

However, some people believe that innate talent is what differentiates a person who has been trained to play a sport or an instrument, from those who become good players. In other words, there is more to the skill than a learned technique, and this extra talent cannot be taught, no matter how good the teacher or how frequently a child practices. I personally think that some people do have talents that are probably inherited via their genes. Such talents can give individuals a facility for certain skills that allow them to excel, while more hard-working students never manage to reach a comparable level. As with all questions of nature versus nurture, they are not mutually exclusive. Good musicians or artists and exceptional sports stars have probably succeeded because of both good training and natural talent. Without the natural talent, continuous training would be neither attractive nor productive, and without the training, the child would not learn how to exploit and develop their talent.

In conclusion, I agree that any child can be taught particular skills, but to be really good in areas such as music, art or sport, then some natural talent is required.

➢《剑桥雅思考试全真试题集6》Test 4 "change"（259 words）

Some people prefer to spend their lives doing the same things and avoiding changes. Others, however, think that change is always a good thing. Discuss both these views and give your own opinion.

Over the last half century the pace of change in the life of human beings has increased beyond our wildest expectations. This has been driven by technological and scientific breakthroughs that are changing the whole way we view the world on an almost daily basis. This means that changes is not always a personal option, but an inescapable fact of life, and we need to constantly adapt to keep pace with it.

Those people who believe they have achieved some security by doing the same, familiar things are living in denial. Even when people believe they are resisting change themselves, they cannot stop the world around them from changing. Sooner or later they will find that the familiar jobs no longer exist, or that the "safe" patterns of behaviour are no longer appropriate.

However, reaching the conclusion that change is inevitable is not the same as assuming that "change is always for the better". Unfortunately, it is not always the case that new things are prompted because they have good impacts for the majority of people. A lot of innovations are made with the aim of making money for a few. This is because it is the rich and powerful people in our society who are able to impose changes（such as in working conditions or property development) that are in their own interest.

In conclusion, I would say that change can be stimulating and energizing for individuals when they pursue it themselves, but that change, including that which is imposed on people, does not necessarily have good outcomes.

四、结论段

结论段不是对正文信息的简单罗列，也不是对开头段的再次复制。而是，它的主要功能在于对前文进行summary式的归纳并进一步强调重申立场。结论段的写法有很多种。但就雅思议论文写作而言，尤其是学术类写作，比较保守的做法是极其简要地概况正文部分提到的要点并重申考生本人的观点。就雅思写作而言，我本人不是太主张开放式的结论段（open conclusion）；毕竟，“节外生枝”并不是什么好事。关于结论段的举例，请广大考生参考本书中收录的所有文章，好好体会。

这里以“出国留学”为例，供大家参考：

题型②	例题	More and more students choose to go to another country to finish their higher education. Do you think the advantages outweigh the disadvantages? (出国留学)
	开头段	These days, a growing number of young people further their studies overseas. (From time to time, people fiercely debate over the pros and cons such an act can bring to young people.) The purpose of this essay is to examine that studying abroad can be a very rewarding experience to young people.
	正文	1) The first point to make is that young people can have access to a different yet usually better education when studying abroad.
		2) The second important point to make is that students can have a golden opportunity to develop their languages skills.
		3) As for the potential problems of studying overseas, I would say it is merely because of culture shock and language barrier. Thus, if students can get themselves familiarized with the new culture through the Internet and learn the language from their foreign teachers and friends, they will easily fit into the new life.
题型②	结论段	In conclusion, young people can gain academic advantages and develop critical skills for future career and life if they further their studies overseas. Overall, it is a positive thing for them. (31 words)

五、检查

在经历了漫长而又痛苦的写作后，很多考生在停笔那一刹都会长舒一口气，心想总算熬到头了，然后便任由考官或者写作老师处置了。仿佛自己亲生的孩子，都不愿看第二眼。其实这是不对的，孩子出生时我们不但要替他擦拭干净，而且还会爱不释手地抱着仔细观看，生怕孩子走了样。对待雅思作文也应该如此，我们在写完作文后一定要养成检查的习惯。如果考生在考场上没有时间检查，起码保证在平时的备考训练中养成检查的好习惯。只要考生平时练就了火眼金睛，哪怕考场上没有充分的时间检查，也可以瞬间纠正时间紧迫造成的笔误。

比较推崇的做法是：每次写完作文都找专业的老师去修改，并认真揣摩被改动的地方。当你写了5篇、10篇甚至20篇作文给老师批改时，请将所有作文放在一块进行比对，你会发现多数的错误都是类似的。比较普遍的错误有以下几类：

（一）语法方面

- 主谓一致出错。
- 句子成分出错：多了或是少了主语、多了或是少了谓语、用句子做主语……
- 标点符号及大小写犯错导致语法出错。
- 过分依赖复杂句导致句子意思怪异。

（二）语言表达

- 太多华而不实的“好词”。
- 过分地使用同义词，但其实不准确。
- 单词的词性词形出错。
- 中式英文。

（三）审题、逻辑结构

- 只回应到题目中的部分信息。
- 结构出错，没能有效论证立场，甚至自相矛盾。
- ……

当你在平时的写作练习过程中一次次出现某类错误时，请务必认真去钻研去揣摩。考场上，也尽量争取时间来检查这些常见错误。

CHAPTER 3
教育篇

教育类话题（有时与青少年结合在一起）绝对是雅思考试中的重中之重，尤其是对于学术类考生来讲。经笔者粗略统计，过去10年至今，每年基本都会考9～13道教育类话题。而对于广大移民类考生而言，官方每年也会从题库中选一些关于青少年教育的话题进行考查。笔者通过跟踪历年考题，将教育类的话题总结为以下几部分：教育的职能；教学的形式；教师的角色；其他。

一、教育的职能

1. Some people think university education should prepare students for employment. Other people think university has other functions. Discuss both views and what you think the function of university education should be.

2. Many people believe that the main aim for university education is to help graduates to find better jobs, while some people believe that university education has wider benefits for individual and society. Discuss both views and give your opinion.

3. Some people think the main purpose of schools is to turn children into good citizens and workers, rather than to benefit them as individuals. To what extent do you agree or disagree with this opinion?

4. Some people think that universities should provide graduates with knowledge and skills needed in the workplace, while others argue that the main function of a university is to teach students theoretical knowledge. What's your opinion?

5. Some people think universities should provide graduates with the knowledge and skills needed in the workplace in the future. Others think the true function of the university is to give access to knowledge for its own sake. What do you think are

the main functions of a university?

6. It is generally believed that education is vital for the development of individuals and the well-being of society. How can education fulfill both of these functions?

7. Some people think that teachers should be responsible for teaching students how to judge right and wrong and how to behave well. Some say that teachers should only teach students academic subjects. Discuss both views and give your opinion.

8. In some countries, secondary schools aim to provide a general education across a range of subjects. In others, children focus on a narrow range of subjects related to a particular career. For today's world, which system is more appropriate?

9. It is often said that the subjects taught in schools are too academic in orientation and that it would be more useful for children to learn about practical matters such as home management, work and interpersonal skills. To what extent do you agree or disagree?

10. Nowadays, more university students choose to study some practical subjects (such as marketing, computer programming, etc.) instead of theoretical subjects (such as economics, math, and chemistry). Some people suggest that universities should focus on practical subjects, but not theoretical subjects. What's your opinion?

11. Some people think secondary students should study international news as a school subject, but others argue that it is a waste of their valuable school time. What's your opinion?

12. Some people believe history has little or nothing to tell people. Others believe people must study history to understand the present. What's your opinion?

13. Children who find the subjects such as maths and philosophy difficult should not be made to study these. These subjects should be optional rather than compulsory. To what extent do you agree with the statement?

14. Schools should teach children some academic subjects which will be beneficial to their future careers. Therefore, other subjects such as music and sports are not important. To what extent do you agree or disagree with this opinion?

15. The qualities of being successful can not be learnt in university. To what extent do you agree or disagree?

万能思路

以上题目仅仅是雅思教育类话题的一个缩影，真正题量远远大于这些。应该说，以上所有题目几乎都是在辩论教育的真正职能到底是什么。是培养学生的工作技能以便他们毕业后顺利就业呢，还是教学生们理论学科让他们变得知识渊博，抑或是培养他们别的能力？这个话题也是教育界一直在争论不下的一点。2011年上半年，互联网上出现一个很激烈的辩论。一位华裔母亲在美国用铁腕的教育方式教育两位女儿成才，被网友唤作“中国虎妈”。据报道，为了让其中的一位女儿能够好好练琴，这位华裔母亲规定女儿练不好就不给饭吃。当然，女儿也果然不负众望，最终小小年纪就在世界顶级音乐演奏厅进行表演。此事在美国也引发了激烈的讨论，即究竟怎样的教育方式才算合理，怎样的教育成果才算成功。

笔者的立场是：一方面，一个好的教育应该赋予学生独立谋生的能力。至少，我们不希望学生经过多年的寒窗苦读后竟然连工作都找不到。试问，如果一个人每天苦于生计，他/她又如何能真正发挥自己的才能呢？中国历史上怀才不遇的例子太多了。再说了，广大的学子在申请大学选专业时应该不仅仅是为了情怀，多数人还是希望通过大学的学习，将来能找个好的工作。所以，我们投入时间精力和金钱去读大学其实是在投资自己的未来，而不是为了满足情怀。从这个意义上讲，学校也应该教一些对学生将来就业有帮助的学科或者技能。另一方面，我也认为，一个成功的大学教育务必要培养年轻人独立思考的能力，培养他们的想象力和创造力。我坚信，只要一个人学会了独立思考，他/她就一定懂得学习，会有很多机会获得成功。那么，究竟什么样的教育可以帮助培养年轻人的这些能力呢？显然，有一些看似理论化并无多大实用性的课程其实是可以很好地培养年轻人的独立思考能力的。英国哲学家弗兰西斯·培根在其著名的随笔《论学习》中说：“读史使人明智，读诗使人灵秀，数学使人精密，科学使人深刻，伦理学使人庄重，逻辑修辞之学使人善辩。”（Histories make men wise; poets witty; the mathematics subtle; natural philosophy deep; moral grave; logic and rhetoric able to contend.①）

此外，还必须强调的一点是，光有这两点，我们还不能真正意义上认为一个国家的教育就是成功的。因为，成功的教育还应当要培养年轻人的社会责任感。我们可以想象，如果年轻人都只顾着自己，丝毫不在意自己在整个社会中所承担的责任，这将是一个何其冷漠的社会！这又将是一个何其可怕而又可悲的民族！

请广大考生永远记住，凡是考到教育的职能类话题，只要灵活转换上述要点，则高分唾手可得。

下面我将这些要点写成英文，供大家参考。希望考生们在应用的过程中能够灵活转换。

---

① 资料来源：http://oregonstate.edu/instruct/phl302/texts/bacon/bacon_essays.html#OF STUDIES

Q1–Q14 教育的职能 · 万能观点

1）要教实用的技能

On the one hand, I would say that it is important for university to teach students practical subjects and skills that are useful for their future careers.

- University is the last buffer for young people between what people call "carefree life" and tough society. No one would like to see them to be humiliated when they enter the job market. So...
- Sooner or later, students will enter the job market and look for a job to support themselves. If they cannot even find work after years of learning in university, I would not say the education is successful. To my best understanding, education must prepare young people to be independent, literally independent. Otherwise, their talent/potential would not be brought into full play when they have to struggle for a living.
- When students apply for university education, they are investing in their future. They invest a lot of money, time and energy not to just have fun. Most of them would hope one day when they graduate they can use what they have learnt to land a decent job.

For all the reasons above, it is important that university teaches students things like computer literacy and presentation skills, as well as how to handle a job interview.

【参考译文】

一方面，我认为大学教育应该教授对工作有用的学科和技能。

- 对于年轻人而言，大学是所谓“无忧生活”与残酷现实的最后缓冲区。任何人都不希望看到他们在职场上惨遭羞辱。所以……
- 迟早有一天，学生需要进入职场求职养活自己。如果读完大学居然连份工作都找不到，我认为这样的教育是不成功的。在我看来，教育必须帮助一个人学会独立，真正意义上的独立。否则，当一个人每天为了生活而奔波时，他/她根本无法充分施展自己的才能。
- 当年轻人申请读大学时，他们是在对自己的未来做投资。他们投入了巨大金钱、时间及精力不仅仅是为了好玩。多数人还是希望有朝一日能够学有所长，找到一个体面的工作。

因此，大学应该教类似电脑技能、作展示的技能以及面试技巧等。

2）要教理论学科

On the other hand, I also believe that a successful（university）education should not be about job training only. Rather, it should also help unlock young people's imagination and creativity, and train them to think critically. As long as a person can think, he or she can learn, and he or she will learn. Obviously, many seemingly useless academic subjects can help fulfill this function. The great British philosopher Francis Bacon once said "histories make men wise; poets witty; the mathematics subtle; natural philosophy deep; moral grave; logic and rhetoric able to contend.[①]"
（注：请广大读者认真写出各门课程的重要性。此外，Q10-14也的的确确是在考查具体某些课程的重要性。）

Furthermore, a strong background in certain academic subjects can lay solid foundations for one's acquisition of practical subjects and skills. For example, without a strong ground in math, it would be difficult for students to learn computer programming and finance well.

【参考译文】

另一方面，我也认为成功的大学教育不应该仅仅局限于技能培训。相反，它还应该帮助开发年轻人的想象力与创造力，并且让他们学会独立思考。一个人只要懂得思考，就一定懂得学习，就一定会学到东西。显然，很多看似无用的理论课程可以帮助实现这些功能。伟大的英国哲学家弗兰西斯·培根曾经说过："读史使人明智，读诗使人灵秀，数学使人精密，科学使人深刻，伦理学使人庄重，逻辑修辞之学使人善辩"。

而且，学好理论学科可以为学好实用性的学科和技能打下扎实的基础。例如，如果学生没学好数学，他们很难学好计算机编程和金融课程。

3）成功的教育其实还应该教会年轻人承担社会责任

Another equally important role of a successful education is that it must turn young people into socially responsible citizens, making them understand that they are part of society and they shall have duties to fulfill. This is vitally important to the improvement of the well-being of society. Therefore, it is important that school authorities make unpaid community service a compulsory part of education.

① 资料来源：http://oregonstate.edu/instruct/phl302/texts/bacon/bacon_essays.html#OF STUDIES

【参考译文】

成功的教育还应将年轻人培养成有责任感的公民，要让他们明白他们是社会的一分子，让他们明白作为社会成员他们需要履行相应的义务。这对于社会的文明福祉来讲至关重要。因此，校方应该将无偿的社区服务作为教育的必备环节。

高分词汇精选 Word Bank

序号	词汇	意思	同义表达（自测）
1	buffer	缓冲区	
2	carefree	无忧无虑的	
3	tough	艰难的；强硬的	
4	humiliate	羞辱	
5	job market	就业市场	
6	be brought into full play	得到充分发挥	
7	struggle for a living	迫于生计	
8	land a decent job	找到一份体面的工作	
9	computer literacy	计算机技能	
10	presentation skill	做展示说明的能力	
11	job interview	面试	
12	unlock one's imagination and creativity	开发某人的想象力与创造力	
13	think critically	独立思考	
14	fulfill	履行，实现	
15	lay solid foundations for	为……打下坚实的基础	
16	acquisition	学习，习得	
17	computer programming	计算机编程	
18	finance	金融	
19	socially responsible	有（社会）责任感的	
20	fulfill duties	履行义务	
21	vitally important	至关重要	

序号	词汇	意思	同义表达（自测）
22	well-being	福祉	
23	school authorities	校方	
24	unpaid community service	无偿的义工	
25	compulsory	强制的	

Q15 音乐&体育 vs 就业（310 words）

Schools should teach children some academic subjects which will be beneficial to their future careers. Therefore, other subjects such as music and sports are not important. To what extent do you agree or disagree with this opinion?

Recent years have witnessed increased criticism on education, particularly when pragmatism is emphasized in many aspects in individuals' daily life. Pragmatics believe that only subjects which are rewarding to young people's future employment should be taught and thus subjects like music and sports are of little significance and should be excluded from the school curriculum. Personally, however, such a claim is quite short-sighted and cannot be justified.

It is understandable for people to expect schools teaching useful subjects. After all, most young people attend university in the hope that they can learn something useful to find a decent job. However, such a viewpoint does not necessarily lead to the conclusion that subjects like music and sports are not important for students.

As is known, sports particularly team sports can always teach young people to compromise, share, cooperate and take responsibility. All these qualities are extremely important no matter what career one pursues in the future. As for music, although it may not benefit a person's career as directly as sports do, it is an effective way for people to handle the increasingly intense pressure in the workplace. Otherwise, things can get quite ugly if one fails to deal with work stress.

In addition, subjects such as music and sports can also benefit young people in other aspects. For instance, music benefits a person in terms of spiritual enrichment. Sports, on the other hand, remind students of the importance of an active life. It is no exaggeration to say that a good physical condition is the prerequisite for everything people wish to achieve.

In conclusion, be it in pragmatic sense or in a broad sense, subjects like music and sports are important for young people. While practical subjects play an important role in students' education, those seemingly less important subjects represented by music and sports should also be taught in school.

【参考译文】

近些年人们对于教育的批评声越来越大，尤其是当实用主义大行其道时。实用主义派认为学校应该只教对于学生未来就业有用的学科，而像音乐和体育这样的课程并不重要，不应该出现在学校课程中。就我而言，这种看法目光短浅并且毫无道理。

我们可以理解为什么人们会希望学校要教实用的学科。毕竟，多数的年轻人上大学是希望能学有所成以便将来找到一份好工作。但是，这样的观点并不意味着音乐和体育这类课程就不重要。

众所周知，体育（尤其是团队体育）可以教会年轻人懂得妥协、分享、合作与承担责任。不管一个人未来从事任何职业，这些品质都至关重要。至于音乐，尽管它不如体育那般直接有益于一个人的职业生涯，但是它是个非常好的帮助人们应对巨大的工作压力的方式。否则，如果一个人无法应对工作压力，情况会很不妙。

此外，音乐与体育这类课程还可以在其他方面让年轻人受益。例如，音乐还可以陶冶情操。体育则提醒学生多锻炼的重要性。毫不夸张地说，好的身体是人们成就如何事情的前提条件（即“身体是革命的本钱”）。

总之，无论是从实用主义的角度讲还是从广义上而言，音乐和体育这类学科对年轻人都至关重要。学校的确应该教授实用性的学科，但像音乐和体育这类貌似不重要的学科也应该要教。

高分词汇精选 Word Bank

序号	词汇	意思	同义表达（自测）
1	criticism	批评	
2	pragmatism	实用主义	

序号	词汇	意思	同义表达（自测）
3	pragmatics	实用主义者	
4	be rewarding to	对……有益的	
5	be excluded from	被从……中剔除	
6	school curriculum	课程	
7	short-sighted	目光短浅的	
8	justified	有道理的	
9	it is understandable that...	可以理解	
10	a decent job	体面的工作	
11	does not necessarily mean...	并不意味着	
12	compromise	妥协	
13	pursue a career in...	以……为职业	
14	intense pressure	巨大的压力	
15	get ugly	变糟糕	
16	spiritual enrichment	丰富精神世界	
17	It is no exaggeration to say that	毫不夸张地说	
18	prerequisite	前提条件	

二、教学的形式

16. Some people think that school should put students in different classes according to their academic ability, while some others believe that students of different abilities should be educated together. Discuss both views and give your own opinion.

17. Some people think that schools should select pupils according to their academic abilities, while others believe that it is better to have pupils with different abilities study together. Discuss both views and give your own opinion.

18. Some people think it is better for children to attend boarding schools while others believe day schools are better. Discuss both views and give your own opinion. (*OR*, Boarding schools are becoming popular. Why is the case? Do

you think it is a positive or negative trend? *OR*, Is it better for students to live at home with their parents or in school accommodations?)

19. Some people think that it is beneficial for students to go to the private secondary school, but other people think that it can have a negative effect. Discuss the two points and give your own opinion.

20. In the past, lectures were used as a way of teaching large numbers of students, but now with the development of technology for education, many people think there is no justification for attending lectures. To what extent do you agree or disagree?

Q16&17 分班学习（325 words）

Some people think that schools should select pupils according to their academic abilities, while others believe that it is better to have pupils with different abilities study together. Discuss both views and give your own opinion.

In some countries, students are grouped into different classes based on their academic abilities. People are divided into two sides in the debate about the justification of such a practice. Based on the situation in my country, I strongly oppose such an act.

When the school authorities put students with different abilities into different classes, they hope that teachers can better prepare their lessons because they will no longer have to struggle between two different groups. It is also expected that those top students would have fewer distractions (from bad students) and so better concentrate on their studies. However, I think such a scheme/practice is discrimination against students with lower grades and should not be practiced.

In my country, when students at different levels are taught separately, those less qualified and less responsible teachers would be allocated to tutor those so-called "bad students". Students with low grades are usually treated like the black sheep and they are just left on their own. This can be extremely detrimental to these students' academic studies and their character building. Such a practice can ruin any chance for them to make change, and it is, by no means, a positive development to the students.

Meanwhile, I think people should understand that even if some students are not good at academic things, yet they can still be very good at other things. When students with different academic abilities learn together, they have the opportunity to learn from each other. At least, they can learn how to interact with different people, which is vitally important in their future life. Once they are taught separately, that opportunity is then taken away.

In conclusion, it is a wrong idea to select students according to their academic abilities as all students deserve an opportunity for a good education. Moreover, giving students a chance to learn with someone who is less advanced academically or smarter also gives them a chance to learn to interact with different people.

【参考译文】

在一些国家，依据其学习程度，学生会被分成不同的小组进行学习。对于这种做法的合理性则是仁者见仁智者见智。基于我们国家的情况，我强烈反对这种做法。

校方之所以将学生按程度分班，是希望让老师更好地备课，而不用夹在两个不同的群体之间无所适从。同时，这么做也可以让程度好的学生可以少一些干扰，更集中精力学习。但是，我认为这种做法是歧视程度不好的学生，不应该提倡。

在我们国家，当对学生进行分班学习时，通常（学校）会分配一些相对差一些的老师来教“坏学生”。这些学生常常被当做害群之马，没人管。这对学生的学习和性格的塑造都十分不利。这种做法使得学生们没有机会去改变，它无论如何都不是个好的做法。

与此同时，人们必须明白一些学生仅仅是学习不好，但他们可能在其他方面做得很好。当不同程度的学生在一起学习时，他们可以相互学习。至少，他们可以学会和不同的人打交道，这对他们以后的人生至关重要。而一旦他们被分开教学，这种机会就会被剥夺掉。

总之，将学生分班学习不是一个明智的做法，因为每个人都有平等的机会接受教育。而且，给予学生一个机会和程度差或者好的同学进行互动可以让他们有机会学会和不同的人打交道。

高分词汇精选 Word Bank

序号	词汇	意思	同义表达（自测）
1	justification/justified	合理	
2	school authorities	校方	
3	top students	好学生	
4	students with low grades	差生	
5	distraction	分心	
6	less qualified	不合格的	
7	be detrimental to	对……不利	
8	mentality	想法	
9	by no means	绝不	
10	interact with	与……交流互动	
11	vitally important	至关重要	

Q19 寄宿学校vs走读学校（285 words）

Some people think it is better for children to attend boarding schools while others believe day schools are better. Discuss both these views and give your own opinion.

In almost every country, parents have two options when sending their children to schools, i.e. boarding schools and day schools. From time to time, people debate over the advantages and disadvantages of each system. In my opinion, neither of these two forms of education is superior to the other. In the following paragraphs, I would elaborate the pros and cons of both types of schools.

Boarding schools, obviously, provide children a prime opportunity to learn about independence. It is self-evident that students in boarding schools will have to learn to take care of themselves and handle things on their own since their parents or guardians are not around to get things arranged for them. In the meanwhile, there can be a more disciplined atmosphere for learning in boarding schools than in day schools. In boarding school there is always a timetable to guide students what they should attend to. This is important also because students can learn to be time-conscious.

On the other hand, however, school accommodations occupy much time that children could have spent with their parents to build relationship. This is also one of the bases for people to argue against boarding schools. If children live at home, they can talk with their parents often, thus they can also get more parenting. In addition, boys and girls are co-educated in day schools whereas many boarding schools are single-sex schools where students of the two sexes are taught separately. Giving children the chance to learn and interact with the opposite sex can be extremely important for their character building.

In conclusion, both boarding schools and day schools can be good or bad. To provide children the best possible education, parents should make their choices wisely.

【参考译文】

每个国家的父母在送孩子上学时都会面临两个选择：寄宿学校还是走读学校。人们经常辩论两种模式的利弊。在我看来，两种模式各有千秋。本文将分别阐述双方的利弊。

显然，寄宿学校给学生提供了一个绝佳的机会锻炼独立。众所周知，由于父母及监护人无法时刻陪在身边处理一切事情，寄宿生不得不自己照顾自己，自己处理事情。同时，寄宿学校的学习氛围比走读学校好。在寄宿学校，始终有一个作息时间表来引导学生时刻应该做什么。这个也有利于培养学生的时间观念。

但是另一方面，寄宿也占据了学生太多的时间，而他们本可以利用这些时间和父母培养感情。这也是很多人为什么反对寄宿学校的原因之一。如果是走读，则学生可以经常和父母交流，从而得到更多的教养。此外，走读学校通常男女混校，而很多寄宿学校则是男女分校。给予年轻人机会和异性交流互动有利于他们的性格的塑造。

总之，两种模式各有利弊。要让孩子获得好的教育，父母应该谨慎抉择。

高分词汇精选 Word Bank

序号	词汇	意思	同义表达（自测）
1	boarding school	寄宿学校	
2	day school	走读学校	

序号	词汇	意思	同义表达（自测）
3	from time to time	经常	
4	debate over...	辩论	
5	be superior to	优于……	
6	elaborate	阐述	
7	pros and cons	利弊	
8	a prime opportunity	绝佳的机会	
9	It is self-evident that...	显然	
10	guardian	监护人	
11	time-conscious	有时间观念的	
12	school accommodation	寄宿	
13	parenting	教养、抚养	
14	single-sex school	单性别学校	
15	character building	性格的塑造	

三、教师的角色

21. Computers are increasingly used in education. In which areas do you think computers are more important and in which areas are teachers more important?

22. Some people believe that computers and the Internet can take the place of schools, while others contend that teachers play an important role in schools. Discuss both views and give your opinion.

23. Many people use distance-learning programs (study material post, TV, the Internet, etc.) to study at home, but some people think that it cannot bring the benefit as much as attending college or university. To what extent do you agree or disagree with this opinion?

24. School teachers used to be the source of information; however, some people

argue that teachers are not as important as before with the increasing variety of information resources. What is your opinion?

25. Some people think students learn far more from classes with teachers than other resources, such as the Internet and television. Do you agree or disagree?

26. Some people believe that the teaching method with a teacher and students in a classroom will not exist by the year 2050. To what extent do you agree or disagree?

27. Once children start school, teachers have more influence than parents on their intellectual and social development. To what extent do you agree or disagree?

万能思路

除了Question 27外（2015年11月7日考题），其余几题几乎都是对比老师和电脑在教育中所扮演的角色，以便论证老师及传统学校是否会被取代。当然，对于这个辩论，仁者见仁智者见智。但是，笔者建议考生先分析为什么人们会认为电脑可以取代老师及学校，然后再对这些人给出的理由进行评论，看是否事实真的如他们所预想的那样。相对老师及学校，电脑（或者说computer-assisted home learning）的优势在于：①方便快捷，便于学生自主安排学习时间；②信息量大，网络能提供的绝对不只是一些学术资源；③成本低廉，至少比起经营学校它的投入更低；④……但是事实果真如此吗？美国常春藤大学（the Ivy League）的视频公开课程放在网上，有多少人去看？又有多少人真正看懂了？考生一定要记住，多数学生都没自觉或者成熟到如此程度。我们可以预见，如果放任学生自己对着电脑学习而父母又不在身边监督，很多学生都会利用这个机会玩电脑游戏或者做其他事情。这些都将违背distance earning的初衷。而相比之下，在传统学校，老师既授业解惑，又扮演了监督的角色。此外，学生接受教育不应该仅仅是学一些理论学科。实际上，他们还应该学会为人处世。这些技能绝非整天面对电脑就能学会。而如果学生在学校跟着老师学，则老师可以扮演role model的角色，对学生进行言传身教。

Q22 电脑取代老师（321 words）

Some people believe that computers and the Internet can take the place of schools, while others contend that teachers play an important role in schools. Discuss both views and give your opinion.

There has been much debate about whether teachers and traditional schools will be replaced by computers and the Internet. Some people predict that it will happen in 2050. As far as I am concerned, teachers are still important even in the information age and will not be replaced.

It is true that computers bring much convenience to learners as they can organize the schedule flexibly and control the learning process as they wish. Also, the Internet boasts larger quantities of information than teachers can provide. Any information that students cannot get from teachers can be accessed on the Internet, be it academic or non-academic. In addition, it is easier and cheaper for the government to organize distance-learning programs than to run schools.

However, these people fail to realize that most students are not sufficiently mature to learn alone. If children learnt with computer on their own, without much self-discipline or/and supervision from parents, chances are they take this opportunity to play computer games or do some other things that are not related to study. In that case, such a well-intended program would simply fail. In contrast, if students learn at school, teachers will not only be the tutor but also the monitor. In other words, in school there is a better atmosphere for students to study in.

In the meanwhile, it is also important to stress that students do not only need to learn academic subjects but also need to master practical skills like interpersonal skills and how to handle things. These skills can barely be picked up if students sit in front of the computer all day long. But in school, they can learn from teachers and classmates all these critical skills.

In conclusion, computers have their advantages, but students are too young to study on their own. Also, many practical skills must be learnt in school environment. Therefore, teachers and schools will continue to play an important role in education.

【参考译文】

人们经常辩论传统的学校好老师是否会被电脑和互联网所取代，一些人甚至预言这会发生在2050年。在我看来，即使是在信息时代，老师都是非常重要的并且不会被取代。

不可否认，电脑给学习者带来了巨大的便利因为他们可以灵活地安排时间、掌控学习进度。同时，互联网提供的信息远比老师提供的多。任何老师无法提供的信息都可以在互联网上获得，无论是学习上的还是其他的。此外，组织远程教育远比经营学校要简捷实惠。

但是，人们没有意识到绝大多数学生都尚未成熟到自主学习。如果学生对着电脑独自学习，由于缺少自律及父母的监督，他们很可能利用这个机会玩电脑游戏或者做一些与学习毫不相干的事。如此，则这个善意的机制就会失败。相比之下，如果学生在学校学习，老师不仅扮演了教师的角色而且起到监督的作用。换言之，学校能够给学生提供更好的学习氛围。

与此同时，还应该强调的是，学生不仅仅要学习理论学科，而且还要掌握类似于交际和独立处事之类的技能。若是学生整天坐在电脑前，他们无法掌握这些技能。而在学校，他们可以从老师和同学那里学到这些重要技能。

总之，尽管电脑有它的优势，但是学生太小无法自主学习。并且，很多实用性的技能只能在学校学到。因此，老师将在学校教育中继续扮演重要角色。

高分词汇精选 Word Bank

序号	词汇	意思	同义表达（自测）
1	There has been much debate about	人们辩论	
2	information age	信息时代	
3	bring much convenience to...	给……带来便利	
4	vast quantities of	大量	
5	distance learning (programs)	远程教育（课程）	
6	fail to realize that...	忽略了	
7	mature	成熟的	
8	self discipline	自律	
9	supervision	监督	
10	Chances are...	很有可能……	
11	well-intended	善意的	
12	tutor	老师	
13	interpersonal skills	人际交往能力	
14	critical	重要的	
15	practical skills	实用技能	

四、其他

28. Some people believe that a country benefits greatly from a high percentage of young people who go to university, while others argue that it only leads to graduate unemployment. Discuss both views and give your opinion.

29. Some people think that studying in college or university is the best way for students to prepare for their future career. But others think they should leave school as soon as possible to develop their career through work experience. Discuss both views and give your own opinion.

30. Students from poor background such as rural areas often find it difficult to access to university education, so people think universities should make it especially easy for them to study at. To what extent do you agree or disagree?

31. Some people think the students should take the subjects which are decided by the government in the university. Others think that students can apply for the subjects they prefer. Discuss the two situations and give your opinion.

32. More and more students choose to go to another country to finish their higher education. Do you think the advantages outweigh the disadvantages?

33. In some countries, some high school leavers are choosing to work or travel for a period of time before going to university. Do the advantages outweigh the disadvantages? Give your own opinion and reasons using your own experience.

34. In some countries parents expect their children to spend long time studying in school and after school. What are the positive or negative effects on children and the society they live in?

说明

以上考题不好归类，下面将分别做分析。不过，说明一下，就考查频率而言，Q29、Q33出现频率较高。

Q29 是否鼓励更多年轻人读大学（276 words）

Some people believe that a country benefits greatly with a high percentage of young people who go to university, while others argue that it only leads to graduate unemployment. Discuss both views and give your opinion.

While some people think that it is a good idea for universities to enroll more and more students as it benefits the country, some others believe that such a practice would only result in unemployment among young people. Personally, I think university education is extremely important for both the young people and the country and thus the enrolment expansion is a positive thing.

It is true that in some countries the expansion of university enrollment leads to unemployment issues. Nevertheless, it should be understood that the root cause for unemployment is due to the poor economy. When the economy is going down, businesses cut jobs, and when the economy takes off, people get jobs. It has never been university education to blame. As a matter of fact, when there are limited employment opportunities the competition in the job market is certainly to getting fierce. Under such circumstances, a higher level of educational background can add to the competitiveness of the job applicants.

In the meanwhile, the country would also reap great benefits when there is a large population of well-educated people. The best way for a country to invest in the future is to spend resources on young people, educational resources in particular. The more young talents a country has, the higher its level of innovation will be, and the stronger the country will be.

In conclusion, it would be a short-sighted act to discourage young people from attending university. Not only would it jeopardize a nation's further development, but also it hinders young people's personal improvement. On the contrary, the more education young people receive, the better young people themselves and the country will be.

【参考译文】

有些人认为大学招收更多学生是好事，因为这对国家有利，而另外有些人则认为这种做法只会导致年轻人失业。在我看来，大学教育对于年轻人自身和国家都有利，所以大学扩招是件好事。

的确，在有些国家，大学扩招导致了失业问题。但是，我们必须明白失业的根本原因在于经济的不景气。当经济衰退时，企业裁员；而当经济腾飞时，人人都有工作。这从来都不是教育的问题。事实上，当就业机会有限时，职场的竞争务必会加剧。如此，更高的学历背景反而增加了求职者的竞争力。

同时，当一个国家有很多人受到良好教育时国家也会受益无穷。对于任何一个国家来讲，投资未来最好的途径就是把资源投资在年轻人身上，尤其是教育资源。一国的年轻人才越多，其创新水平就越高，它就会越强大。

总之，反对年轻人读大学是个目光短浅的做法。这不仅会危害到国家的长远发展，而且会阻碍年轻人的个人提升。相反，年轻人接受的教育越多，他们就会变的越好，国家也会越好。

高分词汇精选 Word Bank

序号	词汇	意思	同义表达（自测）
1	expansion of university enrolment	大学扩招	
2	root cause	根本原因	
3	job cuts	裁员	
4	employment opportunity	就业机会	
5	fierce competition	激烈的竞争	
6	job market	职场	
7	under such circumstances	在这种背景下	
8	competitiveness	竞争力	
9	job applicants	求职者	
10	reap great benefits	获得巨大好处	
11	well-educated	受过良好教育的	
12	talents	人才	
13	innovation	创新	
14	jeopardize	损害	
15	hinder	阻碍	

Q30 就业：高中毕业后vs大学毕业后（296 words）

Some people think that studying in a college or university is the best way for students to prepare for their future career. But others think they should leave school as soon as possible to develop their career through work experience. Discuss both these views and give your own opinion.

A decent employment is desired by everyone, but the key to it is fiercely debated by people. While some say the key is to join the job market straight after school, others believe the best way is to study beyond school level. Personally, I believe people would stand a better chance if they attend university or college before diving into the work world.

On the surface, high school graduates can invest more time to accumulate working experience and build professional contacts, something considered as career facilitator in today's world. There are also examples to prove this like the stories of the Silicon Valley superheroes Bill Gates and Steve Jobs.

However, what people fail to realize is that time has changed and that in today's society anyone who only holds a high school diploma can only be qualified to manual work like those salary makers on the assembly line for big manufactures like Nike and Foxconn. These jobs are not successful at all. What's worse, with the proliferation of automation, these manual workers will finally be replaced one day.

In contrast, attending university would earn people a degree, which is like a passport in the job market, opening door to opportunity. Without such paper qualification, it would be difficult to imagine one would be employed by a good company unless of course for some physically-demanding work. For example, it is almost impossible to be a university professor or a doctor or lawyer if one does not hold a university degree. All these professions are considered decent and successful in most societies.

In conclusion, people who work straight after school will only stand a slim chance if they wish to pursue a successful career. The key, as elaborated above, is to future one's studies beyond school level first.

【参考译文】

人人都渴望一份体面的工作，但是如何获得这样一份工作则仁者见仁智者见智。有些人认为秘诀在于高中毕业后直接参加工作，而另外一些人则认为最好的办法是继续求学深造。就我而言，如果人们工作之前先读大学则找到好工作的机会更大。

表面上，高中毕业后工作可以有更多时间积累工作经验和人脉，这些都有利于职业的发展。而且，比尔·盖茨和史蒂夫·乔布斯等硅谷英雄们的事迹也证明了这点。

但是，人们忽略的是世道变了。当今时代，任何只有高中文凭的人基本上只能做苦力，例如耐克及富士康等巨头流水线上的薪水工。这些工作都不够成功。更糟糕的是，随着自动化的普及，体力劳动者最终将会被淘汰。

相反，上大学可以获得学位；它就像是职场的通行证，可以创造机会。若是缺少这个学历资质，很难想象除了体力劳动之外还会有谁愿意雇佣这样的员工。例如，如果一个人没有大学学历，几乎不可能成为大学教授或是医生及律师，而所有这些工作在绝大多数国家都是非常成功和体面的。

总之，高中毕业后直接参加工作的人很难成功；正如上文所论述的，读大学才是成功之道。

高分词汇精选 Word Bank

序号	词汇	意思	同义表达（自测）
1	a decent employment	体面的工作	
2	job market	职场	
3	a slim chance	机会渺茫	
4	On the surface,	表面上，	
5	accumulate	积累	
6	professional contacts	人脉	
7	diploma	文凭	
8	degree	学位	
9	manual work	体力劳动	
10	physically demanding work	体力劳动	
11	manual workers	体力劳动者	
12	open door to opportunity	带来机会	
13	paper qualification	学历	
14	the proliferation of...	……的普及	

Q31 农村娃读书难(283 words)

Students from poor background such as rural areas often find it difficult to access to university education, so people think universities should make it especially easy for them to study at. To what extent do you agree or disagree?

It is an irrefutable fact that children from rural regions often fail to secure a university place. This is a shame and extremely unfair. In my opinion, universities should take action to help those children.

Two leading factors result in such a phenomenon. First of all, the primary and secondary education in rural areas is very poor and thus rural students can hardly compete against their urban counterparts in university entrance examinations. Take China for example. In rural areas, the teaching faculty is less qualified than in the city. School facilities, meanwhile, are also extremely poor. In contrast, students in the city have easy access to much better teachers and facilities. Under such circumstances, rural students have little competitiveness against urban students. Soaring tuition fee is the other big obstacle for rural students to the higher education. Each academic year, the tuition costs thousands of Chinese Yuan in China, a huge financial burden to poor families.

To address the issue, I believe it is important and feasible for universities to make effort to help poor students to receive adequate formal education. Specifically, universities can cut down or even exempt the school fee for students in poverty. In the meanwhile, it is also an effective act to provide scholarships and part-time jobs to those students so that they can work through university. Lowering the threshold for entry exam would also be possible to give poor students an equal chance to receive education.

In conclusion, poor students deserve an equal opportunity for further education. They do not get it not because they lavish their chance but because they are deprived of it. Therefore, I would suggest universities play their role to help these eligible students.

【参考译文】

农村孩子上大学难是个不争的事实。这很遗憾也和不公平。在我看来，大学应该采取措施帮助他们。

两个主要因素导致了这一现象。首先，农村的基础教育极为落后，这导致农村孩子在高考中很难与城里的孩子竞争。以中国为例，乡下的师资力量不如城里，与此同时其教学设施又极其简陋。而相比之下，城里的学生轻而易举便可以获得更好的师资和设施。在这个背景下，农村的学生几乎毫无竞争力。高昂的学费是阻碍农村孩子上大学的另一个障碍。每年，大学学费高达数千人民币，这对贫穷的家庭无疑是个巨大的经济负担。

我认为，要应对这个问题，非常重要而又切实可行的做法是大学采取措施帮助农村孩子接受教育。具体而言，大学可以给贫困学生减免学费。同时，给他们提供奖学金或者兼职机会也是个很有效的让他们勤工俭学的办法。降低入学门槛也可以给贫困学生提供一个平等的机会接受教育。

总之，贫困学生同样享有平等的机会接受高等教育。他们没能接受教育不是因为他们肆意挥霍自己的机会，而是因为他们被剥夺了这个机会。所以，我认为大学应该帮助这些学生。

高分词汇精选 Word Bank

序号	词汇	意思	同义表达（自测）
1	It is an irrefutable fact that...	……是个不争事实	
2	rural regions/areas	农村地区	
3	university places	大学名额	
4	primary and secondary education	中小学教育	
5	university entrance examination	高考	
6	compete against sb.	与……竞争	
7	under such circumstances	在这个背景下	
8	competitiveness	竞争力	
9	higher education	高等教育	
10	rural/urban students	农村/城里孩子	
11	tuition/school fee	学费	
12	academic year	学年	
13	financial burden	经济负担	

序号	词汇	意思	同义表达（自测）
14	make effort to...	努力……	
15	poverty	贫穷	
16	exempt	赦免	
17	scholarship	奖学金	
18	work through university/college	勤工俭学	
19	lavish	挥霍	
20	deprive sb. of sth.	剥夺	
21	eligible	合格的	

Q32 大学生自由选课vs政府调控（311 words）

Some people think the students should take the subjects which are decided by the government in the university. Others think that students can apply for the subjects they prefer. Discuss the two situations and give your opinion.

本题基本等同于Chapter 6政府篇话题第三类“政府干预”类话题；同时，答题思路也可以结合本章第一类话题“教育的职能”Q11。例如，Questions 32答题思路为：①确实，如果学生能够选择自己喜欢的课程，那么兴趣将激发他们极大的学习热情。在中文里我们常说，兴趣是最好的老师。只要学生有兴趣了，他们会更愿意主动去学，会更愿意投入时间和精力去学，这对他们的学业是非常有利的。②但是与此同时，我们要注意到另外一个现象：年轻人几乎都不喜欢学理论学科，他们往往选择那些实用性的热门学科。就像Q11里所提到的“university students choose to study some practical subjects (such as marketing and computer programming) instead of theoretical subjects (such as economy, math, and chemistry)”。如果政府真的放任这种自由，那么最后的结局对政府和大学生都不利。毕竟，国家的长远发展需要各行各业的优秀人才，所以某些领域的人才短缺将十分不利于国家的建设。与此同时，对于广大大学生来讲，当几乎所有人都选择热门专业时，供给将大于需求，毕业后他们将面临巨大的就业问题。③实际上，更理想的做法应该是政府或者说相关的机构从大局上考虑国家长远发展所需要的人才及相关领域的就业前景，然后大致确定大学里每个专业或学科的招生名额。在这个基础上，我们再鼓励大学生自主选择专业并辅以自己感兴趣的学科。这既不与国家的发展相冲突，又能够鼓励学生在公平竞争的基础上按照自己的兴趣进行学习。If so, everyone wins.

➢ 范文

In some countries, the government decides what subjects students should take in university. Some people think this is wrong and that students should have their own freedom to choose the subjects they like. From where I stand, I think the government should plan the enrollment for each subject first and then encourage students to choose the subjects they like.

Interest is the fuel for learning. If one is really interested in learning something, he or she will be driven hard to learn. For example, for students who have a real enthusiasm for computer science, with passion and a positive attitude, they will devote their full energies into it. This explains why there are so many computer geeks as well as computer geniuses like Mark Zukerberg, the CEO and co-founder of Facebook.

Yet in the meanwhile, I think it is important that the government sets fixed enrollment of university subjects. This is because when students have the own choice to take the subjects they prefer, most of them would take practical subjects (such as marketing, computer programming, etc.) instead of theoretical subjects (such as math and chemistry etc.) . If things like happen, there will be unemployment issues for students in certain fields and more importantly, for the country there will be shortage of talents in certain fields. Any government cannot afford this.

Therefore, it would be better if the government plans on the future development of the country and notifies universities how many students it expects for each subject. Universities then take over form there and encourage students to apply for subjects they prefer.

In conclusion, university students shall have their own choice of subjects they wish for, but it does not mean that the government should do nothing about it. It is not because the government has the power, but that it has the obligation to ensure the country's sustainable development.

【参考译文】

在有些国家，政府会决定大学生应该学什么课程。一些人认为这种做法不对，学生应该自由选课。在我看来，我认为政府应该先规划好招生名额，然后再鼓励学生自由选课。

兴趣是最好的老师。如果一个人对某事感兴趣，他/她就会主动去努力学。例如，如果一个学生对计算机很感兴趣，他/她就会带着激情端正态度全身心地投入其中。这就是为什么有那么多的电脑怪才和电脑天才，例如Facebook的联合创始人和CEO马克·扎克伯格。

但是与此同时，政府应该设定各学科的招生名额。毕竟，如果放任学生自由选课，则多数人会选实用性的学科（如市场营销、计算机编程等），而放弃理论学科（如数学、化学等）。若此，某些领域就会有失业问题；而更重要的是，另一些领域就会存在人才短缺的问题。任何国家都无法承担得起这样的后果。

因此，更好的做法是由政府做好国家发展规划并告知各高校其各领域的人才期望，然后再由大学接手来鼓励学生自由选课。

总之，大学生的确有他们的自由选择学科，但这并不意味着政府就应置身事外。倒不是说政府有权干涉，而是政府有责任确保国家的可持续发展。

高分词汇精选 Word Bank

序号	词汇	意思	同义表达（自测）
1	enrolment	录取	
2	Interest is the fuel for learning.	兴趣是最好的老师。	
3	be driven to...	努力……	
4	enthusiasm	热情	
5	devote one’s full energies to...	全身心地……	
6	practical subjects	实用学科	
7	theoretical subjects	理论学科	
8	More importantly,	更重要的是，	
9	take over	接管	
10	apply for	申请	
11	have the obligation to do sth.	有义务……	
12	sustainable development	可持续发展	

Q33 出国留学（302 words）

More and more students choose to go to another country to finish their higher education. Do you think the advantages outweigh the disadvantages?

Recent years have witnessed a growing number of young people going abroad to study. From time to time, people fiercely debate over the pros and cons such an act can bring to young people. In this essay, I will examine why the benefits of studying overseas far outweigh its downside.

The first point to make is that young people can have access to a different yet usually better education when studying abroad. It is self-evident that everyone would choose a place that offers a more competitive education as the destination for his or her overseas studies. This explains why so many Chinese students flood into countries like US. It is important to stress that in today's society, a better education usually promises a brighter future for young people.

The second important point to make is that students can have a golden opportunity to build their languages skills. After years of learning and living abroad, most young people usually fluently speak the official language of that country. Being bilingual greatly adds to one's competitiveness in the job market, particularly in this increasingly globalizing world. For example, when many Chinese students finish their education and return home from UK, they are very popular among those prospective employers like P&G China and many other local corporations.

As for the potential problems of studying overseas, I would say they can be easily taken care of. For example, most people would worry about the cultural differences and language barrier. However, if students can get themselves familiarized with the new culture through the media and take some language classes, they will easily fit into the new life.

In conclusion, young people can gain academic advantages and develop critical skills for future career and life if they further their studies overseas. Overall, it is a positive thing for them.

【参考译文】

近些年，越来越多的年轻人出国留学。人们经常激烈地辩论该现象会给年轻人带来的利弊。本文将具体阐述为何这个现象利大于弊。

首先，年轻人可以获得不同但通常更好的教育。显然，人们都会选择能够提供更好的教育的地方作为留学目的地。这就是为何那么多的中国学生涌入美国或是其他英联邦国家如英国、澳大利亚及新西兰留学。而且必须强调的是，当今社会更好的教育通常意味着更好的未来。

其次，学生可以获得一个绝佳的机会来锻炼自己的语言技能。经过几年的国外留学生活，多数学生都可以流利地说一口该国的官方语言。会讲两门语言可以极大地增加一个人在职场上的竞争力，尤其是在这个日益全球化的时代。例如，很多中国的留学生从英国回国后都成了像宝洁（中国）或其他国内企业的抢手目标。

至于出国留学的潜在问题，我认为可以克服。例如，多数人会担心文化差异和语言障碍。不过，只要学生通过媒体提前了解国外文化并参加一些语言课程，他们可以很快适应国外的生活。

总之，年轻人出国留学不仅可以接受好的教育，而且可以为以后的工作和生活积累重要的技能。总体上讲，这是个积极的事情。

高分词汇精选 Word Bank

序号	词汇	意思	同义表达（自测）
1	Recent years have witnessed...	近些年见证了……	
2	pros and cons	利弊	
3	access	权限、获得	
4	It is self-evident that...	显然	
5	competitive	有竞争力的	
6	destination for overseas studies	留学目的地	
7	flood into...	涌入……	
8	It is important to stress that...	必须强调的是	
9	a golden opportunity	绝佳的机会	
10	build one's language skills	锻炼语言技能	
11	bilingual	双语的	
12	job market	职场	

序号	词汇	意思	同义表达（自测）
13	prospective employers	潜在雇主	
14	corporations	企业	
15	cultural differences	文化差异	
16	language barrier	语言障碍	
17	get oneself familiarized with...	熟悉……	
18	critical	重要的	

Q34 间隔年（401 words）

In some countries, some high school leavers are choosing to work or travel for a period of time before going to the university. Do the advantages outweigh the disadvantages? Give your own opinion and reasons using your own experience.

It has been noticed that some high school graduates take one year off to work or travel before starting university. From my perspective, such a practice is positive and can benefit young people remarkably.

First of all, doing a gap year can offer a golden opportunity for young people to develop independence. As is known, when students work or travel to a different place, their parents or custodians will be unable to stay around and get things organized for them. As a consequence, these young people will have to learn to take care of themselves and handle things on their own. All these experiences, I believe, can push them to be independent. For example, if a British student takes one year off to travel to China, he or she will at least learn to book international flights and overcome culture shock to fit in. It can also be expected that s/he learns to organize time on his or her own.

In the meanwhile, doing a gap year also helps young students have a better understanding about themselves and society, which can be a fairly rewarding experience to their future studies, careers and life as well. Young people are always ambitious and expect overnight success. In this fast-paced society, they tend to mistakenly believe that they can easily succeed by attending reality TV shows or winning a lottery. The world, unfortunately, is a tough place. No matter students work or travel, they will get to know what the work world is like and what skills employers are expecting from them; students will also know better what they are capable of and what they are truly interested in. Such knowledge plays a vitally important role in guiding young people to decide on their major in university and their future employment after graduation. Otherwise, they are just wasting their time in university and someday they will regret. This explains why so many Chinese students have no idea about what they want and what they should do to achieve it. If these students did a gap year, their life would be completely different.

In conclusion, I am confident that doing a gap year before starting university is a positive practice for young students because it enables them to see clearer who they are and what the real life is like as well as helps them develop good qualities to better prepare themselves for future life.

【参考译文】

我们注意到一些高中毕业生在上大学前会休整一年出去工作或者旅游。在我看来，这个做法非常的积极并且可以让年轻人受益无穷。

首先，间隔年提供了一个绝佳的机会让年轻人锻炼独立。众所周知，当学生出去工作或旅游时，他们的父母或监护人无法陪在身边替他们打理事情。因此，这些年轻人将不得不学会自己照顾自己、处理事情。我相信，所有这些经历都会使得年轻人变得独立。例如，如果一个英国学生在间隔年期间到中国旅游，他/她至少可以学会预订国际航班，学会克服文化冲击适应新环境。我相信他/她也会学会安排时间。

与此同时，间隔年也可以帮助年轻的学生更好地了解自己和社会，这对他们以后的学习、工作以及生活都很有好处。年轻人总是雄心壮志并且期望一夜成名。在这个快节奏的社会，很多年轻人天真地以为只要参加选秀节目或者买彩票就可以成功。遗憾的是，社会很残酷。无论学生是去工作或是旅游，他们都会明白职场是什么、雇主在期待什么；学生也会更好地明白自己的能力和兴趣。这些都可以引导年轻人更好地决定他们的大学专业以及毕业之后的职业规划。否则，他们很可能只是浪费时间，迟早会后悔。这也是为什么那么的中国学生完全搞不清自己的目标也弄不懂如何去实现这些目标。如果这些学生当初经历过间隔年，他们的人生将完全不同。

总之，我坚信大学前休学一年是一个非常积极的做法，因为它可以帮助学生更好地认清自己和现实生活，并且有助于他们锻炼一些好的品质，来更好地为以后做准备。

高分词汇精选 Word Bank

序号	词汇	意思	同义表达（自测）
1	It has been noticed that...	我们注意到	
2	such a practice	这种做法	
3	gap year	间隔年	
4	a golden opportunity	绝佳的机会	
5	develop independence	锻炼独立	
6	as is known,	众所周知	
7	custodians	监护人	
8	as a consequence,	因此	
9	culture shock	文化冲击	
10	fit in	融入、适应	
11	organize one's time	安排时间	
12	rewarding	有益的	
13	ambitious	有抱负的	
14	overnight success	一夜成名	
15	fast-paced	快节奏的	
16	mistakenly believe	错误/天真地以为	
17	reality TV shows	选秀节目	
18	win a lottery	赢彩票、中奖	
19	be capable of	能	
20	play a vitally important role in...	扮演重要角色	
21	I am confident that...	我坚信	
22	prepare oneself for...	为……做准备	

CHAPTER 4
环境篇

相比教育类考试话题而言，环境类的考题在雅思考试中的比重要轻得多。不过，它却是雅思考试中一个不容忽视的题材，尤其是当人们的环保意识越来越强而我们的环境却在日益恶化时，环保则显得尤为重要。需要指出的是，尽管移民类的写作也考环保类题目，但这类考题更多的是集中在学术类考试中，平均每年2-4题左右。

通过对比分析，环境类的历年考题可以总结为以下几部分：①飞机航班造成的能源消耗及空气污染，②日常生活中人们如何做环保，③经济发展/工业生产对环境的影响，④其他。

一、飞机飞行造成的能源消耗及空气污染

1. Many people think cheap air travel should be encouraged because it gives ordinary people freedom to travel further. However, others think this leads to environmental problems, so air travel should be more expensive in order to discourage people from having it. Discuss both views and give your own opinion.

2. Some people believe that air travel should be restricted because it causes serious pollution and uses up the world's fuel resources. To what extent do you agree or disagree?

3. Long distance flight uses more fuel than car and brings pollution to the environment. We should discourage non-essential flight (such as tourist travel) rather than limit the use of car. To what extent do you agree or disagree?

4. Some people think it is beneficial that traveling by air is becoming cheaper and cheaper, while other people think it has drawbacks to environment and the recourses of the world. Discuss both views and give your own opinion.

万能思路

尽管问法不尽相同，不过，上述题目核心内容都是在谈到底该如何看待air travel（航空旅行）。如果撇开题目，泛泛来谈这个话题的话，我们可以总结出以下几个信息：①相对地面交通而言，飞机航班确实更加方便快捷；②飞机的油耗远比私家车要大得多；故，如果能明确什么航班是不必要的，应该采取适当的措施予以应对或者限制；③在可预见的将来，人们长距离的出行会越来越频繁，这意味着相关的环境的问题会持续存在甚至恶化；④仅凭提高油价或者提高机票价格来减少人们乘坐飞机出行的做法根本就是在逃避问题，因为富人及企业有能力承受，真正受影响的只有普通老百姓，这不公平；而且提高油价或者机票价格反而会造成新的问题：对航空业及旅游业的打击、航空运输成本的提升导致的物价抬升；⑤所以，更好的做法一定是开发利用清洁能源和可再生能源，研发节能的交通工具。

就雅思写作而言，考生只需根据题目从上述要点中摘取相关信息进行拓展重组即可。下面，我将这些要点写成英文，供考生参考。

① 相对地面交通，飞机航班确实更加方便快捷。Air travel brings people the freedom to travel further. Compared with surface transport/other types of transportation, air transport is much faster, thus people can better organize their time in terms of traveling. In the meanwhile, there are occasions when only aero planes can bring people to their destinations while it is almost impossible for them to drive there. For example, it would be ridiculous for a Chinese businessman to drive all the way to Australia or New Zealand on a business trip, while it only takes ten hours or so to reach there by air.

② 飞机的油耗远比私家车要大得多。Statistics show that a 550-seat Airbus 380 consumes 1040 kilograms of fuels per hundred kilometers while an average car consumes 8 litres of petrol every hundred kilometers, less than 3 gallons. Therefore, increased use of air travel will ultimately add to energy problems. And so if non-essential flights could be identified, they should be discouraged. That said, however, it does not mean that the use of private cars should not be limited. After all, automobiles also consume fossil fuels. The picture can get uglier when more and more people can afford to drive cars.

③ 可预见的将来，人们长距离的出行会越来越频繁，这意味着相关的环境的问题会持续存在甚至恶化。The use of flights and cars will not only consume large amounts of fuels but also jeopardize the environment, resulting in environmental problems like global warming. What's worse, it is almost for sure that people will travel more in the future, and so the situation will deteriorate if no effort is made to address it. There are reasons to support this statement. First of all, people will make more money in the future. Once they have the spending power they would travel. Second, increased globalization and economic activities mean business trips are also expected to increase in the future. In addition, more and more international marriages will also encourage people to fly to see their relatives and friends. This list can go on.

④ 仅凭提高油价或者提高机票价格来减少人们乘坐飞机出行的做法根本就是在逃避问题，甚至会带来新的问题。To increase the cost of fuels or simply increasing the ticket prices is a short-sighted way to deal with this issue. The strategy of price hike will barely work because corporations and wealthy people can still afford the bill and for ordinary people, if they have to travel by air they will still stick to it. Surely, some people will not take flights as frequently as they used to, but this is not enough to change the whole situation. As a matter of fact, to increase the cost of fuels or ticket price will be a strong blow to the air transport industry and once the cost of transport goes up, the prices of many consumer goods also pick up. This is by no means a positive development for society. That is not to say that the cost of fuels must be low, but that it must stay at a reasonable level, not too high and not too low.

⑤ 所以，更好的做法一定是开发新能源，研发节能的交通工具。For the sake of sustainable development of human society, alternative energy sources should be explored. For instance, solar energy or biofuels should be used to replace, or at least decrease our reliance on, fossil fuels. Since biofuels are green and renewable, there will be no need to be concerned about air pollution and energy shortage. In the meanwhile, fuel-efficient cars should also be designed and mass-produced., like those of hybrid cars.

有了以上的这些要点，考生只需根据题目做出灵活改动，则任何涉及飞机航班类的雅思作文高分作文唾手可得。

Q1 廉价航空旅行（326 words）

Many people think cheap air travel should be encouraged because it gives ordinary people freedom to travel further. However, others think this leads to environmental problem, so air travel should be more expensive in order to discourage people from having it. Discuss both these views and give your own opinion.

Thanks to cheap air travel, ordinary people are now able to travel around as they please. While many people applaud the convenience brought by it, it is also argued that these cost-effective flights jeopardize the environment and should be discouraged by raising the ticket prices. While I agree that it is important to protect the environment, I would say that increasing the ticket price is not a wise idea.

On the one hand, I praise the freedom that air travel brings to people. Compared with other types of transportation, air transport is much faster, thus people can better organize their time in terms of traveling. In the meanwhile, there are occasions when only aero planes can bring people to their destinations while it is unrealistic for them to drive there. For example, it would be ridiculous for a Chinese businessman to drive all the way to Australia or New Zealand on a business trip, while it only takes ten hours or so to reach there by air.

On the other hand, I would also admit that flights bring emission of greenhouse gases like carbon dioxide to the environment, but simply raising the price of air travel is not an effective way to address the issue. In most cases, this strategy of price hike can barely work because corporations and wealthy people can still afford the bill and for ordinary people, if they have to travel by air they will still stick to it. Furthermore, it is important to stress that hiking the cost of fuels or ticket price will push up the cost of transport, and the prices of many consumer goods also pick up. This, by no means, is a positive development for society.

In conclusion, it is important that people stay environmentally conscious while enjoying the great convenience of cheap air travel, yet it is a short-sighted act to make air travel more expensive to keep people away from it.

【参考译文】

得益于廉价航班，普通老百姓如今可以随心所欲地到处游玩。尽管很多人对这种便利性表示欢迎，但是也有人认为这些廉价航班破坏了环境，因此需要涨价来限制人们乘坐。在我看来，保护环境确实很重要，但提高机票价格并不是个有效的应对方法。

一方面，我对航空给人们带来的自由出现表示赞许。同其他交通方式相比，飞机航班要快速的多，因此人们可以在出行时更好地安排时间。同时，有时只要飞机航班能将人们送往目的地，而要自己开车去则几乎不现实。例如，如果一位中国商人去澳大利亚或者新西兰出差时自己驾车过去，这个就太荒谬了；而如果是坐飞机的话，则十小时左右就可以到。

另一方面，我也承认飞机航班会带来温室气体的排放（如二氧化碳），但仅仅靠提高机票价格并不是个有效的途径来应对这个问题。通常，涨价的策略都收效甚微。因为企业和富人照样能够承担得起这笔费用；而对于普通老百姓而言，如果他们不得不乘坐飞机，他们也将继续乘坐。而且，需要强调的是，提高燃料价格或者票价会推高运费，从而推高很多消费品的价格，而这无论如何都不是个积极的现象。

总之，人们在享受廉价航班的便利性的同时必须要有环保意识，但是通过涨价来限制人们乘坐飞机航班是个目光短浅的做法。

高分词汇精选 Word Bank

序号	词汇	意思	同义表达（自测）
1	thank to	由于	
2	applaud	鼓掌欢迎	
3	cost-effective	省钱的	
4	jeopardize	破坏，损害	
5	discourage sb. from doing sth.	劝阻	
6	praise	赞许	
7	organize one's time	安排时间	
8	destination	目的地	
9	business trip	出差；商务旅行	
10	emission	排放	
11	greenhouse gases	温室气体	
12	carbon dioxide	二氧化碳	
13	in most cases	通常	
14	strategy	战略，策略	
15	price hike	涨价	
16	corporations	企业，公司	
17	by no means	绝不	
18	environmentally conscious	有环保意识的	

Q3 长途航班vs私家车（255 words）

Long distance flight uses more fuel than car and brings pollution to the environment. We should discourage non-essential flight rather than limit the use of car. To what extent do you agree or disagree?

The act that EU imposed carbon tax on flights from countries including US, Canada and China earlier in 2012 has once again reminded people of the environmental damages that long-distance flights can bring. Considering the huge consumption of fuels and heavy pollution brought by long-distance air travel, some people propose that non-essential flights should be discouraged instead of limiting the use of cars. From my perspective, however, I think both of them should be discouraged.

On the one hand, long-distance flights mean heavy consumption of fossil fuels and huge emissions of greenhouse gases like carbon dioxide. This is environmentally damaging as it adds to global warming. In this sense, if certain flights can be identified as non-essentials, they should be restricted. For example, when an airline's tourist flight is only booked by a few people, these passengers should be encouraged to fly with other airlines.

On the other hand, the use of private cars also brings similar consequences on the environment and should thereby be limited. Car exhaust is the leading cause for air pollution in the city and it also contributes to greenhouse effect. What's worse, more and more people are able to afford automobiles and if all of them drove cars, the damage it does to the environment would be even worse than flights do. For these reasons, there should be limits on the use of private cars.

In conclusion, people should be dissuaded to use both long-distance flights and private cars as both types of transport consume fuels and bring environmental problems.

【参考译文】

2012年初欧盟对来自美国、加拿大和中国的航班强制征收碳排放税的行为再一次提醒人们长途航班会造成的环境破坏。考虑到长途航班所消耗的巨大燃料及严重污染问题，一些人主张我们应该限制不必要的航班，而非限制私家车的使用。不过在我看来，长途航班和私家车都应该要被限制。

一方面，长途航班意味着大量化石燃料的消耗和巨大的温室气体的排放（如二氧化碳）。这是很不环保的因为它加剧了全球变暖。从这个意义上讲，如果我们能够确定什么航班是不必要的，这些航班就应该被限制。例如，如果只有一些人预订了某航空公司的旅游航班，则我们应该鼓励这些乘客改成其他航空公司的航班。

另一方面，私家车的使用也会对环境造成同样的影响，所以也应该加以限制。汽车尾气是城市空气污染的主要因素，并且它也会导致温室效应。更糟糕的是，越来越多的人有能力购买车辆。如果每个人都开车的话，由此造成的环境问题相对航班来讲将会有过之而无不及。由此，我们必须限制私家车的使用。

总之，我们应该劝阻人们乘坐长途航班和使用私家车，因为这两种交通方式既会消耗燃料又会带来环境问题。

高分词汇精选 Word Bank

序号	词汇	意思	同义表达（自测）
1	impose sth. on sb.	将……强加于	
2	environmental damages	环境问题	
3	heavy consumption of	大量消耗……	
4	fossil fuels	化石燃料	
5	greenhouse gases	温室气体	
6	carbon dioxide	二氧化碳	
7	environmentally damaging	破坏环境的	
8	global warming	全球变暖	
9	in this sense	从这个意义上讲	
10	airlines	航空公司	
11	car exhaust	汽车尾气	
12	leading cause	主要原因	
13	greenhouse effect	温室效应	
14	dissuade	劝阻	

二、日常生活如何做环保

5. Many people think it is very important to protect the environment but they make no effort to do it themselves. Why does it happen? How to solve this problem?

6. Many people realize the importance of protecting the environment. But they still make no effort to do it. Why is the case? What can individuals do to improve the situation?

7. Individuals can do nothing to improve the environment. Only governments and large companies can make a difference. To what extent do you agree or disagree with this opinion?

8. Some people believe that environmental problems are too big for individuals to deal with, while others think that individuals should take some actions. Discuss both views and give your opinion.

9. Environmental problems are too big for individual countries and individual people to address; we have reached the stage where the only way to protect the environment is at an international level. To what extent do you agree or disagree with this opinion?

万能思路

谈到环境话题，基本上都会涉及环保的具体措施。相对而言，有些话题是从政府或者企业角度考查，而更多话题都是让考生回答普通老百姓应该如何保护环境。我们不妨先撇开这些题目，就事论事地从各方面谈谈应该如何保护环境。

- 国际合作与环保：international cooperation plays a vitally important role in resolving environmental issues. 不过，这个巨大的话题很难三言两语将其写完整，此处只谈全球变暖。Global warming has become increasingly serious over the past few years, and international effort must be made so as to reverse the situation. Currently, carbon emission is still of substantial quantities. Statistics show that in 2008 the top 5 countries that brought the most carbon dioxide emissions were China, the United States, European Union, India and Japan. The consequences of global warming could be serious, like the rise of sea level and climate change globally. One of the good things is that climate talks are now held regularly. For example, there was the climate talk（气候大会）in Germany in 2011. There is also the Kyoto Protocol（《京都议定书》）to urge countries to cut carbon emission.

• 国家与企业：国际合作确实很重要，但是说到底，这需要各国政府的大力配合。否则，再多的协议也是一纸空文。所以，环境问题的解决很大程度上依赖于政府的监管才能得以实施。至于企业，除了很有环保意识的企业外，多数的企业可能都无暇顾及环保，尤其是在发展中国家。从这个意义上讲，政府和企业的环保措施应该放在一块写。①政府要做的第一件事情应该提高企业及公众的环保意识。Efforts should be made to increase public awareness of environmental protection. For example, relevant campaigns or educational programs can be launched and public service advertisements can be broadcast on TV. ②立法约束企业的行为。Laws should be introduced to regulate the business behaviour of certain industries so that they do not pollute the environment as they wish. For example, the government should encourage businesses to use biodegradable materials for packaging. Also, factories should be encouraged to introduce better facilities such as water purification system to minimize the damages they bring to the environment. If businesses fail to meet those targets, penalties such as large fines or heavier taxes should be imposed on them. ③成立环保基金。Environment fund should be established by every government. In theory, every single person pollutes, so does every business. Accordingly, the government can levy tax on both parties and use the money to set up environment and conservation fund. ④企业研发环保的产品。Environmentally friendly products should be designed and put into mass production. Nowadays, almost every person wants to own his or her own car, refrigerator and TV that sort of thing. All these products can bring environmental damages. Since we cannot ask people to give up on these items and go back to simpler lifestyles, we must work on technology to decrease the potential damages that such items bring to the environment. For example, electric cars should be mass produced and promoted among consumers.

• 个人与环保：正如前文所说，每个人都会污染环境，所以人人都有责任为环境保护贡献一份力量。而且，国家的很多环保政策的贯彻于落实最终还是要回归到每个人身上。尽管每个人的力量单薄，但是，united, people can always make a difference (in what they want to achieve) . ①First, individuals can reduce the consumption of disposable products, such as plastic bags. For instance, they can bring their own re-usable bags when they go shopping. ②Second, people can try to lead a low-carbon life to cut their carbon footprint. This can be easily achieved if they use public transport instead of driving private cars. ③In the meanwhile, recycling is also extremely important. Rather than simply throwing all recycling into one bag, as with trash, people should sort out different types of recyclables before delivering them to a recycling center. For example, newspapers and cardboard should be put away separately. People should not simply throw them in the same dustbin.

需要指出的是，上述观点仅仅是抛砖引玉，供广大考生参考。一方面，以上观点足以保证考生完成一篇高质量的雅思作文；另一方面，也希望考生们细心观察，多补充些其他要点；同时，也借此呼吁大家一同保护环境，从身边做起，坚持不懈。

Q7 个人vs环保（276 words）

Many people realize the importance of protecting the environment. But they still make no effort to do it. Why is the case? What can individuals do to improve the situation?

Most people realize it is vitally important to protect the environment. However, few of them take action to do it. The purpose of this essay is to analyze the two principal causes, which are people's misconception about environmental protection and their selfishness.

There is a popular misconception that environmental issues are too big for individuals and only the government and large companies have the ability to combat these problems, such as global warming and deforestation. In the meanwhile, most people are selfish not to change their lifestyles to protect the environment. The most common evidence is that few people choose public transport over private cars when they go to work, hence jeopardizing the environment.

I think people must understand that when it comes to environmental protection, every person has the obligation to contribute and every little bit counts. First, individuals can reduce the consumption of disposable products, such as plastic bags. Specifically, they can bring their own re-usable bags when they go shopping. Second, people can try to lead a low-carbon life to cut their carbon footprint. This can be easily achieved if they use public transport instead of driving private cars. In the meanwhile, to sort recycling and rubbish also helps environment. Rather than simply throwing all recycling into one bag, as with trash, people should sort different types of recyclables before delivering them to a recycling center. For example, newspapers and cardboard should be put away separately. People should not simply throw them in the same dustbin.

In conclusion, better late than never. As long as people bear in mind those tiny things mentioned above, they can make the environment change for the better.

【参考译文】

绝大多数人都明白环保很重要，但却很少有人付诸行动。本文的目的是分析导致这种现象的主要原因，即人们错误的环保观念及他们的自私行为。

人们往往存在一个普遍的错误理念，即环境问题对于公众来讲太大了，只有政府和大企业有能力解决，像全球变暖和森林退化便是如此。与此同时，多数人都过于自私，不愿意通过改变自己的生活方式来保护环境。最为明显的例子是，当人们去上班时，人们往往使用私家车而非公共交通，从而破坏了环境。

我认为人们必须明白，只要涉及环保任何人都有义务贡献出自己的力量，并且他们的每一分努力都是有意义的。首先，人们可以减少使用一次性产品如塑料袋。具体而言，人们可以在购物时带上自己的循环购物袋。其次，人们可以尽量过低碳的生活以减少自己的碳足迹。只要人们尽量使用公共交通而非私家车便可做到这一点。同时，将垃圾分类也有助于保护环境。人们应该在将垃圾送到回收站之前将不同的可回收物品分类放置，而非将它们与垃圾一道通通丢进同一个垃圾袋。例如，报纸和硬纸盒就应该分开放置，而非丢在同一个垃圾桶。

总之，迟做总比不做好。只要人们时刻牢记上面提到的小事情，他们就可以让环境变得更好。

高分词汇精选 Word Bank

序号	词汇	意思	同义表达（自测）
1	vitally important	很重要	
2	misconception	错误的观念	
3	principal	主要的；校长，领队	
4	There is a misconception that...	有些人误以为……	
5	combat	解决；战斗	
6	global warming	全球变暖	

序号	词汇	意思	同义表达（自测）
7	deforestation	森林退化	
8	jeopardize	破坏，损害	
9	have the obligation to do sth.	有义务做某事	
10	Every bit counts.	每个点点滴滴都很重要。	
11	consumption	消费，消耗	
12	disposable products	一次性产品	
13	plastic bags	塑料袋	
14	re-usable bags	循环袋	
15	specifically	具体而言	
16	a low-carbon life	低碳的生活	
17	carbon footprint	碳足迹	
18	recyclable	可循环的（物品）	
19	Better late than never.	迟做总比不做好。	
20	bear in mind	时刻牢记	
21	change for the better	变得更好	

三、经济发展/工业生产对环境的影响

10. An increase in production of consumer goods results in the damage of the natural environment. What are the causes and possible solutions?

11. An increase in the production of popular consumer goods can damage the natural environment. To what extent do you agree or disagree?

12. Pollution and other environmental problems are resulting from a country's developing and becoming richer. Some think this cannot be avoided. To what extent do you agree or disagree?

13. Some people think the international cooperation has brought benefits to the world environment protection, while some people think more benefits have been brought to the international business. Discuss both views and give your own opinion.

答题思路

从考试频率上讲，以上题目考得不多。就答题内容而言，或多或少，与前面的题目也存在部分相似的地方。Q10-Q11明显是同一个内容，Q12则可以写国家在发展工业、经济的过程中可以进行立法来规范工业及企业的行为，具体参照第二部分“日常生活如何做环保”中万能思路之“国家与企业”的相关内容。至于Q13，国际合作到底对环保更有利还是对国际贸易更有利，考生只要停下来想一想自己究竟能数得出几个国际性的环保机构或者会议，又数得出几个国际性的经济贸易组织或者会议，答案就一目了然了。

Q11 消费品生产vs环境（351 words）

An increase in production of consumer goods results in damage of the natural environment. What are the causes and possible solutions?

Human activities have brought many damages to the natural environment, and increased production of consumer goods is one of those on the list. This essay will examine how different procedures of the production jeopardize the environment.

Many raw materials for the production of consumer goods come directly from the natural environment, and when the demand for them increases with the expansion of the production there is a possibility of damaging the environment. For example, to mass produce papers or wooden items like furniture, substantial amounts of timber must be supplied. When the demand for such items expands, more trees would be cut, hence possible deforestation appears. In the meanwhile, harmful chemicals or industrial waste can be discharged in the production of certain consumer goods, such as in the cases of cosmetics production or the manufacture of electronic products. In addition, when consumer goods are produced and packaged, huge amounts of packaging materials will be used, which in many cases are plastic. This is by no means an environmentally friendly thing.

I think the government should play the leading role in reversing this situation. First, the government should, either through legislation or via taxation, encourage industries to buy better facilities (such as water purification system) to minimize the damages they bring to the environment. The government can also introduce laws to urge businesses to use biodegradable materials for packaging. If industries and businesses fail to meet those targets, penalties such as large fines should be imposed on them, i.e. whoever makes profits at the cost of the natural environment should be punished. More importantly, effort should be made to increase public awareness of environmental protection. For example, relevant public service advertisements should be put in national newspapers to remind people what role they can play in protecting environment. As long as the people realize the importance of protecting the environment, the whole situation will change for the better.

In conclusion, any stage involved in the production of consumer goods can bring environmental issues, yet as long as laws are introduced to regulate the business behaviour of industries, the problems will be alleviated.

【参考译文】

人类的活动已经极大地破坏了自然环境，消费品生产便是其中的一部分。本文将论证消费品生产的各个环节是如何破坏环境的。

很多消费品的原材料直接来自于大自然，而当生产扩张导致对原材料的需求扩大时，便有可能造成环境破坏。例如，大批量生产纸张或者木制家具需要使用大量的木材，当需求增长时，更多的树会被砍掉从而可能造成乱砍滥伐。同时，某些消费品的生产过程中（如化妆品或电子产品的生产制造）也会排放出有害的化学物质或者工业废料。此外，消费品生产出来后，也要使用大量的包装材料，而这通常都是用塑料。这绝不会环保。

我认为政府应该扮演主导性的角色来扭转这一局面。首先，政府应该通过立法或者征税来鼓励工业引进更好的设施（如污水净化系统）将其造成的环境问题最小化。政府也可以引入立法敦促企业使用可降解的包装材料。如果工业企业没能实现这些目标，则可以对其处以巨额罚款等惩罚。换言之，如何以牺牲环境为代价赚取利润的人都应该收到惩罚。最重要的是，我们应该采取措施提高公众的环保意识。例如，可以在全国性的媒体上投放相关的公益广告来提醒人们人们如何保护环境。只要公众意识到环保的重要性，整个情况就会好转。

总之，消费品生产的任一环节都会造成环境破坏。不过，只要引入立法来规范各行各业的商业行为，这些问题将会得到极大的缓解。

高分词汇精选 Word Bank

序号	词汇	意思	同义表达（自测）
1	examine	检查；分析	
2	jeopardize	破坏，损害	

序号	词汇	意思	同义表达（自测）
3	raw materials	原材料	
4	mass produce	批量生产	
5	substantial amounts of	大量的	
6	deforestation	乱砍滥伐	
7	packaging materials	包装材料	
8	by no means	绝不	
9	environmentally friendly	环保的	
10	play the leading role in	扮演重要角色	
11	legislation	立法	
12	taxation	征税	
13	introduce laws to	引入立法	
14	biodegradable	可降解的	
15	penalties	惩罚	
16	fine	罚款	
17	at the cost of	以……为代价	
18	public service advertisements	公益广告	
19	change for the better	变好	
20	regulate	规范	
21	alleviate	减轻，缓解	

四、其他

14. Many people say that we have developed into a "throw-away" culture, because we are filling up our environment with so many plastic bags and rubbish that we cannot fully dispose of. To what extent do you agree or disagree with this opinion and what measures can be taken to reduce this problem?

15. We have entered a throw-away society and fill the environment with rubbish. What are the causes and what are your solutions?

16. Now the increased demand of fresh water has became a global problem.

Discuss the causes of the increased demand and what measures the government and individuals should do to solve this problem.

17. The consumption of the resources on the earth such as oil, forests and fresh water is increasing at an alarming rate and above a dangerous level. What are the causes of this? What can be done to solve the problem?

18. Fossil fuels (coal, oil, natural gas) are the main sources in many countries, but in some countries the use of alternative sources of energy (wind energy and solar energy) are encouraged. To what extent do you think it is a positive or negative development?

19. The increasing level of noise pollution has affected people's life significantly. What factors caused this problem? How to solve this problem?

20. The best way to solve the world's environmental problems is to increase the price of fuel. To what extent do you agree or disagree? Use your own experience and give an example to support your idea.

21. The development in technology causes environmental problems. Some people believe the solution to these problems is everyone accepts a simpler way of life, while others say that technology can solve these problems. Discuss both views and give your own opinion.

22. Many tourist attractions such as mountains, rivers and beaches are heavily polluted by visitors. Why is the case? What can be done to change it?

说 明

关于上述题目，最近的考试是Q21，于2015年考过；Q19几乎都是移民类在考。至于其他考题，由于考试频率很低，加上部分题目可以从之前的章节中找到相应的内容加以参考，此处略去不表。

Q22 旅游景区被污染（281 words）

Many tourist attractions such as mountains, rivers and beaches are heavily polluted by visitors. Why is the case? What can be done to change it?

With the boom of tourism over the past few years also comes a downside, i.e. many tourist sites have been jeopardized seriously. I think the reasons are tourists' low awareness of the environment and the poor management of related authorities.

Many tourists, especially in developing countries, still have this mentality that they only spend money to have fun and environmental protection should be the government's responsibility. This misconception persuades them to behave as they please. For instance, if throwing garbage everywhere suits them well, they will just do it.

Meanwhile, poor management of the tourist attractions is also to blame. In many places, there is a lack of tourist facilities. When there are not enough trash cans for people to leave their garbage or there are no signs to warn visitors about the bad consequences of not behaving themselves, it is only logical that visitors litter everywhere.

To combat the situation, I think the solution lies with the authorities. First of all, they should invest to improve tourist facilities, ensuring at least enough dustbins and public toilets. Visual signs should also be set up to deter any uncivilized behavior. Once visitors cross the line and damage the environment, severe penalties such as huge fines should be imposed on the violators. Such policies have been working effectively in Singapore and it should be working everywhere. If necessary, an upper limit should also be set on the number of visitors that every tourist attraction can receive.

In summary, the destruction of tourist spots should be blamed on visitors' selfishness and governments' poor management. The improvement of the situation, however, would be for the government to tighten up rules to discipline visitors.

【参考译文】

近些年，随着旅游业的繁荣，也出现了一定的弊端：很多旅游景区的环节遭到严重破坏。我认为，主要原因是游客淡薄的环保意识以及有关部门的疏于管理。

很多游客，尤其是在发展中国家，总以为他们是来花钱享受的；至于环保，那是政府的事。这种错误的观念使得他们想做什么就做什么。假设随地乱扔垃圾让他们开心，他们会不假思索地就丢。

与此同时，景区糟糕的管理也难逃其责。在很多地方，旅游设施不够完善。倘若人们找不到足够的垃圾桶来扔垃圾，又或者景区没有警示牌警示游客肆意乱来的不良后果，那么游客随手乱扔垃圾就不足为奇了。

我认为，要解决这些问题，终究还是要靠政府。首先，政府应该投入财力去完善旅游设施，至少应确保有足够的垃圾桶和公厕。还应该设立标志牌来杜绝任何不文明的行为。一旦游客过界并破坏环境，我们应当对其处以严厉惩罚，例如处以巨额罚款。这些措施在新加坡效果显著，应该推广开来。此外，如果有必要的话，各景区还应对其可接待的游客人数设立上限。

总之，旅游景区的破坏主要是归咎于游客的自私和政府糟糕的管理。不过，应对措施则有赖于政府加强规章制度来约束游客（的行为）。

高分词汇精选 Word Bank

序号	词汇	意思	同义表达（自测）
1	boom	繁荣	
2	jeopardize	破坏	
3	awareness of the environment	环保意识	
4	authorities	当局	
5	mentality	思想、想法	
6	misconception	错误观念	
7	behave as they please	随心所欲	
8	tourist facilities	旅游设施	
9	logical	合理的	
10	litter	乱扔垃圾	
11	to combat the situation	解决该问题	
12	visual signs	标志牌	
13	uncivilized	不文明的	
14	cross the line	越过界	
15	severe penalties	严厉的惩罚	
16	huge fines	巨额罚款	
17	impose ... on	将……强加于	
18	violator	违规者	
19	tighten up	加强	
20	discipline	约束；管教	

CHAPTER 5
科技篇

科技类的话题也是雅思写作的常客。科技可以和教育结合出题，也可就生活的方方面面出题。笔者认真对比了近10年的雅思写作题库，将这一类别的话题总结成以下六类，逐一进行讲解。

一、科技 vs 社交

1. The development of technology changes the way people connect with each other. In which way does the development of technology change the types of relationships among people? Does it have positive or negative effects on the relationships?
2. Some people think technology such as mobile phones are destroying the social interaction. Do you disagree or not? Give your reasons and relevant examples.
3. Someone believes that modern telecommunication devices have many benefits to human, while others think otherwise. What is your opinion? Please discuss and use examples to support your own ideas.

万能思路

这3道题目尽管问法不同，但是归根到底都是在谈科技（尤其是手机和电脑）对人际关系的影响。通常，很多人都会认为人们对科技的依赖会导致面对面的交流的减少。我们不否认当今社会人们确实不如以前那样经常坐下来面对面地拉家常。但是大家认真想想：现代人缺乏面对面的交流真的是因为科技的广泛使用吗？难倒不是因为现代社会人人都比以前更忙于工作忙于生计所致？而且，面对面的交流的减少就一定意味着人际关系变的疏远吗？设想一下，你和你的家人或者朋友分居大洋两岸或者身处南北半球，如果不借助科技的力量保持经常性的联系，你还认为距离产生美吗？事实上，一切都是借口。只要我们懂得合理地利用科技，它就能为我们所用。它带来的好处就可以最大化，而它可能造成的负面影响也会被最小化。

Q1 科技vs社交（307 words）

The development of technology changes the way people connect with each other. In which way does the development of technology change the types of relationships among people? Does it have positive or negative effects on the relationships?

Breakthroughs in modern technology have brought remarkable positive changes and negligible negative consequences to people's lives. The two most important innovations are in the way they interact with each other: mobiles and computers. Through the extensive use of mobile phone and computers, the consequences of which are hotly debated.

In the past, people used to pay a visit to each other for their social interaction. Nowadays, however, they are becoming more reliant on modern communication technology, particularly instant messaging technologies on their mobile phones and computers. People tend to text each other or interact with each other on social networks like Facebook in the virtual cyber world. This saves valuable time in an otherwise hectic world.

Some people may worry that the reliance on social media reduces face-to-face contacts among individuals and can decrease the sense of closeness between each other. However, simply because people do not see each other often does not mean that they would be alienated from each other. In an age when people are occupied with work and tend to be mobile, the use of modern technology can actually help them stay in touch with each other so that their bonds can be tied and forged. Otherwise, people's relationships might become disconnected. Also, it is noticed that people now have more interaction with strangers than ever before. On the Internet, they talk with thousands of people that they have never met before and yet they become good friends while exchanging ideas in a safe and anonymous way.

In conclusion, I do not think the use of modern technology makes people feel distanced from each other. People may not have much time to see each other, yet they can still maintain their relationship thanks to improved technology. As long as people can be creative about using technology, the benefits it brings can be maximized.

【参考译文】

现代科技的突飞猛进给人们的生活带来了深远的积极改变和微不足道的负面影响。最重要的创新主要是人们交流方式的改变。随着手机和电脑的广泛应用，人们正激烈地辩论着由此带来的影响。

以往，人们的社交互动都是彼此拜访。但是现在，人们变得依赖现代通讯科技，尤其是即时通讯技术。人们往往彼此发短信或者在社交网络如Facebook上的虚拟网络世界进行互动。在忙碌的社会，这无疑节约了宝贵的时间。

有些人会担忧对社交媒体的依赖减少了人们之间面对面的交流，从而降低了彼此间的亲密关系。但是，仅仅因为人们不长见面并不意味着他们就会彼此疏远。如今，人们都忙于工作，而且流动性也很强，科技是使用实际上可以帮助他们保持联系，从而得以维持彼此之间的联系和交流。否则，人们之间的关系可能会断掉。而且，我们也注意到人们现在和陌生人的互动也比以前要多。在互联网上，人们和成千上万的陌生人安全、匿名地交流想法，他们素未谋面，但却成了好朋友。

总之，我认为科技不会让人们变得彼此疏远。或许人们没时间见面，但是他们仍可以借助科技得以维持关系。只要人们懂得合理利用科技，其带来的好处就可以最大化。

高分词汇精选 Word Bank

序号	词汇	意思	同义表达（自测）
1	breakthroughs in technology	科技的发展	
2	negligible	微不足道的	
3	innovations	创新；改变	
4	the extensive use of	……的广泛应用	
5	pay visit to	拜访	
6	social interaction	社交	
7	reliant	依赖的	
8	instant messaging	即时通讯	
9	social networks	社交网络	

序号	词汇	意思	同义表达（自测）
10	text sb.	给某人发短信	
11	virtual	虚拟的	
12	cyber world	网络世界	
13	hectic	繁忙的，忙乱的	
14	be occupied with	忙于	
15	mobile	流动的	
16	anonymous	匿名的	
17	social media	社交媒体	
18	face-to-face contacts	面对面的交流	
19	the sense of closeness	亲密感	
20	alienate	疏远	

二、科技的影响

4. It is now possible to perform everyday tasks, such as bank transaction, shopping or even office work, without meeting people face to face. What are the effects it may have on individuals and the society as a whole?

5. There are social, medical, and technical problems associated with the use of mobile phones. What forms do they take? Do you agree that the problems outweigh the benefits of the mobile phone?

6. More and more work is done by machines. Do you think the positive impact on the development outweighs the negative impact on individuals or the society?

7. Anyone can use a mobile phone to answer the work call and home call at any place, 7 days a week. Some people think this development has negative effects on both individuals and the society. Do you agree or disagree?

8. There are more workers who work from home and more students who study from home. This is because the computer technology is more and more easily accessible and cheaper. Do you think it is a positive or negative development?

9. Many employees may work from home with modern technology. Some people claim that it can benefit only the workers, not the employers. Do you agree or disagree?

10. The speeding up of life in many areas such as travel and communication has negative effects on society at all levels—individual, national and global. To what extent do you agree or disagree?

万能思路

这些题目的写作观点都不尽相同。但是核心一点可以是：虽然科技会带来一些负面影响，但是只要我们懂得合理使用科技，则负面影响可以被最小化而积极的影响能被最大化。

Q4 在线交易·范文（310 words）

It is now possible to perform everyday tasks, such as bank transaction, shopping or even office works, without meeting people face to face. What are the effects it may have on individuals and the society as a whole?

With improved technology, individuals now are able to get many daily tasks done without leaving home. Such convenience has remarkably changed people's life and has also exerted big effects on society as a whole.

For individuals, many positive effects can be produced. To illustrate, people do not need to travel all the way to banks or shopping malls if they wish to settle financial transactions or make purchases. All they need to do is to lie back on the couch, click the mouse and have the deal closed. If the job allows, people may even work from home. Such convenience can be extremely helpful to people as they can better organize their time and enjoy life with ease, particularly for those new mothers who tend to struggle between family and work.

For society, however, there can be both positive and negative consequences. On the bright side, the easy access to the Internet and convenient services it promises brings higher efficiency in business. There will be faster money circulation and more people will sell and buy online. Consequently, a large volume of trade will be contributed to. For example, on November 11 2013 the Alibaba group（the largest online retailer in China）alone accounted for more than $5.7bn（£3.5bn）worth of transactions, far surpassing the big shopping days in the US or Europe. Yet on the other hand, the boom of e-commerce also pose great threats to traditional retail trade, forcing/pushing huge amounts of companies and physical stores out of business and leading to many job cuts. (*That said, however, there is no doubt that the employment opportunities that e-business creates far offset the possible problems it brings.*)

To reiterate, although there can be potential challenges, it should not be a big issue as facts have shown that both individuals and society can benefit greatly from the extensive use of technology.

【参考译文】

随着科技的发展，人们现在可以不用出家门就完成很多日常事务。这种便利性极大地改变了人们的生活并且对整个社会也产生了深远的影响。

对于人们来讲，会有很多积极的影响。具体来说，如果人们要处理金融交易或者购物，人们不再需要长途跋涉赶到银行和商场。人们只需躺在沙发上，点点鼠标就完成整个交易。如果工作允许，人们还可以在家办公。这种便利性极其重要因为人们可以更好地安排时间、享受生活，尤其是对于那些夹在工作和家庭之间苦苦挣扎的年轻的妈妈们来讲。

至于社会影响，我则认为有利有弊。从积极的方面讲，便捷的网络及其服务带来了更高的工作效率。资金流通将更为迅速，网络交易将更为频繁。由此，会带来巨大的交易量。例如，2013年11月11日，仅阿里巴巴集团一家的交易量便超过57亿美元（35亿英镑），远远超过欧美的主要购物日。但是另一方面，电子商务的繁荣也会对传统的零售业造成巨大的冲击，迫使大量企业及实体店破产和公司裁员（*不过话说回来，电子商务创造的就业机会远大于它所带来的问题*）。

总之，尽管存在潜在的风险，但是科技的广泛应用并不会造成大的问题，因为事实证明人们和社会都会从中受益无穷。

高分词汇精选 Word Bank

序号	词汇	意思	同义表达（自测）
1	exert effects on...	对……产生影响	
2	make purchases	购物	

序号	词汇	意思	同义表达（自测）
3	work from home	在家办公	
4	organize one's time	安排时间	
5	enjoy life with ease	享受生活	
6	On the bright side,	从积极方面讲，	
7	money flow	资金流通	
8	consequently	因此	
9	the boom of e-commerce	电子商务的繁荣	
10	pose threat to...	对……构成威胁	
11	retail trade	零售业	
12	physical stores	实体店	
13	be pushed out of business	破产	
14	job cuts	裁员	
15	employment opportunities	就业机会	
16	offset	抵消	
17	challenges	挑战、问题	
18	the extensive use of...	……的广泛应用	

Q9 在家办公是否对雇主无益？（322 words）

Many employees may work at home with the modern technology. Some people claim that it can benefit only the workers, not the employers. Do you agree or disagree?

The improvement of technology makes it possible for people to get their work done from home. Yet some people say that this new work pattern only benefits employees. Personally, however, I think both employees and the employer can reap benefits from it.

Apparently, home office saves employees long commutes to and back from the office, which can be a great relief to them. They can also organize their time better to take care of some personal matters. This is particularly important for new mothers as they do not need to struggle between work and family. Instead, they can take care of both simultaneously.

For employers, some people argue that computer-assisted home office benefits them little on the basis that when employees work from home, without the monitor of the employer or superior, chances are the employees slack off. However, I think these people ignore one thing, i.e. most employers are result-oriented, and when the employer assigns tasks to his or her subordinates, a deadline will also be attached. In other words, there is no need to worry about the way the employees organize their time at home. As a matter of fact, employers can also benefit remarkably from such a working style.

It is obvious that distance working makes the management of business more flexible and efficient. When the task is set, all the employer needs to do is to check on staffers' performance by the deadline. Thus, he or she can better organize his or her own time to take care of other equally or even more important issues. In addition, a flexible schedule for employees also does the employer credit and enhances employees' loyalty to the business, let alone the money saved from rent.

In conclusion, as long as clear directions are given for each task assigned and modern technology can be used in a creative way, the benefits of home office for employees and the employer can be maximized.

【参考译文】

科技的发展使得在家办公成为可能。有些人认为这种新的工作模式只对员工有利，不过在我看来，员工和雇主都可以从中受益无穷。

显然，在家办公节省了员工上下班的通勤，让他们如释重负。他们也可以更好地处理自己的私人事情。这对年轻的妈妈们尤为重要，因为她们不再需要在工作和家庭之前苦苦挣扎，而是可以两者兼顾。

对于雇主，有些人认为计算机辅助的在家办公对他们几乎不会让他们受益。因为如果缺少雇主或是上司的监督，员工很可能偷懒。不过我认为他们忽略了一个事实，即多数雇主都是只注重结果。当他们给下属布置任务时，他们也会设定相应的截止日期。换句话说，没有必要担心员工在家如何安排时间。事实上，这种工作模式可以让雇主受益无穷。

显然，远程办公使得雇主的管理更加灵活高效。一旦布置好任务，雇主要做的只是在截止日期验收一下员工的业绩。如此一来，雇主自己也可以更好地安排自己的时间去处理其他同样重要甚至更为重要的事情。此外，弹性的工作安排也可以加强员工的忠诚度，让雇主受益，更别提还可以节省租金。

总之，只要每个任务都给出清晰的指令并且充分利用科技，在家办公就可以给员工和雇主带来最大化的利益。

高分词汇精选 Word Bank

序号	词汇	意思	同义表达（自测）
1	work/employment pattern	工作模式	
2	reap benefits from...	从……中受益	
3	home office	在家办公	
4	commute	通勤	
5	organize one's time	安排时间	
6	personal matters	私事	
7	simultaneously	同时	
8	...on the basis that...	因为	
9	be superior to...	比……优异	
10	Chances are...	很可能	
11	slack off	偷懒	
12	result-oriented	结果导向型	
13	subordinates	下属	
14	deadline	截止日期	
15	In other words	换言之	
16	distance working	远程办公	
17	flexible schedule	弹性的工作时间	
18	do sb. credit	对某人有利	
19	loyalty (to)	忠诚	
20	let along...	更别提……	

三、科技vs食物生产

11. Food can be produced cheaper if we use improved fertilizers and better machinery. However, some of the methods may be dangerous for human health, and have negative effects on local communities. What is your opinion?

12. The range and quality of the food have been improved by the advancement of science and technology. Discuss the advantages and disadvantages about this and present your view.

13. Some people support the developments in agriculture such as factory farming and creations of new types of fruits and vegetables, while others oppose this view. Discuss both views and give your opinion.

万能思路

说到底，这三题都是在讨论究竟要不要利用科技进行食物生产。正如笔者一贯所主张的那样，考生们先不要急着去写到底要不要用科技，或者用科技会带来什么利弊。不急！我们先来分析一下有些人的担忧：①使用农药、化肥会对人体健康带来危害；②利用科技培养创造出来的新食品（尤其是转基因食品）会对人体健康构成威胁；③利用机械化进行大规模的农业生产会给农业人口带来“失业”的问题。好了，对方的疑虑已经找到，我们接下来要做的事情就是去分析这些担忧是否站得住脚——①没错，农药及化肥的残留的确对人体健康有害。但是，请认真想想，绝大多数农作物都是这么栽培出来的。我们天天吃餐餐吃，为什么我们依然健壮如牛？因为我们吃之前会将水果蔬菜“洗刷刷”？非也。每个国家都有食品安全部门对食品安全进行检疫与监督，以确保食品安全无公害。尽管我们发生过三聚氰胺、塑化剂等食品安全事故，但我们还是要相信政府有能力有决心杜绝类似事情的再次发生；②谈到转基因食品，很多人闻之色变。由于究竟转基因食品会对人体健康造成什么样的影响目前尚未定论，所以很多人强烈反对转基因食品进入市场。美国是转基因食品最多的国家，60%以上的加工食品含有转基因成分，90%以上的大豆、50%以上的玉米、小麦是转基因的[①]。在我国，转基因食品还比较罕见，到目前为止，经农业部生物工程安全委员会准许商业化的转基因作物仅有6个，其中有3个涉及食品，即两种西红柿、一种甜椒[②]。但是，食用转基因食品将成为不可回避的事实。美国、加拿大两国的消费者虽然大多数已接受了转基因食品，但多数欧洲人仍然对转基因食品持怀疑态度。我们不想去评论这场连政府和科研人员都无法定论的辩论；但是至少，多数国家的政府都有出台相关规定，

① 资料来源：http://finance.jrj.com.cn/consumer/2010/07/1320287755513.shtml

② 资料来源：http://www.docin.com/p-503582652.html

在明确转基因食品对人体健康的影响前不轻易让其进入市场流通，并且要求转基因食品一旦进入市场，其包装上必须表明是转基因食品。这样，·是否适用这类食品其实完全取决于消费者本人。所以，我并不认为消费者会蒙受极大的健康危害；③至于机械化的农业生产，我认为这是大势所趋。而且考生们请考虑以下事实：早在2009年，联合国粮食及农业组织的数据显示全球饥饿人口超过10亿，且仍处于增长态势[①]；《2010年世界人口状况报告》称，世界人口总数为69.09亿[②]；此外,《2010年世界人口状况报告》预测，到2050年，世界人口将超过90亿[③]。试问，如果不利用高科技进行大规模的农业生产，我们的食物供应将如何满足日益膨胀的人口爆炸？所以，即使真的有人要因此“失业”，我也认为这个代价是我们必须付出的，而且是值得的。况且，随着科技的进步和社会的发展，一定会有新型产业浮现，转移一部分过剩的农业人口。

一旦有了上述的思路和背景知识，相关的作文就变得相当简单了。

Q11 化肥、机械化农业（268 words）

Food can be produced cheaper if we use improved fertilizers and better machinery. However some of methods may be dangerous for human health, and have negative effects for local communities. What is your opinion?

Despite the fact that the use of modern technology in food production has already brought enormous benefits to human society, some people still concern themselves about food safety as well as other ramifications it brings to local communities. Personally, I think people are just over-reacting to such a trend.

It is understood that excessive use of chemicals like fertilizer or pesticide can jeopardize human health. However, in every country, there are food safety inspections to ensure that the chemicals in foodstuffs do not exceed safety limits. In other words, there is no need to worry about the health risks that fertilizers pose to us.

When it comes to the use of better machinery in food production, I agree that it can bring negative effects for local communities as fewer people will be required to farm land, and thus the labor workers in the rural areas will be replaced. Many of them will have to leave for urban areas to seek a living while old people and children are left on their own. However, I think we need to understand that with population explosion, we

---

① http://wenku.baidu.com/link?url=LDjXuLWsLaMKgzMcQkHAdt7n2pqdq0ffnfbRh9uKmgOSm2cIMBTi_eExJZqUsPQGuP18FhBmkMkXuokhL0sbpH35TKW0bgz8R3VaPFPZrZC

② http://www.gaoxinedu.net/ThreeAndOne/components/News/CommShow.aspx?cmtid=254307

③ http://www.chinadmd.com/file/oouwoivrp3rvsuuiesvrztix_1.html

have to guarantee that there is an abundant food supply, which, I believe, cannot be achieved without the use of machine and technology. In addition, I believe there will be new industries to absorb the surplus of labor force in rural communities.

In conclusion, the use of improved technology in food production is an irreversible trend. I do not agree that there would be health hazards. As for the negative effects to local communities I do not think they should be a concern.

【参考译文】

尽管将科技用于食物生产已经给人类社会带来了巨大好处，一些人仍然担忧食品安全问题和一些地方所遭受的影响。在我看来，人们有些反应过激了。

我能理解过量的使用化学物质例如化肥和杀虫剂会有害健康。不过，世界上的每个国家都会有食品安全检查机制来确保食品中的化学物质不会超出安全标准。换言之，我们没有必要担心化肥给我们带来的健康问题。

至于食物生产中的机械化，我承认机械化农业会对一些地方造成负面影响。由于不需要很多人进行农业生产，农村的劳动力会被取代。很多人会因此背井离乡进城谋生，而老人和小孩则被留在乡下无人照料。不过，我认为我们必须明白，人口爆炸需要充足的食物供应，而我认为这必须得依赖机器和科技。此外，我相信会有新兴的行业吸收这些剩余的劳动力。

总之，利用科技进行食物生产是大势所趋。我不认为会有什么健康问题。至于对一些地方造成的消极影响，我认为也没有必要担忧这些问题。

高分词汇精选 Word Bank

序号	词汇	意思	同义表达（自测）
1	concern oneself with	担忧	
2	food safety	食品安全	
3	ramification	影响	
4	overreact (to)	(对……) 反应过激	
5	excessive use of	过量的使用	
6	jeopardize	损害	
7	labor workers	劳动者	

序号	词汇	意思	同义表达（自测）
8	seek a living	谋生	
9	abundant	充裕的	
10	food supply	食物供应	
11	population explosion	人口爆炸	
12	rural communities	农村地区	
13	absorb	吸收	
14	an irreversible trend	大势所趋	
15	health hazards	健康问题	

四、科技vs想象力&创造力

14. Many people believe that the increasing use of modern technology at work and in leisure is reducing people's creativity. To what extent do you agree or disagree?

15. Leisure is a growing industry. Nowadays, more modern technology is used in entertainment, which may lead people to be less creative. Do you agree or disagree?

说 明

关于这两题，我认为考生需要注意的是在举例时一定要选好角度。很多考生会在不同段落中写到Google、苹果、微软等科技巨头的创新。不过，细想一下，这些公司都是属于同一类型的公司，倒不如只保留其中一个例子，并从其他方面补充相关事例。例如，可以写写日常生活中普通人是如何利用科技进行创新的。又或者在回应Q14时，分别从工作和娱乐休闲的角度来举例。这样，文章的逻辑会显得更为严谨。

Q14 科技扼杀创造力（321 words）

Many people believe that the increasing use of modern technology at work and in leisure is reducing people's creativity. To what extent do you agree or disagree?

Some people claim that we are too relied on modern technology in our work and leisure activities and thus our creativity is decreasing. As far as I am concerned, such a statement cannot be justified.

I think when people say the extensive use of modern technology suffocates people's creativity they must base their argument on the fact that we are becoming increasingly relied on the Internet for almost everything. It is observed that many people nowadays tend to plagiarize/steal ideas from the Internet. This is why the Internet search giant Google becomes so popular across the world. Many people actually cannot live without it. However, I think we should also notice that not every one is kidnapped by the Internet. There are many people who actually condemn such a behavior. If anything, I would say that millions of examples prove that people's imagination and creativity has been boosted with the use of technology.

For many ordinary people, they have shown their talent in arts with the use of user-friendly computer programs such as Photoshop. They modify the pictures of celebrities to spoof/mock these people. This cannot be done without creativity. We can also see this creativity in magic. Magicians across the world employ cutting-edge technology to create illusions and show people a magical world. Again, this cannot be achieved without imagination. For technicians, technology also increases their creativity beyond the wildest imagination of ordinary people. A case in point is that people can talk to their smart-phones because of built-in voice-activated assistant like Siri whereas they could only use mobile phones to make calls in the past.

In conclusion, while only a few stories show that some people are losing their creativity because of technology most examples have proven that human being's imagination and creativity have been remarkably unlocked with the extensive use of it.

【参考译文】

有些人认为我们在工作和休闲娱乐中过于依赖现代科技，以至于我们的创造力在下降。在我看来，这个说法没道理。

我认为，人们之所以认为过分地使用科技会扼杀我们的创造力是因为我们现在过于依赖互联网了。我们注意到很多人如今上网剽窃，这就是为何像谷歌这样的网络搜索巨头在全世界如此的受欢迎。很多人已经无法离开谷歌了。但是，我们也必须意识到不是每个人都被网络所绑架了。很多人事实上是在指责这种行为的。我认为无数的例子都证明了人们的想象力和创造力借助科技得到了提升。

很多普通老百姓借助像Photoshop这样的实用软件挖掘出了自己的艺术才能。他们恶搞名人照片。如果没有创造力，这不可能实现。魔术也可以很好地展示这点。全世界的魔术师们利用最前沿的科技来创造各种幻象给人们呈现一个梦幻的世界。同样，如果没有想象力，这一切不可能完成。对于技术人员来讲，科技也以最超乎常人想象力的方式激发着他们的创造力。例如，人们以前只能用手机打电话，可是现在接着内置语音助手人们可以和他们的智能手机进行对话了。

总之，尽管少数人由于科技而丧失了创造力，更多的事例表明人类的想象力和创造力都在科技的广泛应用下得到了开发。

高分词汇精选 Word Bank

序号	词汇	意思	同义表达（自测）
1	cannot be justified	不合理	
2	suffocate	扼杀	
3	plagiarize	剽窃	
4	kidnap	绑架	
5	condemn	谴责	
6	boost	推动、促进	
7	ordinary people	普通人	
8	user-friendly	容易操作的、好用的	
9	computer programs	电脑程序/软件	
10	modify	修改	
11	celebrity	名人	
12	spoof/mock	嘲弄	
13	cutting-edge technology	前沿的科技	
14	smart-phones	智能手机	
15	built-in	内置的	
16	voice-activated assistant	语音助手	
17	unlock one's imagination	开发想象力	
18	the extensive use of...	……的广泛应用	

五、科技/互联网是否取代……

16. Some people believe that computers and the Internet can take the place of schools, while others contend that teachers play an important role in schools. Discuss both views and give your opinion.

17. Some people claim that public museums and art galleries will not be needed because people can see historical objects and works of art by using a computer. Do you agree or disagree with this opinion?

18. Maintaining public libraries is a waste of money since the computer technology is now replacing their functions. To what extent do you agree or disagree?

19. It is inevitable that as technology develops traditional cultures must be lost. Technology and tradition are incompatible—you cannot have them both together. To what extent do you agree or disagree?

20. With the increasing use of mobile phones and computers, less people tend to write letters. Some people even think the skill of writing letters will disappear completely. To what extent do you agree or disagree? How important do you think letter writing is?

21. It is not necessary to travel to other places to learn about other cultures. We can learn just as much from books, films and the Internet. To what extent do you agree or disagree?

万能思路

之所以人们会认为电脑能够取代学校、老师、博物馆及图书馆等，无非是因为电脑具备以下优势：①方便快捷。人们可以随时随地进行相关的活动；②信息量巨大。无论如何，互联网上能够共享的信息远远大于任何一所学校或者一座博物馆或图书馆所能提供的书面信息。③廉价。相比营运学校或者博物馆，互联网要做的主要是开发并维护相关的程序；相对而言政府无需为此投入巨大的财政扶持。但是考生们一定不要忘记：①电脑优势再大，人们不一定会也不一定能够自觉去利用这些优势；②电脑始终无法取代人际交往；③学校、博物馆、图书馆、旅行有其独特优势。实际上，电脑与现有物之间的关系应该共存，相互补充。

Q16 电脑取代学校&老师（321 words）

Some people believe that computers and internet can take the place of schools, while others contend that teachers play an important role in schools. Discuss both views and give your opinion.

There has been much debate about whether teachers and traditional schools will be replaced by computers and the Internet. Some people predict that the day is 2050. As far as I am concerned, teachers are still important even in the information age and will not be replaced.

It is true that computers bring much convenience to learners as they can organize the schedule flexibly and control the learning process as they wish. Also, the Internet boasts larger quantities of information than teachers can provide. Any information that students cannot get from teachers can be accessed on the Internet, be it academic or non-academic. In addition, it is easier and cheaper for the government to organize distance-learning programs than to run schools.

However, these people fail to realize that most students are not sufficiently mature to learn alone. If children learnt with computer on their own, without much self-discipline or/and supervision from parents, chances are they take this opportunity to play computer games or do some other things that are not related to study. In that case, such a well-intended program would simply fail. In contrast, if students learn at school, teachers will not only be the tutor but also the monitor. In other words, in school there is a better atmosphere for students to study in.

In the meanwhile, it is also important to stress that students do not only need to learn academic subjects but also need to master practical skills like interpersonal skills and how to handle things. These skills can barely be picked up if students sit in front of the computer all day long. But in school, they can learn from teachers and classmates all these critical skills.

In conclusion, computers have their advantages, but students are too young to study on their own. Also, many practical skills must be learnt in school environment. Therefore, teachers and schools will continue to play an important role in education.

【参考译文】

人们经常辩论传统的学校与好老师是否会被电脑和互联网所取代，一些人甚至预言这会发生在2050年。在我看来，即使是在信息时代，老师都是非常重要的并且不会被取代。

不可否认，电脑给学习者带来了巨大的便利因为他们可以灵活地安排时间、掌控学习进度。同时，互联网提供的信息远比老师提供的多。任何老师无法提供的信息都可以在互联网上获得，无论是学习上的还是其他的。此外，组织远程教育远比经营学校要简捷实惠。

但是，人们没有意识到绝大多数学生都尚未成熟到自主学习。如果学生对着电脑独自学习，由于缺少自律及父母的监督，他们很可能利用这个机会玩电脑游戏或者做一些与学习毫不相干的事。如此，则这个善意的机制就会失败。相比之下，如果学生在学校学习，老师不仅扮演了教师的角色而且起到监督的作用。换言之，学校能够给学生提供更好的学习氛围。

与此同时，还应该强调的是，学生不仅仅要学习理论学科，而且还要掌握类似于交际和独立处事之类的技能。若是学生整天坐在电脑前，他们无法掌握这些技能。而在学校，他们可以从老师和同学那里学到这些重要技能。

总之，尽管电脑有它的优势，但是学生太小无法自主学习。并且，很多实用性的技能只能在学校学到。因此，老师将在学校教育中继续扮演重要角色。

高分词汇精选 Word Bank

序号	词汇	意思	同义表达（自测）
1	There has been much debate about	人们辩论	
2	information age	信息时代	
3	bring much convenience to...	给……带来便利	
4	vast quantities of	大量	
5	distance learning (programs)	远程教育	
6	fail to realize that...	忽略了	
7	mature	成熟的	

序号	词汇	意思	同义表达（自测）
8	self discipline	自律	
9	supervision	监督	
10	Chances are...	很有可能……	
11	well-intended	善意的	
12	tutor	老师	
13	interpersonal skills	人际交往能力	
14	critical	重要的	
15	practical skills	实用技能	

Q17 互联网 vs 博物馆 & 艺术馆（347 words）

Some people claim that public museums and art galleries will not be needed because people can see historical objects and works by using computer.
To what extent do you agree or disagree?

It has been suggested that with the proliferation of computer and the Internet, people will no longer have to visit museums and art galleries to see historical objects and works of art. As I see it, there is little justification in such a statement.

I understand that computer boasts a series of advantages over real museums and art galleries as it can give people the freedom to get close to arts whenever they want to. People also save the trouble of lining up in real museums.

However, I still believe that public museums and art galleries will still be important and irreplaceable. Firstly, public museums and art galleries offer average visitors the first-hand experience, which I think is far better than the virtual experience computer provides. In public museums and art galleries, visitors can lean forward and step back to observe a particular item from different angles. More importantly, in museums and art galleries there is such an authentic atmosphere that visitors may even feel like they were on the spot/scene to witness a particular historical event or the creation of certain works of art. For instance, online technology can never show people the magnificence of the Terra Cotta Warriors in China unless they travel there to see those life-like art works with their own eyes.

Another reason that public museums and art galleries will still be needed is that they serve educational functions which computers fail to achieve at a comparative level. As has been illustrated, with such an immersive atmosphere and the items exhibited in (front of) visitors' face out there visitors of all ages can always learn a lot about a country's culture and history when they visit museums and art galleries. In contrast, only independent learners can learn with computer while most visitors especially children and senior citizens will find it boring and unappealing to stay around computer.

In conclusion, museums and art galleries bring visitors a better experience and serve a better educational function than computer does. They have played an important role in human society and will remain important in the future.

【参考译文】

有些人认为随着电脑和互联网的普及，人们无需再去博物馆和画廊欣赏文物和艺术品。在我看来，这个看法不靠谱。

我理解相对于博物馆和画廊，电脑有一系列优势，因为它使得人们可以随时都接触到艺术。而且，人们也省去了在博物馆排队的麻烦。

尽管如此，我坚信博物馆和画廊仍会很重要并且不可取代。首先，博物馆和画廊给游客带来了亲身体验，这远比电脑所能提供的虚拟体验要好得多。在博物馆和画廊里，游客可以凑近或者退后并从不同的角度来欣赏某个物品。更重要的是，博物馆和画廊中的氛围是如此的逼真以至于游客仿佛身临其境地见证了某个历史事件或者见证了某个艺术品的创作过程。例如，在线科技始终无法呈现秦始皇兵马俑的宏伟壮观，除非人们去到现场感受。

博物馆和画廊会继续存在的另一个理由是他们可以起到教育的功能，而电脑则无法做到同样的效果。正如前文所言，博物馆和画廊的氛围如此逼真而且物品就陈列在游客面前，因此各个年龄段的游客都可以从中了解一个国家的历史和文化。相比之下，只有真正懂得独立学习的人才能利用电脑进行学习，而多数游客尤其是老人和小孩通常都会认为整天围着电脑转既无聊又无趣。

总之，博物馆和画廊能提供比电脑更好的体验和教育。它们在人类社会中始终扮演着重要角色，而且将来也将继续扮演重要角色。

高分词汇精选 Word Bank

序号	词汇	意思	同义表达（自测）
1	It has been suggested that...	有些人认为	
2	the proliferation of...	……的普及	
3	historical objects	文物	
4	work of art	艺术品	
5	boast	拥有、炫耀	
6	a series of	一系列	
7	save the trouble of doing sth.	省去……的麻烦	
8	irreplaceable	无可替代的	
9	average visitors	游客	
10	first-hand experience	亲身体验	
11	virtual	虚拟的	
12	More importantly, ...	更重要的是	
13	authentic	原汁原味的	
14	As has been illustrated, ...	如上所述	
15	immersive	浸泡式的	
16	senior citizens	老年人	

六、其他

22. Children spend much time on TV, video and PC games. Some people believe it is good for them while others believe that is bad. Discuss these two views and give your own opinion.

23. Mobile phones and the Internet are very useful. However, it is rare for old people to use them. In what ways could mobile phones and the Internet be useful to old people? How to encourage the old people to use this new technology?

24. Some people believe that robots will play an important role in future society, while others argue that robots might have negative effects on society. Discuss both views and give your opinion. (OR, Some people think that robots are very

important for human's future developments, while others argue that they are dangerous and have negative effects on society. Discuss the advantages and disadvantages brought by intelligent robots.)

25. Lately, more and more work has to be done by machines. To what extent do you think the positive effects of this development outweigh the negative effects on individuals and society?

说 明

除Q24-Q25外，以上题目的答题思路各不相同，请考生认真备考。

Q22 小孩vs电视＆电脑（314 words）

Children spend much time on TV, video and PC games. Some people believe it is good for them while others believe that is bad. Discuss these two views and give your own opinion.

Television and computer play an important role in people's daily life and they help people learn about many things. However, people now are debating whether children should be encouraged to spend much time on television and computer games. Personally I think children can reap benefits from it as long as they do not become addicted to those things.

First, TV programs can tell children many things about the real life and widen their horizons. This is extremely important for children to prepare for future life. For example, many TV programs teach children how to behave well and how to get along with others. Those skills can be very useful in the future when children grow up and step into society. As for computer games, they can do good to children's intellectual development. We know that in those games, children need to use their imagination and creativity to employ both strategies and tactics to conquer their rivals and achieve the task.

Yet on the other hand, it should be pointed out that children should understand that they should not spend too much time on video games and television. Otherwise, there will be problems. For one thing, students' time will be wasted. For another thing, some TV programs and computer games contain too much violence. They can be very misleading to children, because children are not sufficiently mature to make judgment and they are very likely to imitate these wrongful acts.

Therefore, I think it would be better if proper guidance is given to children so that they can know what types of computer games and TV programs are good for them. If possible, parents can stay with children when they watch TV or play video games and tell them what is right and what is wrong.

In conclusion, I would say that television and computer have both advantages and disadvantages to children. It depends on how they use these items. As long as they can receive guidance to judge, they will benefit from modern technology.

【参考译文】

电视和电脑对于人们的生活非常重要，并且他们帮助人们了解很多事情。但是，人们如今纠结于究竟应不应该鼓励小孩花很多时间看电视或者玩电脑游戏。在我看来，只要小孩子不沉迷于其中，他们就能从中受益。

首先，电视帮助小孩更了解生活并拓展视野，这对他们适应未来至关重要。例如，很多电视节目教会小孩如何处世、如何与人相处。这些技能在他们成年步入社会后会变得至关重要。至于电脑游戏，它们则有利于小孩的智力发育。我们知道，玩电脑游戏需要运用想象力和创造力并且使用战略战术来击败对手赢得比赛。

但另一方面，必须指出的是小孩子应该要明白他们不应该花太多时间玩游戏和看电视，否则会有问题。首先，会浪费时间；其次，一些电视节目和游戏过于暴力，这会误导小孩。因为他们尚未成熟，缺少判断，很容易去模仿这些糟糕的行为。

因此，我认为如果能够给小孩子给予适当的引导，让他们了解什么类型的电脑游戏和电视节目对他们有益，这会更好。可能的话，家长可以陪着小孩看电视或者玩游戏，并告诉他们是非对错。

总之，我认为电视和电脑有利有弊，取决于小孩怎么利用它们。只要给他们指导让他们学会判断，他们就能从中受益。

高分词汇精选 Word Bank

序号	词汇	意思	同义表达（自测）
1	reap benefits from...	从……受益	
2	be addicted to...	沉迷于	

序号	词汇	意思	同义表达（自测）
3	widen one's horizon	拓展视野	
4	do good to...	对……有利	
5	step into society	踏入社会	
6	intellectual development	智力发展	
7	imagination and creativity	想象力和创造力	
8	strategy	战略	
9	tactics	战术、策略	
10	not sufficiently mature	尚未成熟	
11	make judgment	判断	
12	imitate	模仿	
13	proper guidance	适当的引导	

Q23 手机&电脑vs老年人（357 words）

Mobile phones and the Internet are very useful. However, it is rare for old people to use them. What ways could mobile phone and the Internet be useful to old people? How can the old people be encouraged using this new technology?

With the proliferation of mobile phones and the Internet in people' daily life, life itself has turned into an amusement park. Yet elderly people are missing in this carnival. What benefits can they gain from those modern devices and how can they be encouraged to use those gadgets?

People may take it for granted that mobile phones and the Internet are useless to the elder, which is not true. First and foremost, senior citizens can use them to keep in touch with their children. We must understand that young people seldom live with their parents; they tend to be mobile and can hardly squeeze time from their tight schedules to visit their parents. Under such circumstances, mobile phones and the Internet can be the best way to get them together. Also, elderly people can use the internet and mobile phones to have fun and drive away boredom. With millions of apps online, old people can always find some user-friendly ones to have fun with, which in the meanwhile happens to be mentally beneficial to them as well. The easy access to the Internet also means senior citizens can keep themselves updated with current affairs around the globe or any other things if that is what interests them.

To encourage elderly people to make the best out of mobile phones and the Internet, the following incentives can be a good start. Mobile phone manufacturers and PC makers as well should be encouraged to design special handsets for the aged population, like phones with big screen and buttons. To make it even better, built-in voice activated assistant and other user-friendly software must be pre-installed. Meanwhile, training programs can be provided at community level. Some old people stay away from modern technology simply because they do not know how to use it. Once someone can volunteer to train them, they will find technology appealing.

In conclusion, mobile phones and the Internet can be important tools for communication and entertainment as well as information sources for old people. All we need to do is to ensure there are customized models for them and programs to train them to use these tools.

【参考译文】

随着手机和互联网在人们日常生活中的普及，生活本身都变成了一个游乐场。不过，这场盛宴中却少了老年人的身影。究竟老年人可以从这些现代设备中享受到什么好处？我们又该如何去鼓励他们使用这些设备呢？

人们可能会想当然地以为手机和互联网对老年人没用，其实不然。首先，老年人可以用它和子女保持联系。我们必须明白，年轻人很少和父母住一块，他们流动性很强而且很难从忙碌的工作中挤时间去看望父母。在这种背景下，手机和互联网是最好的方式将他们联系在一起。此外，老年人也可以利用手机和互联网进行娱乐，打发无聊。老年人可从网上无数的app应用中挑选一些好用的来消遣，而这同时又有利于他们的头脑。轻松上网还意味着老年人可以了解时事或其他他们感兴趣的事物。

要鼓励老年人充分利用手机和互联网，以下措施可以开个好头。我们可以鼓励手机和PC制造商设计一些特殊的型号给老年人这个群体，例如大屏幕大按键。更理想的是，在里面内置语音助手和预装其他实用的软件。同时，我们可以在社区内提供培训。有些老年人远离科技仅仅是因为他们不懂怎么使用，一旦有人志愿去教他们怎么用，老年人就会喜欢科技。

总之，对于老年人来讲，手机和互联网可以是非常重要的通讯和娱乐工具，以及信息渠道。我们所要做的就是确保有为他们量身定做的机型和相应的培训项目。

高分词汇精选 Word Bank

序号	词汇	意思	同义表达（自测）
1	with the proliferation of...	随着……的普及	
2	amusement park	游乐场	
3	senior citizens	老年人	
4	carnival	狂欢、嘉年华	
5	modern devices/gadgets	现代设备	
6	take it for granted that	想当然地认为	
7	live under the same roof（with）	一起住	
8	be mobile	流动性强	
9	squeeze time	挤时间	
10	tight schedules	忙碌的工作/安排	
11	pay visit to	拜访	
12	under such circumstances	在这种背景下	
13	drive away boredom	排挤孤独	
14	apps	应用	
15	user-friendly	好用的、用户友好型的	
16	be mentally beneficial to	对头脑有益	
17	access	权限；获得	
18	keep oneself updated with	了解	
19	current affairs	时事	
20	make the best out of	充分利用	
21	incentives	（激励）措施	
22	manufacturer	制造商	
23	handset	设备	
24	built-in voice-activated assistant	内置语音助手	
25	pre-install	预装	
26	volunteer to do sth.	志愿做某事	
27	information source	信息渠道	
28	customize	定制	

Q24 机器人（257 words）

Robots have been used widely in human society. Discuss the advantages and disadvantages brought by intelligent robots.

Technological breakthroughs have greatly revolutionized human society and one example of it has been the extensive use of intelligent robots. Like any other innovations, there are both positive effects and undesirable consequences with the use of robots.

On the bright side, intelligent robots can release human beings from endless time-consuming and/or physically-demanding work. Thanks to this, we can better manage our time and enjoy life with ease. We can also have more time to do other more creative things. Meanwhile, the automation and mass production brought by robots have remarkably boosted the productivity in all human activities. In addition, robots can save human workers from performing dangerous tasks as in the rescue work in an earthquake. Thanks to robots, worker safety can be remarkably increased in hazardous conditions.

Yet there is also the dark side of the picture. While robotic automation earns people more leisure time, it also results in a sedentary life among all of us. This is not a good sign as statistics show that globally each year more than two million people lose their lives because of a less active life. On the other hand, automation in manufacturing may seem to boost productivity, yet it also leads to huge job cuts. In the war, robots and drones can be turned into killing machines, literally killing machines. Once these machines are abused, innocent lives will be claimed.

In conclusion, there are both benefits and problems with the proliferation of robots. Humans must be very careful and creative to if maximized benefits are to be expected.

【参考译文】

科技的发展已经革命性地改变人类社会，机器人的广泛应用便是其一。与以往任何创新一样，机器人的使用既能带来好的影响，也能造成消极的后果。

从积极的方面讲，智能机器人可以将人从无尽的耗时间及耗体力的事情中解放出来。正因如此，我们可以更好地安排时间，享受生活。我们也有了更多时间投入其他更有创造力的事情中去。同时，机器人所带来的自动化和大规模生产也已极大地提高了人们社会的效率。此外，机器人还能避免人从事危险的工作从而拯救生命，例如地震中的援救工作。正是得益于机器人，危险的工作环境中员工的人身安全得到了极大提高。

但是这个现象也有不好的一面。尽管自动化给人们带来了更多的休闲时间，这却导致了久坐不动的生活方式。这不是什么好的现象，因为统计表明全球范围内每年因久坐不动的生活而死亡的人数超过二百多万。另一方面，尽管制造业的自动化提供了生产效率，但这也导致了大量的裁员。在战场上，机器人和无人机会被编程杀人机器，真正的杀人机器。一旦它们被滥用，则无辜的生命将被随意剥夺。

高分词汇精选 Word Bank

序号	词汇	意思	同义表达（自测）
1	technological breakthroughs	科技的发展	
2	revolutionize	改变	
3	the extensive/wide use of	……的广泛应用	
4	the proliferation of	……的普及	
5	innovation	创新	
6	undesirable consequences	负面/消极影响	
7	On the bright side, ...	从积极方面来讲，	
8	Yet there is also the dark side.	但也有消极的一面。	
9	free sb. from sth.	将……从……中解放	
10	time-consuming	耗时间的	
11	physically-demanding	耗体力的	
12	manage one's time	安排时间	
13	enjoy life with ease	享受生活	
14	automation	自动化	
15	mass production	大规模生产、批量生产	
16	boost	推动、促进、提高	

序号	词汇	意思	同义表达（自测）
17	productivity	效率、	
18	rescue work	援救工作	
19	worker safety	员工的人身安全	
20	hazardous	有害的；危险的	
21	a sedentary life	久坐不动的生活	
22	Statistics show that...	统计表明……	
23	job cuts	裁员	
24	drone	无人机	
25	killing machines	杀人机器	
26	claim a life	剥夺生命	
27	innocent	无辜的	
28	maximized	最大化的	

备注：Q25（machines）的答题思路可基本参照Q24（robots）一文。

CHAPTER 6 政府篇

政府职能类话题在雅思写作中属于常考题目。这类考题对于国内考生有较大的难度。一是因为这些话题都涉及大的社会问题，而随着雅思考生的低龄化以及学校繁重的课业，很多学生平时很少关注相关社会问题；二是由于我们国家的体制与国情都不一样，所以当考生用我们国家的国情来分析西方社会的事务时，往往很难说服考官。例如，我们由于实行的是民主集中制，所以政府很有魄力和财力去处理一些社会问题，而西方国家的政府往往财力有限，即使想做事，往往都是心有余而力不足，甚至我们看到2013年9月美国芝加哥政府因财力不济决定关闭50所小学；英国某地方政府考虑未来让一些地方的学生轮流去学校上课，理由同样是财政吃紧。理论上讲，雅思写作考得只是考生的英语表达能力，不涉及考生内容的正确与否，但是评分标准中的Task response一项却涉及考生能否充分地扣题，并将个人观点/理由拓展，而这或多或少都会关系到考生内容的说服力。

根据对近10年雅思写作题库的跟踪与分析，笔者将政府类话题重新整理分为以下几个板块：①为某事务买单：government VS individuals；②政府是否应资助某事物；③政府是否应介入某项事物；④城市规划；⑤是否只有政府能够解决某问题；⑥是否只有政府有资格/权利做某事；⑦其他。

一、究竟应该谁买单：政府vs个人?

1. Some people think the government should pay for those who go to university while others believe students should pay themselves. Discuss both views and give your own opinion.

2. Some people say that governments should pay for the public health care and education, while others say that it is not the government's responsibility. Please discuss both views and give your own opinion.

3. As the number of cars increases, more money has to be spent on road systems.

Some people think the government should pay for these. Others, however, think that the user should pay for the cost. Discuss both views and give your own opinion.

4. In some countries, when someone gets old they often go to live in a home with other old people where there are nurses to look after them. Sometimes the government has to pay for this care. Who should pay for this care, the government or old people themselves?

5. Some people argue that the companies and private individuals should pay the bill of cleaning up the pollution they produced, while others believe that it is the government's responsibility. What is your opinion?

万能思路

对于上述题目中所涉及的事业，由于基本上属于民生工程，所以考生当然可以写成应该由政府买单。而且，在一些社会制度相对完善的发达国家，政府也确实在为公众提供免费的相关福利。但是，广大考生也不要忽略另外的事实：那就是这些国家已经为此承受巨大的财政压力。高福利真的就可以解决所有社会问题吗？2010年世界杯期间，全法国罢工，导火索便是政府将退休年龄从60岁推迟到62岁，并且降低公职人员的福利；2011年，英国首相卡梅伦宣布削减800亿英镑的公共开支，涉及医疗、教育等方方面面；2013年10月，美国奥巴马政府关门，原因无外乎是两院在公共开支的预算方面无法达成共识。类似的例子还有很多。它们都折射出一个社会现实，即其实政府不像公众所想象的那样财源滚滚；相反，政府在很多方面都面临财政的空缺。所以，如果考生能将上述题目中涉及的议题写成双方应该共同承担责任则会更好地展示自己的逻辑。

以Q1（大学学费）为例，我建议考生在回答这类题目时，先认真思考以下几个问题。当所有问题都想通了，我们的作文也就写好了。

1. 人们是否有义务自掏腰包？显然是这样的，因为人们（这里指大学生）接受大学教育是为了自身的提升与发展。既然他们直接从中受益，他们理所当然需要支付相应的学费；

2. 是否所有人都有能力自费？当然不是。那么，由此导致的不公平又该谁来负责？例如，很多贫困家庭的孩子明明考上了大学，却因为无法承担高昂的学费而放弃读书的机会，这是非常遗憾的。我认为政府应该采取措施给人们提供帮助。

3. 既然政府有责任提供帮助，那这是否意味着政府需要给所有人都提供帮助呢？如果是政府提供免费的大学教育，政府是否会破产？如果政府只给贫困学生交学费，是否又对有能力承担学费的同学和家庭不公平呢？

4. 基于上述谈论，我们是否可以找到一个两全其美的做法？一方面，我们需要保证所有人平等享有某项服务的权利；另一方面，我们还得保证不让政府承受巨大的财政负担以免政府在其他事物上举步维艰。就大学学费而言，我认为我们可以要求学生及其家长自行承担学费，但政府可以出台相应的政策发放助学贷款来帮助贫困学生，这不失为一个双赢的做法。

由此，Q1（大学学费）我的立场为：I would say that university students should pay the tuition fee themselves, yet the government must provide help to those in need.

Q1 大学学费（350 words）

Some people think the government should pay for those who go to university while others believe students should pay themselves. Discuss both these views and give your own opinion.

While compulsory education in many countries is free, many people say it is also the government's obligation to offer free higher education. From my perspective, however, university students should pay the tuition fee themselves, yet the government must provide help to those in need.

It is natural for students to pay for their own education in the sense that they receive university education for the sake of personal development. Since they benefit directly from it, I think we have every reason to ask them to pay for what they gain. However, it is also observed that in many places many eligible students fail to access to university education merely because of the soaring school fee. This is completely unfair and should not be acceptable to any responsible governments. In these cases, the governments need to take action to help these children get the opportunity for formal education.

However, it should be noted that even if the government has the responsibility to help it does not (necessarily) mean that the government should pay the tuition fee for all students. After all, facts have shown that the government has to work under a tight budget and it has to take care of a wide range of other important issues, such as the infrastructure and healthcare service. If the government were to pay school fee for all students, it would be broke and that would be a disaster to the country.

As a matter of fact, I think it would be better if the government can offer student loans to those who could not afford the tuition. Not only can such a practice ensure students an opportunity for university education, but also it does not bring huge financial burden to the government, since not every student can be granted a loan.

In conclusion, going to university is a personal option and thus the government has no obligation to pay for students. The best scenario, however, would be that while students are paying the bill themselves the government should create a mechanism to help those who are academically qualified yet financially weak.

【参考译文】

由于很多地方的义务教育免费，很多人认为政府也有义务提供免费的高等教育。不过在我看来，大学生应该自己交学费，而政府可以给需要帮助的人提供帮助。

让学生自行负担学费是很正常的，因为他们是为了自身的提升而接受大学教育。既然他们直接从中受益，我们就有充分的理由让他们为自己的所得支付费用。当然，我们也注意到在很多地方一些符合条件的孩子仅仅因为日益高涨的学费而无法获得大学教育。这是极其不公平的，不应该为任何负责任的政府所容忍。像这些情况，政府应该采取措施来帮助这些孩子获得接受正规教育的机会。

但是，需要指出的是即使政府有责任帮忙并不意味着政府就得为所有学生支付学费。毕竟，事实表明政府预算有限。而且政府还有很多同样重要的事情需要处理，例如基础设施建设、医疗服务等等。如果政府给所有学生支付学费，政府可能会破产，而这将是个灾难。

事实上，我认为如果政府能够给贫困学生提供助学贷款则会更好。这个做法不仅可以确保学生能够平等地享有接受大学教育的机会，而且也不至于给政府带来巨大的财政负担，毕竟不是每个学生都能获得贷款。

总之，读大学是个人的选择，所以政府没有义务为学生支付学费。最好的做法是，由学生承担费用，而政府创造机制帮助那些学习好但家境差的学生。

高分词汇精选 Word Bank

序号	词汇	意思	同义表达（自测）
1	compulsory education	义务教育	
2	obligation	义务	

序号	词汇	意思	同义表达（自测）
3	higher education	高等教育	
4	from my perspective	在我看来	
5	tuition fee	学费	
6	people in need	需要帮助的人	
7	natural	自然的；正常的	
8	...in the sense that...	因为	
9	for the sake of...	看在……的份上	
10	personal development	个人的发展	
11	have every reason to do sth.	有充分的理由做某事	
12	It is observed that...	我们注意到	
13	eligible	合格的	
14	access	权限；得到	
15	work under a tight budget	预算有限	
16	a wide range of...	许多	
17	infrastructure	基础设施	
18	broke	破产	
19	student loans	助学贷款	
20	grant	批准	
21	scenario	方案	
22	mechanism	机制	
23	academically strong/qualified	学习好的	
24	financially weak	贫穷的	

备注：只要考生掌握了上面这个思路，那么这组题目中剩下的题目就可迎刃而解了。比方说Q4提到的养老问题，考生只要顺着上述思路去论证，并在倒数第二段提出一个新的方案即可。什么方案呢？相信考生们已经注意到了我们现行的社保制度：国家成立养老基金，老百姓只要在参加工作后连续缴纳一定年限的费用后便可在退休后领取相应的生活补贴。

二、政府是否应该资助某事物？

6. Some people believe that people who work for arts, such as painting, theatre or music should be supported financially by the government. Some people believe that they should find other financial support resources instead. Discuss both views and give your opinion.

7. Some people think it is wrong for the government to spend much money on artistic projects such as sculptures and art galleries. Do you agree or disagree?

8. Some people say the government shouldn't put money on art such as music and painting; they should spend more money on the construction of public facilities. Do you agree or disagree?

9. Some people say the government shouldn't put money on building theaters and sports stadiums; they should spend more money on medical care and education. Do you agree or disagree?

10. Some people believe governments should spend money on saving languages of few speakers from dying out completely. Others think this is a waste of financial resources. Discuss both views and give your position.

11. Maintaining public libraries is a waste of money since the computer technology is so advanced that the Internet and computer can replace them. To what extend do you agree or disagree?

12. Most countries spend a large amount of money in weapons to defend themselves though they are not at war. To the countries it should spend money to help the citizens who are poor and disadvantaged. Do you agree or disagree?

13. The first time when man arrived on Moon, he said: "It's a big step for mankind". But some people think it only made a little impact on our daily life. Millions of dollars has been spent on space research. But somebody says space research wastes money; they suppose money should be used to improve life consumption. To what extent do you agree or disagree?

14. It is more important for the government to spend money on promoting healthy lifestyle to prevent the illness rather than on the treatment for people who are already ill. Do you agree or disagree?

15. Money for postgraduate research is limited. Therefore some people think financial support from governments should be provided only for scientific research rather than research for less useful subjects. Do you agree or disagree?

16. Some people believe that national sports teams and individual men and women who represent their countries should be financially supported by the government. Others think they should be funded by non-government organizations (business, scholarship). Discuss both views and give your position.

17. Many people think that we are spending too much time and money on protecting animals. The money should be spent on human. Do you agree or disagree?

18. The restoration of old buildings in major cities in the world spends numerous government expenditures. This money should be used in new housing and road development. To what extent do you agree or disagree?

万能思路

这类题目是政府类话题中最重要的考题，其中又以“政府是否应资助艺术/艺术家”这类尤为重要。整个这类题目大同小异，出题思路基本都是：①政府应该花钱资助A而非B；②政府不应该花钱资助A。对于第①类，我们先别急着去写到底要不要资助B。我们先分析一下为什么人们认为应该资助A而非B，理由不外乎两点：一是A比B重要，二是政府财力有限，无力资助。弄懂了这两点理由，我们接下来的论证就很好写了。我们可以承认A重要，但这并不意味着B不重要。考生接着可直接论证B为什么重要。如果论证不来，我建议采取以下思路：几十年前A也不重要，正是由于有了政府的资助，A才变得如此重要；同理，B此刻貌似不重要，但是如果政府能够持续予以资助，将来势必会在人们日常生活中扮演重要角色。从这个意义上讲，或多或少，B理所当然要得到政府的财政扶持。当然，如果考虑到政府的确财力有限，我们也不强求一定要政府出钱；我们可以鼓励一些私人企业参与进来，予以财政资助。至于政府，它只要做好立法监管工作，确保各方合法受益即可。对于第②类题目，写作思路大同小异，此处略去不表。

还有一个思路来回答这类问题，即老百姓往往希望政府的每一分钱都投到与他们生活息息相关的领域去，让他们切身感受到受益。我们能理解老百姓的这种心情，但是我们必须强调多少普通老百姓还是比较没有远见的。他们往往只注重眼前的好处而忽略了长远的理由。如果处处由着普通老百姓的逻辑来治国安邦，则极有可能“后果很严重”。

Q7 政府资助艺术（374 words）

Some people think it is wrong for the government to spend much money on artistic projects such as sculptures and art galleries. Do you agree or disagree?

The way the government allocates its public spending has always been one of the top concerns of the general public. Considering the tight budget of the government, some people think that financial resources of the government should not be wasted on artistic projects like sculptures and art galleries. Personally, I think it would be shame on the government should it turn a blind eye to arts.

People always kidnap the government by saying that its revenues come from the taxes they pay and thus the government, the fund manager they say, should always put them above everything, which is true. But I think it is also important to stress that ordinary people are short-sighted not to put long term concerns ahead of short term profits. If all policies are formulated by their will, the consequences can be catastrophic.

On the surface, the investment in artistic objects like sculptures and art galleries does not improve people's living standard, and the money may seem to be better spent on public services like healthcare and infrastructure. However, people must understand that art is an important aspect of a nation's culture and history, and that it is important that the government preserve it for future generations. Otherwise, things can get fairly ugly. For example, there are so many sculptures of historical figures in the China-Japan War (also known as the Second Sino-Japan War, 1937-1945) across China to remind people what happened between these two Asian neighbours so that they cherish what they have today and that they can understand why these two countries have such a sensitive and vulnerable relationship. Money invested in these things is worthwhile, and I do not think it is a waste of financial resources. Plus, sculptures and art galleries spice our life up. Without them and such, human civilization would be dull. Imagine one day when the British Museum and the Louvre Palace are gone. Will people still be joyful? Will life still be as beautiful as it is today? I doubt it.

To reiterate, ignoring arts is a dangerous act because it not only jeopardizes the preservation of culture, but also turns people's life into a boring pond of dead water. Thus, it is important that the government sponsors artistic projects.

【参考译文】

政府如何支配公共开销始终是公众最为关心的事情。鉴于政府预算有限，一些人认为我们不应该在艺术工程如雕塑和画廊上浪费钱。就我个人而言，如果政府真的对艺术置之不理，那将是非常遗憾可耻的。

人们总是绑架政府，理由是政府的财政收入都是来自他们交的税。因此，政府必须始终将人民摆在第一位。我不否认这个，但我认为必须强调的是老百姓是目光短浅的。绝大多数人都只注重眼前利益，而忽略长远的利益。如果政府按照人们的意愿制定所有政策，后果将会是灾难性的。

表面上，资助艺术不会提高人们的生活水平，这笔钱若是用在公共服务如医疗和基础设施上会更好些。但是，人们必须明白艺术也是一个国家历史文化一个方面，所以政府需要为下一代保护好它。否则，情况可能会变得很糟糕。例如，中国各地有很多关于抗日战争（1937年——1945年）的历史人物的雕塑。这些雕塑能够提醒人们中国和日本这两个亚洲邻居的历史，从而让人们学会珍惜他们目前所拥有的，学会理解为什么中日两国的关系为何如此敏感与脆弱。我认为把钱投在这方面是值得的，并不浪费钱。此外，雕塑和画廊可以丰富我们的生活。如果没有它们，人类的文明将会变得黯淡。设想一下如果有一天大英博物馆和巴黎卢浮宫消失了，人们还会欢乐吗？生活还会像今天这般精彩吗？

最后重申一下，忽略艺术是很危险的，因为它不仅仅会破坏文化的保护，也会让生活变成一潭死水。因此，政府应该资助艺术项目。

高分词汇精选 Word Bank

序号	词汇	意思	同义表达（自测）
1	allocate	分配	
2	public spending	公共开销	
3	top concern	最关心的事	
4	tight budget	有限的预算	
5	financial resources	财政资源、钱	
6	shame on sb.	为某人感到羞耻	
7	turn a blind eye to...	对……置之不理	

序号	词汇	意思	同义表达（自测）
8	kidnap	绑架	
9	revenue	收入	
10	fund manager	基金经理	
11	ordinary people	老百姓	
12	short-sighted	目光短浅的	
13	current benefits	眼前利益	
14	to formulate policies	制定政策	
15	consequences	影响；结果	
16	catastrophic	灾难性的	
17	On the surface, ...	表面上，……	
18	investment	投资	
19	living of standard	生活水平	
20	be better spent on...	更好地用在……	
21	healthcare	医疗	
22	infrastructure	基础设施	
23	preserve	保护	
24	get ugly	情况不妙	
25	historical figures	历史人物	
26	cherish	珍惜	
27	sensitive	敏感的	
28	vulnerable	脆弱的	
29	worthwhile	值得的	
30	spice...up	改善；让……变得更好	
31	... and such	……和类似的事物/事情	
32	civilization	文明	
33	jeopardize	损害；破坏	
34	a pond of dead water	一潭死水	
35	sponsor	赞助	

说明：Q7 ~ Q10的答题思路与Q6大同小异。

Q14 推广健康生活方式vs治疗病人（283 words）

It is more important for the government to spend money on promoting a healthy lifestyle to prevent illness rather than on treatment for people who are already ill. Do you agree or disagree?

It is suggested that the government should invest more to encourage people to lead a healthy life to prevent illness instead of provide treatment for those who already suffer. From where I stand, this is a ridiculous statement because there is no conflict between these two acts.

It is important to promote a healthy life among people. Nowadays modern lifestyles have remarkably reduced people's levels of fitness and health. Many people work long hours everyday or sit in front of their computers to have fun all day long. They seldom work out. To make things worse, they eat a lot of fast food and swallow in huge amounts of calories and fat. Heavy consumption of fast food like French fries and sedentary lifestyles keep increasing the obesity rate and diabetes rate. If the government can stage campaigns to get people live a more balanced life, many people would have not had health issues.

However, preventing illness does not necessarily mean that treating people who are already ill is less important. We have to understand that sometimes no matter how healthy a person's lifestyle is, s/he can still fall sick. There multiple reasons for this. If the government makes less effort to provide timely treatment for them, things can go out of control. AIDS serves as a compelling example. Willing or not, governments must work hard to find or at least try to find the cure to treat those carriers because the virus is out there and if we pretend it is not, let's envision a world besieged by HIV.

In conclusion, I believe it is a dangerous act to attach more importance to promoting healthy lifestyles and fail to take the treatment seriously.

【参考译文】

有些人认为政府应该投入更多财力去推广健康的生活方式来预防疾病，而不是给那些已经患病的人提供治疗。在我看来，这是个非常荒谬的说法，因为这两件事之间根本不存在冲突。

是有必要提供健康的生活方式。如今的生活方式已经极大地降低了人们的健康水平。很多人每天长时间地工作或者玩电脑，他们很少锻炼。更糟糕的是，人们大量吃快餐，摄入大量的热量和脂肪。这个加上久坐不动的生活使得肥胖率和患糖尿病的比率一直在升高。如果政府可以发起运动来让人们过更加均衡的生活，很多人就不会有健康问题了。

不过，预防疾病并不意味着治疗疾病就不重要。我们必须明白，无论一个人的生活方式多么健康，他/她仍会生病，这里面有很多原因。若是政府不努力提供及时的治疗，情况可能会失控。艾滋病是个非常好的例子。无论愿不愿意，政府都应该寻找或者至少要努力寻找治疗的方法来救助这些病毒携带者。病毒就在外面肆虐，如果我们装作视而不见，我们预计整个世界都将遭受艾滋病的围困。

高分词汇精选 Word Bank

序号	词汇	意思	同义表达（自测）
1	It is suggested that...	有些人认为	
2	invest	投资；资助	
3	From where I stand, ...	在我看来	
4	conflict	冲突	
5	modern lifestyles	现代的生活方式	
6	levels of fitness and health	健康水平	
7	work long hours	长时间地工作	
8	work out	锻炼	
9	To make things worse, ...	更糟糕的是	
10	swallow	吞；下咽	
11	calories	热量、卡路里	
12	heavy consumption of fast food	吃太多快餐	
13	a sedentary life	久坐不动的生活	
14	obesity	肥胖	
15	diabetes	糖尿病	
16	campaign	活动	

序号	词汇	意思	同义表达（自测）
17	a balanced life	均衡的生活	
18	AIDS/HIV	艾滋病	
19	a compelling example	很好的例子	
20	carriers	携带者	
21	virus	病毒	
22	envision	预见	
23	besiege	烦扰，纠缠；围攻	
24	attach importance to...	重视	
25	take...seriously	重视	

Q15 科研经费（273 words）

Money for postgraduate research is limited. Therefore some people think financial support from governments should be only provided for scientific research rather than research for less useful subjects. Do you agree or disagree?

The way the government allocates its public spending has always been one of the top concerns of the general public. Considering the tight budget of the government, some people think that funding from the government should merely go to scientific research rather than those less important subjects. From my perspective, however, the government should never ignore those seemingly less useful subjects.

It is true that scientific research like medicine test plays an extremely important role in society and thus financial support from the government should never be suspended. However, it does not necessarily mean that other issues are not useful and should be neglected by the government. No one can actually tell what is really not important to us. Decades ago, space research was regarded meaningless and a waste of taxpayer's money. Yet it has now become one of the top priorities on many governments' agenda. Many ordinary people also consider space exploration important for human society. By the same token, it is important that governments do not really ignore anything when allocating budget for public issues.

That said, however, governments do not necessarily have to fund those relatively less urgent issues alone. Instead, it can encourage the private sector to play a role. In this case, the government will just need to introduce legislation to ensure that the private sector does nothing illegal to make profit so that a multiple-win situation can be achieved.

In conclusion, both useful scientific research and those seemingly less important subjects deserve financial support. To ignore something simply because it is currently not important is a short-sighted thing that any government does not want to do.

【参考译文】

政府如何分配其公共开销始终是公众最为关注的话题。鉴于政府预算有限，一些人认为政府仅仅应该资助科研项目，而非一些不重要的课题。不过在我看来，政府绝不应该忽略这些貌似无用的课题/学科。

确实，诸如药物测试之类的科研对于我们的社会至关重要，因此政府绝不应该停止资助它们。但这并不意味着其他的事情就不重要，就可以被忽略。没有任何人可以真正分辨什么是不重要的。数十年前，太空探索被认为是浪费纳税人的钱，而如今它却成为很多国家政府工作议程上的重中之重，甚至很多普通老百姓也认为太空探索对人类很重要。同理，政府在为公共事务做预算时不应该随意忽略一些事物。

当然话说回来，政府倒不必任何事物都独自资助，而是可以鼓励一些私人单位参与。这样，政府只需要引入立法确保私人企业不非法盈利即可实现多赢的局面。

总之，有用的科研和看似不重要的课题都应该得到资助。仅仅因为某事物目前不重要就忽略它是种目光短浅的行为，没有政府会这么做。

高分词汇精选 Word Bank

序号	词汇	意思	同义表达（自测）
1	allocate	分配	
2	top concern	最关注的事情	
3	a tight budget	有限的预算	
4	funding	资金；资助	
5	seemingly	看似	

序号	词汇	意思	同义表达（自测）
6	play an important role in...	在……中扮演重要角色	
7	suspend	延缓；暂停	
8	neglect	忽视	
9	taxpayer	纳税人	
10	space research	太空探索	
11	priority	优先事物	
12	agenda	议程	
13	by the same token	以此类推	
14	That said, however, ...	但话说回来……	
15	fund	基金；资助	
16	introduce legislation to do sth.	引入立法做某事	
17	illegal	非法的	
18	a multiple-win situation	多赢的局面	
19	short-sighted	目光短浅的	

三、政府是否应该介入某事物？

19. Some people think the government should encourage a healthy lifestyle while others believe that people can choose to live the way they like. Discuss both views and give your own opinion.

20. Violence in TV programs and movies results in juvenile delinquency. Therefore, the government should impose censorship on the violence in TV programs and movies. To what extent do you agree or disagree?

21. Some people think students should take the subjects which are decided by the government in the university. Others think that students can choose the subjects they prefer. Discuss the two situations and give your opinion.

22. Creative artists should always be given the freedom to express their own ideas (in words, pictures, music or film) in whichever way they wish. There should be no government restrictions on what they do. To what extent do you agree or disagree?

23. Some countries have introduced a law to limit working hours for employees. Why is the law introduced? Do you think it is a positive or negative development?

24. Nowadays many people enjoy dangerous sports such as mountain climbing or parachuting. Governments should ban these sports to protect the safety of people. To what extent do you agree or disagree with this opinion?

万能思路

除Q24外，所有这些题目都是在探讨政府是否应对某种行为进行介入/干预。对于这类题目，我们可以这样思考：理论上讲，只要人们的所作所为不违反法律且不违背道德，他们就应该有自由选择的权利，若是政府一味地限制约束人们的行为则是不尊重人权。但事实上，人们必须明白凡事没有绝对的自由。放任自由最后必然导致适得其反的后果，而这正是政府需要立法约束规范人们行为的原因。对于上述考题，为什么政府要介入干预呢？肯定是因为人们的所作所为已经造成了负面的社会影响，政府不得不出面予以干预。只是，在这个过程中，政府应该扮演引导的角色，而不应该是强权监控的角色。

需要额外注意的是，Q24直接说政府应该禁止极限运动，这就有些矫枉过正。太过头了就不见得是好事，所以这道题目比较适合写反面的立场。

Q19 推广健康的生活方式（290 words）

Government should encourage a healthy lifestyle while others believe that people can choose to live the way they like. Discuss both views and give your own opinion.

Modern lifestyles have brought many health problems to individuals while promising them free ways of living. Thus some people say it is the government's responsibility to promote healthy lifestyles among individuals while others insist they shall have the freedom to pursue their own lifestyle.

On the one hand, I think as long as what people do is not against the law, nor is it morally wrong, they shall have the choice to do whatever they want. For instance, if young people like extreme sports, I do not see why they should not be allowed to pursue these activities. Yet on the other hand, I would also say that people should realize modern lifestyles have not only exerted many negative effects on individuals themselves but also on society as a whole. Apparently, the government needs to take action to bring things to the correct track.

It has been observed that people nowadays tend to lead less active lives and they also have unhealthy diet. Sedentary lifestyles and heavy consumption of fast food have proven to be blamed for increasing obesity issues and higher risks of cancer-related health hazards. Statistics show that one third of Americans are obese. If these figures are correct, then the government will have to invest a big fortune to provide adequate medical resources for the people, which could have been avoided if people live a healthy life. As a consequence, it is important for the government to stage campaigns to encourage people to go for healthier lifestyles.

In conclusion, facts have shown that the way people live not only jeopardizes their own health; it can also pose challenges to the government and sustainable development of society. Therefore, intervention from the government is necessary and should be accepted.

【参考译文】

现代的生活方式在给他们带来便利的同时已经给人们造成了很多健康问题。由此一些人认为政府有责任在公众中推广健康的生活方式，而另外一些人则认为人们有自由追求自己想要的生活方式。

一方面，我认为只有人们的所作所为不违反法律并且不违背道德，他们就有权做自己喜欢的任何事情。例如，如果年轻人喜欢极限运动，我不明白为什么要去禁止他们这么做。但是另一方面，我也认为人们必须明白现代的生活方式不仅仅给人们自身造成了很多负面影响，而且对整个社会也造成影响。显然，政府需要采取措施将事情扳回到正确的轨道上。

我们注意到人们往往久坐不动并且饮食不健康，而久坐不动的生活方式和吃太多快餐是导致肥胖率上升和其他与癌症相关的健康风险升高的罪魁祸首。统计表明，三分之一的美国人肥胖。如果这些数据属实，则政府将不得不投入巨资来提供充足的医疗资源，而这本可以通过人们的健康生活方式予以避免。因此，政府应该发起运动来鼓励公众过更加健康的生活。

总之，事实表明人们的生活方式不仅仅危害自己的健康，而且会对政府和社会的可持续发展构成巨大的挑战。因此，政府的干预是必要的，应该被公众接受。

高分词汇精选 Word Bank

序号	词汇	意思	同义表达（自测）
1	modern lifestyles	现代的生活方式	
2	promote	推广；推销	
3	pursue	追求	
4	be against the law	违法	
5	morally wrong	道德败坏的	
6	extreme sports	极限运动	
7	exert effect on...	对……产生影响	
8	a less active life	久坐不动的生活	
9	a sedentary life	久坐不动的生活	
10	unhealthy diet	不健康的饮食	
11	heavy consumption of fast food	吃太多快餐	
12	obesity	肥胖	
13	health hazards	健康问题	
14	Statistics show that...	统计表明	
15	obese	肥胖的	
16	invest a fortune to do sth.	投入巨资做某事	
17	As a consequence, ...	因此	
18	jeopardize	危害；破坏	
19	pose challenges to...	对……构成挑战	
20	sustainable development	可持续发展	
21	intervention	干预	

说明

若字数不够，考生可以补一段写到政府应该具体做什么来引导公众过健康的生活方式。这样，本文的逻辑也会更严谨更完整。

当然，也请广大考生明白，以上万能思路也仅仅是这类文章的切入点之一。只要考生能够自圆其说地论证自己的看法，高分作文并非遥不可及。下面收录的是《剑桥雅思4》Test 3中的一篇7分的考生作文。供考生们借鉴。

Q22 艺术创作vs政府约束（342 words）

Creative artists should always be given the freedom to express their own ideal (in words, pictures, music or film) in whichever way they wish. There should be no government restrictions on what they do. To what extent do you agree or disagree?
（《剑桥雅思考试全真试题集4》Test 3，7分）

I agree with the statement that there should be no government restriction on creative artists who express themselves in the way they do and that they must be given freedom for the same. Expression has always been the keynote in a person's life. It is the result of were expression of our thoughts that we are able to communicate. Restrictions on how we present our thoughts is senseless.

Creative artists play a major role in our society, be it the government, old people, the youth or the children. Their works enlighten our minds, no matter if is factual or entertainment based. It is disserving that aster a days work when we want to take some time off for ourselves, we look out for some leisure. For instance: either pleasant music or a family movie which soothes the mind. Entertainment give us an overview of a new side of life which every individual respects. There is almost everything good in what is given to us through the media world which is made up of artists.

On the contrary sometimes these artists tend to be unscrupulous. They convert rumors into facts and present them before us. This might impair the reputation of some illustrious people in today's society. On such occasions, certain restrictions are understandable. Nevertheless we all do know what is right or wrong. Rules and regulations not always are the solution to how artists present their own ideas. Hence it is doltish to be impetuous and the government should enforce alterative ways to control the media.

Respect for ones ideas is not only hypothetical but must be practiced. It is through respect that each one of us can be recognized as a unique person in the world. This can be achieved by looking at the bright side of what media i.e. the creative artists display for us. Not a day can go by when we don't look out for colorful dreams and a beautiful life which we can find either through music, poetry, films, pictures; everything that the creative artists offer us.

考官点评

This answer considers the main issues raised by the question and presents a definite opinion about the statement. However, the response tends to over-generalize and sometimes the examples used to support ideas seem rather confusing. Ideas are generally clearly organized, and paragraphing is clear but the argument is difficult to follow in places. A range of linking words and expressions is used, but there are occasional mistakes. The candidate uses an ambitious range of vocabulary and sentence patterns, but has some problems with word choice and collocations. There are very few spelling errors and only minor grammar mistakes, but there are many examples of expressions used inappropriately.

Q23 政府立法约束工作时间（318 words）

Some countries have introduced a law to limit working hours for employees. Why is the law introduced? Do you think it is a positive or negative development?

In this fast-paced society, many people are pushed to work hard and long hours because of the increasingly fierce competition in the job market and the soaring cost of living. Under such circumstances, some governments introduce legislation to limit the working hours for employees. Though controversial to some people, I think such a practice can produce many positive effects.

When we take a look at the job market we can see that many people are forced to be stuck there. They have to handle intense work pressure and work overtime because they are struggling to make enough money to make ends meet. Many people can barely squeeze time from their tight schedules to stay with their family. It is ironic that people work against the clock to support their family and yet they do not have time to have quality family life. Some of them even lose their marriage, and their children hate them.

To make things worse, some employers take advantage of this and ask employees to do extra work without paying them. This is why governments introduce laws to set upper limits on employee's workload, or working hours. By doing this, governments are actually safeguarding the rights and interests of ordinary people.

Some people may worry that such laws or rules can bring negative impacts and jeopardize the interest of employers, especially those who work in the private sector, and it can bring difficulties to the management of business. Yet we should realize that people have different priorities in life, and as long as related benefits can be guaranteed, I am confident that someone would be willing to work long hours.

In conclusion, society is based on laws and rules; people also need rules in their economic activities, and the job market is no exception. While some people need to compromise their interest with the enforcement of the above-mentioned law, the majority of people will benefit.

【参考译文】

在这个快节奏的社会，由于职场竞争激烈以及生活成本的上涨，很多人被迫长时间努力工作。如此一来，一些国家引入立法限制员工的工作时间。尽管这一做法饱受争议，我认为它会带来许多积极的影响。

关注职场的话，我们会注意到很多人被迫努力工作。他们需要应对巨大的工作压力和加班，因为他们必须努力维持收支平衡。很多人几乎无法从忙碌的工作中挤时间陪家人。令人讽刺的是，人们努力工作养家糊口却没时间享受家庭生活。有些人甚至由此婚姻破裂，遭子女憎恨。

更糟糕的是，一些雇主利用员工加班却拒付加班费。这就是为什么政府需要立法来限定员工的工作量/工作时间。这样一来，政府其实是在保护普通老百姓的权益。

有些人可能会担忧类似的法律法规会带来负面影响并危害雇主的利益，尤其是私人企业，而且这会给企业的管理造成困难。不过人们必须明白不同人有不同的重要事情，只要相关的福利能够得到保障，我相信一定会有人乐意长时间地工作。

总之，社会是建立在法律法规的基础上。人们的经济生活需要法律法规，职场也不例外。随着上述法律的贯彻执行，尽管有些人需要妥协自己的利益，但绝大多数人都会从中受益。

高分词汇精选 Word Bank

序号	词汇	意思	同义表达（自测）
1	fast-paced	快节奏的	
2	fierce competition	激烈的竞争	

序号	词汇	意思	同义表达（自测）
3	job market	职场	
4	cost of living	生活成本	
5	under such circumstances	在这种背景下	
6	introduce legislation/laws to	引入立法	
7	controversial	有争议的	
8	intense pressure	巨大的压力	
9	work overtime	加班	
10	to make ends meet	维持收支平衡	
11	squeeze time	挤时间	
12	a tight schedule	忙碌的工作/日程安排	
13	It is ironic that...	具有讽刺意味的是	
14	work against the clock	努力工作	
15	quality	高质量的	
16	lose one's marriage	婚姻破裂	
17	To make things worse, ...	更糟糕的是	
18	take advantage of	利用	
19	workload	工作量	
20	safeguard	维护、保护	
21	right and interest	权益	
22	ordinary people	老百姓	
23	jeopardize	危害、损害、破坏	
24	bring difficulties to	给……造成麻烦	
25	priority	优先	
26	benefits	福利；好处	
27	guarantee	保障	
28	I am confident that...	我相信	
29	work long hours	努力工作	
30	...is no exception.	……也不例外。	
31	compromise	妥协	
32	enforcement	贯彻执行	
33	the majority of	大多数的	

Q24 政府禁止极限运动（297words）

Nowadays many people enjoy dangerous sports such as mountain climbing or parachuting. Governments should ban these sports to protect the safety of the people. To what extent do you agree or disagree with this opinion?

It is reported that many people lose their lives when doing extreme sports. Thus, some people propose that such activities should be banned for the sake of people's safety. Although I agree that there are dangers associated with extreme sports, I think it is wrong to ban these pursuits.

Some people would say that extreme sports can cause injuries or even death to participants and this is not good to society. For this reason, the government needs to stop people from doing such activities. Personally, I would not deny such facts. However, simply because there are dangers associated with extreme sports does not necessarily mean that such activities should be banned. I believe it is necessary to keep extreme sports as long as actions can be taken to restrict and regulate these pursuits.

It is important to stress that, for some people, extreme sports help them handle the intense pressure from work or life; and it is individuals' basic right to do what they like as long as it is not against the law, nor is it morally wrong. Should these sports be banned, it would be an infringement upon people's right.

Yet it should be noted that certain sports should be restricted and regulated by means of license or certification. For instance, if one decides to go parachuting, the authority should insist that he or she undergoes some training. If necessary, a license should be obtained. The government should also ensure that companies or clubs running extreme sports are regularly supervised so that they meet the safety standards.

In conclusion, I do not see any reason to impose a ban on extreme sports despite the potential risks to individuals. As long as both participants' behavior and related associations' business can be regulated, extreme sports should be kept.

【参考译文】

据报道，很多人由于极限运动而丧命。有些人因此主张出于公众安全的角度政府应该禁止这些运动。尽管我承认极限运动有危险，但我反对禁止它们。

可能有人会说极限运动导致人们受伤甚至死亡，这对社会不好。因此，政府应该禁止人们做这些。我倒不否认这些事实，但是仅仅因为极限运动的危险性并不意味着就必须禁掉它们。我认为只要能够采取相关的措施来限制和规范这些活动，它们就应该保留。

必须强调的是，极限运动可以帮助一些人应对工作或者生活的压力。而且，只要人们的所作所为不违反法律并且不违背道德，人们就有权做自己想做的事情。若是政府禁止极限运动，这会侵犯人们的权利。

当然应该指出的是，有些极限运动确实应该通过颁发执照或者授予凭证的形式予以限制和规范。例如，如果有人想跳伞，他/她必须先获得执照。政府也应该确保定期监督经营极限运动的公司或俱乐部以确保他们达到安全标准。

总之，尽管极限运动有一定的危险性，但我认为没有任何理由去禁止它们。只要能够规范参与者和相关机构的行为，极限运动就应该被保留。

高分词汇精选 Word Bank

序号	词汇	意思	同义表达（自测）
1	extreme sports	极限运动	
2	propose	主张，建议	
3	for the sake of...	看在……的份上	
4	associated with	与……有关的	
5	oppose to	反对	
6	pursuits	追求	
7	injury	伤害	
8	participants	参与者	
9	regulate	规范	
10	It is important to stress that...	应该强调的是，	
11	intense pressure	巨大的压力	
12	go against the law	违反法律	
13	morally wrong	道德败坏的	
14	infringement (upon)	侵犯	

序号	词汇	意思	同义表达（自测）
15	Yet it should be noted that...	但是应该注意的是，	
16	by mean of	通过……方式	
17	license	执照	
18	certification	证书	
19	go parachuting	跳伞	
20	authority	权威；当局	
21	supervise	监督	
22	safety standards	安全标准	
23	impose...on...	将……强加于……	

四、城市规划

25. In some countries, governments are encouraging industries and businesses to move out of large cities and into regional areas. Do you think the advantages of this development outweigh its disadvantages? Give reasons for you answer and include examples from your knowledge or experiences.

26. In many cities, planners locate schools, homes, offices and shops in specific areas which are widely separated from each other. Do you agree the advantages of this policy outweigh the disadvantages?

万能思路

近些年，城市规划的题目在雅思写作中考的频率很高。我建议考生们按下面的写作的基本思路备考：通常，政府都是出于更好的城市规划才会进行一些拆迁、市政工程，所以只要合理规划，这些做法还是可以带来很多积极的影响的。对于城区本身来讲，这可以极大地缓解由于人口过分集中而导致的诸多问题；对于郊区来讲，其经济会腾飞。当然，为了完善我们的逻辑，我建议再加上一段话——当然政府在这个过程中一定要完善配套设施（如公共交通），并尽量将环境问题降到最低限度。

对于Q25，考生很容易接受这个思路。但是对于Q26，很多考生不太理解为什么也可以套用这个逻辑。我的解释是这样：如果政府将学校、住宅、办公室（即写字楼）及商店（购物区）按功能区进行划分并且彼此之间相隔很远，这必然意味着所有这些版块不可能全部集中在市区，一定会有些版块需要被划分在郊区（例如各大城市的大学城、工业园区等等）。既是如此，它就缓解了城区由于过度拥挤导致的诸多问题，同时又盘活带动了郊区的发展，也就是Q25的思路。需要提醒考生的是，由于Q26并没有明确提到将一些版块安置在郊区，所以需要考生在写作时重新定义一下这个行为，这样再去套用Q25的思路就顺理成章了。例如，考生可以在开头段说，It has been observed that in many cities, schools, homes, offices and shops are located in designated zones that are separate and far away from each other; some like schools and offices are relocated in suburban areas. From my perspective, such an act can produce far more positive effects than negative impacts.

Q25 工业/企业搬迁（318 words）

In some countries, governments are encouraging industries and businesses to move out of large cities and into regional areas. Do you think the advantages of this development outweigh its disadvantages? Give reasons for you answer and include examples from your knowledge or experiences.

It is reported that many governments are relocating industries and businesses in suburban areas. To my best understanding, those governments come up with such a practice for the sake of better town planning and I think many positive effects can be produced.

For large cities, such a relocation project can greatly alleviate a variety of problems caused by overpopulation. As is known, the concentration of industries and businesses in the city has already brought a series of problems to urban areas. For example, increased traffic issues and housing shortage mean that the infrastructure in the city is under huge burden. Deteriorating air quality is also a nightmare to people. Therefore, once industries and businesses are moved out, those problems can be significantly overcome and people's life will be much better.

In reference to suburban areas, when industries and businesses are moved in, the local economy can be presented a golden opportunity to take off. There will be more employment opportunities for the local residents as well as more tax incomes for the local governments. The infrastructure in the local communities would also be remarkably improved.

Yet in the meanwhile, it is also important to stress that governments must ensure that all plans are carried out properly and effort should be made to minimize the environmental impact to the suburbs. Otherwise, the short-sighted act to develop economy at the cost of local environment will prove to be a disaster to society. At the same time, public transport linking the urban areas and suburban regions must be improved so that commuting should never be a problem for people who live in downtown yet work outside it.

In conclusion, any responsible government would be devoted to serving the best interest of the general public and so people should have faith in it. As long as proper plans are devised and stuck to, the practice mentioned above can be a positive development.

【参考译文】

据报道，很多地方的政府将工业和企业搬迁至郊区。在我看来，政府这么做都是出于一个好的城市规划，并且我认为这会带来很多积极的影响。

对于大城市，这个搬迁项目可以极大地缓解人口过剩带来的一系列问题。众所周知，工业和企业集中在城区已经给城市带来了一系列问题。例如，日益增长的交通问题和住房短缺都意味着城市的基础设施正承受巨大的压力。日益恶化的空气质量也是人们的一个梦魇。因此，一旦工业和企业搬出城市，这些问题便得到极大的克服，人们的生活也会越来越好。

至于郊区，当工业和企业迁进时，当地经济将得到一个绝佳的机会得以腾飞。当地居民会有更多的就业机会，而当地政府也将获得更多的税收。同时，当地的基础设施也将得到巨大完善。

不过与此同时，需要强调的是政府必须确保恰当地执行所有计划，并且努力将环境影响降到最低。否则，这种以牺牲当地环境为代价来换取经济发展的做法必将给社会带来巨大灾难。同时，政府必须完善公共交通连接城市和郊区以确保那些住在城市而在郊区工作的人不会操心通勤问题。

总之，任何负责任的政府都会努力为广大老百姓服务，所以人们应该相信政府。只要指定好规划并认真实施，上述措施就会带来积极影响。

高分词汇精选 Word Bank

序号	词汇	意思	同义表达（自测）
1	relocate	搬迁，重新安置	
2	suburban areas	郊区	
3	To my best understanding, ...	在我看来	

序号	词汇	意思	同义表达（自测）
4	town planning	城市规划	
5	...can produce positive effects.	……会带来积极的影响	
6	alleviate	减轻、缓解	
7	overpopulation	人口过剩	
8	As is known, ...	众所周知	
9	concentration	集中	
10	a variety of	一系列	
11	a series of	一系列	
12	traffic issues	交通问题	
13	housing shortage	住房短缺	
14	infrastructure	基础设施	
15	deteriorate	恶化	
16	nightmare	梦魇	
17	In reference to...	至于	
18	a golden opportunity	绝佳的机会	
19	take off	起飞；腾飞	
20	employment opportunity	就业机会	
21	tax incomes	税收	
22	carry out	执行	
23	make effort to do sth.	努力做某事	
24	short-sighted	目光短浅的	
25	at the cost of	以……为代价	
26	commuting	通勤	
27	downtown	市区	
28	be devoted to	致力于	
29	have faith in	信任	
30	devise	制定；设计	
31	stick to	坚持	

五、是否只有政府能够解决某问题

27. Some people believe that environmental problems are too big for individuals. Only governments and big companies can make a difference. To what extend do you agree or disagree?

28. The shortage of housing in big cities can cause severe consequences and only governmental actions can solve the problem. Do you agree or disagree?

万能思路

显然，相对个人而言，政府的确有其优势：政府可以通过立法或者征税的方式鼓励企业或者公众各尽所能，齐力克服或者解决某问题。鉴于此，我建议考生们在正文第一段先承认这些。接着从正文第二段开始笔锋一转，指出承认政府的优势并不代表个人或者其他有关各方就束手无策，从而强调后者也可以做出巨大贡献。

Q27 环保：个人vs政府/企业（276 words）

Some people believe that environmental problems are too big for individuals, only governments and big companies can make a difference. To what extend do you agree or disagree?

Recent years have witnessed a worsening environmental situation in many places. Some people think we have reached a stage where only the government and large businesses can make a difference in solving environmental issues. Personally, however, I think individuals can also contribute greatly in environmental protection.

It is self-evident that compared with individuals, the government has the power to introduce legislation or levy taxes to encourage people and businesses to make effort to improve the environment. In the meanwhile, big companies can also try to be environmentally friendly in their production or business activities. For example, the use of biodegradable materials in industrial production can be a big step in protecting the environment.

However, it is important to point out that individuals can also play an extremely fundamental role in the combat against the deteriorating environment. Above everything else, ordinary people can try to lead a low-carbon life so as to reduce their carbon footprint. For instance, instead of driving private cars, people can use public transport as much as possible because this can bring much less carbon emission.

When less greenhouse gases are emitted, the environment will be improved remarkably. Also, if individuals stick to their own reusable bags when they go shopping, and reduce the consumption of disposable products such as paper cups, the world would be much cleaner. In addition, people can also sort out garbage for recycling to contribute to environmental protection.

In conclusion, when united, the general public can also make great contributions to the improvement of environment. While the government and big companies can play the leading role in this campaign, individuals' supporting role shall never be neglected.

【参考译文】

近些年，很多地方的环境在恶化。一些人认为要解决环境问题，我们只能依靠政府和大企业。但是，我认为人们也可以在为环保做出巨大贡献。

相对人们而言，政府显然有权通过立法或者征税来鼓励人们和企业努力保护环境。与此同时，大企业也可以努力使其生产环节和其他商业活动变得环保。例如，通过使用可降解的材料进行工业生产对环境保护是个巨大的进步。

但必须强调的是，人们在对抗日益恶化的环境问题中同样可以扮演极其重要的角色。首先，人们可以过低碳的生活来减少自己的碳足迹。例如，人们可以尽可能地使用公共交通而非私家车，因为这可以减少碳排放。只要温室气体排放少了，环境就会得到改善。同时，如果人们购物时坚持重复使用自己的袋子，并减少使用诸如塑料袋之类的一次性物品，世界也会更干净。此外，人们也可以通过将垃圾分类回收利用来为环保做贡献。

总之，当人们团结一致时他们也可以为环保做出巨大贡献。尽管政府和大企业可以在整个活动中起主导性的作用，但老百姓所扮演辅助性角色也不应该被忽视。

高分词汇精选 Word Bank

序号	词汇	意思	同义表达（自测）
1	witness	目击；见证	
2	make a difference (in)	有所作为	
3	It is self-evident that...	显然	
4	introduce legislation to	引入立法	
5	levy taxes	征税	

序号	词汇	意思	同义表达（自测）
6	environmentally friendly	环保的	
7	biodegradable	可降解的	
8	play a role (in)	发挥作用	
9	combat	应对，解决；战斗	
10	deteriorate	恶化	
11	a low-carbon life	低碳的生活	
12	carbon footprint	碳足迹	
13	carbon emission	碳排放	
14	greenhouse gases	温室气体	
15	emit	排放	
16	reusable bags	可重复利用的购物袋	
17	disposable products	一次性物品	
18	paper cups	纸杯	
19	sort out	分类、整理	
20	make contribution to	为……做贡献	
21	play the leading role (in)	起主导地位	
22	a supporting role	辅助性角色	
23	campaign	活动	
24	neglect	忽视	

提示：Q28考试频率相当低。截止到本书稿完成为止，上一次考到这题还是在2006年5月13日。就像前文所说的，基本的写作框架可以参考Q27。

六、是否只有政府有权利/资格做某事

29. Some people think that good health is very important to every person, so medical services should only be run by the government, not profit-making companies. Do you agree or disagree? (OR, Some people think that good health is a basic human need, so the medical service should not be run by profit-making companies. Do you think the disadvantages of the private health care outweigh the advantages?)

30. Some people think scientific research should be controlled by governments rather than private companies, Do you agree or disagree?（OR, Governments should be responsible for funding and controlling the scientific research rather than private organizations. To what extent do you agree or disagree?）

万能思路

我在上课时有时会布置这类题目作为家庭作业让学生写，结果很多学生将题目理解错了。很多学生的答题思路为：我同意只能让政府来做。因为老百姓给国家交税了，所以政府有责任有义务为人民服务；而且，政府有钱来做这些，私人企业没钱。

显然，学生没有认真思考为什么会有人提出题目中的看法，即只能让政府来做而不允许私人企业来做。首先，需要声明的是，企业的财力不会输给政府的。在国外，反倒是政府经常很拮据。我们来设身处地地想，之所以人们认为只能让政府做而将私企拒之门外，其主要原因就是政府有公信力。人们相信政府不会胡来，而私人企业则未必了。在人们心目中，私人企业唯利是图，若是让私企参与，则人民遭殃。

事实果真如此吗？我们需要问自己几个问题：1．政府是否有财力和精力独自承担某项任务，尤其是当它涉及所有老百姓的切身利益时？2．政府垄断某个行业一定就好吗？3．私人企业一定就会胡来吗？政府难道没有立法监管？

就Q29而言，我认为人们的担忧其实没有必要。因为如果私人企业提供的医疗服务很糟糕，人们为什么会放弃公费医疗而自费去接受糟糕的服务呢？换句话讲，多数企业为了存活为了盈利，一定会尽可能提供最好的服务。再说，即使有私企想要不择手段地追求利益，政府的立法监管务必会至其于死地。所以没必要担忧私企的胡作非为。想到了这层，剩下的就是将私企参与医疗服务所带来的双赢甚至多赢局面阐述清楚即可。

Q29 医疗：政府vs私企（285 words）

Some people think that good health is very important to every person, so medical services should only be run by the government, not profit-making companies. Do you agree or disagree?

People have different opinions about whether medical services should be provided by private companies. Some people insist that such programs should only be run by the government. As I see it, however, such a statement cannot be justified.

When profit-making companies run healthcare services, the most common concern for ordinary people is that those companies might do whatever it takes to seek maximized profits, which would jeopardize people's interest. However, I think those people fail to realize that every government would introduce legislation to ensure that those corporations' business behaviour is regulated. In the meanwhile, if a business wants to survive and thrive, it would provide the best possible service. Otherwise, why would someone pay to have poorer service when they can have access to free and better healthcare services with public hospitals? Thus I think in most cases people's concerns are unnecessary.

Moreover, it is important to stress that the provision of healthcare service by the private sector overcomes the shortage of medical resources when only the government is the service provider, particularly when the government is working under a tight budget. The National Health Service (NHS) in U.K serves as a very good example. For lack of funding and manpower, the NHS fails to provide timely treatment to people, leaving tens of hundreds of patients suffering on their own. In addition, for wealthy people, they have the right to enjoy better services as long as they can afford the bill.

In conclusion, I think private healthcare service alleviates the government's burden and brings individuals more options. As long as laws are introduced to regulate it, a multi-win situation can be arrived at for the profit-making companies, the government and most importantly the people.

【参考译文】

对于是否应该让私人企业提供医疗服务，仁者见仁智者见智。一些人坚持这些服务应该完全由政府承担。不过在我看来，这样的看法没道理。

当私人企业提供医疗服务时，公众最大的担忧是这些企业可能会为了追求最大化的利润而不择手段，而这会危害到人们的利益。但是我认为人们并未意识到其实政府会有立法来监管这些企业的商业行为。同时，如果一家企业想要存活并发展壮大，它必然会提供尽可能好的服务。否则，人们为什么会放弃公费医疗而自费去接受更糟糕的服务？所以，我认为多数人其实是在杞人忧天。

而且，必须强调的是私人企业提供的医疗服务克服了当只有政府一方提供服务时的医疗资源短缺问题，尤其是当政府预算有限时。英国的全民医疗体系（NHS）便是个很好的例子。由于缺乏资金和人手，英国的全民医疗体系无法给人们提供及时的治疗，导致无数人苦苦遭殃。此外，对于有钱人来说，只要他们有能力支付费用他们就有权利享受更好的服务。

总之，我认为私人企业提供的医疗既减轻了政府的负担，同时也给老百姓带来更多的选择。只要能够引入立法对其进行监管，对于私企、政府，尤其是人民来说就可以实现多方的共赢。

高分词汇精选 Word Bank

序号	词汇	意思	同义表达（自测）
1	People have different opinions about...	见仁见智	
2	As I see it, ...	在我看来	
3	such a statement cannot be justified.	这个看法不靠谱	
4	profit-making companies	盈利性企业	
5	do whatever it takes to...	不惜一切地	
6	jeopardize	危害，破坏	
7	introduce legislation/laws to	引入立法	
8	corporation	企业	
9	business behaviour	商业行为	
10	regulate	规范	
11	survive	存活	
12	thrive	繁荣	
13	have access to	得到	
14	in most cases	通常	
15	the private sector	私企	
16	work under a tight budget	预算有限	
17	funding	资金	
18	manpower	人手	
19	alleviate	减轻，缓解	
20	options	选择	
21	arrive at a multi-win situation	实现多赢	

七、其他

31. Many governments in developing countries are expanding tourism. Do the problems outweigh the advantages?

32. Some people say that giving aid to poor countries has more negative effects than positive effects. To what extent do you agree or disagree?

33. Some people think that the way to judge the success of a nation is the quality of average person's life, while some others insist a promising economy should be most essential. What is your opinion?

34. More and more young people hold important positions in government. Some people think it is not suitable but others think otherwise. Discuss both views and give your own opinion.

说明

政府类话题中还存在一些零散的题目，不适合套用前面六类的思路。不过由于前面六大类已经基本覆盖整个写作题库中绝大多数的政府类考题，所以剩下的一些零散考题其实并不多。本节就给考生们提供部分考题的范文，供大家参考。

Q31 发展中国家发展旅游业（281 words）

An increasing number of developing countries are expanding their tourism industry. Why do you think is the case? And do you think it is a positive development?

Recent years have witnessed the boom of tourism in developing countries. People are wondering why these countries would like to make such a big effort to do this, and also about the consequences such a practice can bring. This essay will examine economic purpose is the most important reason for such a situation and how it can positively affect developing countries.

As is known, the development of tourism can boost related industries and create huge tourism revenue for the government so that it can be financially strong enough to take care of a wide range of issues like improving infrastructure and alleviating poverty in particular areas. Employment opportunities, in the meanwhile, can also be created in related industries such as tour guides and hotel housekeeping.

As for the effects of developing tourism, there are multiple benefits for developing countries. Not only can it boost economy, as is elaborated above, but also it provides a golden opportunity for those less developed countries to showcase their unique cultures and the friendliness of the people. In other words, developing tourism can be a way to change the poor image that developing countries leave on foreigners. For example, some people may take it for granted that Thailand is a poor and dirty place, and that Thai people are lazy. But once they travel there, they will realize that Thailand is a country with natural beauty and amazing culture, and that people there are as diligent as any other nations across the world.

In conclusion, growing tourism is an effective way for developing countries to boost the economy and it also creates a platform for the world to get to know more about those countries.

【参考译文】

近些年见证了发展中国家旅游业的繁荣。人们很好奇究竟为何这些国家会如此下工夫去发展旅游业，以及由此带来的影响。本文将论证经济因素是造成这一现象的最主要原因，以及发展中国家会如何从中受益。

众所周知，旅游业的发展可以推动相关产业的发展并给政府创造巨大的旅游收入。这样，政府才有足够的财力来处理很多其他事物，如完善基础设施和给某些特定的地方扶贫。与此同时，导游及酒店客房服务等相关产业将产生大量的就业机会。

至于发展旅游业带来的影响，发展中国家可以从多方面受益。除了上文提到的经济发展外，发展中国家也会得到一个绝佳的机会来展示自己独特的文化和人民的友好。换句话说，发展旅游业是个很好的途径来改变发展中国家留给外人的糟糕形象。例如，一些人总是想当然地以为泰国是个贫穷、肮脏的地方，并且泰国人很懒。但如果他们去泰国旅游，他们会明白泰国是个风景优美、文化奇特的国家，并且泰国人也同世界上任何一个民族一样勤劳。

总之，发展旅游业是个很好的发展经济的途径；同时，它也为发展中国家搭建了一个平台来让世界更了解它们。

高分词汇精选 Word Bank

序号	词汇	意思	同义表达（自测）
1	boom	繁荣	
2	make effort to do sth.	努力做某事	
3	consequences	影响；后果	
4	such a practice	这种做法	
5	examine	检查；分析；论证	
6	boost	推动	
7	tourism revenue	旅游收入	
8	financially strong	财力雄厚的	
9	a wide range of	一系列	
10	infrastructure	基础设施	
11	alleviate	减轻	
12	employment opportunities	就业机会	
13	tour guide	导游	
14	hotel housekeeping	酒店客房服务	
15	multiple	多重的	
16	as is elaborated above	正如前文所述	
17	a golden opportunity	绝佳的机会	
18	showcase	展示	
19	unique	独特的	
20	take it for granted that	想当然地以为	
21	natural beauty	（美丽的）自然风景	
22	diligent	勤劳的	
23	platform	平台	

Q32 国际援助（326 words）

Some people say that giving aid to poor countries has more negative effects than positive effects. To what extent do you agree or disagree?

Each year billions of dollars are spent delivering aids to poor countries so that people there can have a better life. While many people applaud those aid programs, some others voice objections to them. Personally, I believe it is ridiculous to say that more negative consequences than positive ones can be produced with those aid programs.

For those recipient countries, international aids can effectively and directly relieve their people from suffering. For example, many people in Africa have no access to clean drinking water and other very basic vaccines, and each day, a lot of them die because of this. If they can receive aids from the outside world, such tragedies can be avoided. In May 2013, when the president of the US Obama promised African countries an aid program worth $8 billion to provide people there electricity in the coming years, were there anyone to question the benefits of it to these countries? No.

For rich countries, helping others also does them credit. Firstly, they can build up a good image in the international community, which will definitely pay off some day. Second, a better world is also in the interest of rich countries. In this global village, everything is connected. When some countries are in trouble, the rest of the world can hardly stay out of trouble. A case in point is that a virus in poor countries can turn into a pandemic swiping the whole world. Thus, it is important that we watch each other's back.

As for the possible problems like poor countries decision making might be influenced by foreign powers, I would say this is mainly because of the poor transparency in those aid programs. If non-governmental organizations (NGOs) can be encouraged to watch what rich countries do, most problems can be combated.

In conclusion, the problems involved with international aids can be overcome. As long as they are carried out properly, both recipient countries and donor countries can benefit greatly.

【参考译文】

每年，数十亿美元被用来资助穷国以帮助当地的人民过上更好的生活。尽管很多人对此表示欢迎，但是仍有些人提出了质疑声。在我看来，认为这些援助项目会造成更多的问题的看法是非常荒谬的。

对于受赠国来讲，国际援助可以有效并立竿见影地减轻当地人民所遭受的苦难。例如，很多非洲人无法得到干净的饮用水和其他一些基本的疫苗。每天，很多人因此而丧生。如果他们可以得到外面的援助，类似的悲剧可以避免。2013年5月份，当美国总统奥巴马承诺给非洲国家提供价值80亿美元的援助项目以帮助非洲人民用上电时，会有人质疑这给非洲国家带来了好处吗？没有。

对于富国来讲，帮助他国也对自己有利。首先，他们可以在国际社会建立一个积极的形象，而这会在未来带来回报。其次，更好的世界也符合富国的利益。在当今这个地球村，任何事物都是相互联系的。如果某些国家受难，其他国家将很难幸免。很明显的一个例子是穷国的某个病毒可以演变成席卷全球的流行病。因此，我们需要相互照应。

至于负面影响，如穷国的决策可能会受到外国势力的干涉，我认为这主要是因为援助项目缺乏透明度。如果非政府组织可以对富国进行监督，绝大多数问题可以得到解决。

总之，国际援助带来的问题是可以克服的。只要这些援助项目得到恰当的执行，受赠国和捐赠国都将受益无穷。

高分词汇精选 Word Bank

序号	词汇	意思	同义表达（自测）
1	deliver	递送；提供	
2	applaud	鼓掌欢迎	
3	voice objections (to)	提出质疑	
4	aid programs	援助项目	
5	recipient countries	受赠国	
6	donor countries	捐赠国	
7	international aids	国际援助	
8	relieve people from sth.	减轻	
9	have no access to	得不到	
10	vaccine	疫苗	

序号	词汇	意思	同义表达（自测）
11	tragedy	悲剧	
12	do sb. credit	对某人有利	
13	international community	国际社会	
14	pay off	带来回报	
15	in the interest of sb.	符合某人的利益	
16	A case in point is that...	（很显然的）例子是	
17	virus	病毒	
18	pandemic	流行病	
19	decision making	决策	
20	foreign powers	外国势力	
21	transparency	透明度	
22	NGOs	非政府组织	
23	combat	战斗；解决	

CHAPTER 7 文化篇

文化类写作话题是很多考生惧怕的一类题目。毕竟，这类题材所涉及的内容非常抽象；而且，它们对学生的词汇量也提出了考验。我在教写作词汇时也时常提醒学生，环境类、犯罪类及文化类这三组题材的单词需要格外关注。理由很简单，因为我们平时接触这些题材的机会不多，从而会认为这些单词都相对专业，一旦改写成简单的表达法，则文章的整体水平也会出现"跳水"现象。不过，比较利好的消息是，这样话题考试频率相对较低。此外，这类考题的内容及词汇都相对固定，因此，只要考生能花些时间和精力把这些常用的思路和相应词汇掌握好，那么考试时就一定能大显身手。例如，cultural heritage（文化遗产）、cultural diversity（文化的多样性）等。

通过对比分析，文化类的常考话题主要分为以下几类：

一、全球化vs文化认同

这可以算是文化类写作话题最重要的题目。常见的出题形式有：全球化对文化认同的影响；国家越来越相似，其原因与影响。

二、旅游业vs传统文化

有些题目会直接考查旅游业是否会破坏当地的（传统）文化；而另外一些题目的题干则只提旅游，并不涉及文化，但考生在答题时又往往会提及文化。

三、科技vs传统文化

比较常见的出题形式是，科技的发展是否会破坏传统文化。

四、语言vs文化

这一类别下主要有三种出题方式：1）要学外语是否应学习了解对方的文化？2）政府是否应花钱拯救/保护小语种？3）全世界是否应该使用一门共同的语言？

五、建筑vs文化

关于建筑与文化的考题，A类与G类共同的题目是：政府是否应翻新、修复古建筑？回答这类题目时，考生难免会提及文化方面的内容。另外，还有一道考题是，是否应该将房子建成传统风格而非现代风格，原因在于这样可以保护传统文化。

六、艺术vs文化

我之所以在这里提及艺术类考题，主要是因为众多考生在答题时会提及艺术是一个国家的文化，需要保护，需要予以资助。这里的关键词是：art/painting/sculptures/statues/artistic projects/art galleries/people who work for art，等等。

▶ 常考话题清单

1. Some people think that traditional culture can be destroyed by using it as money-making attractions to tourists. However, others believe that it is the only way to save traditions. Discuss both views and give your opinion.
2. Some people suggest when people move to a new country, they should accept the new culture as their own. To what extent do you agree or disagree?
3. As mass communication and transport continue to grow, societies are becoming more and more alike, leading to a phenomenon known as globalization. Some people fear that globalization will inevitably lead to the total loss of cultural identity. To what extent do you agree or disagree with this statement?
4. Some people say that the increasing business and cultural contact between countries is a positive development, while others think that many countries will lose their national identities. Discuss both views and give your opinion.
5. Some people think that increasing business and cultural contacts have positive influences on development; others think that it has negative effects on national

identities. Discuss both views and give your opinion.

6. Exposure to international media, e.g. films, TV and magazines, has an impact on the local culture. Please discuss whether the advantages outweigh the disadvantages.

7. Multi-cultural societies, which are a mixture of different ethnic groups, bring more benefits than drawbacks to a country. To what extent do you agree or disagree with this conclusion?

8. It is inevitable that as technology develops traditional cultures must be lost. Technology and tradition are incompatible—you cannot have them both together. To what extent do you agree or disagree?

9. Modern buildings have greatly changed the appearance of the city. Yet some people think that buildings should be built in traditional styles to protect the traditional culture. To what extent do you agree or disagree with this opinion?

10. Government should protect the culture; some people believe new buildings should be built in traditional styles. Do you agree or disagree?

11. To learn a language well, we should also learn about the country as well as the cultures and lifestyles of the people who speak the language. To what extent do you agree or disagree?

12. Some people think it is wrong for the government to spend much money on artistic projects such as sculptures and art galleries. Do you agree or disagree?

13. Several languages are in danger of extinction because they are spoken by very small numbers of people. Some people say that governments should spend public money on saving these languages, while others believe that it would be a waste of money. Discuss both views and give your opinion.

14. Some people think that a common language should be adopted globally to improve international communication and understanding. Others, however, think it would lead to the loss of cultural identity. Discuss both views and give your own opinion.

15. Some people think that a new language should be invented for people from different countries to use for international communication. To what extent do you think its advantages far outweigh disadvantages?

万能思路

泛泛而谈，文化类考题能用到的普遍观点为：

- 旅游业一定程度上也帮助了传统文化的复兴，毕竟当地政府需要投入巨资对其传统文化进行保护和宣传。至少，当一些地方为了满足游客的需求而经常举行民俗表演时，其传统习俗多少都在延续。（contributes to the revival of traditional culture...culture shows/performances）

- 另一方面，过多的商业行为也对文化的保护构成威胁。毕竟，当人们更加关注物质财富而开始忽略自己的传统文化时，文化的地位也就显得无足轻重了。（too commercialized...pay more attention to material wealth）

- 全球化/国际旅游/看外国电影/…/一方面有利于促进文化交流，增进交流和了解，从而消除对彼此的偏见。（facilitate cultural exchanges and improve mutual understanding between each other...remove prejudice against each other）

- 与此同时，在全球化/国际旅游过程中，发展中国家的文化又处于相对弱势的地位，原因在于人们总是倾向模仿发达国家的生活方式。逐渐地，发展中国家的一些传统便会被遗忘，而他们的文化或习俗也会被冲淡。（to imitate the lifestyles of people in developed countries...be diluted/watered down）

以下为考生们提供部分范文，供参考。

Q1 旅游业vs传统文化（320 words）

Some people think that traditional culture can be destroyed by using it as money-making attractions to tourists. However, others believe that it is the only way to save traditions. Discuss both views and give your opinion.

It has been observed that many places are expanding their tourism industry based on their local culture. People wonder what effects this can exert on the culture. Although I do not believe this is the only way to preserve traditions, I think it can bring positive effects to the local culture.

On the one hand, using traditional culture as money-making attractions can bring rebirth of traditions. If the government wishes to boost the local tourism based on the traditional culture, it would invest a big fortune to protect and promote the traditional culture. This can be a prime opportunity for the traditions to revive and thrive. For example, residents of some minority ethnic groups in the southwest of China stage cultural performances regularly to satisfy visitors' curiosity. Thanks to this, many local traditions are maintained. Otherwise, these traditions would have not survived. Also, visitors who are fascinated by the local culture tend to share their experience with others, which can further spread the name of the local culture. Once local people realize the importance of it, they will also make efforts to protect the culture.

On the other hand, I certainly disagree that developing tourism is the only way to save traditions. Firstly, I think culture-related activities organized by non-governmental organizations (NGOs) can be an effective way to remind people of the importance of protecting traditions. Secondly, public holidays based on traditions can be established so that public celebrations always remind people of the traditions. This has been proven to be effective in China. In the meanwhile, building museums is another good way to achieve such an aim. People never forget what their cultural identity is when they visit relevant theme museums.

In conclusion, developing tourism brings a golden opportunity for traditional culture to revive. However, it is not the only way to cultural protection. After all, building museums and organizing public celebrations can also remind people to save traditions.

【参考译文】

我们注意到很多地方利用当地的文化发展旅游业。人们很纳闷这到底会对文化造成什么影响。尽管我认为这不是保护传统的唯一途径，但可以对当地的文化带来积极的影响。

一方面，利用传统文化作为盈利产业来发展可以复苏传统文化。如果政府想利用传统文化发展旅游业，就会投入巨资来保护和宣传传统文化。例如，中国西南地区的一些少数民族经常进行民俗文化表演来满足游客的好奇心。正是得益于此，一些当地的习俗得以维持；否则，这些习俗可能会消失。此外，喜欢当地文化的游客也常常同他们身边的朋友分享自己的经历，从而进一步帮助宣传当地的文化。一旦当地人意识到其重要性，便会努力去保护当地文化。

另一方面，我并不认为发展旅游业是保护传统的唯一途径。首先，民间文化活动对提醒人们保护传统的重要性非常有效。其次，基于传统文化的公休假期也可时刻提醒人们不要忘本。这种做法在中国取得了不错的效果。与此同时，修建博物馆也是一个很好的途径来实现这一目标：只要人们逛各类主题博物馆，就永远不会忘记自己的文化认知。

总之，发展旅游业为传统文化提供了绝佳的复兴机会。但是，这并不是保护传统的唯一途径。毕竟，修建博物馆及组织公共庆典活动也都可以提醒人们去保护传统。

高分词汇精选 Word Bank

序号	词汇	意思	同义表达（自测）
1	It has been observed that...	我们注意到	
2	exert effect on...	对……产生影响	
3	preserve	保护	
4	boost	提高、促进	
5	invest a big fortune to do sth.	花巨资做某事	
6	promote	宣传；推销	
7	a prime/golden opportunity	绝佳的机会	
8	cultural performances	文化表演	
9	satisfy one's curiosity	满足……的好奇心	
10	spread the name of...	传播……的美名	
11	make efforts to do sth.	努力做某事	
12	NGOs	非政府组织	
13	cultural identity	文化认知	
14	theme museums	主题博物馆	
15	revive	复兴	
16	thrive	繁荣	
17	survive	存活	

注：本题为2015年12月19日剑桥雅思考题。

Q2 移民vs入乡随俗（291 words）

Some people suggest when people move to a new country, they should accept the new culture as their own. To what extent do you agree or disagree?

It is interesting to see that people even debate over the attitude immigrants should hold to the new culture when they relocate overseas. For me, I think it is self-evident that whoever moves to a foreign country should follow the local customs and traditions.

The first reason is that accepting the new culture is the easiest and irreplaceable way for immigrants to fit in. Imagine a Chinese person moves to New York and yet s/he refuses to follow local customs. His/Her life would be totally messed up because of his/her negative attitude to those "expected" cultural differences. Plus, people in the neighbourhood would also stay away from him/her because refusing to accept the local lifestyle makes them from two different worlds and for some it is simply rude to always say no to local culture.

The second reason is related to the purpose for people to move in. For most immigrants they move to an exotic land is to experience what the locals live: the culture, traditions and the local cuisine, etc. If they finally turn their back on those things when they set their feet on the land, what is the point of relocating?

Of course, I understand some people's concern, i.e. what should they do with their own culture if they suddenly dive into the new culture? The answer is simple: keep it. I do not think that the new culture and people's own background are incompatible with each other. Chinese New Year and Christmas can co-exit well— that is what China Town shows us.

In conclusion, it is important that people do not leave their mother culture behind no matter what happens, yet this does not necessarily keep people away from accepting and learning about a new culture.

【参考译文】

有意思的是，人们居然在辩论移居国外后对当地的文化到底应该持何种态度。在我看来，所有移民显然应该遵循当地的习俗与传统。

首先，接受当地的文化是最简单也是不可替代的方式来帮助外来移民融入当地。设想一下，如果一个中国人移民纽约后却拒绝遵循当地的习俗，他/她的生活将会因此而变得一团糟。而且，周围的人也会对其敬而远之，原因在于拒绝接受当地的生活方式将使得他们成为来自两个不同世界的人；再者，拒绝接受当地的文化也是对一些当地人的不尊重。

其次与人们移民的原因有关。绝大多数人移民国外都是想体验当地的生活：文化、传统、饮食，等等。如果他们踏上这片陌生的土地后却不融入当地的生活，那他们移民的意义何在？

当然，我能理解一些人的担忧：如果他们突然接受一种新文化，那他们自己的文化怎么办？答案其实很简单：保留它。我认为新的文化和人们原有的文化并非水火不容。唐人街证明，中国的春节和西方的圣诞节其实可以共存。

总之，无论发生什么人们都不应该丢弃自己的文化，但这并不妨碍他们去接受和了解一种新的文化。

高分词汇精选 Word Bank

序号	词汇	意思	同义表达（自测）
1	It is interesting that...	有意思的是	
2	immigrants	移民	
3	relocate	搬迁；搬家	
4	It is self-evident that...	显然，……	
5	customs	习俗	
6	irreplaceable	不可替代的	
7	fit in/into...	融入/适应	
8	mess up	弄砸	
9	cultural differences	文化差异	
10	be related to...	与……有关	
11	exotic land	异域	
12	local cuisine	当地的饮食	
13	turn one's back on...	对……置之不理	
14	set one's feet on...	踏足于……	
15	dive into...	一头扎进……	
16	be incompatible with...	与……不兼容	
17	mother culture	原有文化	
18	leave...behind	将……丢弃	

Q3 全球化vs文化认知（305 words）

As mass communication and transport continue to grow, societies are becoming more and more alike leading to a phenomenon known as globalization. Some people fear that globalization will inevitably lead to the total loss of cultural identity. To what extent do you agree or disagree with this statement?

Improved transportation and communication technology have turned the world into a tiny global village. In this village, people are sharing more and more similarities, like they consume the same brands, watch the same movies and eat the same food.

Pessimists are concerned that this trend will finally lead to the loss of cultural identity, while I think it would only prove to be a false alarm.

On the surface, globalization has narrowed the cultural differences among people around the globe. For example, people in every corner of the world drink coca cola, wear Nike and celebrate Christmas as westerners do. These parallels among countries show that people in other places like China and Japan are giving up their own dietary habit and dressing code.

However, what people fail to realize is that simply because someone changes the way he or she dresses or the things he/she eats and drinks (it) does not mean that he/she is losing his or her cultural identity. Cultural identity is based on the shared values that people pass down from generation to generation and these core values cannot be easily changed. For example, Chinese people may drink as much coke as they wish, but deep inside they are a nation that work long hours and do anything they can to please their children. People in US do not do this, neither do the Australians; not that Americans and Aussies do not love their work and children, (but that) they simply do not go that far as the Chinese do.

In conclusion, I do not think globalization will lead to the death of culture identity because it is not something that changes with the way people eat or dress; cultural identity is the values that bond people together, and they are in people's blood ever since they were born in their mother land.

【参考译文】

完善的交通与通讯科技已经将世界变成了一个小小的地球村。在这里，人们之间的相似性越来越多，例如，消费相同的品牌，看同样的电影，吃同样的食物。悲观主义者担忧这种趋势最终会扼杀我们的文化认知，但我认为这只是耸人听闻而已。

表面上，全球化缩小了不同国家之间的文化差异。例如，全球范围内人人都在喝着可口可乐，穿耐克衣服，庆祝圣诞节。这些相似性表明，像中国、日本等一些地方正在放弃自己的饮食习惯和着装法则。

但是，人们没有意识到的是，仅仅因为人们的饮食习惯和着装方式的改变并不意味着他们就失去了自己的文化认知。文化认知的根基在于人们代代相传的共同价值观，而这些核心价值观并不会轻易改变。举例来说，中国人可以尽情地喝可口可乐，但是内心深处他们仍是那个努力工作并且为了取悦孩子可以牺牲一切的民族。美国人做不到这点，澳大利亚人也做不到。倒不是说美国人和澳大利亚人不爱自己的工作和孩子，但是他们就是做不到像中国人那样。

总之，我认为全球化不会扼杀文化认知。因为文化认知并不会随着人们的饮食和着装而改变，它是将人们紧密相连的价值观；从人们在故土出生的那一刻起，这些价值观就深深融入到了他们的血液中。

高分词汇精选 Word Bank

序号	词汇	意思	同义表达（自测）
1	global village	地球村	
2	similarities/parallels	相似性	
3	pessimists	悲观主义者	
4	cultural identity	文化认知	
5	a false alarm	耸人听闻、虚惊一场	
6	On the surface, ...	表面上，	
7	narrow	缩小	
8	around the globe	全球	
9	every corner of the world	全球	
10	dietary habit	饮食习惯	
11	dress code	着装法则	
12	core values	核心价值观	
13	work long hours	长时间/努力工作	
14	sacrifice	牺牲	
15	deep inside	内心深处	
16	not that...but (that)...	不是因为……而是……	
17	Aussie	澳大利亚人（俚）	
18	bond	联系	
19	mother land	故乡	

注：Q4～Q5的答题思路也可适当参考Q3的内容。

Q8 科技vs传统文化（278 words）

It is inevitable that as technology develops, traditional cultures must be lost. Technology and tradition are incompatible —— you cannot have them both together. To what extent do you agree or disagree?

It is argued that modern technology and traditional culture cannot coexist no matter how hard people try to protect the latter from being endangered. Some people even claim that all our efforts are doomed to be in vain. Yet in my opinion, it depends on what the traditions are and how the technology is employed.

On the one hand, modern technology has brought individuals different forms of entertainment under whose impact some traditional art forms are losing their vitality. Chinese Peking Opera is a typical example. This art form that used to make billions of Chinese proud is now losing ground to modern entertainments such as 3D movies and computer games. Most young people choose 3D movies over Peking Opera because such movies like Hollywood blockbusters bring them stunning audio-visual enjoyment. The exciting scenes of Hollywood movies stand in marked contrast to the slow moves of Peking Opera and it is almost impossible that the latter could win the battle.

On the other hand, there are also occasions when modern technology has been employed by traditional art forms to revive and thrive (themselves). A case in point is that Chinese martial arts take advantage of blockbusting movies to create breathtaking fighting to attract audiences as in movies like KUNG FU PANDA (2008) and THE MATRIX RELOADED (2003). Over the past few years, Chinese Kung Fu has been gaining increasing popularity both at home and abroad.

In conclusion, it depends on how people make use of technology if desirable outcomes are to be expected. It might be difficult, but as long as people are creative about using it, the development of technology does not necessarily have to suffocate traditional culture.

【参考译文】

有些人认为，现代科技和传统文化是不能共存的，不管人们多么努力去保护后者都无济于事。有些人甚至认为，我们所有的努力注定是徒劳的。但在我看来，这得取决于什么样的传统，以及我们如何利用科技。

一方面，现代科技为人们提供了各种各样的娱乐方式，在这些娱乐方式的冲击下，一些传统的艺术形式正在失去生命力。中国京剧就是典型的例子，这种曾让无数中国人引以为豪的艺术形式正将其阵地输给3D电影和电脑游戏等现代娱乐。大多数年轻人看3D电影而非京剧，原因在于这些电影（如好莱坞大片）给他们带来了令人惊叹的试听享受。这些刺激的场面与京剧的慢动作形成鲜明对比，想让京剧赢得这场对抗几乎不可能。

另一方面，传统艺术形式有时借助现代科技被来复兴并发展壮大自己。一个很明显的例子是，中国武术结合大片来制作一些扣人心弦的打斗场面以吸引观众（如《功夫熊猫》、《黑客帝国3》）。最近这些年，中国功夫在国内外越来越受欢迎。

总之，是否有好的结果取决于我们如何利用科技。尽管有一定的困难，但是只要人们能够灵活应用，科技的发展就不一定会扼杀传统文化。

高分词汇精选 Word Bank

序号	词汇	意思	同义表达（自测）
1	It is argued that...	有人认为	
2	coexist	共存	
3	be doomed to...	注定……	
4	in vain	徒劳	
5	traditional art forms	传统艺术形式	
6	vitality	生命力	
7	lose its ground to...	失去阵地	
8	blockbusters	大片	
9	blockbusting movies	大片	
10	stunning audio-visual effect	令人惊叹的试听效果	
11	stand in marked contrast to...	与……形成鲜明对比	
12	There are occasions when...	有时	
13	take...on board	接受、利用	
14	revive	复兴	

序号	词汇	意思	同义表达（自测）
15	thrive	繁荣	
16	A case in point is that...	例如	
17	take advantage of...	利用……	
18	Chinese martial arts	中国武术	
19	Chinese Kung Fu	中国功夫	
20	gain popularity	受欢迎	
21	both at home and abroad	国内外	
22	desirable outcomes	好的结果	
23	suffocate	扼杀	

Q9 现代建筑vs传统文化（317 words）

Modern buildings have greatly changed the appearance of the city. Yet some people think that buildings should be built in traditional style to protect traditional culture. To what extent do you agree or disagree with this opinion?

With city development, the skyline in many cities has been remarkably changed by record high skyscrapers. While some people applaud this trend, others voice objection as they believe buildings should be in traditional styles for the sake of protecting traditional culture. In my opinion, it is ridiculous to reject innovation in the name of protecting the old.

I do not deny that architecture and culture are closely related and the style of a nation's buildings is a reflection of the people's lifestyle, which is also a part of the culture. However, I think people should also realize that culture is not something that remains constant over time. Instead, it changes. Consequently, there is no need to always stick to traditions because of cultural protection.

In the meanwhile, it is important to point out that modern buildings and traditional culture are not mutually exclusive to each other. Instead, they can be integrated with each other. Facts have shown that traditional culture can be employed well in ultramodern designs. Taipei 101 is a typical example. On the surface of this high-rise monster, there are wide eaves in traditional style and huge circles in the form of

Chinese ancient money, both of which were extensively used in ancient buildings in China and are widely considered a part of Chinese culture.

In addition, buildings in modern style also boast their own advantages. Compared with those short buildings in traditional style, modern skyscrapers can provide more accommodations for a larger population with a smaller piece of land. They are also more resistant to natural forces and they are the future of architecture.

In conclusion, it is important to save traditions, but it does not mean all buildings must be built in traditional style. For me, there is always a balance that can be stricken between the appearance of a building and its function, and I see that in creative high-rise buildings.

【参考译文】

随着城市的发展，很多城市的天际线被越来越高的摩天大楼大幅改写。有些人对此拍手称好，而有些人则表示反对，因为他们认为，建筑应该建成传统风格来保护传统文化。在我看来，打着保护传统的口号而一味地拒绝创新是非常荒谬的行为。

一方面，我不否认建筑和文化是密切相关的，并且一个国家的建筑可以反映人们的生活方式，而这也是文化的一个重要部分。但我认为，人们也应该意识到文化并不是一成不变的。随着时代的发展，文化也会发生改变，因此，我们没有必要为了保护文化的而一味地守旧。

与此同时，应该指出的是，现代建筑和传统文化并非相互排斥，而是可以相互融合。事实表明，传统文化可以很好地应用到超现代的设计中，台北101大楼便是典型的一例。在这个巨型怪物的表面有宽大的传统屋檐和巨大的中国古钱币，这些都被广泛地应用到中国的古建筑中，也被广泛地看作中国的文化。

此外，现代风格的建筑还有其独特的优势。与传统风格的低矮建筑相比，现代的摩天大楼可以用更少的土地给更多的人提供更多的住宿。它们也更为牢固，它们才是建筑的未来。

总之，保护传统固然重要，但这并不意味着所有的建筑都应该建成传统风格。在我看来，我们永远可以在建筑的外观与功能上找到平衡点，而我认为，创意无限的摩天大楼正是这一平衡点的典范。

高分词汇精选 Word Bank

序号	词汇	意思	同义表达（自测）
1	skyline	天际线	
2	record high	创纪录高的	
3	skyscrapers	摩天大楼	
4	applaud	鼓掌欢迎	
5	voice objection to...	对……表示反对	
6	innovation	创新	
7	architecture	建筑	
8	reflection	反映	
9	remain constant	保持不变	
10	stick to...	坚持……	
11	in the name of...	以……的名义	
12	mutually exclusive to each other	相互排斥	
13	integrate	结合	
14	employ	利用	
15	ultramodern	超现代的	
16	high-rise buildings	（超）高建筑	
17	boast	炫耀；拥有	
18	accommodation	住宿	
19	be resistant to natural forces	坚实牢固	
20	strike a balance between A and B	寻找A与B的平衡点	

说明

Q10的答题思路同Q9。若考题为“The appearance of a building is more important than its function. Do you agree or disagree?”，则考生也可灵活改写“建筑风格”一文。大致的思路为：人们之所以认为建筑的外观比其功能更重要，一个最主要的原因是外观可以体现生活方式、时代背景、民族文化。这个我不否认，例如……。但是，人们也必须明白，建筑的外观并不是全部。时代的发展和现代的城市规划需要我们充分利用有限的土地……所以摩天大楼这种以功能为导向的（function-oriented）建筑才应该被提倡。而且，现代的超高建筑同样可以将文化融入到其独特的外观中。……

Q11 学语言vs学文化（303 words）

In order to learn a language well, we should also learn about the country as well as the culture and lifestyles of the people who speak it. To what extent do you agree or disagree?

To be bilingual or even multilingual has been a trend in this increasingly globalized world. Thus, the secret of learning a language well is something that language learners are always looking for. From my experience, it is important that we learn the culture and lifestyles of the native speakers if we want to have a good command of their language.

The most important reason is that language is a constituent part of culture. They are not mutually exclusive to each other; instead, they are closely connected. Thus, knowledge of the culture can facilitate one's linguistic acquisition. For instance, in some western societies dragon stands for evil whereas in the Chinese culture it stands for power, authority and auspiciousness. If a foreigner has this cultural background, he or she will understand that almost all phrases or idioms that contain this particular Chinese character carry good meanings.

The other reason is that the ultimate purpose for most people to learn a foreign language is to use it to talk with others especially those native speakers. And it is extremely important to point out that cross-cultural communication means (far) more than language fluency. Rather, language learners must have a good knowledge of the culture of the target language as well as the lifestyles of the people who speak the language to improve mutual understanding. For example, in western countries, people should not break the taboo to ask about other people's incomes or religious beliefs the first time when they meet each other, whereas in China it is not that a big deal to talk about these issues.

In conclusion, language learners need to learn about the culture and lifestyles of native speakers. Not only because culture is the base of the language but also (because) cross-cultural communication means more than the language itself.

【参考译文】

在这个日益全球化的社会，人人都想会至少两门甚至更多门语言。因此，语言学习者们始终都在找寻语言学习的奥秘。以我个人的经验来看，若想要把语言学好，则应该要学习了解当地人的文化和生活方式。

我认为最重要的原因在于，语言是文化的一个组成部分，他们并不彼此排斥，而是密切相连的。因此，了解文化有利于促进语言的习得。例如，在一些西方文化中，龙是邪恶的象征，而在中国文化中，龙则代表了权力、权威与吉祥。如果一个老外了解了这层文化背景，他/她就会明白几乎所有包含了“龙”这个中国汉字的词语和成语都是积极的意义。

（学习了解文化的）另一个原因是，多数人学外语的最终目的是为了同他人进行交流，尤其是老外，而必须强调的是，跨文化交流绝不仅仅是语言本身流畅不流畅的问题，而是语言学习者必须了解对方的文化背景及生活方式，如此才能更好地相互理解。例如，在西方国家，人们首次见面时不会冒昧地询问对方的收入或宗教信仰。而在中国，即使人们谈论这些事情，也不会有太大关系。

总之，语言学习者应该学习了解当地人的文化及生活方式。这不仅仅是因为文化是语言的基础，还因为跨文化交流远不只是语言本身的问题。

高分词汇精选 Word Bank

序号	词汇	意思	同义表达（自测）
1	bilingual/multilingual	双语的/多语的	
2	increasingly globalized world	日益全球化的世界	
3	have a good command of...	熟练掌握……	
4	a constituent part of...	……的组成部分	
5	mutually exclusive to each other	相互排斥	
6	facilitate	促进	
7	linguistic acquisition	语言习得	
8	auspiciousness	吉祥	
9	idiom	成语、习语	
10	It is important to point out that...	应该指出的是……	
11	cross-cultural communication	跨文化交流	
12	language fluency	语言的流畅度	
13	mutual understanding	相互理解	

序号	词汇	意思	同义表达（自测）
14	break the taboo to do sth.	打破禁忌做某事	
15	religious beliefs	宗教信仰	
16	a big deal	大事	

Q12 政府资助艺术（381 words）

Some people think it is wrong for the government to spend much money on artistic projects such as sculptures and art galleries. Do you agree or disagree?

The way the government allocates its public spending has always been one of the top concerns of the general public. Considering the tight budget of the government, some people think that financial resources of the government should not be wasted on artistic projects like sculptures and art galleries. Personally, I think it would be shame on the government should it turn a blind eye to arts.

People always kidnap the government by saying that the government revenues come from the taxes they pay and thus the government, the fund manager they say, should always put them above everything, which is true. But I think it is also important to stress that ordinary people are short-sighted and most of them only care about current benefits and ignore what is important in the future. If all policies are formulated by their will, the consequences can be catastrophic.

On the surface, the investment in artistic objects like sculptures and art galleries does not improve people's living of standard, and the money may seem to be better spent on public services like healthcare and infrastructure. However, people must understand that art is an important aspect of a nation's culture and history, and that it is important that the government preserve it for future generations. Otherwise, things can get fairly ugly. For example, there are so many sculptures of historical figures in the China-Japan War (also known as the Second Sino-Japan War, 1937-1945) across China to remind people what happened between these two Asian neighbours so that they cherish what they have today and that they can understand why these two countries have such a sensitive and vulnerable relationship. Money invested in these things is worthwhile, and I do not think it is a waste of financial resources. Plus, sculptures and art galleries spice our life up. Without them and such, life would be boring. Imagine one day when the British Museum and the Louvre Palace are gone.

Will people still be joyful? Will life still be as beautiful as it is today? I doubt it.

To reiterate, ignoring arts is a dangerous act because it not only jeopardizes the preservation of culture, but also turns people's life into a boring pond of dead water. Thus, it is important that the government sponsors artistic projects.

【参考译文】

政府如何支配公共开销始终是公众最为关心的事情。鉴于政府预算有限，一些人认为我们不应该在艺术工程如雕塑和画廊上浪费钱。就我个人而言，如果政府真的对艺术置之不理，那将是非常遗憾可耻的。

人们总是绑架政府，理由是政府的财政收入都是来自他们交的税。因此，政府必须始终将人民摆在第一位。我不否认这个，但我认为必须强调的是，老百姓是目光短浅的。绝大多数人都只注重眼前利益，而忽略长远的利益。如果政府按照人们的意愿制定所有政策，后果将会是灾难性的。

表面上，资助艺术不会提高人们的生活水平，这笔钱若是用在公共服务如医疗和基础设施上会更好些。但是，人们必须明白，艺术也是一个国家历史文化的组成部分，所以政府需要为下一代保护好它。否则，情况可能会变得很糟糕。例如，中国各地有很多关于抗日战争（1937年—1945年）的历史人物的雕塑。这些雕塑能够提醒人们中国和日本这两个亚洲邻居的历史，从而让人们学会珍惜他们目前所拥有的，学会理解中日两国的关系为何如此敏感与脆弱。我认为把钱投在这方面是值得的，并非浪费。此外，雕塑和画廊可以丰富我们的生活。如果没有它们，生活会变得很无趣。设想一下，如果有一天大英博物馆和巴黎卢浮宫消失了，人们还会欢乐吗？生活还会像今天这般精彩吗？

最后重申一下，忽略艺术是很危险的，因为它不仅仅会破坏文化的保护，也会让生活变成一潭死水。因此，政府应该资助艺术项目。

高分词汇精选 Word Bank

序号	词汇	意思	同义表达（自测）
1	allocate	分配	
2	public spending	公共开销	
3	top concern	最关心的事	
4	tight budget	有限的预算	

序号	词汇	意思	同义表达（自测）
5	financial resources	财政资源、钱	
6	shame on sb.	为某人感到羞耻	
7	turn a blind eye to...	对……置之不理	
8	kidnap	绑架	
9	revenue	收入	
10	fund manager	基金经理	
11	ordinary people	老百姓	
12	short-sighted	目光短浅的	
13	current benefits	眼前利益	
14	to formulate policies	制定政策	
15	consequences	影响；结果	
16	catastrophic	灾难性的	
17	On the surface, ...	表面上，……	
18	investment	投资	
19	living of standard	生活水平	
20	be better spent on...	更好地用在……	
21	healthcare	医疗	
22	infrastructure	基础设施	
23	preserve	保护	
24	get ugly	情况不妙	
25	historical figures	历史人物	
26	cherish	珍惜	
27	sensitive	敏感的	
28	vulnerable	脆弱的	
29	worthwhile	值得的	
30	spice...up	改善；让……变得更好	
31	...and such	……和类似的事物/事情	
32	jeopardize	损害；破坏	
33	a pond of dead water	一潭死水	
34	sponsor	赞助	

Q13 保护小语种

关于Q13，大致的思路是：language is not just a means of communication. Behind it there is so much culture. Once a language disappears, the culture it carries will also be gone. 若是真的发生这样的事情，我们的cultural diversity will be jeopardized；并且，对于人类社会的cultural heritage and human civilization也将是个disaster.

当然，光上述要点并不足以支撑一篇文章。所以，考生可以在正文的下一段举例来证明。

Q14 全球统一语言vs文化（275 words）

Some people think that a common language should be adopted globally to improve international communication and understanding. Others, however, think it would lead to the loss of cultural identity. Discuss both views and give your own opinion.

Many people often complain that the language barrier has become the obstacle of globalization. They claim that international communication would be remarkably improved if a common language were spoken globally. Others, however, worry that cultural identity would be lost because of this.

I think there is no need to create a new language. For one thing, there should be cultural base for a language and we do not create it out of nothing. For another, English has already become the dominant language in international communication. That said, however, even if English has already been so popular it does not mean that it should be imposed on every single person. People shall have their own choice to use the language they want. If two people can understand each other in Chinese, I do not see why they have to speak English.

In the meanwhile, I also do not agree that culture would be lost if people spoke languages other than their mother tongue. Millions of Chinese people are learning and speaking English, yet their culture does not collapse. History also shows that when people have to speak other languages instead of their native language, they do not forget who they are. A case in point is that those colonies of the Great Britain such as India never really lost their own cultural identity. When people meet an Indian person, they do not say he or she is English even if he/she speaks English, because Indian culture is in his or her blood.

In conclusion, adopting a globally spoken language would be unrealistic and unnecessary. But should it be really done, it would not destroy cultural identity.

【参考译文】

很多人经常抱怨语音障碍阻碍了全球化的进程，他们认为，如果全球通用同一门语言，国际交流将得到大幅提升。但是，另一些人则担忧这会导致文化认知的丢失。

我认为没有必要去创造一门新语言。一方面，语言必须依托文化，我们不能凭空创造语言。其次，英语已经成为了国际交流的主导语言。不过，即便是英语已经如此普及，也不意味着必须将它强加在每个人头上。人们应该可以自由选择自己想说的语言。如果人们能用中文进行交流，我不明白为什么强迫他们讲英文。

与此同时，我也不认为如果人们讲外语而非母语就会导致文化丢失。无数中国人都在学习和使用英语，但他们的文化并未因此崩溃。历史也表明，当人们使用外语而非母语时，他们并不会真正忘记自己的身份。例如，各个英国的殖民地（如印度）从未丢失过自己的文化认知。当人们在街上碰到印度人时，没有人会说他/她是英国人，尽管印度人讲的是英语，因为印度文化已经融入到了他/她的血液中了。

总之，全球讲同一门语言既不现实也没必要。但即使万一真的讲了，也不会摧毁（各国的）文化认知。

高分词汇精选 Word Bank

序号	词汇	意思	同义表达（自测）
1	language barrier	语言障碍	
2	obstacle	障碍	
3	cultural identity	文化认知	
4	dominant	主导的	
5	That said, however, ...	但是（话又说回来）	
6	impose sth. on sb.	将……强加于某人	
7	mother tongue	母语	
8	native language	母语	
9	collapse	崩溃	

序号	词汇	意思	同义表达（自测）
10	A case in point is that...	例如	
11	colony	殖民地	

说明

- 考生在回应Q14时，其实也可以参照Q13的答题思路。即，同意如果全球使用同一种语言会导致cultural identity的丢失。因为language is not just a means of communication. Behind it there is so much culture. Once a language disappears, the culture it carries will also be gone. …
- Q15的答题思路基本参照Q14。

CHAPTER 8 犯罪篇

犯罪类的话题每年都考，不过考试频率相对较低。笔者做了粗略统计，这类考题通常每年2～4题。通过跟踪题库，笔者将犯罪类考题分为两大类：一类是考查犯罪的原因及对策，为主流考题；另一类则为其他犯罪类真题。

一、犯罪的原因及对策

1. Crime is a problem all over the world and there is nothing that can be done to prevent it. To what extent do you agree or disagree?
2. Many people are afraid to leave home because of crime. Some believe that more actions should be taken to prevent crime, but others feel little can be done. What's your view?
3. Some people think the best way of reducing crime is to give longer prison sentences. Others, however, think there are other better ways to reduce crime. Discuss both views and give your own opinion.
4. Some people think that all the lawbreakers should be sent into the jail, while others believe that they should also be made to do some work or learn some skills in the community. What is your opinion?
5. Putting criminals into prison is not so effective in dealing with them. Instead, education and job training should be offered to them. To what extent do you agree or disagree?
6. Some people think the only purpose of prison is to punish crime. Others think it has other functions. Discuss the two views and give your opinions.
7. More and more measures to improve the security in the urban area have been introduced because of the increased crime. Do the benefits of the measures outweigh the drawbacks?

8. It is reported that most/many criminals commit crime again when they are released from prison. What are the causes and how can we solve this problem?

9. Some people think the media should not report details of crimes to the public. To what extent do you agree or disagree? (OR, Detailed reporting on crime in the mass media can have bad effects on society. To what extent do you agree or disagree?)

10. In some countries, young criminals are not put into prison; instead, they are required to do unpaid work in community. Do you think it has more advantages or disadvantages?

11. Statistics suggest that nowadays an increasing number of crimes are committed by the young people. What are its causes and how can we solve this problem? (OR, In some countries, the rate of teenagers' criminal acts is increasing. What are the reasons? Give your measures to reduce it. OR, What are the possible causes for, and solutions to, juvenile delinquency?)

12. Violence in TV programs and movies results in juvenile delinquency. Therefore, the government should impose censorship on the violence in TV programs and movies. To what extent do you agree or disagree?

13. Today there is a general increase in anti-social behaviors. What might have caused this situation? How to improve it?

14. Many scientists believe that now we can study the behavior of a three-year-old child to see whether they will grow up to be criminals. To what extent do you think the human nature produces crime? And how can we prevent children from growing up to be criminals?

15. Young people who commit serious crimes should be punished in the same way as adults. Do you agree or disagree?

万能思路

尽管上述15道题目的问法各不相同，但是多数题目都需要烤鸭们写如何有效地降低社会的犯罪率。实际上，考生可以将上述考题串成一条线来回答。具体为：Q1 ~ Q2是在找降低犯罪率的措施，而Q3为其提供了一条线索，即延长坐牢期限，增加威慑力。但与此同时，Q3又抛出了一个新问题：除了长期的牢狱，是否有其他方式减少犯罪呢？该问题的答案在Q4 ~ Q5中可以找到，即想办法让犯罪分子学到谋生技能；有了一技之长，一定会有犯罪分子改邪归正，从而降低犯罪率。而这实际上也是Q8在寻找的答案。为什么很多犯罪分子刑满释放后又去犯罪？除了自身的恶性、社会的歧视外，另一个重要原因也许是他们中有很多人根本没有一技之长赖以谋生，所以如果能够在惩罚他们的同时让他们掌握一定的技能，则很大程度上可以避免重复犯罪。再看Q6，监狱的唯一职能就是惩罚犯罪分子吗？其实不然。Q5提示我们，提供教育与技能培训也是一个不错的选择。对于Q7，考生们首先得找出究竟采取了什么措施来增强城市的安全。很明显的事实是，现在几乎每个城市都被监控录像给保护了起来。由于监控录像可以记录犯罪现场，为警方提供确凿的证据来惩治犯罪分子，所以这确实极大地威慑了犯罪活动。另外，我们注意到特殊时期特殊场合，更多的警力被安排到大街上执勤。尽管这会加大政府和纳税人的财政负担，但确实极大地了维护了社会治安。Q7的两项措施也可以用来回答Q1～Q2；此外，Q10、Q12也都为Q1～Q2提供一定的答题思路。接着我们来看Q11（青少年犯罪的增长）。究其原因，当然是各方面都有，不过Q12则为青少年犯罪率的上升提供了一个原因及相应的解决方案。而Q12实际上也在部分地回应Q13：反社会行为增多的原因及对策。毕竟，当媒体越来越充斥着各种暴力，且如今又无孔不入地渗透到生活的方方面面时，不明真相的围观者及缺乏判断力的年轻人会被误导和利用而做出一些愚蠢的行为。还记得《蝙蝠侠》首映式枪击案引发的血案吗？（百度百科：2012年7月20日美国科罗拉多州奥罗拉市举行《蝙蝠侠前传3：黑暗骑士崛起》首映式的“世纪16”电影院发生严重枪击案，导致12人死亡，58人受伤。警方称，该名枪手身份为24岁的科罗拉多大学神经学博士James Holmes①。）说到这里，考生们可以回头想想Q9的答题思路了。至于Q14，我想提醒的是，如果犯罪可以被预测，世界就会天下太平了。但是事实呢？远非如此。这里向广大考生推荐一部充满未来主义的电影：《少数派报告》，英文名为Minority Report（2002）。电影里面描述的就是犯罪可以被预测之后的社会。Q15则参考前面题目，尤其是Q10。

至此，关于犯罪类的主流题目全部串讲完毕。下面将犯罪的常见原因、相应对策及其可行性翻译成英文，供考生们学习参考。

① Some people break the law because they are poorly educated. They do not know much about the law. Thus, weak law awareness makes them fail to realize what they do is against the law. →相应的措施：Educational programs should be launched so as to increase public consciousness of the law. In addition, I think some law courses should be a compulsory part of school education.（评论：客观地讲，很多受过正规教育的人都没有接受过一定的法制教育，这势必造成很多人不懂法律，更遑论那些没有接受过正规教育的人。）

① 资料来源：http://baike.baidu.com/link?url=j2GpFIvuQ85Dk2z9PpulDmUuMEieSxBTXsbLU4XbGQXiMLJBVCmyEagE6iGDnaFjF_yhGbZ_gut-o9d8tLaYTK

② In some cases, people commit crime because they are pushed/tested to their limits by the injustice they have been through. Those who fail to safeguard their legal rights and interests might resort to violence to demand justice. →相应的措施：Both the law system and social system should be reconsidered. At least, there should be a transparent law system so that corrupt officials are punished and justice is served.（评论：我们一直强调要以法治国。有了透明的法律制度，有了政府的公信力做保证，我们相信，这类犯罪现象会日渐减少。）

③ Some people offend the law because they are greedy such as in the cases of tax evasion, embezzlement or taking bribes. For most of these law offenders, they are well-educated. They have the power and ability to make money and lead a decent life. Yet their desires are never satisfied. They just expect more, regardless of the price. → 相应的措施：Severe penalties should be given so that more similar criminal acts will be deterred. For instance, longer term of prison sentence should be given. If people realize the price to pay, they will think twice/harder before they do anything criminal.（评论：在某些地方，犯罪成本的低廉导致部分人铤而走险，知法犯法。对于这样的情况，如果我们能够加大惩罚力度，对此类违法犯罪活动严惩不贷，我相信一定可以极大地降低政治犯罪及经济犯罪。）

④ Some people, particularly those illiterate or poorly-educated people, commit crime like stealing because they have no life skills. They need money yet they do not have the skills to earn it. Therefore, they take the wrong way. → 相应的措施：For these people, I do no think imprisonment is an effective way to deal with them. They might regret and reform after the prison sentence. Then what? When they are released, they will still have to struggle for a living. It is highly possible that they commit crime again and go back to jail. For them, I would say that, besides severe punishments behind bars, education and job training programs can also be given（based on their performance）. This, I believe, can help prevent recidivism, or repeated crimes.（评论：相当一段时间内，监狱的“回笼率”相当高。原因之一就是犯罪分子重新进入社会后，由于缺乏谋生技能或者不被人们接受，导致他们再次失足，重返监狱。所以，我认为，在可能的前提下，我们可以在改造囚犯时努力培养他们的谋生技能以帮助他们出狱后自食其力，避免重复犯罪。）

⑤ For the increasing juvenile delinquency, the violence in the mass media, to some extent, should be blamed. When there are too much violent scenes in TV programs and movies, it is possible that some teenagers imitate those wrongful acts and do something against the law. Juveniles are not sufficiently mature to judge things.

Out of curiosity or being misled, they can go astray. → 相应的措施：Some people propose strict censorship on the violence in TV programs and movies, but I doubt it works. I think this is unfair for related industries and people who work in these industries. Also, I do not think it is a good idea to infringe upon people's right for information. To my best understanding, the root cause for juvenile-related crime is not the violence in TV programs. I think if we can work more on education, and more parental guidance can be given, things can change for the better. Besides, despite the current rating system for movies in many countries, it can still be improved.（评论：过多地审查影视作品反而会适得其反。在网络如此无孔不入的时代，任何被删除或封杀的作品都会因为人们的好奇心和叛逆的本能驱使而被找到并被广泛传阅。而且，事实证明，当政府过多地对信息进行干预时，它会失去公信力，这是很悲哀的。事实上，只要更合理地去引导、教育青少年，他们反而更能以平常心去对待这些事物。《无间道》说得好：出来混，迟早是要还的。这个道理青少年也懂。所以，我们应该更自信。我始终相信教育的力量，相信沟通的力量。）

⑥ In some countries and places, the increasing unemployment is also one of the factors that lead to criminal activities and anti-social behaviours, particularly when the economic crisis hit these countries or places the hardest. → 相应的措施：When the economy is going down, it would be hard for the government to create jobs, yet that should be the direction. In the meanwhile, the government should also try to improve the social security system such as increasing minimum wage for ordinary people. This would not have a negative effect on the economy yet it can give people an income boost and increase their ability to check inflation. This, I believe, is an effective way to prevent some anti-social behaviours.（评论：2008年的金融危机再一次重创了世界各国。一些欧美国家的经济持续衰退，失业率居高不下。老百姓待业在家，生活步履维艰，于是开始吃“霸王餐”，据统计，2010年英国吃“霸王餐”的人创历史新高[①]。当人们对政府失去了耐心和信任时，便开始抗议游行，结果部分国家的反社会行为开始增长，一些人甚至出国到其他国家就业。例如，2010年，由于在美国就业很难，一些美国人就到澳大利亚寻找工作机会。）

⑦ 降低犯罪率的其他措施：CCTV cameras can be set up in public places like shopping malls and city squares. Though some people are concerned that this can invade people's privacy, I think there should not be much privacy in public places. If anything, the installation of security cameras can exert a deterring effect on crime. It can also record the crime scene and present hard evidence to convict criminals.（评

① 资料来源：http://gb.cri.cn/27824/2011/01/26/5311s3137602.htm

论：我认为，在公共场合不应该有太多隐私可言，安装摄像头势必可以起到威慑作用。而且，一旦有犯罪活动出现，摄像头记录下来的影像资料便可作为证据，为法院的判决提供依据。）

以上内容只是针对人们犯罪的原因和对策泛泛而谈，但这是个社会问题，涉及方方面面，无法面面俱到。不过从备考角度而言，上述要点足以帮助广大考生拿到自己的目标分数。考生只要从上述要点中选取自己需要的，再适当增补即可。

下面提供部分范文供考生们参考。

Q1 如何降低犯罪率（289 words）

Crime is a problem all over the world and there is nothing that can be done to prevent it. To what extent do you agree or disagree?

Crime is a big social problem afflicting the whole world. In some places, the crime rate keeps increasing all the time. Some people say that nothing can be done to reverse such a situation. Personally, however, I think these people are completely wrong because there are so many ways to bring down the crime rate.

First of all, CCTV cameras can be set up in public places like shopping malls and city squares to prevent crime. Though some people are concerned that this can invade people's privacy, I think there should not be much privacy in public places. The installation of security cameras, if anything, can exert a deterring effect on crime because it can record the crime scene and present hard evidence to convict criminals.

Also, if severe penalties can be imposed on offenders, many criminal acts will be deterred. For instance, longer term of prison sentence can and should be given to punish criminals who are greedy such as in the cases of tax evasion, embezzlement or taking bribes. If people realize the price to pay, they will think harder before they do anything criminal.

Another way to reduce the crime level is to provide education and job training to inmates. This, I believe, can help prevent recidivism, or repeated crimes. Some people, particularly those illiterate or poorly-educated people, commit crime like stealing because they have no life skills. Therefore, they take the wrong way to get money. For these people, the provision of job training can prevent most of them from committing crime again.

In conclusion, whenever there is a problem there is a solution, and so is crime. Precautious actions and heavy punishments as well as job training are all keys to the issue.

【参考译文】

犯罪是个困扰全世界的社会问题。在某些地方，犯罪率一直都在上升。有些人认为我们无法改变这一局面。不过，我认为这些人完全错了，因为有很多方法可以降低犯罪率。

首先，在公共场合安装监控录像可以阻止犯罪。尽管有人担心这会侵犯人们的隐私，但我认为公共场合不应该有什么隐私。更可能的是，安装监控录像可以震慑犯罪，因为它可以记录犯罪现场并提供确凿的证据惩治犯罪分子。

同时，如果对犯罪分子处以严厉的惩罚措施，很多犯罪行为也会被震慑住。例如，我们可以而且应该对于逃税、挪用公款、贪污受贿等案件中的那些贪婪的罪犯判刑更久。如果人们意识到这种惨重的代价，就会在犯罪前三思而后行。

降低犯罪率的另一个方法是为囚犯提供教育和工作培训。我认为这可以避免重复犯罪。一些人犯罪主要是因为他们没有谋生的技能，尤其是那些文盲和没接受过良好教育的人，所以他们走上不归路。为这些人提供工作培训可以避免其中多数人再次犯罪。

总之，任何问题都会有解决办法，犯罪也不例外。提前预防、严厉惩罚及工作培训都是解决这一问题的关键。

高分词汇精选 Word Bank

序号	词汇	意思	同义表达（自测）
1	afflict	困扰	
2	crime rate/level	犯罪率	
3	reverse	扭转；改变	
4	CCTV	监控录像	
5	security cameras	摄像头	
6	invade one's privacy	侵犯某人的隐私	

序号	词汇	意思	同义表达（自测）
7	if anything	更可能的是	
8	installation	安装	
9	exert a deterring effect on...	对……产生威慑力	
10	record the crime scene	记录犯罪现场	
11	hard evidence	确凿的证据	
12	convict	审判	
13	severe penalties	严厉的惩罚	
14	deter	威慑	
15	prison sentence	徒刑	
16	tax evasion	逃税	
17	embezzlement	挪用公款	
18	take bribes	贪污受贿	
19	think hard/twice	认真思考；三思而后行	
20	inmates	囚犯	
21	recidivism	重复犯罪	
22	illiterate	文盲	
23	commit crime	犯罪	
24	life skills	谋生的技能	
25	precautious actions	预防措施	
26	heavy punishments	严厉的惩罚	

Q5 囚禁vs就业培训（319 words）

Putting criminals into prisons is not so effective in dealing with them. Instead, education and job training should be offered to them. To what extent do you agree or disagree?

Everyone realizes it is important to take action to rehabilitate criminals yet they are widely divided regarding how to do it. While some people think prison sentence should be given, others insist that education and job training programs are much better. Personally, however, I would say it depends on the motivation for and the effect of the crime.

Some people break the law because they are greedy such as in the cases of tax evasion, embezzlement or taking bribes. For most of these law offenders, they are well-educated. They have the power and ability to make money and lead a decent life. Yet their desires are never satisfied. They just expect more, regardless of the price. For them, severe penalties like prison sentence should be given so that more similar criminal acts will be deterred. If people realize the price to pay, they will think twice before they do anything criminal.

On the other hand, some people, particularly those illiterate or poorly-educated people, commit crime like stealing because they have no life skills. They need money yet they do not have the skills to earn it. Therefore, they take the wrong way. For these people, I do no think imprisonment is an effective way to deal with them. They might regret and reform after the prison sentence. However, when they are released, they will still have to struggle for a living. It is highly possible that they commit crime again and go back to jail. For them, I would say that the provision of education and job training is a better approach to deal with them because it can help prevent recidivism, or repeated crimes.

To reiterate, it is difficult to judge which way is the best way to deal with criminals. What should be truly considered when deciding on the way to punish or reform them is the motivation for, as well as the effect of, their crime.

【参考译文】

人们都意识到了需要采取措施改造犯罪分子，但是具体如何做则出现分歧。有些人认为应该对罪犯处以徒刑，而另一些人则认为应该依靠教育和工作培训。在我看来，其实得依据他们的犯罪动机及犯罪的影响程度而定。

一些人违法犯罪是因为他们太贪婪了，如那些逃税、挪用公款又或者是贪污受贿等案件。这类犯罪分子绝大多数都是受过良好教育的，他们有权力有能力挣钱过体面的生活，但是他们的欲望始终得不到满足。他们总想要更多，而不考虑代价。对于这些人，我们应该处以严厉的惩罚如徒刑。这样的话，更多类似的犯罪行为就可以被震慑住。如果人们意识到要为犯罪行为付出惨重的代价，就会三思而后行。

另一方面，有些人犯罪如偷窃是因为他们缺少谋生的技能，尤其是那些文盲和没有受过良好教育的人。这些人需要钱却挣不到，所以走上歧途。对于他们而言，徒刑未必行之有效。他们可能会后悔并改过自新。但是，刑满释放后他们还是难以谋生，所以很可能会再次犯罪，然后又被送回监狱。对于这些人，我认为更好的办法是为他们提供教育和工作培训，因为这可以避免重复犯罪。

总之，重申一点，我们很难判断哪种办法才是对待犯罪分子最好的方式。在采取措施时，我们真正需要考虑的是其犯罪动机和犯罪的影响程度。

高分词汇精选 Word Bank

序号	词汇	意思	同义表达（自测）
1	rehabilitate	改造	
2	reform	改造，改过自新	
3	People are divided by...	就……，见仁见智。	
4	prison sentence	徒刑	
5	motivation for crime	犯罪动机	
6	break the law	违反法律	
7	tax evasion	逃税	
8	embezzlement	挪用公款	
9	take bribes	贪污受贿	
10	law offenders	违法者	
11	a decent life	体面的生活	
12	severe penalties	严厉的惩罚	
13	deter	威慑，震慑	
14	think twice	三思	
15	illiterate	文盲	
16	commit crime	犯罪	
17	life skills	谋生的技能	
18	imprisonment	囚禁	

序号	词汇	意思	同义表达（自测）
19	struggle for a living	苦苦谋生	
20	approach	方式，途径	
21	recidivism	重复犯罪	
22	reiterate	重申	

Q7 加强城市安全（330 words）

More and more measures to improve the security in the urban area have been introduced because of the increased crime. Do the benefits of the measures outweigh the drawbacks?

The increasing crime rate in the urban area has drawn people's attention to the issue of how to improve the security in the city. Thus, a series of measures have been introduced and people are wondering about the real effects of these acts. Overall, I believe there are more benefits than drawbacks with the introduction of the measures.

One of the most common ways of improving the security in the city is to set up CCTV cameras in public places such as shopping malls and city squares. These security cameras can record the crime scene and present hard evidence to convict criminals. Therefore, such a practice can help deter crime and bring down the crime rate. Some people may say that the installation of video cameras can invade people's privacy. However, I do not think there should be much privacy thing in public places.

Also, in some cities, the local government increases security forces and encourages the police to increase patrols. Though it means taxpayers would have to pay more to keep the police on the street, this practice, like the above-mentioned act, can also have a deterring effect on crime and improve urban security.

Another way for some cities to improve the urban security is to give detailed reporting on crime in media so that the general public can stay alert to the tricks criminals employ and better protect themselves from falling victim to crime. While some fear the easy access to details of criminal activities can give other criminals an opportunity to improve their skills and reduce the city security, I think it is unnecessary to worry about this because the government will be smart enough not to disclose every single detail to the media. Instead, it will ensure that this approach works for the good of the people.

In conclusion, despite the potential drawbacks, most measures to improve urban security have proven to be effective and help create a good world for people to live in.

【参考译文】

城市日益上升的犯罪率使得人们关注如何改善城市的安全。由此，也采取了一系列措施，并且人们想弄清楚这些措施的真正效果。总体上，我认为这些措施的利好大于其弊端。

改善城市安全最常见的方法是在公共场合安装监控录像，例如购物中心及城市广场等。这些摄像头可以记录犯罪现场，为惩治犯罪分子提供确凿的证据。因此，这一做法可以震慑犯罪并且降低犯罪率。有人会担心摄像头的安装会侵犯人们的隐私，但我认为公共场合不应该有太多隐私可言。

同时在有些城市，当地政府增派安保力量并且增加警察巡逻。尽管这意味着纳税人将为此负担更多的费用，但正如上述方法一样，这也可以对犯罪活动产生威慑力，从而提高城市安全性。

改善城市安全的另一个做法是媒体更多地对犯罪活动进行详细报道。这样，公众对犯罪分子所使用的小伎俩保持警惕，从而更好地保护自己，避免自己成为犯罪活动的受害者。尽管有人担心如此轻而易举就接触到犯罪细节会使得其他犯罪分子有机会完善自己的手法，降低城市安全性，但我认为没必要担心，因为政府不会无知到向媒体透露所有细节。相反，政府会确保这一做法对公众有利。

总之，尽管存在隐患，但事实证明，绝大多数改善城市安全的措施都是有效果的，并且为人们创造了一个美好的环境。

高分词汇精选 Word Bank

序号	词汇	意思	同义表达（自测）
1	crime rate	犯罪率	
2	draw people's attention to...	让人们关注……	
3	a series of	一系列	
4	set up CCTV cameras	安装监控录像	

序号	词汇	意思	同义表达（自测）
5	security cameras	摄像头	
6	record the crime scene	记录犯罪现场	
7	hard evidence	确凿的证据	
8	convict	审判；惩治	
9	deter	威慑，震慑	
10	invade one's privacy	侵犯隐私	
11	security force	安保力量	
12	patrol	巡逻	
13	taxpayer	纳税人	
14	have a deterring effect on...	对……产生威慑力	
15	urban security	城市安全	
16	detailed reporting on crime	详细报道犯罪	
17	stay alert to...	对……保持警惕	
18	access（to）	权限；得到	
19	fall victim to...	成为……的受害者	
20	disclose	公布，披露	
21	every single	每一个	
22	approach	方法	
23	for one's good	为了某人好	

Q12 审查影视作品（264 words）

Violence in TV programs and movies results in juvenile delinquency. Therefore, the government should impose censorship on the violence in TV programs and movies. To what extent do you agree or disagree?

Many people are concerned about the negative effects that violent scenes in TV programs and movies bring on teenagers and propose strict censorship on the media. From my perspective, however, such an act cannot be justified.

It is understood that when teenagers are not sufficiently mature to distinguish right from wrong, they, out of curiosity or being misguided, can imitate some wrongful acts in TV programs. This is believed to be one of the causes for increased juvenile-related crimes. It is also the basis for media censorship.

However, it should be pointed out that the violence in TV programs and movies is not the root cause for juvenile delinquency. Plus, the violence in TV programs and films can actually serve educational purposes as most villains in those shows only have tragic ending. I think once juveniles realize the price to pay for violent acts, they will understand that violence shall never be the solution to issues.

In addition, individuals have the right to enjoy great movies and TV shows. If the government were to impose censorship on the media, it would infringe people's rights. People may even lose faith in the government. Meanwhile, TV production and film industry would also suffer massively because many great TV programs and movies will be blocked and talented people in this business will never be motivated to create any more.

To sum up, I strongly object to the censorship on TV programs and movies because it does not necessarily reduce juvenile delinquency and yet it jeopardizes people's right for entertainment as well as the development of related industries.

【参考译文】

很多人担心电视电影的暴力场景会给青少年带来负面影响，主张严厉审查媒体。但在我看来，这种做法站不住脚。

我们能理解，当青少年没有足够成熟到明辨是非时，出于好奇或者被误导，他们会模仿电视中的错误行为。人们认为这是青少年犯罪增多的原因之一，这也是人们主张审查媒体的原因。

但是，必须指出的是，电视电影中的暴力并非青少年犯罪的根本原因。而且，这些暴力实际上可以带来教育意义，因为影视中的多数反派人物最终都悲剧收场。我认为一旦年轻人意识到犯罪行为的代价，他们就会理解暴力永远都不是解决问题的办法。

此外，公众有权利享受好的影视作品。如果政府对媒体进行审查，这会侵犯人们的权利。人们甚至会因此对政府失去信任。与此同时，电视制作及电影产业也将因此遭受重创，因为很多伟大的作品将因此被封杀，从而导致该行业的精英毫无创作的动力。

总之，我强烈反对审查电视电影。因为这非但不能减少青少年犯罪，还会损害人们娱乐的权利及相关产业的发展。

高分词汇精选 Word Bank

序号	词汇	意思	同义表达（自测）
1	be concerned about	担忧	
2	censorship	审查	
3	from my perspective	在我看来	
4	cannot be justified	站不住脚	
5	not sufficiently mature to	尚未足够成熟到	
6	distinguish right from wrong	明辨是非	
7	out of curiosity	出于好奇	
8	misguide	误导	
9	imitate	模仿	
10	wrongful acts	错误的/违法的行为	
11	juvenile-related crimes	青少年犯罪	
12	juvenile delinquency	青少年犯罪	
13	root cause	根本原因	
14	serve educational purposes	起到教育的意义/功能	
15	villains	反派角色	
16	tragic ending	悲剧的结局	
17	juveniles	青少年	
18	have the right to do sth.	有权利做某事	
19	impose...on sb.	将……强加于某人	
20	infringe	侵犯	
21	film industry	电影产业	
22	suffer massively	遭受重创	
23	block	封杀	
24	be motivated to	被激励着去做某事	
25	object to	反对	
26	jeopardize	损害，破坏，伤害	

二、其他犯罪类真题

16. Society is based on rules and laws. It could not function if individuals were free to do whatever they want. To what extent do you agree or disagree?

17. Some people think there should be fixed punishments for each type of crime while others think the motivation and the effects of the crime should be considered while deciding on the punishment. What's your opinion?

18. Some people believe that the police force carrying guns would cause a high level of violence. Do you agree or disagree?

说 明

这些算是犯罪类考题中的非主流。开玩笑地说，除非“幸运”，否则比中奖的几率还低。需要指出的是，Q17被收录在《剑桥雅思考试全真试题集7》一书中，所以考试概率基本为零。考试真正需要备考的是Q16与Q18，而其中Q16的写作思路基本可以参考Q17一文。关于Q18，考生们可以上网搜索一下美国警察配枪所带来的利弊作为参考。

Q17 是否要有固定的惩罚措施（299 words）

Some people think there should be fixed punishments for each type of crime while others think the motivation and the effects of the crime should be considered while deciding on the punishment. What's your opinion?（《剑桥雅思考试全真试题集7》Test 2——7.5分作文）

Fixing punishments for each type of crime has been a debatable issue. There are many arguments supporting both views, those for and those against fixed punishments.

On the one hand, fixed punishments will have a deterring effect on society. Individuals knowing that they will be subject to a certain punishment if they are convicted with a given crime, will reconsider committing this act in the first place.

This deterring effect also leads to social stability and security, through minimising the number of crimes committed.

If people knew they would be able to convince the court or the jury of a reason for having committed the crime they are accused of, penal decisions would be largely arbitrary. This would result into criminals getting away with their crimes and into a high level of injustice caused by the subjective approach of different courts.

On the other hand, taking the circumstances of a crime and its motivation into consideration is a prerequisite for establishing and ensuring justice and equity.

A person killing in self-defense can not be compared to a serial killer, moving from one victim to the next. In my opinion an intermediary position between both solutions is the perfect way to establish and ensure justice and equity.

There has to be fixed punishment for all crimes. However, criminal laws have to provide for a minimum and maximum for the punishment and the laws also have to foresee certain cases of exemptions.

An example for setting minimum and maximum penalties is competition law where a person being held liable of a crime under this law will be convicted to pay a fine, according to the harm caused by the violation and the profit gained by the violator through committing the crime.

As for the exemptions, in some countries the law exempts thiefs stealing food during a period of famine taking into consideration the distress and hunger.

Also, a person killing in self-defense will be exempted from punishment.

考官点评

This is a thoughtful and well-argued response to the task. The candidate examines the opposing views of the topic and gives a clear opinion that is well developed and supported. To reach the highest band a more clearly-signaled conclusion would be needed. The argument is well organized and linking is well managed throughout. The development of the answer is not helped, however, by poor control of paragraphing which sometimes confuses the links across different sections. This is a weak feature of the script which limits the overall rating. In contrast, an excellent range of vocabulary is used with a sophisticated level of control and only rare slips. The range of structures is also wide and most sentences are accurate and precise, but there are some errors and omissions. These, however, are only minor and do not affect communication.

CHAPTER 9
社会生活篇

社会生活类话题是雅思写作的重中之重，无论是对于学术类考生还是移民类考生都是如此。那么究竟什么是社会生活类的话题呢？基本上，除去本书前面章节所涉及的题材，其余考题都可以看做是社会生活类话题。

大体来讲，社会生活类话题包括以下类别：

- 广告
- 媒体
- 工作
- 城市
- 健康
- 老年人
- 其他

在历年的雅思写作中，考试频率最高、考查范围最广、考题最多的便是社会生活类话题。正是由于这类考题的多样性和不可预测性，考生往往在备考过程中显得很茫然。笔者通过跟踪对比历年考试真题，从题库中筛选出以下核心母题，建议考生认真备考这些高频考题。

一、广告

1. Today, the high sales of popular goods reflect the power of advertising and not the real needs of the society in which they are sold. To what extent do you agree or disagree?
2. If a product is good or it meets people's needs, people will buy it. So advertising is unnecessary and no more than an entertainment. Do you agree or disagree?
3. Advertising encourages consumers to buy in quantity rather than promoting quality. To what extent do you agree or disagree?

4. Consumers are faced with increasing numbers of advertisements from competing companies. To what extent do you think consumers are influenced by advertisements? What measures can be taken to protect them?

5. The society would benefit from a ban on all forms of advertising because it serves no useful purpose, and can even be damaging. To what extent do you agree or disagree with this opinion?

6. Advertising discourages people from becoming different individuals and makes them look the same. Do you agree or disagree?

7. There is an increasing amount of advertising directed at children which encourages them to buy goods such as toys and snacks. Many parents are worried that these advertisements put too much pressure on children, while some advertisers claim that they provide useful information to children. Discuss both views and give your opinion.

万能思路

广告类话题基本上每年必考，而且有些年份考查2～3次。泛泛而谈，这类话题多是考查广告是否会影响人们的行为，以及如何影响。

从备考的角度讲，建议考生们记住以下万能思路：

- 广告之所以对人们的行为产生影响，原因如下：①邀请名人代言（endorsement），由于名人效应（celebrity effect），歌迷影迷们就会进行大量购买；②使用植入广告（product placement），导致很多人也进行购买；③使用吸人眼球的（eye-catching）图片或者漂亮模特（slim-trim models）打广告，吸引一部分人购买；④使用夸大其词的广告语或者文案（copy），诱导（lure）或者误导（mislead）人们消费；⑤反复播放广告，对公众进行洗脑（mind-wash/brainwash），使公众在潜意识里（subconsciously）记住它。

- 既然广告会造成这么大的影响，应该如何保护消费者的利益呢？建议考生记住以下思路：政府立法规范广告行业。如果企业提供虚假信息误导消费者，有关管理部门应对其处以巨额罚款，甚至吊销执照。与此同时，代言人也应被追究相应责任以增加法律法规的威慑力。【Governments should introduce legislation to regulate advertising industry. If advertisers provide misleading information, governments should impose huge fines on them or even revoke their license. Meanwhile, the entertainment star should also be responsible if the product he/she endorses goes wrong.】

- 有时，考题还会涉及广告带来的积极影响。若此，建议考生们掌握：①广告可以是个重要的信息来源（information source），为人们提供某方面的有用讯息，如口腔/牙齿护理（dental care）等；②某些广告可以为人们提供一定的创意（ideas）或者是激励人们坚持自己的追求；③在经济活动中，广告是非常重要的催化剂/润滑剂（catalyst），撬动相关商业活动的发展。同时，也创造了大量的就业机会（employment opportunities）与税收（tax revenues）。

关于广告类的考题，本章节使用《剑桥雅思考试全真试题集6》Test 1所收录的考生作文供读者参考。请大家认真研读，并对照文章后面附上的考官评语来揣摩一下本文哪些方面做得好，而哪些方面又有待改进。

Q1 购物：广告vs真实需求（331 words）

Today, the high sales of popular goods reflect the power of advertising and not the real needs of the society in which they are sold. To what extent do you agree or disagree?

Nowadays, there are lots of advertisements on television or on the streets. Some people think that advertising boosts the sales of goods and it encourages people to buy things unnecessarily. This arguments may be true. In my country many advertising companies produce advertisements with famous and popular actors or singers. People, especially youngsters, buy goods that their favourite singer advertise, although they do not really need the products.

Also, on the television screen, a product may look gorgeous and good quality. As a result of it, people often buy goods without enough consideration. Consumers may not actually need it but they buy goods impulsively soon after they watch the advertising. Furthermore, as many customers buy a particular product due to its advertising campaign, the other people may be affected by the trend, even if the product is not of the real needs of the society.

On the other hand, there are various aspects against these arguments. Moreover, it is people's choice to make a decision to buy goods. Advertising may be not a cause of customers' buying habits. Individuals have their own spending habits. If they have got enough disposable income, then the right to make a decision is given to them.

No one actually can judge whether the goods sold are the real needs of the society or not.

In addition, as there should be a limited amount of disposable income consumers are able to spend, people try to allocate their budgets. They cannot be simply swayed by those advertisements.

In conclusion, as customers have their own strong opinions and standard of good quality goods, it is better to leave them to make their own decision in buy goods. It is fairly difficult to say everyone is swayed by advertising and buy good impulsively. However, in sensitive area of businesses such as toy industries, it may be necessary to band advertising to those children as children have not got enough ability to control themselves or to know what they need.

【参考译文】

如今，电视里大街上到处都是广告。一些人认为，广告促销商品，并且鼓动人们购买一些非必需品。该看法可能是对的。在我国，很多广告公司请著名的演员或流行歌手代言。人们，尤其是年轻人，就会去购买他们最喜欢的歌手代言的物品，尽管这些并非是他们真正需要的。

同时，产品在电视屏幕上看起来非常漂亮，且质量上乘。因此，人们经常不假思索地购买。消费者可能并不需要该产品，但是他们看完广告后便冲动购买。而且，当很多人由于广告促销而购买了某种产品时，其他人便会受到影响而跟风，即使这也不是他们真正需要的。

另一方面，也有很多看法与上述看法相。况且，购不购买是人们自己的决定。广告可能并不是促使大家购买行为的原因。人们有自己的消费习惯。如果他们有足够的可支配收入，就有购买的权利。没人能够判断所售物品是否是社会的真正需求。

此外，由于消费者的可支配收入有限，他们总是尽量合理地分配预算。他们不会轻易受到广告的影响。

总之，每个人都有自己的看法和标准来衡量好的物品，所以最好由他们自己做出购买决定。很难定论说每个人都是被广告说服而去冲动消费。但是，在一些敏感的行业譬如玩具行业，有必要禁止针对小孩子的广告。因为小孩子没有足够的判断能力或者他们并不知道自己需要什么。

高分词汇精选 Word Bank

序号	词汇	意思	同义表达（自测）
1	boost	提高，促进	
2	impulsively	冲动地	
3	advertising campaign	广告宣传活动	
4	disposable income	可支配性收入	
5	allocate	分配	
6	budget	预算	
7	sway	动摇；说服	

说明

这是《剑桥雅思考试全真试题集6》Test 1中收录的一篇7.5分的考生作文[①]。

考官的评语为

The way in which the candidate has responded to the task is a strong point of this script. It is a well-developed answer that addresses the issues relevantly and at length. The writer introduces the topic, examines both sides of the argument and expresses a clear position. Points are well-argued and supported with examples.

The answer is well-organized and the message is easy to follow with clear paragraphing and linking of ideas. There are too many errors, however, and some linkers are not always fully appropriate, so this limits the rating for this criterion.

A wide range of vocabulary is used accurately and precisely, in spite of one or two awkward expressions and some rare errors. Similarly, a sophisticated range of structure is used but there are too many minor errors and omissions (such as in the use of prepositions and basic subject/verb agreement) to reach Band 8. Nevertheless these mistakes do not reduce the clarity of the answer and overall a wide range of language is used with a high level of proficiency.

① 资料来源：《剑桥雅思考试全真试题集6》(Cambridge IELTS 6) Test 1。

二、媒体

8. Every day people are presented with different news reports. Some people think we should not trust these reports. To what extent do you agree or disagree with it? What qualities should journalists have?

9. News media is more influential nowadays. Some people think it is a negative development. To what extent do you agree or disagree?

10. News media are important in modern society. Why are they important? Are their influences generally positive or negative?

11. Newspapers have become an enormous influence on people's ideas and opinions. Why is this case? Is it a positive or negative situation?

12. Today, there are more and more reports on violence and disasters in the media. Why is the case? What effects can this have?

万能思路

上述考题中，Q8～Q9的考试频率相对偏高；其中，Q9最新的考试日期为2016年1月23日。媒体类的话题不少，除了这几题外，考查频率相对较高的还有本书中政府篇所涉及的“censorship on the violence in TV programs and movies”一文，以及犯罪篇“detailed reporting on crime”与“more and more news reports on violence and disasters”两篇作文。请广大考生认真备考。

Q8 是否应相信新闻报道（353 words）

Every day people are presented with different news reports. Some people think we should not trust these reports. To what extent do you agree or disagree with it? What qualities should journalists have?

In this information era, we are bombarded with news reports of all types every day. However, we are always caught in a dilemma: if we read, we are probably misinformed; but if we do not, we are uninformed. What needs to be clarified then is should we trust the media or should we be suspicious of everything they say? From where I stand, it depends on the news source.

Some news media are manipulated by the government and I think their credibility should be questioned. Obviously, these news agencies can always be abused to serve the best interest of the authorities or a few influential people. Likewise, if a news organization always fights against the government, then it is highly possible that it is also in the interest of those powerful people. In that case, we should also be careful before accepting what they say.

On the other hand, however, some news agents have built a good reputation of presenting the truth and have stood the test of time. Their reliability should not be easily challenged. For these news organizations, what they do is to show us the truth as it is and they have earned themselves the name that they deserve, such as the New York Times. Wikileaks, meanwhile, also enjoys a high credibility among people even though it is just a whistle-blowing website founded in 2006.

As for the qualities that journalists should have, I think being investigative shall always be on top of the list. Journalists should always be brave to dig out the truth, even if that means they might put their own lives at risk. They should also be objective, telling people nothing but the truth. Last but not least, they should have a good command of words so that they can always keep it brief and keep it to the point when expressing things.

In conclusion, while journalists are supposed to simply presenting the truth, it would be judgmental for us to blindly reject or accept what they say. What we should do is to read, compare and think critically so that we do not get misguided.

【参考译文】

在这个信息时代，我们每天都受到各种新闻报道的狂轰滥炸。但是，我们也经常陷入困境：如果我们阅读，可能会被误导；而如果我们放弃阅读，则又会变得孤陋寡闻。因此，我们必须弄清楚的是，对于媒体我们到底是应该相信还是应该怀疑？在我看来，这取决于信息的渠道来源。

有些媒体受到了政府的操控，我认为它们的可信度应该受到质疑。显然，这类新闻机构总是被滥用于为当局或者一小部分有影响力的人谋利。同样，如果某家新闻机构始终与政府保持对立，则很可能也是为那些有权势的人谋利的。如此，我们也应该谨慎对待它们的言论。

另一方面，有些新闻机构已经赢得了一个只呈现真相的好名声并且经受住了时间的考验。它们的可信度不应该轻易受到质疑。对于这些机构而言，它们具备新闻记者应有的品质，我认为富有调查精神永远应该摆在首位。新闻记者一定要勇于挖掘真相，即使这意味着其生命可能会受到威胁。记者还应该公正客观，只用事实说话。此外，他们还应该有很好的文字功底，以便在表达事情时言简意赅。

总之，当新闻记者要呈现客观事实时，我们不应该盲目地拒绝或者接受其报道。我们真正要做的，是批判性地进行阅读、对比和思考，以免被误导。

高分词汇精选 Word Bank

序号	词汇	意思	同义表达（自测）
1	information era	信息时代	
2	be bombarded with	充斥着	
3	be caught in a dilemma	陷入困境	
4	be suspicious of	怀疑	
5	from where I stand	在我看来	
6	news source	新闻渠道/来源	
7	manipulate	操控	
8	credibility/reliability	可信度	
9	question	质疑	
10	abuse	滥用	
11	serve the interest of...	为……服务	
12	influential	有影响力的	
13	powerful	有权势的	
14	news agents/agencies	新闻机构	
15	reputation/name	名声	
16	whistle blow	爆料	
17	investigative	富有调查精神的	
18	dig out the truth	挖出真相	
19	have a good command of...	熟练掌握	
20	judgmental	武断的	
21	think critically	批判性地思考	

说明

Q8需要考生对西方的主流媒体有所了解。

关于Q9，这道题有陷阱，很多考生写跑题了。

注意，题目问的是“媒体的影响力在增强”好不好，而很多考生往往只是泛泛而谈媒体对人们会造成什么样的影响。实际上，这道题的答题思路可以参考Q8——当被某些机构或者个人所操控的媒体的影响力在增大时，这绝对不是个好的现象；但如果是那些为公众服务的媒体的影响力在增强，则可以促成好的结果，因为这可以传递民意，对各行各业起到强有力的监督作用。对于广大的考生而言，接受这些观点并不难，难的是到底能不能一一举例论证。这需要考生具有一定的阅读量和国际视野。加油吧，小伙伴们！

三、动物

13. Some people think that the use of animal for experimentation is cruel. Others think it is good for the development of science. Discuss the two sides and give your opinion.

14. It is no longer necessary that animals should be slaughtered and made into either human foodstuffs or non-foodstuffs, such as fur and medicine. Do you agree or disagree?

Q12 动物实验（260 words）

Some people think that the use of animal for experimentation is cruel. Other think it is good for the development of science. Discuss the two sides and give your opinion.

It has been suggested that experiment on animals, despite its scientific intention, should be ceased because of its cruelty. Personally, however, such experiments should always be continued.

The most important reason for people to argue against animal experiments is because of the pains that animals have to endure. For instance, many animals are tortured or even lose their lives in some scientific experiments. However, I think people must realize it is only natural for those on top of the food chain to take advantage of those at lower levels for their own good. Survival of the fittest, as people call it.

Moreover, there are regulations to ensure that scientists do not dissect a lab rat for fun. In some places, there are even rules to ask lab researchers to conduct euthanasia on animals if they suffer too much. In other words, there is no need to be concerned about animal abuse.

Furthermore, it is important to stress that animals' sacrifice has great values. They do not die in vain because they help human beings find the cure to certain diseases, which can help save lives, not just human lives but animal lives as well. For instance, the invention of antibiotics was attributed to animal experimentation, without which it would be difficult for human beings to cure smallpox and millions of lives would not have been saved①.

In conclusion, the cruelty of animal testing can be justified. Moreover, such scientific research is vitally important in saving humans and animals. Consequently, I think it is reasonable to carry on animal experimentation.

【参考译文】

一些人认为，尽管动物实验是用于科研目的，但是由于其残忍性应该予以终止。不过在我看来，这类实验应该永远保留。

人们反对动物实验的最主要的原因是动物遭受到巨大的痛苦。例如，在一些科学实验中很多动物被折磨甚至是死亡。但是，我认为人们必须明白食物链顶层的物种利用更低级别的物种是很正常的。这就是人们所说的“适者生存”。

此外，有规章制度来确保科学家不会无缘无故只是为了好玩便解剖一只小白鼠。在一些地方，甚至有条例要求研究人员在动物遭受巨大痛苦时对其实施安乐死。换句话讲，没有必要担心虐待动物的情况。

而且，必须强调的是，动物的牺牲是有价值的。它们没有白死，因为它们帮助人类找到一些疾病的治疗方法，而这不仅仅是治病救人，也可以拯救动物。例如，抗生素的发明就得归功于动物实验。如果没有动物实验，我们将很难治愈天花，而成千上万的生命也将难以幸免于难。

总之，动物实验是残忍，但这是出于正当理由的。而且，这类实验对于拯救生命（人和动物）都至关重要。因此，我认为我们有理由继续进行动物实验。

① 资料来源：http://www.bio1000.com/experiment/zoology/2242.html

高分词汇精选 Word Bank

序号	词汇	意思	同义表达（自测）
1	cease	停止	
2	cruelty	残忍	
3	endure	经受，承受	
4	torture	折磨	
5	food chain	食物链	
6	take advantage of	利用	
7	survival of the fittest	适者生存	
8	dissect	解剖	
9	lab rat	小白鼠	
10	euthanasia	安乐死	
11	animal abuse	虐待动物	
12	sacrifice	牺牲	
13	in vain	徒劳	
14	antibiotics	抗生素	
15	be attributed to	归功于	
16	smallpox	天花	
17	animal testing	动物实验	
18	vitally important	至关重要的	
19	consequently	因此	
20	animal experimentation	动物实验	

四、其他

15. In many countries, the proportion of older people is steadily increasing. Does this trend have more positive or negative effects on the society?

16. Some people say that workers over 55 must retire while some disagree. What's your opinion?

17. Some people believe that personal happiness is directly related to one's material wealth. Others believe there are other factors. Discuss the two sides and give your opinion.

18. In modern society, fashion is becoming more and more popular in people's choice of clothes. Why? Do you think it is a positive development or a negative development?

19. An increasing number of people change their career and place of residence several times during their lives. Is this a positive or negative development?

20. Some people say job satisfaction is more important than job security, while others think people cannot always expect to enjoy their work so finding a permanent job is more important. Discuss both views and give your own opinion.

21. In some countries, small town-centre shops are out of business because people are driving to large out-of-town stores. As a result, people without cars have limited access to shops, so more and more people buy cars. Do you think the disadvantages of this development outweigh the advantages?

22. Some people say that it brings more negative effects when rich countries help poor countries. To what extent do you agree or disagree?

23. Many people are optimistic about the 21st century and see it as an opportunity to make positive changes to the world. To what extent do you agree or disagree with their optimism? What changes would you like to see in the new century?

24. Modern lifestyles make many people hard to lead active and healthy lives. What are the factors contributing to that? How to suggest the governments and other large companies helping them do more exercise?

25. In recent years, traffic jam has become a headache problem around the world. In order to solve this problem, some people think governments have to build wider roads to satisfy and solve the traffic jam. Do you agree or disagree?

26. The quality of life in the city is getting worse and worse. What are the possible reasons and what can be done to improve the situation?

说明

以上为近些年的高频考题，涉及老年人、工作职场、城市问题、国际援助等方方面面。至于未提及的健康问题，我们将在下一章节进行探讨。

Q20可参照《剑桥雅思考试全真试题集7》Test 3的考官范文；Q24则可参考本书中"cause + solution"章节针对《剑桥雅思考试全真试题集8》Test 4所写的作文，同时《剑桥雅思考试全真试题集9》Test 3的考官范文也非常具有参考价值。Q26也将在"cause + solution"章节进行讨论。

Q15 人口老龄化（341 words）

In many countries, the proportion of older people is steadily increasing. Does this trend have more positive or negative effects on the society?

Recent years have witnessed an expansion in the aged population in many countries across the world. Facts have shown that such a trend can bring far more undesirable consequences than positive effects.

First and foremost, the aging trend poses enormous financial challenges to the government and taxpayers. As is known, the government needs to provide retirement benefits such as pensions and health care services to the aged people. When there are a higher percentage of senior citizens in society, the government will have to invest more public funds in these issues. Unfortunately, governments at all level are working under a tight budget and cannot handle such a burden. For example, in China decision makers propose that there should be a-few-year delay before people can really claim their pensions. Should this truly happen, old people's life would be a mess.

Meanwhile, with a higher percentage of elderly people in society, it will ultimately result in a series of social and economic problems. Statistics show that in aged societies, the birth rate is very low and there will not be sufficient young workers in the job market. Because of labour shortage, old people will be left no choice but to stay in the job market. This is one of the reasons why some countries have increased the retirement age from 65 to 67. Moreover, the shortage of workforce will push the government to introduce immigrant workers from overseas, which would bring visa issues and the management of these expats would also be a challenge to the authorities.

Some people might say that there can be positive effects with the aging trend. For example, the increase of aged populations can create business opportunities for certain industries. However, as has been elaborated, the government will have to spend more to take care of elderly people because the tax revenues generated by those businesses cannot cover the whole paycheck.

In conclusion, the aging trend can bring huge problems to both the government and ordinary people, compared with which the possible benefits of it can be simply written off.

【参考译文】

最近这些年，很多国家的老年人群体越来越大。事实表明，这一现象造成的负面影响远远超过其积极影响。

首先，人口老龄化会对政府构成巨大的财政负担。众所周知，政府需要为老年人提供退休福利如退休金及医疗服务。当老年人群体扩大时，政府将不得不投入更多的公共资金到这些领域。不幸的是，各级政府都预算有限，无力承担这一负担。例如，中国的决策者建议人们退休后推迟几年领退休金。如果这个真的发生，老年人的生活将会一片混乱。

同时，老年人群体的扩大最终会导致一系列社会问题和经济问题。统计表明，在老龄化的社会，出生率非常低，职场将来会没有足够的年轻劳动力。由于劳动力短缺，老年人将不得不继续工作。这就是为什么有些国家将退休年龄从65岁推迟到67岁。而且，劳动力的短缺会迫使政府从国外引进劳务，而这势必带来签证及外籍人口的管理问题。

有人可能会认为人口老龄化会带来积极影响。例如，老年群体的扩张会给某些行业带来商机。但是，正如前文所述，政府仍将花费更多来照顾好老年人，因为这些商机所带来的税收不并足以抵消所有开销。

总之，人口老龄化不仅给政府而且给普通老百姓带来巨大的问题。相比之下，其积极影响基本不值一提。

高分词汇精选 Word Bank

序号	词汇	意思	同义表达（自测）
1	aged population	老年人群体	
2	Facts have shown that	事实表明	
3	undesirable consequences	消极影响	

序号	词汇	意思	同义表达（自测）
4	the aging trend	人口老龄化	
5	financial challenges	财政问题	
6	taxpayers	纳税人	
7	retirement benefits	退休福利	
8	pension	退休金	
9	senior citizens	老年人	
10	public funds	公共资金	
11	work under a tight budget	预算有限	
12	decision makers	决策者	
13	claim	领取；索要；声称	
14	Statistics show	统计表明	
15	job market	就业市场；职场	
16	labour shortage	劳动力短缺	
17	retirement age	退休年龄	
18	workforce	劳动力	
19	immigrant workers	外来务工人员	
20	expat/ expatriate	外籍旅居人士	
21	tax revenues	税款	
22	write off	注销；忽视	

Q17 幸福是什么（341 words）

Some people believe that personal happiness is directly related to material wealth. Others believe there are other factors. Discuss the two sides and give your opinion.

The pursuit of happiness has always been a frequent topic of discussion among people. But what defines happiness? Some people would say that material wealth can determine whether a person is happy or not. Although I would not deny the importance of money, I believe there are other factors that can contribute to people's happiness.

On the one hand, material wealth plays a vitally important role in people's pursuit of happiness. After all, money promises people the right to choose, which is considered a prerequisite for a happy life. Otherwise, people will be frustrating and not content with their life. In China, for example, many of those born in the 1980s now have to work long hours to save money for an apartment. Unfortunately, no matter how hard they work, they still find it difficult to save enough. At the end of the day, these young people will have to use up all the savings of their own and their parents' as well just to pay the down payment and spend the rest of their lives working hard to pay off the mortgage. Many of these people live a pathetic life and they are not happy.

Yet on the other hand, it would be judgmental for us to say that money is the only thing that people care about a happy life because there are many other contributing factors. First of all, health has a say. Many people become pessimistic and lose their faith in life when they contract an incurable disease. Most of these people eventually die depressed. Secondly, religious beliefs also impact people's contentment at life. For those who have religious beliefs, what they care about is not material wealth, but the spiritual meaning in life. As long as they feel God is still with them, and as long as they believe they can still help others, they will be happy and grateful.

In conclusion, money is only one of the factors that people care about when pursuing happiness; other issues such as health and religious beliefs also matter.

【参考译文】

追求幸福始终是人们关注的话题。但究竟什么是幸福？有些人会认为物质财富决定了一个人幸不幸福。

尽管我不否认金钱的重要性，我认为有其他因素会影响人们的幸福感。物质财富在人们追求幸福方面至关重要。毕竟，金钱给予人们选择权利，而这是幸福的前提条件之一。否则，人们可能会很沮丧并且对生活不满意。例如，中国的很多八零后必须长时间地工作赚钱买房。不幸的是，无论他们多么努力工作，仍旧无法存到足够多的钱。最终，他们不得不花光自己和父母的所有积蓄交首付，然后下半辈子努力偿还贷款。他们中的很多人生活悲惨，活得并不开心。

但另一方面，如果我们认为金钱是人们唯一关注的因素则未免太武断了。首先，健康很重要。很多人染上不治之症后便变得悲观，对生活失去信念。他们中的多数人最后都郁郁而终。其次，宗教信仰也会影响人们对生活的满意度。有宗教信仰的人往往不在乎物质财富，他们更在乎精神生活。只要他们认为上帝仍与他们同在，只要他们相信他们仍旧可以帮助他人，他们就会很开心并心存感激。

总之，金钱不是追求幸福的唯一因素，其他诸如健康和宗教信仰等因素也很重要。

高分词汇精选 Word Bank

序号	词汇	意思	同义表达（自测）
1	pursuit of happiness	追求幸福	
2	a frequent topic of discussion	经常谈论的话题	
3	material wealth	物质财富	
4	play an important role in...	扮演重要角色	
5	prerequisite	前提条件	
6	those born in the 1980s	八零后	
7	work long hours	长时间地工作	
8	unfortunately	不幸的是；遗憾的是	
9	at the end of the day	终究	
10	savings	积蓄	
11	down payment	首付	
12	pay off	偿还，还清；有回报	
13	mortgage	抵押贷款	
14	pathetic	可悲的	
15	judgmental	武断的	
16	have a say	有发言权	
17	pessimistic	悲观的	
18	contract	感染上	
19	incurable diseases	不治之症	
20	die depressed	郁郁而终	
21	religious beliefs	宗教信仰	
22	contentment	满意	
23	the spiritual meaning in life	精神生活	
24	be grateful	心存感激	

Q18 时尚（267 words）

In modern society, fashion is becoming more and more popular in people's choice of clothes. Why? Do you think it is positive development or negative development?

It has been a trend that people buy famous and fashionable brands when they go shopping, especially for clothes. I believe that the reason behind it is the impact of advertising and I do not regard this is a positive development.

Advertisers always lure people to buy what they believe is good. They either invite entertainment stars to endorse their products or pay gorgeous models to convince people how good their products are. These TV commercials and eye-catching pictures make young people mistakenly believe that they are not cool enough unless they dress the way those "successful" people do. Once some young people buy those fashionable clothes, others just follow suit. It is like virus and few can escape.

I do not think it is a positive thing that a growing number of young people are buying fashionable clothes. First of all, staying in fashion costs money and most young people simply do not have enough financial resources for it. Thus, this is a waste of parents' money, which is not funny. Secondly, such a trend, though not necessarily, can make young people materialistic and superficial. It is good to look presentable, but when young people only focus on their appearance and ignore what is really important for personal improvement, they will be judging each other simply by the way they dress and this can be extremely negative.

In conclusion, advertising lures young people to stick to fashion when they buy clothes. But no matter how good young people may feel about themselves, this trend can be negative as it wastes their money and makes them materialistic.

【参考译文】

人们在购物时往往选择名牌和时尚的牌子，尤其是购买衣服时。我认为究其原因，主要是受到广告的影响，而且我认为这一现象很不好。

广告商总是诱导人们去购买他们认为好的产品。他们要么邀请娱乐明星代言，要么雇漂亮的模特来说服人们其产品很好。这些电视广告和吸引人的图片使得很多年轻人误以为他们必须同那些“成功人士”一样穿衣打扮，否则就不够酷。而一旦有人这么做了，其他人便跟风。就像病毒一样，没有人能够逃脱。

越来越多的年轻人购买时尚的衣服，我认为这并不是个好现象。首先，追求时尚需要花钱，而年轻人根本就没这个财力。因此，这会浪费父母的钱，而这是个很严肃的事情。其次，这一趋势会让年轻人变得物质、肤浅，尽管这并不是必然的。穿着得体是好事，但是如果年轻人只注重外表而忽视内在的提升，他们就会以貌取人，而这是个非常不好的现象。

总之，广告诱使年轻人购买衣服时追求时尚。但无论年轻人自我感觉多么良好，这一趋势也是很不好的，原因在于其既浪费钱又让人变得物质。

高分词汇精选 Word Bank

序号	词汇	意思	同义表达（自测）
1	lure sb. to do sth.	诱导某人做某事	
2	entertainment stars	娱乐明星	
3	endorse	背书，代言	
4	gorgeous	美貌的	
5	convince	说服	
6	TV commercials	电视广告	
7	eye-catching	吸引眼球的	
8	mistakenly believe that	误以为	
9	follow suit	跟风	
10	virus	病毒	
11	a growing number of	越来越多的	
12	financial resources	财力	
13	not necessarily	并非必然地	
14	materialistic	物质的	
15	superficial	肤浅的	
16	look presentable	穿着得体	
17	personal improvement	个人的提升	

Q21 小商店vs大卖场（340 words）

In some countries, small town-centre shops are out of business because people are driving to large out-of-town stores. As a result, people without cars have limited access to shops, so more and more people buy cars. Do you think the disadvantages of this development outweigh the advantages?

With city sprawl, more and more outlets are set up by retail giants such as Wal-Mart, Tesco and Carrefour, which pushes many town-center shops out of business. While governments may welcome this trend as those large out-of-town stores bring huge tax revenues and create huge tons of employment opportunities, I believe there is a dark side with it.

First of all, ordinary people will no longer enjoy the convenience as they used to when those corner shops or community-based groceries are replaced. For those who do not have a car, it can be quite frustrating to travel all the way to the outskirts just to buy a pan. For those who have a car, the shopping experience can also be annoying because it is fairly time-consuming. Moreover, in main shopping days when all residents flood into those large stores, parking and queuing up to pay can be a nightmare.

Secondly, many people will buy cars when they are tired of catching buses out of town just for shopping. This can open a sort of Pandora box, resulting in a series of problems. For one thing, it will definitely increase the traffic volume, making the already horrible traffic in town even worse. For another, the increasing use of private cars will bring environmental damages, not just air pollution because of carbon emission but also huge consumption of ir-renewable energy sources like oil.

Thirdly, while those large out-of-town stores bring economic benefits to governments and people, they also create financial problems. Specifically, while the government can collect more taxes from these stores, it will also have to invest a fortune to take care of the traffic issues and environmental destruction when the volume of cars shoots up. For ordinary people, despite the discounts they get from supermarkets, they will also need to pay more oil money for driving.

In conclusion, I believe there are reasons for town-center shops to exist; if all of them are replaced by large out-of-town stores, it can cause a lot of trouble to people and the city.

【参考译文】

随着城市的扩张，零售巨头（如沃尔玛、特易购和家乐福等）开了越来越多的分店，从而使得很多市中心的小商店倒闭。尽管政府可能会因为城外这些大卖场所带来的巨大税收和就业机会而欢迎它们，但我认为这一现象有其弊端。

首先，当街角商店和社区的杂货店被取代后，普通老百姓就无法再像过去那样享受到购物的便利。对于没车的人，辛辛苦苦赶到市郊只是为了买一个平底锅是件非常沮丧的事；而对于有车一族来讲，其购物体验也会很烦人，因为很耗时。而且，在主要的购物时节，当所有人都涌向这些大卖场时，停车和排队付账将是个噩梦。

其次，当人们厌倦了挤公车出城购物时，很多人会购买私家车。这将打开潘多拉魔盒，带来一系列问题。一方面，这会增加交通量，从而使得城市已经很糟糕的交通变得更糟；另一方面，私家车的增多会破坏环境，这不仅仅是由于碳排放导致的空气污染，也包括耗费大量的不可再生资源，如石油。

此外，城外这些大卖场在给政府和老百姓带来经济回报的同时，也会带来财政问题。具体而言，政府在获取税收的同时也将不得不投入巨资来整治私家车造成的交通问题和环境问题。对于老百姓而言，尽管可以从超市获得打折优惠，但他们也将为此支付大笔的油钱。

总之，我认为市区的小商铺有其存在的理由；若是它们都被郊区的大卖场取代，将给人们和整个城市造成很大问题。

高分词汇精选 Word Bank

序号	词汇	意思	同义表达（自测）
1	city sprawl	城市扩张	
2	outlet	分店	
3	retail giants	零售巨头	
4	tax revenues	税收	
5	employment opportunities	就业机会	
6	corner shops	街角商店	
7	community-based groceries	社区杂货店	
8	outskirts	市郊	
9	time-consuming	耗时的	
10	flood into	涌入	
11	queue up	排队	
12	be tired of	厌倦	
13	Pandora box	潘多拉魔盒	
14	traffic volume	交通量/车流量	
15	carbon emission	碳排放	
16	ir-renewable	不可再生的	

序号	词汇	意思	同义表达（自测）
17	specifically	具体而言	
18	invest a fortune to	投入巨资	
19	environmental destruction	环境破坏	
20	shoot up	迅速上升	
21	oil money	油钱	

Q23 乐观看待21世纪（318 words）

Many people are optimistic about the 21st century and see it as an opportunity to make positive changes to the world. To what extent do you agree or disagree with their optimism? What changes would you like to see in the new century?

It is suggested that the 21st century be a golden opportunity to make the world a better place. While I agree with such a statement, I also believe the world is far from perfect and changes must be made to turn it even better.

On the one hand, people have reasons to hold an optimistic attitude toward the new century. Among the reasons are, first of all, technological breakthroughs in many fields have been and will continue to be benefiting human society remarkably. For example, 3D printing will someday make it possible to print human organs and organ transplantation will no longer be a problem afflicting patients. Meanwhile, there is more international cooperation in the new century, which will help combat tons of global issues and make the world better. Now countries are working closer more than ever to address environmental destruction, economic problems and political issues. This is why climate talks are organized regularly, new economic agreements are reached under WTO framework, and the EU is expanding.

On the other hand, it would be blind for us to say that the world is now a perfect place. There are so many things that remain to be improved in the 21st century. Firstly, terrorism is still threatening the world. Each year, many innocent lives are killed because of this. Superpowers are still dominating the world, imposing their will on other nations. Meanwhile, statistics released by the UN show that nearly one billion people are living in hunger, which is almost one seventh of the world population. In addition, AIDS and cancer are still incurable, thus claiming tens of millions of lives each year.

In conclusion, technological growth and increased international cooperation bring people the confidence in the 21st century. However, to turn the world a better place, further effort must be made to counter terrorism, increase food supply and improve medical services, just to name a few.

【参考译文】

人们认为21世纪是个绝佳的机会让世界变得更美好。尽管我同意这一观点，但我也认为我们的世界远非完美，还有很多方面需要改变。

一方面，人们有众多理由对新世纪抱以乐观的态度。首先，科技在众多领域取得突破性发展，正在并将继续造福人类社会。例如，未来3D打印技术将实现人体器官的打印，从而让病人免受器官移植的烦恼。同时，21世纪会有更多的国际合作，而这将帮助解决诸多国际问题从而让世界变得更加美好。如今，国家之间正史无前例地密切合作应对环境破坏、经济问题和政治问题。这也是为什么气候大会在定期召开，新的经济协议在WTO的框架下达成及欧盟在扩张。

另一方面，我们不能盲目地认为世界已经很完美了，因为有太多事情亟待完善。首先，恐怖主义仍威胁着全世界。每年，很多无辜生命因此丧生。超级强国仍旧主宰着世界，并将自己的意愿强加给其他国家。与此同时，联合国公布的数据显示，有将近10亿人生活在饥饿中，而这约为世界总人口的七分之一。此外，艾滋病和癌症仍是不治之症，每年夺走成百上千万条性命。

总之，科技的进步和日益频繁的国际合作增强了人们对于21世纪的信心。但是，要让世界变得更加美好，我们还需要在反恐、增加食物供应和提高医疗水平方面做出更大努力。路漫漫其修远兮。

高分词汇精选 Word Bank

序号	词汇	意思	同义表达（自测）
1	It is suggested that...	人们认为	
2	a golden opportunity	绝佳的机会	
3	technological breakthroughs	科技的进步	
4	3D printing	3D打印	
5	human organs	人体器官	

序号	词汇	意思	同义表达（自测）
6	organ transplantation	器官移植	
7	afflict	折磨，困扰	
8	combat	解决	
9	address	应对，处理	
10	climate talks	气候会议	
11	framework	框架	
12	blind	盲目的	
13	terrorism	恐怖主义	
14	innocent lives	无辜的生命	
15	superpowers	超级强国	
16	impose one's will on sb.	将意志强加于某人	
17	Statistics show...	统计表明	
18	incurable	无法治愈的	
19	claim	夺走	
20	just to name a few	略举几例；路漫漫其修远兮①	

Q25 交通拥挤（386 words）

In recent years, traffic jam has become a headache problem around the world. In order to solve this problem, some people think governments have to build wider road to satisfy and solve the traffic jam. To what extent do you agree or disagree?

Traffic congestion has been a nightmare in many cities, particularly in metropolises such as Beijing and Los Angles. Some people propose that the key to the problem is to widen roads. While I agree that this practice can exert certain positive effects on traffic, it is definitely not the best way.

One thing that many city planners in the early days failed to foresee is that the car ownership in cities would increase so dramatically, and they did not build wide roads back then. This is why so many municipal governments are now expanding the road

① 路漫漫其修远兮：It is a long road.

system so desperately to satisfy the increasing traffic demand. In China, for example, many cities are demolishing those buildings alongside narrow roads and turn them into six- or even eight-lane roads. For a while, the traffic in those cities improves remarkably.

However, with city sprawl more and more people are flooding in and the use of private cars is seeing an explosive growth. Under these circumstances, simply building wider roads seems not to be a sustainable way to address the issue. Personally I would say that the best way is to improve public transport and discourage car use. The most important reason for people to drive cars is that it brings them convenience. If public transport can serve this purpose then people will have no reason to drive cars. Hong Kong is doing an amazing job in this with public transport accounting for around 90% of the daily traffic. This is also why cities like Beijing and Singapore are expanding their subway systems.

Other ways to combat traffic problems include levying high taxes on car purchases and car use in city center during rush hours. High cost of using and maintaining cars will discourage people from using cars. Controversial though it sounds, it can actually be justified because car users jeopardize the environment and worsen the traffic to waste other people's time. Meanwhile, car pooling can also be encouraged to reduce car use in the city. This is not difficult, but it can effectively reduce the traffic by two thirds or even three fourths. It is a simple math question.

In conclusion, building wider roads can only ease the traffic temporarily; more effort should be made to work on public transport and legislation to minimize the use of private cars.

【参考译文】

交通拥挤在很多城市都是个噩梦，尤其是在北京和洛杉矶这样的国际大都市。一些人主张解决问题的关键是拓宽道路。尽管我认为这么做可以一定程度上改善交通，但这根本上并不是最好的办法。

早期的城市规划者没能预见的是，城市的私家车拥有量会增长如此迅速，因此他们没有修建很宽的道路。这便是很多市政府都在疯狂拓宽道路的原因，目的是为了满足交通需求。例如，在中国，很多城市拆除狭窄街道两旁的建筑，然后将道路改造成六车道甚至是八车道。短期内，这些城市的交通得到了极大改善。

但是，随着城市的扩张，越来越多的人涌入城市，而私家车的数量也呈现出爆炸性的增长。如此一来，仅靠拓宽道路似乎无法长远地应对该问题。在我看来，最好的办法是改善公共交通和限制私家车的使用。人们之所以开车最为重要的原因是它很方便，而如果公共交通也能实现这种便利性，人们就没有理由再开车了。香港在这方面做得非常好，以至其公共交通占到每天总交通量的90%左右。这也是北京和新加坡等城市都在改造其地铁系统的原因。

解决交通问题的其他途径还包括征收高额的车辆购置税和高峰期的车辆使用税。高额的用车成本和养车成本会让人们减少用车的。尽管这听上去有些争议性，但实际上是有道理的，因为私家车主破坏了环境并且造成交通问题浪费了他人的时间。与此同时，还可以提倡拼车来减少私家车的使用。这其实并非难事，但却可以有效地减少三分之二甚至是四分之三的车流量。这是道非常简单的数学题。

总之，修建更宽的道路只能暂时缓解交通问题。更多的精力应该用来完善公共交通和立法来减少私家车的使用。

高分词汇精选 Word Bank

序号	词汇	意思	同义表达（自测）
1	traffic congestion	交通拥挤	
2	nightmare	噩梦	
3	metropolis	大都市	
4	exert effects on...	对……产生影响	
5	city planners	城市规划者	
6	foresee	预见	
7	car ownership	私家车拥有量	
8	municipal government	市政府	
9	desperately	绝望地；疯狂地	
10	demolish	拆除，摧毁	
11	for a while	短期内；一阵子	
12	city sprawl	城市扩张	
13	flood (in/into)	涌入	

序号	词汇	意思	同义表达（自测）
14	an explosive growth	爆炸性的增长	
15	under these circumstances	在这样的背景下	
16	sustainable	可持续的	
17	discourage sb from (doing) sth.	劝阻	
18	car use	用车	
19	subway system	地铁系统	
20	levy taxes on...	对……征税	
21	car purchases	购车	
22	rush hours	高峰期	
23	controversial	富有争议的	
24	justified	合理的	
25	jeopardize	破坏，损害	
26	car pooling	拼车	
27	ease	减轻，缓解	
28	temporarily	暂时地	
29	legislation	立法	

CHAPTER 10
cause+solution essays

纵观雅思历年写作，大作文除了考前面章节所涉及的议论文（argumentative essays），也会考查cause + solution型、cause + effect型、effect + solution型，以及其他混合型的作文。例如：

▶ cause + solution型

①In some countries young people have little leisure time and are under a lot of pressure to work hard in their studies. What do you think are the causes of this? What solutions can you suggest?

②In some countries today young people are less respectful and polite to others. What could be the reasons behind such behaviour? What can be done about it?

▶ cause + effect型

In some parts of the world, old people are not duly respected. Why does this happen? What effect can this have?

▶ effect + solution型

①Consumers are faced with increasing numbers of advertisements from competing companies. To what extent do you think are consumers influenced by advertisements? What measures can be taken to protect them?

②Increasing the price of petrol is the best way to solve growing traffic and pollution problems. To what extent do you agree or disagree? What other measures do you think might be effective?

▶ 其他混合型

①Some people think that economic progress is the only way to measure a country's success, while others think that there are other factors which can be used to measure a country's success. What are these factors? And among them, which one is more important than others?

②In recent years, people watch more movies from overseas. What are the reasons for this? Should the government give financial support to local cinema to produce local films?

尽管雅思大作文的出题形式千变万化，但是我认为只要考生真正掌握了议论文（argumentative essays）及cause + solution类型作文的写法，其余的就不足为虑了。毕竟，其他各种作文都是这两类的灵活组合。由此，本章节只讲cause + solution大作文的写法。一旦考生掌握了这类作文的写作套路与框架，剩下的则是对这类考题题库的熟悉。故，本章节的第二个版块便是给广大考生总结cause + solution类型大作文的历年真题。

一、cause + solution类型大作文的写法

例题：In some countries the average weight of people is increasing and their levels of health and fitness are decreasing. What do you think are the causes of these problems and what measures could be taken to solve them?（《剑桥雅思考试全真试题集8》Test 4）

▶ 开头段：改写题目+简要指出原因

同议论文一样，这种题目的开头段也需要考生对题目进行改选。很多考生都喜欢先写个大的背景，然后再逐步缩小导向题目。这本身是个很多好的写作方法，不过我不主张考生怎么做，原因是很多考生在写背景时往往写得很啰唆，其内容与考题关联不够紧密而且缺少内容逻辑。我建议考生开门见山式的对题目进行改写即可。

同时，很多考生会在改写完题目后加上一句：In this essay I will analyze the possible reasons for such a phenomenon and provides some suggestions to solve the problem. 我也很反对考生写这种句子，除非考生只要5.0-5.5分的写作。表面上，这句话指出了本文的写作意图，但实际上这完全是句极其空洞的废话。与其这样，倒不如直截了当地将原因写出，好让考官明了你要从哪几个方面来展开。

例如《剑桥雅思考试全真试题集4》Test 4就有一篇作文，题目是：In many countries

schools have severe problems with student behavior. What do you think are the causes of this? What solutions can you suggest? 考官的开头段为：Poor student behavior seems to be an increasingly widespread problem. I think that modern lifestyles are probably responsible for this. 非常简洁明了。

再如，《剑桥雅思考试全真试题集8》Test 4中Task 2某考生的开头段是：In some countries the average weight of people is increasing and their levels of health and fitness are decreasing. I think that the cause of these problems is the unhealthy lifestyle and the lack of exercise. 尽管这个开头段前面是在抄题目，但是它明确指出是不健康的生活方式和缺少锻炼这两个因素导致了问题的出现，而且该考生在正文中也是从这两个角度来分析的。那么最后这篇作文拿了多少分呢？6.5分。对于国内雅思考生来说，6.5分其实是个比较理想的雅思写作分数。

当然，如果该考生在写开头段时能够自行改写，而不是照抄题目，效果一定会更好。例如：Many countries are reporting an increasingly high obesity rate and the rise of related health hazards. In this essay I would examine how unhealthy diet and sedentary lifestyles have resulted in such a phenomenon.（34 words）

▷ 正文段：分析原因+给出对策

由于题目要求考生去分析某现象/某社会问题的成因及解决方案，所以考生只要照办即可。需要指出的是，考生决不能像列购物清单似地罗列原因，而应该加以拓展分析；写解决方案时，也决不能像作报告似地空喊口号，而是要给出具体的措施。有两种方式来写正文：①原因全部写完后再另起一段写对策；②每写完一个原因就将相应的对策写好。两种方式无所谓孰优孰劣，各有千秋罢了。以《剑桥雅思考试全真试题集8》Test 4的题目为例，两种方式分别大抵为：

方式一：原因全部写完后再另起一段写对策

原因段：First of all, people nowadays eat too much fast food and seldom do physical exercise, hence their expanding waistline and poor health. As is known, there are too many calories and fat in fast food and thus heavy consumption can lead to health issues like obesity. Also, many people consume too much sugar, be it sugary drinks or treats. This not only leads to weight gain but also diabetes. To make matters worse, many people lead a less active life. Everyday they just drive to work and sit in the office for hours. When they come back home, they stick to their couch and watch sitcoms, and they just cannot stop eating. There is actually a phrase to describe these people, i.e. "couch potato".（124 words）

对策段：Unless measures are taken (to combat the problem), many people will be fatter and resources be wasted. Firstly, people must cut out fast food and turn to a balanced diet. Eating more fruits and vegetables will suffice to provide the human body with the vitamins it needs. In the meantime, people should work out more often. This can be easily achieved if people use the public transport when they go to work because they will have to walk to the stations. Also, when people use the stairs to go upstairs and downstairs it will burn some extra fat and keep them fit. Aerobic exercise such as jogging or brisk walking can also help people stay healthy.（116 words）

方式二：每写完一个原因就将相应的对策写好

正文1）Firstly, unhealthy diet, particularly heavy consumption of fast food is the principal cause for the problems. Whatever the reason is, people nowadays are relying on fast food and other convenience food for its convenience. Unfortunately, eating too much these types of food also means swallowing huge amounts of calories and fat. This is why people are gaining weight. The solution to this, however, is quite simple. As long as people can cut out fast food and eat more fruits and vegetables, they will find themselves losing weight and becoming healthy.（90 words）

正文2）In the meantime, less active lifestyles also jeopardize people's health. As is demonstrated above, people swallow so many calories and fat, and yet they seldom do exercise. Unless people can burn these layers of extra fat, they will become overweight and some other health risks arise. However, it should be stressed that if people can try to lead a more active life, things would be quite different. If, for example, people use stairs to go to the office and walk for a while on their way back home they will be healthier. Aerobic exercise such as jogging or brisk walking can also help people stay healthy.（105 words）

▶ 结论段：简要总结前文提及的原因及对策

无论如何，切忌在结论段空喊口号："总之我们必须立刻采取措施，否则这个问题会持续恶化。因此，让我们一起努力，携手共同解决这个棘手的问题！"试问，有多少考生是用类似的方式来做总结的？还是那句话，除非写作目标分数不高，否则，这么写就只有死路一条了：Bam! 5.0. Stay in China. See you next time.

雅思作文的结论段简要对前文做个小结即可，不用太花哨。实际上，官方在评分标准里讲得很清楚，即使是6分的写作，其结论段都可以是对前文的重复：presents a relevant position although the conclusions may become unclear or repetitive[①]。

就前面的例题而言，我们可以这么写：In conclusion, modern lifestyles should be responsible for the health problems people have. Yet as long as they change their dietary habits and live a more active life, these problems will be overcome and people will find themselves fit and healthy.（41 words）

二、cause + solution类型大作文历年真题总结

掌握了cause + solution类型大作文的写作方法和结构后，考生只需对历年真题有所了解就可以获得写作高分了。通过对比近10年的雅思写作题库，可将这类题目总结为三个类型：青少年篇、环境篇、社会生活篇。根据我多年的授课经验及考试跟踪可知，考试范围基本如此。

（一）青少年篇

1. In some countries, the rate of teenagers' criminal acts is increasing. What are the reasons? Give your measures to reduce it.
2. The incidence of violence/crimes for young people is increasing. Give possible reasons and recommendations of punishment and measures to the situation.
3. Recent research shows that the majority of the criminals who are sent into the prison continue to commit crimes after they are set free. What do you think about the case? What should be done to solve this problem?
4. Many schools have problems with student behavior. What are the possible causes? What measures can be taken to improve the situation?
5. Young people are now less respectful and polite than before. What are its causes and what solutions can be taken to solve this problem?
6. Teenagers have problems at both home and school. What difficulties are they facing now? What should parents and schools do to help them?
7. In some countries young people have little leisure time and are under a lot of

① 详见雅思考试中文官网

pressure to work hard at their studies. What do you think are the causes of this? What solutions can you suggest?

8. Many young people nowadays leave school with negative attitudes towards learning. Why does this happen? What do you think would encourage young people to have a positive attitude?

9. Many children spend much time on watching TV and seldom do active and creative activities. Why do you think this is a case? What measures will be helpful to change this situation?

10. In many countries, after young people graduate, they still have little chance to find a job. What do you think are the reasons for this from individual and social angles? What solutions would you suggest?

11. Nowadays children are becoming lazier and lazier while in the meantime they are getting fatter and unsociable. Give reasons and solutions.

12. Today, fewer and fewer young people pursue a career in teaching. Why is the case? What can be done to change the situation?

说明

教育类与青少年类话题是每年雅思写作考查的重点。此前，教育类的考题在本书的Chapter 3中得到了较为详细的论述。本章节将着重分析青少年类的考题。通过浏览题目，考生们会发现，青少年类的考题通常都是围绕他们的学习、行为、生活及健康等方面展开的。

Q1 青少年犯罪（309 words）

In some countries, the rate of teenagers' criminal acts is increasing. What are the reasons? Give your measures to reduce it.

Everyday there are reports about juvenile delinquency in the mass media. It seems that this issue has become more serious over the past few years. I believe that the increase of violence in the media and the parents' and schools' negligence of duty should be blamed for it.

To attract audience, TV and movie producers put an increasing amount of violence into TV programs and movies. Unfortunately, while this spices up the shows it also contributes to the increase of juvenile delinquency. Many teenagers blindly imitate what they see on TV or in movies because they are not sufficiently mature to make the right judgment. They mistakenly believe that it is cool if they behave as those movie characters do, and fail to realize sometimes what they do is against the law.

The other reason is that parents and teachers attach too much importance to teenagers' academic studies and ignore the importance of education about legal knowledge and morality. Parents and teachers fail to discipline and supervise these young people. And when their children do something wrong, they over-protect them. In my country, this happens quite often.

One solution to this issue is that the government imposes strict censorship on the violence in TV programs and movies. A good censorship system will not destroy those works but can limit young people's exposure to violence. Once the access is limited, it can bring down the crime level among young people. In the meantime, if schools include certain law subjects in the curriculum and parents spend some time in guiding their children to distinguish right from wrong, the situation will also change for the better.

In conclusion, negative media influence and poor parenting and schooling should be blamed for the rise in youth crime. Therefore, the cure lies in the government intervention and the improvement of parental guidance and school education.

【参考译文】

媒体中每天都有关于青少年犯罪的报道。这个问题在过去的几年似乎变得越来越严重了。我认为这应该归咎于媒体中暴力的增加以及家长和学校的失职。

为了吸引观众，电视和电影制片人在影视作品中增加了越来越多的暴力。遗憾的是，尽管这会让节目本身变得更精彩，但它也导致了青少年犯罪的增长。由于青少年尚未成熟到可以明辨是非，所以他们会盲目地模仿他们在电视、电影中看到的场景。他们会误以为模仿剧中人物的行为是件很酷的事情，而忽略了有时他们的行为会触犯法律。

另外一个原因则是父母和老师过于重视青少年的学习成绩，而忽略了法律知识以及道德教育的重要性。家长和老师没能好好地管教年轻人，而当孩子们做错事时，他们会过度地保护他们。这在我的国家非常普遍。

对策之一是政府强制审查电视、电影中的暴力。好的审查制度不会破坏作品本身，但却可以限制年轻人过多地接触暴力。一旦他们接触暴力的途径得到限制，青少年犯罪率就会降低。与此同时，如果学校教授一些法律课程，并且父母多花些时间引导孩子分辨是非，情况也将得到好转。

总之，媒体的负面影响、糟糕的家庭教育及学校教育是导致青少年犯罪率上升的罪魁祸首。因此，应对措施有赖于政府的干预以及父母引导和学校教育的改善。

高分词汇精选 Word Bank

序号	词汇	意思	同义表达（自测）
1	juvenile delinquency	青少年犯罪	
2	negligence of duty	失职	
3	spice up	调味；使……变得精彩	
4	imitate	模仿	
5	not sufficiently mature	尚未成熟	
6	mistakenly believe	误以为	
7	movie characters	电影人物/角色	
8	attach importance to	重视	
9	legal knowledge	法律知识	
10	discipline	纪律；管教	
11	over-protect	过度保护	
12	censorship	审查	
13	access	权限	
14	school curriculum	课程	
15	distinguish right from wrong	分辨是非	
16	change for the better	改善	
17	parenting	家教，育儿	
18	youth crime	青少年犯罪	
19	cure	对策	
20	intervention	干预	

Q4 学生行为差（257 words）

Many schools have problems with student behavior. What are the possible causes? What measures can be taken to improve the situation?

Poor student behavior seems to be an increasingly widespread problem, and I think that modern lifestyles are probably responsible for this.

In many countries, the birth rate is decreasing so that families are smaller with fewer children. These children are often spoilt, not in terms of love and attention because working parents do not have time for this, but in more material ways. They are allowed to have whatever they want, regardless of prices, and to behave as they please. This means that the children grow up without consideration for others and without any understanding of where their financial support comes from.

When they get to the school age they have not learnt any self control or discipline. They have little respect for their teachers and refuse to obey school rules in the way that their parents did.

Teachers continually complain about this problem, so measures should be taken to combat the situation. I think the solution to the problem lies with the families, who need to be aware of the future consequences of spoiling their children. If parents could raise them to be considerate of others and to be social, responsible individuals, the whole community would benefit.

Perhaps parenting courses are needed to help them to do this, and high quality nursery schools could be established, which would support families more in terms of raising the next generation. The government should fund this kind of parental support, because this is no longer a problem for individual families, but for the society as a whole.

【参考译文】

糟糕的学生行为似乎成为了一个越来越普遍的问题。我认为现代的生活方式或许应该为此负责。

在很多国家，出生率的下降使得家庭规模变小，每个家庭的孩子变少，而这些孩子经常被宠坏。倒不是说他们得到了爱和关注，因为上班族父母无暇顾及这些，而是他们往往在物质上被宠坏。这些孩子可以得到他们想要的任何东西，不管价格如何；他们可以随心所欲，为所欲为。这意味着他们在成长过程中完全不考虑他人，也完全不明白支持他们挥霍的钱从何而来。

当这些孩子到了入学年龄时，他们没有任何自控及自觉能力。他们不太尊敬老师，也不像他们的父母那样遵守学校的规章制度。

老师们对此经常抱怨，因此必须采取措施来解决这一局面。我认为应对之策在于家庭，他们需要明白溺爱孩子的后果。如果父母能够将小孩抚养成体贴他人、善于社交并且勇于承担责任的人，整个社会都将因此受益。

或许应该开设育儿课程来帮助实现这些目标。同时，也应该开设高品质的幼儿园来帮助家庭更好地抚养下一代。政府应该资助这种对父母的支持，因为这不再是单个家庭的问题，而是整个社会的问题。

高分词汇精选 Word Bank

序号	词汇	意思	同义表达（自测）
1	widespread	普遍的	
2	birth rate	出生率	
3	spoil	溺爱，宠坏	
4	regardless of	不管，不顾	
5	behave as they please	随心所欲	
6	financial support	财政支持	
7	self control or discipline	自控、自律	
8	combat the situation	解决这一局面	
9	consequence	后果	
10	be considerate of	体谅	
11	parenting course	育儿课程	
12	high quality	高品质	
13	nursery school	托儿所，幼儿园	
14	raise the next generation	抚养下一代	

说明

Q4是《剑桥雅思考试全真试题集4》Test 4考官的范文[①]。

Q5基本参考Q4。不同之处在于Q5没有将青少年的问题限定在学校范围内。

① 资料来源：《剑桥雅思考试全真试题集4》（*Cambridge IELTS 4*）Test 4。

Q8 学生厌学退学（286 words）

Many young people nowadays leave school with negative attitudes towards learning. Why does this happen? What do you think would encourage young people to have a positive attitude?

In some countries many students quit school because they run out of patience with the education system. I think two factors result in such a phenomenon. The first is the poor school curriculum and the second is the intense pressure from parents and teachers.

Many schools provide a wide range of subjects and encourage students to sign up for them. Unfortunately, a high proportion of the curriculum is about academics, which students believe is boring and useless for their future careers. When students do not see the value of investing time and energy in these subjects, it is fairly natural that they withdraw from school.

To make matters worse, parents and teachers always expect young people to come up with an impressive academic record so that someday these young people can get a ticket to prestigious universities. Some parents even arrange extra tuition for their children every day（as in China）. Such high expectations exert considerable pressure on young people, and they just cannot bear it.

Solutions to the issue lie in the school. Specifically, if the school curriculum could stop being so theoretical in nature and focus more on practical subjects instead, students would come around. After all, young people always want to see the practical side of their investment in education. In the meantime, schools can also encourage students to organize more student societies so that their campus life can be spiced up with extracurricular activities. Once young people find out the fun part of school life, they would like to stay.

In conclusion, the fundamental cause for students' negative attitudes toward learning are associated with the education system. If the school curriculum can be more practical in nature, things will change for the better.

【参考译文】

在一些国家，很多学生由于厌学而退学。我认为有两个因素导致了这个现象：一是糟糕的学校课程，二是家长和老师施加的巨大压力。

很多学校开设一系列课程鼓励学生选择学习。遗憾的是，大部分课程都是些学生们认为很无聊并且对未来职业毫无用处的学术课程。当学生看不到为这些学科投入时间和精力可以带来价值回报时，他们选择退学就显得很正常了。

更糟糕的是，家长和老师总是期望年轻人学习成绩优异，这样他们有朝一日才能进入名牌大学。一些家长甚至每天都给孩子安排补课（例如在中国）。如此高的期望值给孩子们造成了难以承受的巨大压力。

这个问题的应对措施取决于学校。具体而言，如果学校课程能够避免过于理论化，而是更侧重实用性的学科，学生会回心转意的。毕竟，年轻人总是希望看到教育投资中实用的一面。与此同时，学校也可以鼓励学生组织更多的学生社团，用课外活动来丰富校园生活。一旦年轻人发现校园生活的乐趣，他们就会愿意留下来。

总之，学生厌学的根本原因与教育制度有关。如果学校课程能够更加实用，情况会好转的。

高分词汇精选 Word Bank

序号	词汇	意思	同义表达（自测）
1	run out of patience	失去耐心	
2	school curriculum	课程	
3	intense pressure	巨大的压力	
4	a wide range of	一系列	
5	unfortunately	令人遗憾的是	
6	a high proportion of	很多	
7	academics	学术	
8	It is fairly natural that...	……是很正常的。	
9	withdraw	回撤	
10	to make matters worse	更糟的是	
11	an impressive academic record	优异的成绩	
12	extra tuition	补课	

序号	词汇	意思	同义表达（自测）
13	exert pressure on...	对……施加压力	
14	specifically	具体而言	
15	come around	回心转意	
16	society	社团	
17	spice up	调味；让……变得精彩	
18	extracurricular activities	课外活动	
19	fundamental	根本的	
20	be associated with	与……有关	
21	change for the better	改善	

说明

Q7、Q8及Q9的观点可以互用。

Q10 年轻人就业难（288 words）

In many countries, after young people graduate, they still have little chance to find a job. What do you think are the reasons for this from individual and social angles? What solutions would you suggest?

Youth unemployment is a big issue in many countries and is on the rise in the past few years. Under such circumstances, it is extremely important to find out what reasons are behind this situation so that remedies can be proposed.

At the individual level, I think many young people simply do not possess the skills and qualities that their prospective employers expect. Many young people complain that the school education is too academic in nature and yet they do not take the initiative to acquire the skills needed in the workplace. When they enter the job market, they are not job-ready, but they all expect good working environment and a decent salary.

From the social angle, the economic crisis should be blamed. The financial crisis in 2008 has hit many countries hard, leading to substantial numbers of layoffs. When those skillful professionals re-enter the job market, the harsh competition nearly leaves nothing to those career rookies. *The Guardian* reports that in 2013 "Spain youth unemployment reaches record 56.1%" ①.

I think it is difficult to bring down youth joblessness when the economy is going down. However, if young people themselves can plan their careers ahead and stop expecting too much from their first job, they will still have opportunities. For example, if they do not mind running errands and starting small, they will at least have a chance for themselves. And when the right time come, they can really shine themselves.

In conclusion, poor economy and young people's lack of skills and qualities are the leading causes for rising youth joblessness. I do not think there are good solutions to it, although if young people themselves can learn to be a bit more career-savvy they will earn themselves a chance.

【参考译文】

在很多国家，年轻人失业都是个很大的问题，并且在过去的几年里呈现出上升趋势。在这种背景下，我们必须找出其背后的原因并提出应对措施。

从个人层面看，我认为很多年轻人只是没有掌握潜在雇主所期望的技能和品质。很多年轻人抱怨学校课程太理论化，但自己却又不主动去学习工作中所需要的技能。等他们进入职场后，他们并没有准备好工作，但他们却期望工作环境好而又高薪的工作。

从社会的角度分析，经济危机难逃其责。2008年的金融危机严重冲击了很多国家，导致大量的裁员。当这些技能娴熟的职业人士重新进入职场时，残酷的竞争使得职业新手几乎毫无机会可言。据《卫报》（英国）报道，2013年"西班牙的年轻人失业率达到了56.1%的创纪录新高。"

我认为当经济不景气时要降低年轻人的失业率是很困难的。不过，如果年轻人自己能提前做好职业规划并且正视第一份工作，他们仍然有机会找到工作。例如，如果年轻人不介意从小事做起干些跑腿的活儿，他们将至少为自己赢得一次机会。等到时机来临时，他们自然会发光。

总之，年轻人失业率上升的主要原因是糟糕的经济以及年轻人缺乏技能和品质。我认为很难有什么好的应对措施。不过，如果年轻人能够变得职业嗅觉敏锐一些的话，他们仍然可以为自己赢得机会。

① 资源来源：http://www.theguardian.com/business/2013/aug/30/spain-youth-unemployment-record-high

高分词汇精选 Word Bank

序号	词汇	意思	同义表达（自测）
1	youth unemployment	年轻人失业	
2	on the rise	上升	
3	Statistics show...	统计表明	
4	under such circumstances	在这种背景下	
5	remedy	对策	
6	possess	拥有	
7	prospective	潜在的	
8	take the initiative to	主动	
9	job market	职场	
10	job-ready	有工作技能的	
11	decent	体面的	
12	substantial numbers of	大量的	
13	layoffs	裁员	
14	professional	专业人士	
15	harsh competition	残酷的竞争	
16	career rooky	职场菜鸟	
17	youth joblessness	年轻人失业	
18	run errands	跑腿，打杂	
19	be career-savvy	有敏锐的职业嗅觉	

温馨提示

雅思写作题库中有一道极为类似但又略有不同的题目，请考生认真看题：In many countries more and more young people are leaving school but unable to find jobs. What problems do you think youth unemployment causes for individuals and the society? What measures should be taken to reduce the level of unemployment among youngsters?

（二）环境篇

13. Many people say that we have developed a “throw-away” culture, because we are filling up our environment with so many plastic bags and rubbish that

we cannot fully dispose of. To what extent do you agree or disagree with this opinion and what measures can be taken to solve this problem?

14. We have entered a throw-away society and fill the environment with rubbish. What are the causes and what are your solutions?

15. Many people think it is very important to protect the environment, but they make no effort to do it themselves. Why does it happen? How to solve this problem?

16. In many tourist attractions such as lakes, mountains and beaches, the environment is polluted because of the rubbish and litters produced by tourists. Why is this? How can we solve the problem?

17. The level of noise around us is constantly increasing, and is affecting the quality of our lives. What causes the noise? What should be done about it?

18. The increasing level of noise pollution has affected people's life significantly. What factors caused this problem? How to solve this problem?

19. Now, more and more people want to buy cars. However, cars cause many problems. What are these problems? How can we encourage people to take public transportation?

20. Traffic is developing rapidly all round the world at present. What are the traffic problems in your country? What causes these problems? Give some recommendations of solution.

21. Some people think building more roads can reduce the traffic problems. What do you think of this solution?

22. The unlimited use of cars may cause many problems. What are those problems? In order to solve the problems, should we discourage people to use cars?

23. The natural resources such as oil, forests and fresh water are being consumed at an alarming rate. What problems does it cause? How can we solve these problems?

24. In many countries around the world, there is a serious shortage of water. What are the causes of and the possible solutions to the scarcity of water resources?

说明

环境篇中的很多题目实际上都要求给出保护环境的具体措施。我在教学过程中一直提醒学生，环境类的考题一般有两个大的方向：一是关于能源消耗及其污染的问题，一是日常生活中人们如何保护环境。把这两个大的方向把握好了，环境类考题备考就会事半功倍。由于本书前面有专门的篇章总结讲解环境类话题，故本章节不再重复。

（三）社会生活篇

25. Many people have unhealthy diet and do not do enough exercises. What are the reasons for this? How can we encourage people to have a healthier lifestyle?

26. Doctors say that in many countries, people do not have enough physical exercise. What are the causes for this problem? What can be done to solve it?

27. Modern lifestyles make many people hard to lead active and healthy lives. Why? How to suggest the governments and other large companies helping them do more exercise?

28. International travel sometimes makes people more prejudiced rather than board-minded. Give out reasons why it cannot bring benefits to those visitors. Do you have ways to improve people's understanding of the countries they visit?

29. People's attitude towards international travel turns to be more prejudiced instead of open-minded. Why is the case? What can be done to improve the situation?

30. Nowadays, many people have to work longer time, and they feel more stressed than before. What are the reasons? What can the employers do to make the employees' life easier?

31. There is too much stress in the workplace. What can employees and employers do about it?

32. Many people change their jobs often. Why is the case? What can the employers do to make the employees stay?

33. Many people want to have both a successful career and a happy family life. What problems are involved in combining a career and the family life? How to

overcome such problems?

34. Many people believe that today there is a general increase in anti-social behaviors and lack of respect for others. What might have caused this situation? How to improve it?

35. Today there is a great increase in anti-social behaviors and lack of respect for others. What are the causes of this? Who should take responsibility for dealing with it?

36. Some people say that it is impossible to live comfortably in big cities. What problems are faced by the people living in big cities? What solutions can be taken to solve those problems?

37. Today, the quality of life in some big cities is getting worse. What are the causes for this problem? What measures should be taken to deal with the problem?

38. What problems for the young people living in major cities are caused by the development of the cities? How to solve those problems?

39. The movement of people from agricultural areas to cities to work can cause serious problems in both places. What are the serious problems and what measures can be taken to solve those problems?

40. The gap between the rich and the poor is widening. Why is the case? What can be done to improve the situation?

41. It is generally acknowledged that families are now not so close as they used to be. What are the possible reasons and what can be done to reverse the trend?

说 明

Q25 ~ Q27考查的是人们的健康问题。这与本章前面“cause + solution类型大作文的写法”中所举的例子，即《剑桥雅思考试全真试题集8》Test 4真题相一致，请考生参考前文。

Q28 ~ Q29是讲国家旅游造成的问题及相应对策；Q30 ~ Q33主要是分析职场压力及其造成的问题；Q34 ~ Q35讨论的是反社会行为；Q36 ~ Q39算是高频考题，要求阐述城市所面临的问题并提出应对措施；Q40与Q41会显得相对“特别”一些，因为它们很少有“同伙”。

Q30 工作压力（364 words）

Nowadays, many people have to work longer time, and they feel more stressed than before. What are the reasons? What can the employers do to make the employees' life easier?

In many countries, the work pressure has been increased over the past few years and people are pushed to stay in the office for longer time. I think there are two reasons to explain this situation, i.e. increasingly fierce competition and higher cost of living.

The competition in the job market is harsher more than ever. With the economy going down, many businesses are shut down or cut jobs to survive. This means people will have to work harder to keep their jobs. In the meantime, more and more well-educated young people join the job market, thus further adding to the difficulty of finding employment. To make things worse, globalization means companies have to compete against international players, which also increases employees' work pressure. Meanwhile, in many industrialized countries, many jobs are outsourced to emerging markets because of the cheaper labour there. Under these circumstances, people will have to work longer time and harder to keep their business alive.

Furthermore, the cost of living increases dramatically, which means people will need to work harder to make the ends meet. This also explains why people now have more work pressure than in the past. For example, many white-collar workers in Shanghai work overtime against their will almost every day. They cannot just quit because they have to pay mortgage, rising rent and water bills etc. Like it or not, these people have to learn to handle tight schedules and work pressure on their own.

What employers can do to help employees is, first and foremost, to promise them job security. When people do not need to worry about where their next meal comes from, they can always rest assured. In the meantime, employers can give employees some paid vacation so that they can take a break and get refreshed. Last but not least, relaxation activities should be organized regularly. In this way, employees will have a lot of fun after a period of long and hard work.

In conclusion, tougher competition and higher living costs are the two principal causes for intense work pressure. Among all the things that employers can do to help their subordinates, promising them job security should be on the top of the list.

【参考译文】

过去几年间，很多国家员工的工作压力越来越大，人们不得不在办公室更长时间地工作。我认为有两个原因可以解释这个现象，即日益激烈的竞争和高涨的生活成本。

如今，职场的竞争比以往任何时候都要残酷。随着经济的衰退，很多企业倒闭或者裁员以维持生存。这就意味着人们必须更加努力地工作来保住饭碗。与此同时，越来越多受过良好教育的年轻人也进入职场，从而进一步增加了就业的难度。更糟糕的是，全球化使得企业必须同一些跨国公司进行竞争，这也增加了员工的工作压力。同时，在一些工业化国家，很多工作被外包到劳动力更为廉价的新兴市场。在这些情况下，人们必须更长时间更努力地工作来维持生计。

而且，生活成本急剧上涨，这意味着人们需要更努力地工作去挣钱。这也解释了为什么现代人的工作压力比以前大。例如，上海的很多白领几乎每天都被迫加班。他们无法辞职一走了之，因为他们要还房贷，还要支付日益上涨的房租和水电费等等。无论是否愿意，这些人不得不学会独自应对繁忙的工作及工作压力。

雇主能帮到员工的是，首先，给员工承诺工作的稳定性。当人们不用担心吃了上顿没下顿时，他们就可以安心（工作）了。与此同时，雇主可以给员工一些带薪假期。这样，员工可以稍加休息并补充精力。最后，可以定期组织一些放松的活动，这可以让员工在长时间辛苦工作后找点乐趣。

总之，工作压力变大的两个主要原因是日益激烈的竞争和高涨的生活成本。在雇主力所能及的所有事情中，给下属保证工作的稳定性最为重要。

高分词汇精选 Word Bank

序号	词汇	意思	同义表达（自测）
1	fierce competition	激烈的竞争	
2	cost of living	生活成本	
3	job market	职场	
4	cut jobs	裁员	
5	international players	国际玩家；跨国公司	

序号	词汇	意思	同义表达（自测）
6	to make things worse	更糟糕的是	
7	industrialized countries	工业化国家	
8	outsource	外包	
9	emerging markets	新兴市场	
10	under these circumstances	在这些情况下	
11	make the ends meet	维持收支平衡	
12	white-collar workers	白领	
13	work overtime	加班	
14	against one's will	违背意愿	
15	tight schedules	忙碌的安排/工作	
16	job security	工作稳定性	
17	rest assured	安心	
18	paid vacation	带薪假期	
19	get refreshed	补充精力	
20	relaxation activities	放松的活动	
21	principal	主要的	
22	subordinate	下属	

Q34 反社会行为（278 words）

Many people believe that today there is a general increase in anti-social behaviors and lack of respect for others. What might have caused this situation? How to improve it?

Over the past few years, anti-social behaviors have been on the rise in many places. In the meantime, people are also becoming less respectful than before. A variety of reasons can be responsible for this.

Firstly, the increase of violence in TV programs and movies should be blamed. To make their shows exciting, more and more TV producers and film makers use violence in their works. The high popularity of such TV programs and movies unconsciously change people's mentality, making them believe it is cool and no big deal to imitate those TV and movie characters. This, unfortunately, leads to the rise of anti-social behaviors.

The second reason is that nowadays many people use the increasingly influential social media to spread rumors, and a lot of Internet users are fooled to do stupid things. In the cyber world, people feel less obliged to follow laws and rules; they judge everything solely on the basis of hearsay and do not take responsibility for their words. Many misinformed "angry young men" are thus misguided and resort to extreme actions to "serve justice".

With regard to the solutions, I think related laws should be reinforced. I always believe that once people have to pay heavy price for what they say and do, they will think twice before doing anything against the social order. For example, anyone who conducts anti-social behaviors, be it in the virtual cyber world or in the real life, should face severe penalty like prison sentence, then similar acts will certainly be deterred.

In conclusion, the increase of anti-social behaviors is mainly caused by the abuse of media. To improve the situation, tougher punishment must be imposed on all offenders.

【参考译文】

过去数年间，很多地方的反社会行为越来越多。同时，人们也不如以前那么尊敬他人。诸多因素导致了这个问题。

首先，电视、电影中暴力的增加应该对此负责。为了让节目更刺激，越来越多的影视制片人在作品中使用暴力。这类影视作品的普及潜移默化地改变了人们的思想，使得人们认为模仿影视人物的行为是很酷的事情，没什么大不了的。遗憾的是，这增加了反社会行为。

第二个原因是如今很多人利用日益有影响力的社交媒体散布谣言，误导很多不明真相的网民做蠢事。在网络世界，人们觉得没有义务遵守法律法规；他们仅仅凭道听途说就做出判断，并且不为自己的言语负责。很多被误导的“愤青”因此诉诸极端行为来“维持正义”。

至于解决方案，我认为应当强化相关的法律。我始终相信，一旦人们必须为自己的言行付出沉重的代价，他们就会在做出有碍社会秩序的行为前三思而后行。例如，无论是在虚拟的网络世界还是在现实生活中，如果任何做出反社会行为的人都应该处以类似于徒刑之类的严厉惩罚，那类似的行为就会被震慑住。

总之，反社会行为增长的主要原因是媒体被滥用了。若要改善这一情况，则必须对所有触犯者处以更加严厉的惩罚。

高分词汇精选 Word Bank

序号	词汇	意思	同义表达（自测）
1	on the rise	上升	
2	respectful	尊敬他人的	
3	a variety of	诸多的	
4	unconsciously	潜移默化地	
5	mentality	想法	
6	imitate	模仿	
7	movie characters	电影角色	
8	influential	有影响力的	
9	social media	社交媒体	
10	rumor	谣言	
11	Internet users	网民	
12	be fooled	被愚弄	
13	cyber world	网络世界	
14	be obliged to	有义务	
15	on the basis of hearsay	依据道听途说	
16	resort to	诉诸，使用	
17	misinform	误导	
18	serve justice	伸张/维护正义	
19	with regard to	至于	
20	reinforce	加强	
21	pay heavy price for	为……付出沉重代价	

序号	词汇	意思	同义表达（自测）
22	think twice	三思	
23	social order	社会秩序	
24	virtual	虚拟的	
25	severe penalties	严厉的惩罚	
26	prison sentence	徒刑	
27	deter	威慑	
28	abuse	滥用	
29	impose sth. on sb.	将……强加于某人	
30	offender	冒犯者	

备注：考生们可在本书的犯罪类章节中找到与反社会行为相关的内容。

Q37 城市生活（339 words）

Today, the quality of life in some big cities is getting worse. What are the causes for this problem? What measures do you think should be taken to deal with the problem?

In most places across the globe, people move to the city for a better life. However, with the development of the city people start to realize that the city life is not as good as expected. What's worse, the quality of life is deteriorating in many big cities. Multiple factors can be blamed for this.

Firstly, there is overpopulation in many big cities, and this makes it difficult to live comfortably there. In metropolises like Beijing and Shanghai, tens of millions of people live there. This leads to the shortage of housing and push up the property prices and cost of living. The competition in the job market also gets increasingly stiff. Infrastructures like road systems are also under huge pressure, making commuting to work a nightmare for people. Under these circumstances, it would be a miracle to live a comfortable life there.

The increase of cars also sheds a shadow on the life in big cities. Unlimited use of cars creates huge environmental problems. Again, Beijing serves as a strong example. In 2013, the capital of People's Republic of China suffered the most serious "smog" issue in its history, which sharply increased hospital admissions. The municipal government blamed it on the overuse of private cars and had to formulate polices to forbid people buying and using cars in certain conditions.

I do not think there are effective solutions to this issue. However, I think if the government can have better urban planning, the problems can be alleviated and people will have a better life. For example, the government can relocate some industries and businesses in regional areas and encourage people to work and live in those specific areas. This will help address the overpopulation issues and environmental issues in big cities so that life there can get improved. For people who choose to stay and those who choose to relocate, their life would also be better.

In conclusion, overpopulation with city sprawl is the main reason that the life in big cities becomes worse. The solution, as is elaborated above, lies in better town planning.

【参考译文】

在全世界的多数地方，人们搬到城市是为了更好的生活。但是，随着城市的发展，人们开始意识到城市生活并不像所预期的那样美好。更糟糕的是，很多大城市的生活质量一直在恶化。很多因素导致了这个问题。

首先，很多大城市人口过剩，这使得城市生活很难舒适。在北京、上海这样的大都市，成百上千万人居住在一起。这导致了住房短缺，并推高了房价和生活成本。职场的竞争也变得更加激烈。道路系统等基础设施正在承受巨大压力，上下班通勤成为人们的噩梦。在这种情况下，若能生活舒适简直是个奇迹。

大城市私家车的增多也给城市生活蒙上了一层阴影。无节制地使用私家车给环境造成了巨大问题。北京仍然可以是个很好的例子。2013年，这座中国的首都城市遭遇了史上最严重的雾霾天气，这使得医院接待的病例迅速增多。北京市政府将此归咎于私家车的过度使用，并且拟定了措施来限制私家车的购买和使用。

我认为很难有好的措施可以解决这些问题。但是，如果政府能够更好地进行城市规划，就可以缓解这些问题，人们的生活也将变得更好。例如，政府可以将一些工业和企业迁到周边地区，并鼓励人们到这些地方上班和生活。这可以帮助解决大城市人口过剩和环境恶化的问题，从而改善城市的生活。不管是对于那些愿意留在城市还是那些愿意搬迁的人来讲，他们的生活都将因此得到改善。

总之，城市扩张导致的人口过剩是大城市生活恶化的主要原因。正如前文所述，对策在于更好的城市规划。

高分词汇精选 Word Bank

序号	词汇	意思	同义表达（自测）
1	across the globe	全世界	
2	deteriorate	恶化	
3	overpopulation	人口过剩	
4	metropolis	大都市	
5	shortage of housing	住房短缺	
6	property price	房价	
7	cost of living	生活成本	
8	job market	职场	
9	stiff competition	激烈的竞争	
10	infrastructure	基础设施	
11	commuting	通勤	
12	shed a shadow on	给……蒙上阴影	
13	municipal government	市政府	
14	urban planning	城市规划	
15	alleviate	缓解	
16	relocate	搬迁	
17	regional area	周边地区	
18	city sprawl	城市扩张	
19	as is elaborated above	正如上文所述	

备注：Q36～Q39这几个话题在内容上有相通之处。也请考生们认真复习本书“政府篇·城市规划”的相关内容，因为可以将其改写成这些题目的应对措施。

Q41 家庭亲密度（338 words）

It is generally acknowledged that families are now not so close as they used to be. What are the possible reasons and what can be done to reverse the trend?

Many people say that family members are having a lower sense of closeness than before. I think there are three reasons for this.

The first reason is that people nowadays have to work longer hours and thus they can hardly squeeze time from their tight schedules to stay with their families. Over time, families do not talk to each other, especially between children and their parents. The solution, I would say, is that people must learn to better organize their time to spend more time with families. If possible, people can try home office or at least ask for flexible hours.

The second reason is related to the proliferation of smart phones and tablet computers. This mainly happens to young people as they have now become slaves to those modern devices. Whenever they have time, they do not talk to their parents; instead, they just stare at screens and bury themselves in their own world of cell phone games. To change this situation, I think parents should learn to use some popular apps and when they have time they can play games with their children on tablets. This way, they will have a lot of quality family time and feel close to each other.

The third reason is that people tend to be more mobile than before. With improved transport and communication technology, people can now choose to work and live anywhere they like. The result of this is that young people always leave their parents and work in other cities or even in other countries. I think distance shall never be the excuse for people to forget their families, and the cure is people should make the best out of the modern technology. With Skype and other instant messaging apps, people can always talk to and see their families.

In conclusion, it seems that heavy work and technology distance people from each other. However, as long as people can be creative about using their time and modern technology, they will overcome those problems and be close to their families.

【参考译文】

很多人说如今家庭成员之间的亲密度比以前低，我认为原因有三。

第一个原因是，人们现在上班时间比以前更长，因此他们没办法从忙碌的日程安排中挤出时间陪伴家人。逐渐地，家人之间很少沟通，尤其是子女与家长之间。至于对策，我认为人们必须学会更好地安排时间，从而挤出时间陪家人。如果可能的话，人们可以尝试在家办公；至少，他们可以申请弹性的工作时间。

【参考译文】

第二个原因与智能手机和平板电脑的普及有关。这主要发生在年轻人身上，因为他们已经成了这些现代设备的奴隶。只要一有时间，年轻人就会盯着手机和电脑的屏幕，沉溺于手机游戏中，而不是同父母交谈。要改变这种局面，我认为父母应该学着使用一些流行的应用软件（apps），并且在他们有空的时候同孩子们一起玩游戏。这样，他们一定会有很多美好的家庭时光，并且感觉彼此之间很亲密。

第三个原因是人们往往比以前流动性更强。随着交通及通讯科技的改善，人们如今可以选择去任何地方工作或是生活。由此，年轻人往往离开父母去其他城市甚至出国工作。我认为距离永远不应该作为遗忘家人的借口。对策其实就是人们充分利用现代科技。有了Skype和其他即时通讯程序，人们随时都能和家人联系并看到对方。

总之，繁忙的工作和科技似乎疏远了人们的关系。但是，只要人们能够合理利用时间和现代科技，他们就能够克服这些问题并同家人保持亲密的关系。

高分词汇精选 Word Bank

序号	词汇	意思	同义表达（自测）
1	sense of closeness	亲密度	
2	work long hours	长时间地工作	
3	squeeze time	挤时间	
4	tight schedule	忙碌的安排/工作	
5	better organize one's time	更好地安排时间	
6	home office	在家办公	
7	flexible hours	弹性的工作时间	
8	the proliferation of	……的普及	
9	smart phone	智能手机	
10	tablet (computer)	平板电脑	
11	modern device	现代设备	
12	app	应用软件	

序号	词汇	意思	同义表达（自测）
13	quality	高品质的	
14	feel close to	感觉亲密	
15	mobile	流动的	
16	make the best out of	充分利用	
17	instant messaging	即时通讯	
18	heavy work	繁重的工作	
19	distance	使疏远	
20	be creative about doing sth.	灵活做某事	

CHAPTER 11
雅思写作Task 1 A类

一、图表作文简介

（一）图表类型

学术类雅思写作Task 1是图表作文，主要分为以下几类：

- Line charts/graphs 曲线图
- Bar charts 柱状图
- Pie charts 饼状图
- Tables 表格题
- Maps 地图题
- Diagrams 示意图（包括process charts/diagrams，也叫flow charts，即流程图）

考试要求20分钟左右至少写150词，俗称小作文。其中，前四类为主流题型，后两类为非主流题型。每次考试有可能考上述图表题型中的任意一种，或是前四类图表的混搭。

▷ 样题

WRITING TASK 1

You should spend about 20minutes on this task.

The graph below shows the consumption of fish and some different kinds of meat in a European country between 1979 and 2004.

Summarise the information by selecting and reporting the main features, and make comparisons where relevant.

Write at least 150 words.

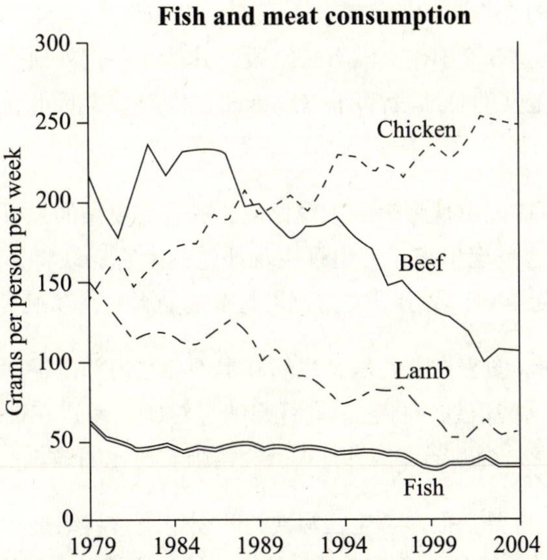

（资料来源：《剑桥雅思考试全真试题集7》Test 2）

（二）评分标准

Task 1图表作文的评分标准包括以下四项：

- Task achievement
- Coherence and cohesion
- Lexical resource
- Grammatical range and accuracy

（详细评分标准请参照本书附录）

（三）注意事项

1. 雅思图表作文并非像传闻中的那样不重要。很多考生误以为Task 1不重要，随便应付一下即可。这种看法是不对的。按照官方的说法，Task 1要求20分钟左右至少写150词，而Task 2要求40分钟至少写250词，从比例上来讲，Task 1的要求反而比Task 2更高。因此尽管确实Task 2的分值要高一些，但不能因此就忽视Task 1。

2. 图表作文的总结段（overview）至关重要。经常听到有人说雅思小作文可以不需要总结，一些学生在写作时也往往不写总结段，但实际上这是个危险的做法。雅思官方评分标准Task achievement一项中讲得非常清楚：5.0分的作文recounts detail mechanically with no clear overview，6.0分的作文是presents an overview with information appropriately selected，而7.0分的作文则是presents a clear overview of main trends, differences or stages。纵观《剑桥雅思考试全真试题集》（1—9）系列

从书中所收录的所有图表作文的考官范文，只有剑1·Test 3、剑2·Test 1和Test 4、剑5·Test 1、剑6·Test 1这5篇小作文没有总结段，其他无一例外地全部都有总结段。另外，几乎所有的考官范文的总结段都用“Overall, ...”开头，因此，建议考生也采用该模式。

3. 雅思图表作文中不应该出现考生的主观评论。考生需要做的，只是客观地将图表所传递的信息有条理性地呈现出来。若出现主观评论，考官建议将其删掉。由此可能产生以下后果：①字数受影响，②上下文的连贯与衔接受影响，③浪费宝贵的考试时间。

4. 一定要用好衔接词。图表作文的信息之间基本不存在内部逻辑，因此考生需要使用各种衔接表达来组织这些信息，将它们进行归纳、对比。考官在批改图表作文时，一定会看考生的作文本身是否顺畅，信息是否分类清晰、对比明确。

5. 信息的准确性极其重要。很多考生在写A类图表作文时就像是在记流水账，不太懂得展现数据背后所传递的信息，又或者是将数据遗漏。这就对应了评分标准5.0分Task achievement里所说的recounts detail mechanically...there may be no data to support the description...there may be a tendency to focus on detail。实际上，考生需要将图表中数据所包含的信息转化成更准确的、更为地道的英文表达，并用图表中的数据予以证明。具体的写法，请参考后文的相关章节及范文。

6. 时态要规范。除diagrams外，所有A类图表作文中都会出现相应的时间，这些时间决定了考生写作所使用的时态。通常，这些图表都是基于过去的数据绘制的，因此要用过去时。若是图表没显示时间，则使用一般现在时。有时，图表中的时间始于过去，终于将来，像这种从过去到将来的图表就显得比较麻烦，也是众多考生难以把握的。强烈建议考生们看一看《剑桥雅思考试全真试题集5》Test 1及《剑桥雅思考试全真试题集9》Test 3和Test 4所收录的图表，其中剑5·Test 1及剑9·Test 4配有考官范文。

二、雅思图表作文写作攻略

图表作文的写法比较模式化，各类图表都大同小异，加上只有20分钟左右的写作时间，因此不太建议考生写太长的篇幅。从《剑桥雅思考试全真试题集》系列丛书中所收录的考官作文来看，基本上每篇都控制在200词以内。因此，建议广大考生将Task 1的词数控制在200词以内。

开头段

雅思图表作文的开头段主要是改写题目。切忌抄题目，否则除了会被扣除相应字数外，还会在第三项评分标准lexical resource（词汇）上受到影响，即有可能会被认为vocabulary is limited。

一般来讲，雅思A类小作文的开头段都遵循“The XX chart illustrates/demonstrates/shows...”这个句型结构来改写题目。此外，考生最好能够对图表中所呈现的时间、地点或者其他信息进行加工。例如，《剑桥雅思考试全真试题集2》Test 4的小作文讲的是1930年到1980年Great Britain, Australia, New Zealand, United States及Canada这五个国家的囚犯人数情况。原题为：The table below shows the figures for imprisonment in five countries between 1930 and 1980. 在这道题目中，我们会发现英国、澳大利亚、新西兰、美国和加拿大全部是说英语的国家；而1930年到1980年正好是50年，可以改写成半个世纪。由此，我们可以改写为：The bar chart illustrates how many people were kept in prison in five English-speaking countries over half a century between 1930 and 1980.

正文

关于正文部分，考生需要做好两件事情：一是保证回应到所有主要信息并且表达准确；二是用好衔接词，保证行文流畅。

line charts, bar charts, pie charts及tables这四类主流题型，正文中有很大部分是在描述各种变化趋势，因此考生务必要掌握相应的词汇及句型结构。

▶ 表示变化趋势的词汇

上升	动词	increase, rise, climb, jump, soar, leap, pick up, go up
	名词	increase, rise, climb, jump, leap, growth
下降	动词	decrease, decline, fall, drop, go down
	名词	decrease, decline, fall, drop
不变	动词	keep/stay the same at（数值）; remain constant at（数值）; level off at（数值）
	名词	no/few changes at（数值）
波动	动词	fluctuate (around)
	名词	fluctuation (around), an up-and-down trend (around)

表示变化程度的词汇

轻微	形容词	slow, slight, moderate
	副词	slowly, slightly, moderately
稳步	形容词	steady, smooth, constant
	副词	steadily, smoothly, constantly
显著	形容词	rapid, quick, remarkable, considerable, sharp, dramatic
	副词	rapidly, quickly, remarkably, considerably, sharply, dramatically

以下将以“2001年—2006年间，A公司的利润急剧上升到500万。”为基础来介绍几类句型。

表示变化趋势的句型结构

① From 2001 to 2006, A's profit increased remarkably to $5 million.

② From 2001 to 2006, A's profit experienced a dramatic growth to $5 million.

③ Between 2001 and 2006, there was a steep climb in A's profit to $5 million.

④ The years from 2001 to 2006 saw a sharp rise in A's profit to $5 million.

表示倍数级增长/下降的句型结构

① From 2001 to 2006, A's profit doubled from $5 million to $10 million.

② From 2001 to 2006, A's profit more than doubled from $5 million to $12 million.

③ From 2001 to 2006, A's profit nearly doubled from $5 million to $9 million.

④ From 2001 to 2006, B's profit halved from $10 million to $5 million.

⑤ From 2001 to 2006, C's profit increased six-fold from $1 million to $6 million.

⑥ From 2001 to 2006, C's profit had a six-fold growth from $1 million to $6 million.

表示极值的句型结构

① From 2001 to 2005, A's profit increased massively to its peak/top at $10 million.

② From 2001 to 2005, A's profit increased massively to a record high at $10 million.

③ From 2001 to 2005, A's profit rose massively, peaking at $10 million.

④ From 2001 to 2005, B's profit decreased quickly to its bottom at $1 million.

⑤ From 2001 to 2005, B's profit decreased quickly to a record low at $1 million.

⑥ From 2001 to 2005, B's profit decreased quickly, bottoming out at $1 million.

▶ 表示倍数的句型结构

A's profit is five times (as big as) that of B's.

▶ 表示交叉点的句型结构

① In 2005, A and B had the same profit, reaching $5 million.

② Starting from 2005, A overtook/replaced B to be the more profitable company.

▶ 衔接词

描述变化趋势时用到的衔接词

- 如图所示：
  - According to the chart, ...
  - As can be seen...
  - As is shown (in the chart)...
- 具体而言：
  - To be more specific, ...
  - Specifically, ...
- 相比之下：In contrast, ...
- 另一方面：On the other hand, ...
- 相　　反：
  - On the contrary, ...
  - In contrast, ...
  - However, ...
- ……而……：句子1 + while + 句子2.（或While + 句子1，句子2.）
- 与此相类似的是：
  - Similarly, ...
  - Similar to A, B...
  - The same as A, B...
- 与此同时：
  - In the mean time, ...
  - At the same time, ...
- 至于……
  - As for/to...
  - When it comes to...
  - As far as A is concerned, ...
  - Regarding...
  - With regard to...
  - In reference to...

强调极值或倍数或相同数值或重要信息时或补充额外信息

- 应该指出的是：It should be noted that...
- 同样也应该提及的是：
  - It is also worth mentioning that...
  - It should also be pointed out that...

有了合适的衔接词和句型结构，图表作文基本上就可以写得比较不错了。但是需要强调的是，以上所有表达只是雅思A类小作文的基础，更好的写作方法及表达法需要考生根据图表及内容做出适当调整。

总结段

前文已经讲过，考生需要给图表作文写个清晰的总结概述。同开头段一样，总结段不需要写太多，只需用一到两句话对图表的主要特征做一个归纳。以前文收录的样题（《剑桥雅思考试全真试题集7》Test 2）为例，官方范文的总结段为：Overall, the graph shows how the consumption of chicken increased dramatically while the popularity of these other foods decreased over the period.

（一）曲线图 line charts

曲线图的重点在于考生必须将各条曲线的变化趋势描述清楚。由于考试至少是考2条线，而每条线的走势又曲曲折折，所以这对考生的语言能力提出了较大的挑战。若是动辄用同样的词汇和句型，那lexical resource及grammatical range and accuracy这两项评分就会很低。

还有一点需要注意，线越多越需要考生突出重点，否则就会沦为记流水账，而这会直接导致出现recounts detail mechanically...there may be a tendency to focus on detail这种低分情况。因此，考生必须在动笔前就规划好相应的内容，该归纳的得归纳，该对比的要对比地写。通常来讲，建议考生将正文的字数控制在130词左右。这样，加上开头段与结论段就刚刚好。

Question 1

You should spend about 20 minutes on this task.

The chart shows the number of people using a London underground station every day.

Write a report for a university lecturer describing the information on the graph.

Write at least 150 words.

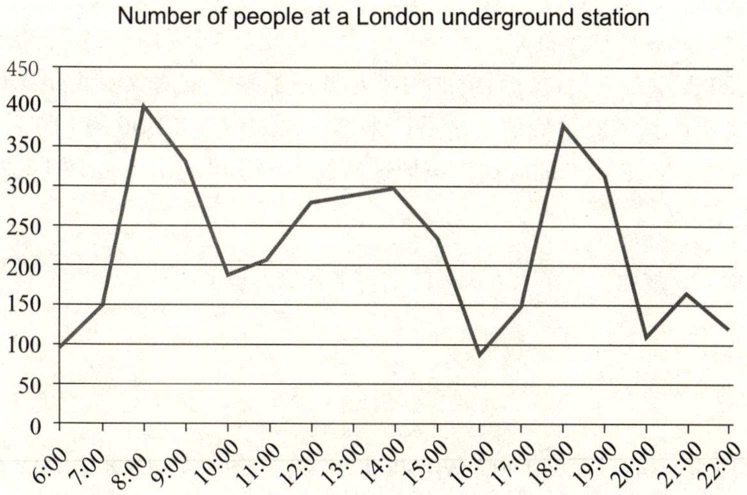

（资料来源：本图表是根据互联网上的相关数据进行绘制，原始来源不详。）

▶ 范文（164 words）

The line graph illustrates how many passengers use a London tube station in a typical day.

As can be seen, at 6:00 only 100 passengers use the subway station, yet the figure jumps sharply to the peak at 400 over the next two hours till 8:00. Afterwards, however, the figure has a remarkable decline to approximately 190 at 10:00 o'clock, followed by a constant rise to 300 over the next four hours, another plateau during daytime.

After 14:00, the subway station receives fewer and fewer passengers as the figure falls massively from 300 to a record low (90 or so) at 16:00. Nevertheless, the following two hours witnesses a steep recovery of passenger flow in the station, peaking at nearly 400 again at 18:00 before it sinks to around 110 at 22:00. It should be noted that there is another plateau at 21:00 with some 170 people using the station.

Overall, the metro station is packed with the most passengers during the rush hours.

【参考译文】

这幅曲线图展现了一天之中有多少乘客使用某个伦敦地铁站。

如图所示，早晨6:00时该地铁站只有100名乘客，但接下来的两个小时内乘客量迅速增长到最高点，在8:00时，达到400人。但是此后10:00时，该数据则迅速降到190人左右，之后的四小时内又持续性地增长到一个小高潮，到300人。

14:00之后，该地铁站的乘客量越来越少，体现在16:00时人数降到了最低值，为90人左右。不过，后续的两小时见证了乘客量的急剧回升，并且在18:00再次回到400的峰值。之后，乘客人数跌落到22:00的110人左右。需要注意的是，21:00的时候，该地铁站的乘客量出现了一个170人左右的小高潮。

总体上而言，该地铁站在上下班高峰期时乘客数量最多。

备注

1. 题目中的everyday被改成了in a typical day，其实还可以写成on a daily basis。
2. 题目中的underground station一词被改写成tube station, subway station及metro station，体现了词汇的丰富性。
3. 第二段没有一上来就大谈特谈乘客人数从多少增长到多少，而是先将起始点的信息改写，然后再将其变化趋势呈现出来。
4. 在词汇层面，全文灵活使用了各类表示上升、下降及变化程度的词汇；而且，也灵活改写了信息，例如第三段的receive fewer and fewer passengers，a steep recovery of passenger flow等。
5. 语法方面，文章使用了状语从句、插入语、非谓语动词等结构。

Question 2

You should spend about 20 minutes on this task.

> ***The graph below shows the changes in the number of West Indians and Indians and Pakistanis immigrating to Britain between 1940 and 1970.***
>
> ***Summarise the information by selecting and reporting the main features, and make comparisons where relevant.***

Write at least 150 words.

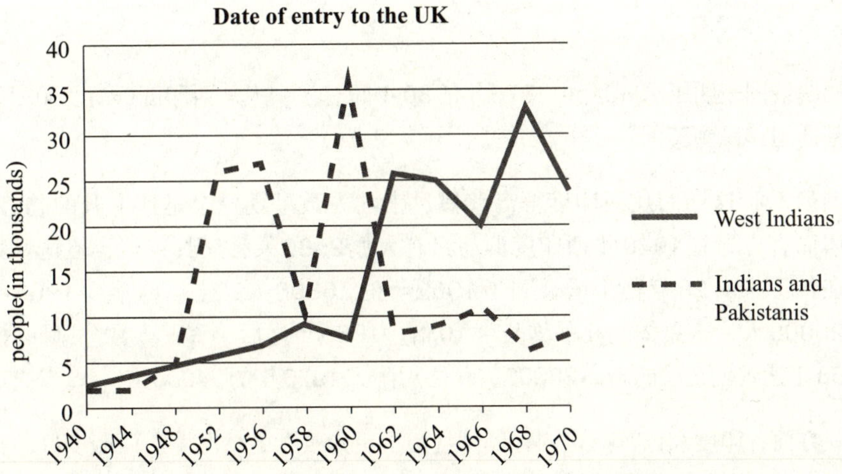

（资料来源：本图根据http://wenku.baidu.com/link?url=9PsJTtCKgrEwzH-4AawfDcOCGHiULpEQaCPnjJYmzse2JEV-pFtT03QCGRkRDP9qw97Y6Z20xe27XShvugze21TP94fzHvJ5ICPAEyHTRpi的图表重新绘制，原始来源不详。）

▶ 范文（210 words）

The line chart illustrates how many West Indians and Indians and Pakistanis immigrated to the UK over the thirty years between 1940 and 1970.

As can be seen, immigrants from West Indies had a rapidly rising trend over the surveyed period. Specifically, while in 1940 only about 2,500 West Indians immigrated to the UK, the figure picked up smoothly in the next two decades and then sharply to 26,000 in 1962 before it fell to 20,000 in 1966, which was almost a tenfold growth. After 1966, the number recovered dramatically to a record high at 33,000 in 1968, followed by a decline to 24,000 in 1970.

Indians and Pakistanis, on the other hand, saw a much more complicated immigration wave to the UK. Similar to West Indies, the number of immigrants from India and Pakistan started at 2,500 in 1940, yet it rose more than tenfold to 26,000 in 1956 before falling to 10,000 in 1958. After that, the immigrants increased dramatically to the peak at 36,000 in 1960 and took a dive to about 8,000 in the next two years, after which the figure fluctuated around at the same level till 1970.

Overall, the line graph demonstrates how West Indies overtook India and Pakistan to be the bigger source of immigrants to the UK.

【参考译文】

这幅曲线图表明了1940年～1970年的30年间有多少人从西印度群岛及印度和巴基斯坦移民到英国。

如图所示，这期间从西印度群岛移民过来的人数呈现一个迅速上升的趋势。具体而言，尽管1940年西印度群岛只有大概2500人移民到英国，但这一数据在接下来的20年稳步增长到了1962年的26000人，之后跌落到1966年的20000人，这总体上几乎增长了10倍。1966年之后，移民人数急剧回升，1968年达到创纪录的新高33000人，之后降到1970年的24000人。

另一方面，印度和巴基斯坦的移民则经历了更为复杂的情况。与西印度群岛相似，来自印度和巴基斯坦的移民人数在1940年也只有2500人。但是，1956年时这个数字增长了10倍以上，达到26000，尽管1958年时降到了10000人。1960年，其移民人数迅速上升到峰值36000人，接下来的两年则又急剧跌落到8000人左右，此后一直到1970年都维持在该水平上下。

总体上，该曲线图展示了西印度群岛是如何反超印度和巴基斯坦，成为移民英国更大的客源国的。

维基百科

*The West Indies, or West India, is a region of the Caribbean Basin and North Atlantic Ocean that includes the islands of the Antilles and the Lucayan Archipelago*①.

▷ 备注

1. 这篇文章篇幅较长。不过这么写倒也给广大考生提供了更为详细的内容作参考，而且只要能在规定时间内完成，过长的篇幅并不是太大的问题。若是要删减字数，可以将文中标下划线的地方（共计25 words）删除，则最后文章的字数为185词。

2. 正文部分并没有一下笔就说某某地方的移民人数从多少增长到多少，而是巧妙地改写了起始点的信息。语法上也用到了非谓语动词、定语从句等结构。

3. 全文的衔接词很好地使用了本书前面章节总结的表达法，使得文章表达很流畅，还包含了归纳、对比。

4. 第二段及第三段都用到了tenfold作为倍数的表达，不同的是第二段作为名词用，而第三段则用作副词。

① 资料来源：https://en.wikipedia.org/wiki/West_Indies

Question 3

You should spend about 20 minutes on this task.

The chart below shows the number of private cars used between the years 1920 to 1980 in three different countries.

Summarise the information by selecting and reporting the main features, and make comparisons where relevant.

Write at least 150 words.

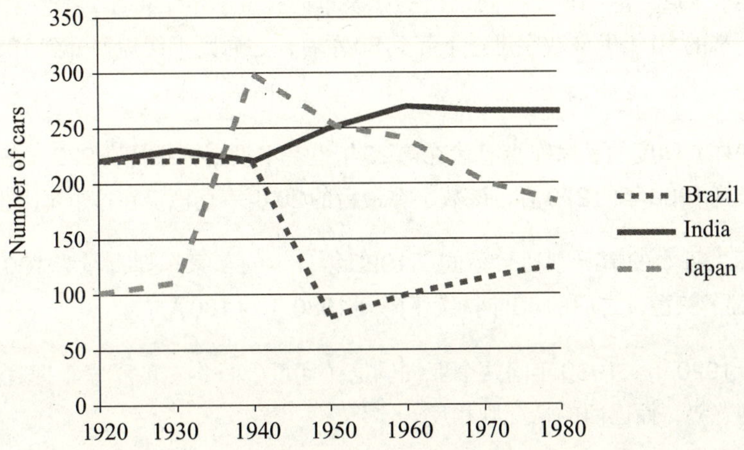

（资料来源：本图表根据互联网上的信息重新绘制，原始来源不详。）

▶ 范文（177 words）

The line graph compares the car ownership in three different countries over sixty years between 1920 and 1980, including Brazil, India and Japan.

As can be seen, the car ownership in Brazil remained constant at around 220 between 1920 and 1940, yet it shrank remarkably to approximately 80 in the next decade, followed by a moderate recovery to 130 over the last thirty years till 1980.

Similar to Brazil, there were few changes in the car ownership in India over the first twenty years as the figure also leveled off at 220. After a gradual growth to 270 in 1960, the number stayed steady in the last two decades.

Japan, on the other hand, had a quite different situation in its car ownership. Starting at 100 in 1920, the number tripled to 300 in 1940, followed by a constant fall to around 180 during the last forty years till 1980.

Overall, while the two Asian countries（i.e. India and Japan）had an upward trend in their car ownership between 1920 and 1980, Brazil had an opposite situation.

【参考译文】

这幅曲线图对比了1920年～1980年这60年间三个不同国家的私家车拥有量，包括巴西、印度和日本。

如图所示，1920年～1940年间巴西的私家车拥有量基本维持在220左右。不过在接下来的10年里该数字迅速下降到80左右，之后则平缓地回升到1980年的130。

同巴西一样，印度的私家车拥有量在前20年也基本没变，维持在220。在后续逐步增长到1960年的270后，该数字在最后的20年一直稳定在这个水平上。

另一方面，日本的情况则比较不同。1920年日本的私家车拥有量为100，到1940年翻了三番，之后的40年持续下降到1980年约180左右。

总体上，1920年～1980年间两个亚洲国家（印度、日本）的私家车拥有量呈现上升的态势，而巴西的情况则相反。

▶ 备注

1. car ownership是本文的亮点之一，避免了一直重复the number of cars的表达。
2. 描述这幅曲线图时，建议考生逐条线写并突出重点，而不是以10年或20年为单位同时对比三条线。否则，考生会写得比较辛苦，而且不利于考官从总体上了解每条线的变化趋势。另外，提醒考生，若线条有3条及以上，可以将趋势相似的线写在一起，可以对比，而趋势不同的线则写在其他段落。这样的例子可以在《剑桥雅思考试全真试题集5》Test 1、《剑桥雅思考试全真试题集7》Test 2、《剑桥雅思考试全真试题集8》Test 4及《剑桥雅思考试全真试题集9》Test 4中找到。
3. 第二段用一个句子将巴西的信息全部描述清楚。考生可以认真分析其句型结构——状语从句加上非谓语动词。
4. 总结段巧妙地将印度和日本概括成the two Asian countries，这也算是对图表信息的对比归纳。

Question 4

You should spend about 20 minutes on this task.

> ***The graphs below show the number of men and women in full and part-time employment in Australia between 1973 and 1993.***
>
> ***Summarise the information by selecting and reporting the main features, and make comparisons where relevant.***

Write at least 150 words.

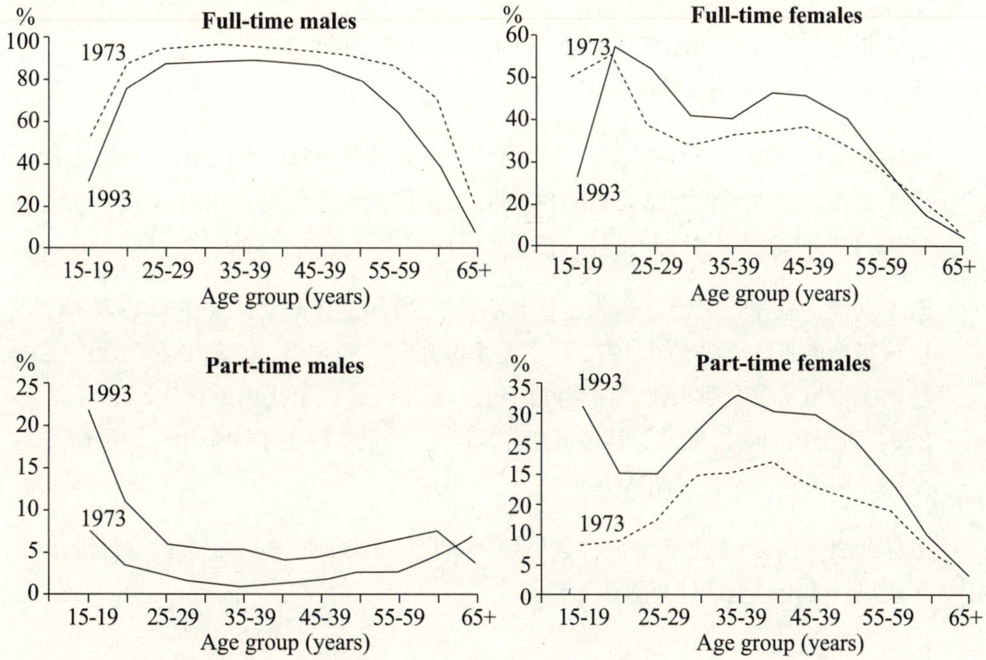

（资料来源：Labour Force Survey）

▶ 范文（191 words）

The line charts illustrate the number of males and females in different employment patterns, i.e. full and part-time work in Australia over twenty years between 1973 and 1993.

As can be seen, in both 1973 and 1993 most males worked full time, particularly those aged between 20 and 59, accounting for more than 80% of the male population. It should be noted that more men worked part time in 1993 than in 1973, by an average of 3% throughout the adulthood.

As for females, in general 1993 saw a higher percentage of them playing a role in both full and part-time employment compared with 1973. It should be pointed out that once women stepped into their twenties, fewer and fewer of them chose full-time employment in both 1973 and 1993, down from some 52% to 3% when they turned 65^{+}. The turning point for part-time females, however, was 35 years old. Once females entered their late adulthood, they were less likely to work even part time.

Overall, while most men worked full time once they turned twenty-five, more and more females quit the job market, be it full-time or part-time employment.

【参考译文】

这些曲线图表明了1973年~1993年的20年间澳大利亚不同工作类型中男女人数的情况，包括全职与兼职工作。

如图所示，1973年与1993年，多数男性（尤其是那些20~59岁的人）都从事全职工作，这占到男性总人数的80%以上。应该注意的是，相对于1973年，1993年兼职工作的男性要更多，在成年男性中大致多出了3%。

至于女性，总体上无论是全职还是兼职，1993年工作的女性要多于1973年。应该指出的是，无论是在1973年还是1993年，一旦女性上了20岁，她们便越来越少地从事全职工作。而当她们超过65岁时，这个比例更是从52%降到3%。对于兼职女性来说，其转折点在35岁。一旦女性上了这个年纪，她们甚至连兼职工作都不大可能从事了。

总体而言，当25岁之后绝大多数男性从事全职工作时，越来越多的女性退出了职场，无论是全职还是兼职工作。

▷ 备注

1. 这是一篇信息量非常大的作文，因为它的图表数量很多。因此，考生不得不舍弃掉很多细节。
2. 本文在写作过程中用不同方式改写了图表内容。例如，第二段的work full-time/part-time、第三段的played a role in full and part-time employment和stepped into their twenties，以及总结段的more and more females quit the job market。
3. 本文只展示了一种写作思路，考生还可以从full-time employment及part-time employment这两个方面分别对比males及females。

（二）柱状图 bar charts

建议考生在柱状图写作中，按标签逐个分析。此时，会有两种情况出现：一是该柱状图可以转换成曲线图，考生只需按照曲线图的方式去写即可；二是该柱状图无法转换成曲线图，此时就需要考生凭着良好的英文功底准确地传达出图表中的内容。

Question 1

You should spend about 20 minutes on this task.

> ***The table below shows the figures for imprisonment in five countries between 1930 and 1980.***
>
> ***Summarise the information by selecting and reporting the main features, and make comparisons where relevant.***

Write at least 150 words.

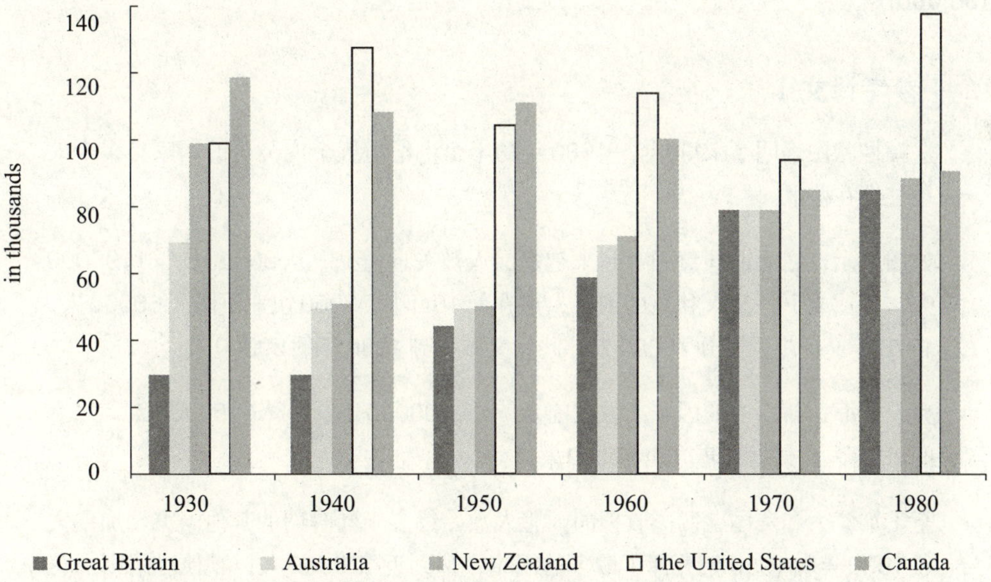

（资料来源：根据《剑桥雅思考试全真试题集2》Test 4图表重新绘制。）

▸ 范文（206 words）

The bar chart illustrates how many people were kept in prison over half a century between 1930 and 1980 in five English-speaking countries.

As can be seen, over this time period a growing number of people were put into prison in Great Britain, up from 30,000 to 90,000. In contrast, the figure for Australia had a quick decline from 70,000 to 50,000 in the first decade before it gradually recovered to 70,000 again in 1970. After that, it went down to about 50,000 in the year of 1980.

New Zealand, on the other hand, saw a rapid fall in its prisoners from 100,000 to 50,000 in the first twenty years, followed by a steady climb to 90,000 in the last thirty years.

When it comes to Canada and the US, both of them had higher percentages of prisoners than the other countries throughout this time period. While Canada had the most prisoners in both 1930 and 1950 with almost 120,000 prisoners, the US topped the list in the other years, fluctuating around 110,000.

Overall, North America always had the most prisoners whereas Great Britain constantly had the smallest number of inmates except in 1980 when Australia replaced Great Britain, becoming the country with the least prisoners (50,000).

【参考译文】

这幅柱状图表明了1930年—1980年的半个世纪里五个说英语的国家有多少人被关押在监狱。

如图所示，在此期间英国有越来越多的人被关进监狱，从30000增长到90000人。相比之下，澳大利亚的囚犯人数在前10年从70000快速下降到50000人，1970年又逐步回升到70000人，此后又减少到1980年的50000人。

另一方面，新西兰的囚犯人数在前20年从100000迅速下降到50000人，之后的30年内该数据稳步升至90000人。

至于加拿大和美国，两国收押的囚犯人数始终多于同时期的其他国家。加拿大于1930年和1950年关押了最多的囚犯，达到近120000人；其他时间则由美国占据榜首，囚犯人数在110000人上下浮动。

总体上，北美的囚犯人数总是最多，而英国始终最少，除了在1980年。这一年，澳大利亚取代英国，成为囚犯人数最少的国家（50000人）。

▶ 备注

1. 这幅柱状图本质上就是一幅曲线图，因此写法与曲线图无异。只是它有五条曲线，因此考生需要做好以下工作：①控制好字数，若正文为130词左右，则每条线平均写20多词；②可以逐条线去写，但若有趋势相似的线，亦可合在一起对比写；③做好衔接过渡；④务必要总体对比这些标签作为总结。

2. 为了保证能将字数控制好，考生需要用到一些比较复杂的句型结构，例如非谓语动词、定语从句等。

3. 考生应注意到，图表中的时间正好是半个世纪，而国家又全部是讲英语的国家。

Question 2

You should spend about 20 minutes on this task.

The charts below show the main reasons for study among students of different age groups and the amount of support they received from employers.

Summarise the information by selecting and reporting the main features, and make comparisons where relevant.

Write at least 150 words.

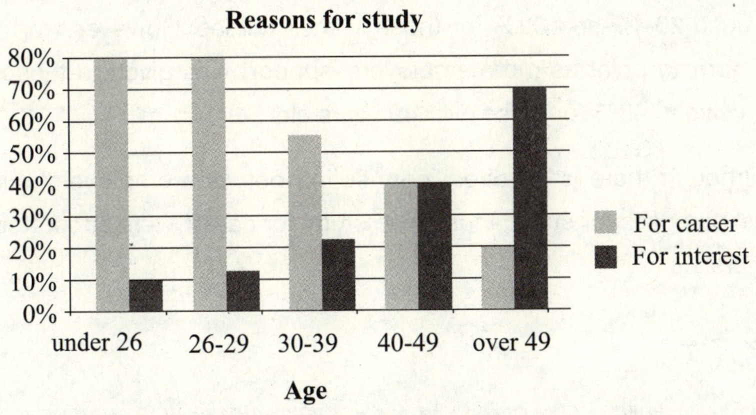

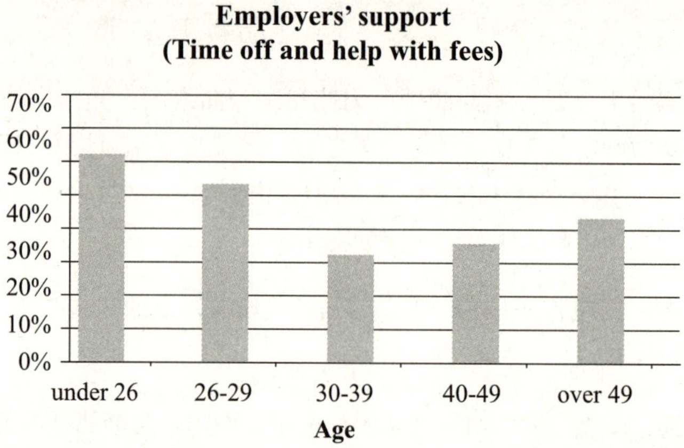

（资料来源：根据《剑桥雅思考试全真试题集5》Test 2的图表重新绘制。）

▶ 范文（184 words）

The bar charts illustrate the purposes people study for and the support given by their employers, by age group.

Specifically, as people turn older, more and more of them study out of interest, from 10% (under 26) to 70% (over 49). In contrast, fewer and fewer people study for career consideration, down from 80% to 20%. In should be noted that there are equal percentage of people (40%) studying for both purposes for those in their forties.

In reference to employers support' (time off and help with fees) people received, young people received the most support from their employers (62%). As people grew older, the employers were less willing to help as the support level went down to 53% for those aged 26~29 and 32% for those in their thirties. However，forty years old seemed a turning point as more employers' support was given to those above 40 years old, rising to 43% for those over 49 years old.

Overall, although there is no direct connection between employers' support and employees' purposes for study, those who study for career were supported the most by employers.

【参考译文】

这些柱状图表明了不同年龄段的人学习深造的目的以及雇主所给予的支持度。

具体而言，人们年龄越大则越多的是出于兴趣而学习，相应的比例从10%（26岁以下）升至70%（49岁以上）。相比之下，越来越少的人会出于职业的考虑去深造，比例从80%降到20%。应该注意的是，40多岁的人出于兴趣和职业而深造的比例是一样的（40%）。

至于雇主的支持度（休假和学费资助），年轻人得到的支持最多（62%）。随着（员工）年龄的增长，雇主的支持意愿在下降，其对于26~29岁的人的支持度降到53%，对30多岁的人的支持度降到32%。不过，40岁似乎是一个转折点，因为40岁以上的人得到的支持度在上升，49岁以上的人为43%。

总体而言，尽管雇主的支持度与员工深造的动机之间并无直接关联，但为了职业而深造的人得到了雇主最大的支持。

▷ 备注

1. 当图表不止一个时，考生可以逐个进行分析。当然，最后务必要将这些图表进行对比，看是否能够找到一些重要的信息作为总结。
2. 正文中，几乎所有句子的主语都不是percentage，而是巧妙地用人做主语。这实际上是在灵活地改写信息，也是考生需要认真去学习和掌握的。
3. 注意相关的地道表达，例如out of interest, people in their forties/thirties等。

Question 3

You should spend about 20 minutes on this task.

> ***The chart below shows the amount of leisure time enjoyed by men and women of different employment status.***
>
> ***Summarise the information by selecting and reporting the main features, and make comparisons where relevant.***

Write at least 150 words.

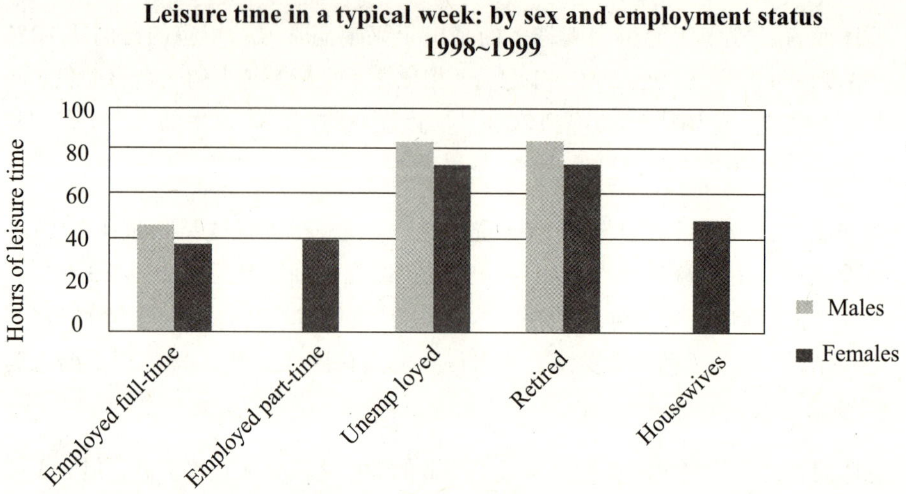

（资料来源：根据《剑桥雅思考试全真试题集2》Test 2的图表重新绘制。）

▶ 范文（163 words）

The bar chart illustrates how much leisure time males and females enjoyed between 1998 and 1999, by employment status.

According to the chart, full-time male workers had approximately 45 hours of leisure time every week, while those who had no employment or retired had 84 hours for leisure activities. For some reason, there were no statistics for males who worked part-time.

Females, on the other hand, had less leisure time than males. Specifically, those who had a full-time job had no more than 40 hours of leisure time, while those who were unemployed and retired could enjoy 75 hours of free time, almost ten hours less than men. In the meantime, 40 hours of leisure time went to females who worked part-time, whereas housewives had about 50 hours for themselves.

Overall, the chart shows that females, employed or retired, failed to enjoy equal amounts of leisure time by a margin of about ten hours.

【参考译文】

这幅柱状图按就业状态呈现了1998年和1999年男性和女性所享有的休闲时间。

【参考译文】

根据图表，全职的男职工每周大致有45小时的休闲时间，而失业或者退休的男性每周的休闲时间达到了84小时。不知为何，图表没有统计兼职男性的休闲时间。

另一方面，女性的休闲时间要比男性少。具体而言，全职女性每周的休闲时间不超过40小时，而失业及退休的女性每周可以享受75小时的休闲时光，这几乎比男性少了10小时。与此同时，兼职女性每周有40小时的闲暇时间，而家庭主妇每周则有大致50小时的休闲时间。

总体上，图表表明女性无论是工作还是退休都无法享受与男性相同的闲暇时光，相差近10小时。

▷ 备注

1. 与前两篇不同，这幅柱状图没有时间轴，也不存在年龄的增长，故无法转换成曲线图来写。此时，需要考生看懂图表，并巧妙地改写信息，避免一直用The leisure time of men/women is...之类的句式表达。
2. 考生只需按标签逐个写出男性与女性的信息，然后再将它们进行对比即可。

（三）饼状图pie charts

饼状图的写法与柱状图并无二异，也是按标签进行分析，也有两种可能：一是可以转换成曲线图去描述其变化趋势，二是单独改写以呈现每个标签的内容。因此，考生只要掌握了柱状图的写法，会写饼状图也是情理之中的事。

就雅思考试中饼状图的数量而言，比较常考的情况是两幅或者两幅以上的饼状图，或者是一个饼状图搭配柱状图/表格/曲线图，以混搭的形式出现。

就饼状图中的数值而言，通常是百分比。如若不是，考生也不用刻意将其换算成百分比，但应提及其总量是多少。

Question 1

You should spend about 20 minutes on this task.

The pie chart below shows the average way in which foreign students learning English in London spend their money over the course of a week.

Summarise the information by selecting and reporting the main features, and make comparisons where relevant.

Write at least 150 words.

Students' spending (pounds)

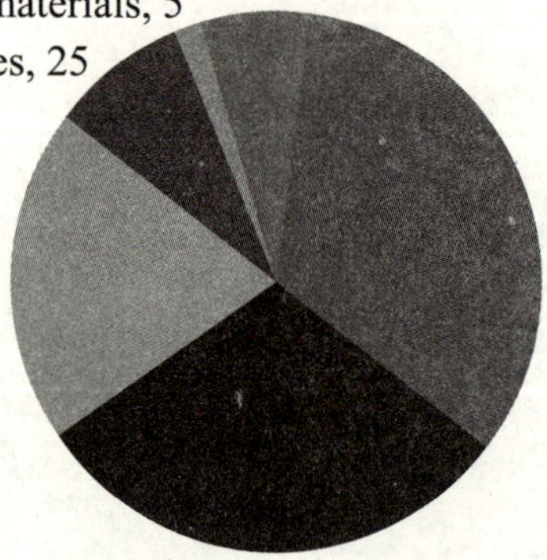

（资源来源：本图根据http://wenku.baidu.com/link?url=enxfiAKKuYpelK2JyT7bK2Q1Ly-s4JsGDwnWKPDMfLXuDahQdQi2Hr0HD8lDj1yic5POJx5SfVyFt6vePmiDNSoAzb5HNBJX51ZOWwsOqCS图表重新绘制，原始来源不详。）

▶ 范文（154 words）

The pie chart illustrates how much money international students who learn English in London spend in a typical week as well as what they use the money for.

According to the pie chart, every week international students spend £300 in total. To be more specific, £100 is used for rent and food, which is also the single largest spending, nearly one third of the total amount. In contrast, students are the least generous when it comes to study materials as they only spend £5 on it.

School fees, on the other hand, cost students £90 on a weekly basis, a huge sum compared with the money students spend on study materials.

Of the remaining one third of the money, £60 is used for entertainment, while another £25 is for underground transport. Finally, students spend the last £25 buying clothes.

Overall, rent and food are the most money-consuming things for those international students in London.

【参考译文】

这幅饼状图表明了在伦敦学英语的留学生每周会花多少钱以及他们花钱做什么。

根据图表，留学生们每周开销共计300英镑。具体而言，租金和伙食费开销为100英镑，这也是最大的一笔单项支出，几乎占到总开销的三分之一。相比之下，学生们在学习材料上花钱最小气，每周只花费5英镑在这上面。

另一方面，留学生的学费平均每周90英镑，与他们花在学习材料上的费用相比，这是个巨额数字。

在剩下的三分之一费用中，学生们将60英镑用作娱乐，25英镑用来乘坐地铁，最后的25英镑则用来购买衣服。

总体上，房租和吃饭是留学生们最耗钱的地方。

▷ 备注

1. 这篇文章有惊无险地超过150词的最低要求，究其原因，主要是图表数量偏少。就雅思考试而言，若只有一幅饼状图，则通常会搭配一幅其他的图表。即使万一真的只有一幅图的话，考生仍可以写到规定字数。一个比较简单的法则是，考生可以将相关标签的信息进行倍数比较。
2. 第二段的思路是将最大的开销与最小的开销进行比对。有两个表达法值得考生关注：which is also the single largest spending以及are the least generous when it comes to。
3. 第三段的思路是将school fees与study materials进行对比，因为两者都与学习/教育有直接关系。此处可以进行倍数比较。
4. 第四段中的各项开销其实没关联，但既然已经剩到最后了，就应想办法巧妙地将它们归个类——110英镑，是总开销的三分之一多一些。

Question 2

You should spend about 20 minutes on this task.

> ***The pie charts below describe the electric energy production, a major source of energy in the US.***
>
> ***Summarise the information by selecting and reporting the main features, and make comparisons where relevant.***

Write at least 150 words.

1970

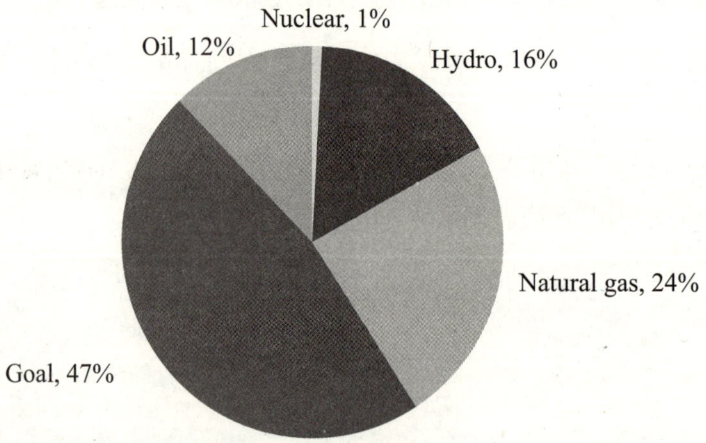

1980

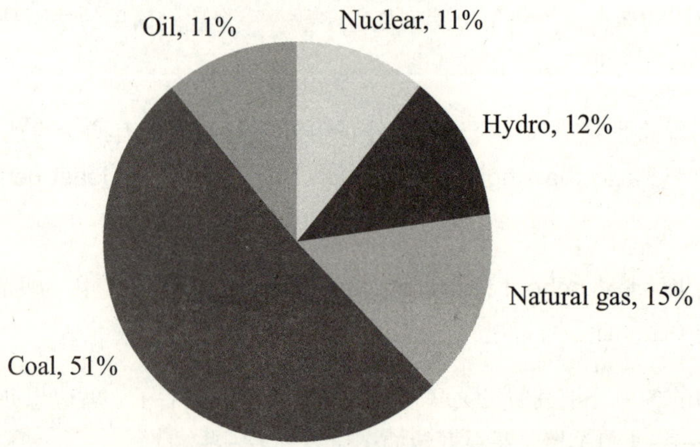

（资料来源：本图根据http://blog.renren.com/share/333410263/5503176463图表重新绘制，原始来源不详。）

▶ 范文（183 words）

The pie charts compare the shares that different sources of energy contributed to the electricity production in the US in the years of 1970 and 1980.

As can be seen, in 1970 47% of the electricity in the US was produced by coal, and this non-clean energy source became more important ten years later as it provided 51% of the total electricity. Similar situation also occurred to the nuclear energy. Although in 1970 only 1% of the power supply was supported by it, the figure jumped to 11% in the year of 1980.

In contrast, the other sources of energy saw a moderate decline of shares in the power supply system of the US. To be more specific, while oil had a slight decline from 12% in 1970 to 11% in 1980, the figures for natural gas dropped the most by 9% to 15% over the same period. Hydro, on the other hand, saw a fall of 4% from 16% to 12% during this time period.

Overall, the US relied heavily on non-clean energy sources in both 1970 and 1980, and coal remained the most important source of the power supply.

【参考译文】

这些饼状图对比了1970年和1980年美国用不同能源发电的份额。

如图所示，1970年美国有47%的电力是靠煤炭供应，并且该非清洁能源在10年后变得更为重要，因为它贡献了51%的总电力。核能的情况也与之类似。尽管1970年只有1%的电力供应来自核能，1980年该数据则增长到11%。

相比之下，其他能源在美国供电系统中的份额则在平缓地下降。具体而言，石油的份额从1970年的12%降到了1980年的11%；天然气降幅最大，直降9%，降到15%；另一方面，水力发电降了4个百分点，从16%降到12%。

总体上，1970年和1980年美国严重依赖于非清洁能源，并且煤炭始终是其最重要的电力供应来源。

▶ 备注

1. 这篇文章其实还可以有另外一个写作思路，即先单独将1970年的信息写出，然后再将1980年的信息写出，最后再将两者进行对比。

2. 按照本文的写作思路，这两幅饼状图其实就是五条曲线，因此建议考生将上升趋势的标签写在同一段，将下降趋势的标签写在另一段。这样，在处理信息方面就显得得很灵活，有归纳和对比。

3. 秉承一贯的风格和原则，本文并未停留在某某的比例上升、下降之上，而是改成了更为通俗、通顺的表达。

4. 由于所有标签都是能源类，所以考生在写作过程中可以将它们进行归类——清洁能源、化石燃料、可再生能源，具体选用哪个根据写作需要而定。

Question 3

You should spend about 20 minutes on this task.

> ***The three pie charts below show the changes in annual spending by a particular UK school in 1981, 1991 and 2001.***
>
> ***Summarise the information by selecting and reporting the main features, and make comparisons where relevant.***

Write at least 150 words.

Total School Spending in 1981

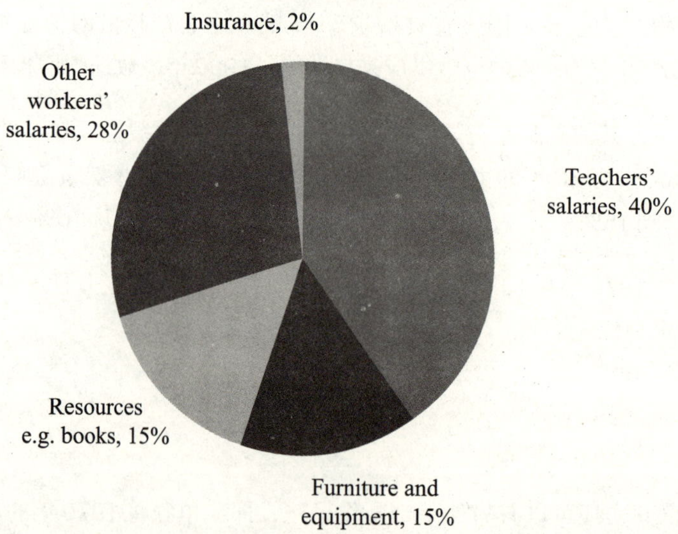

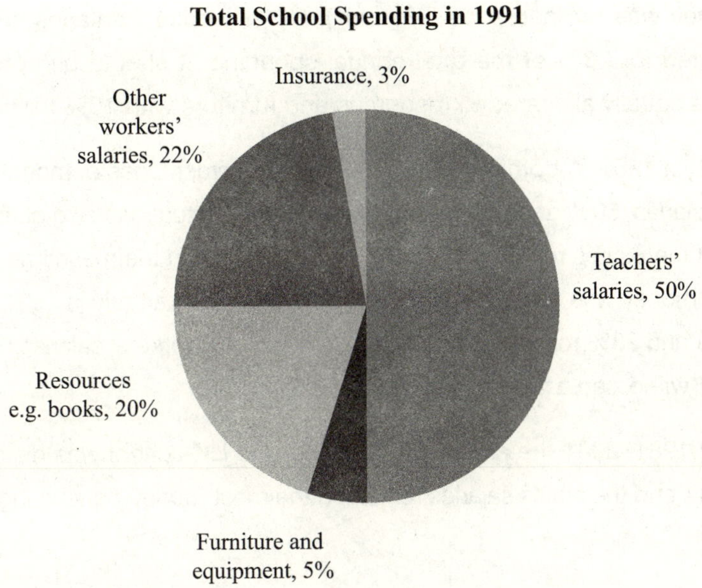

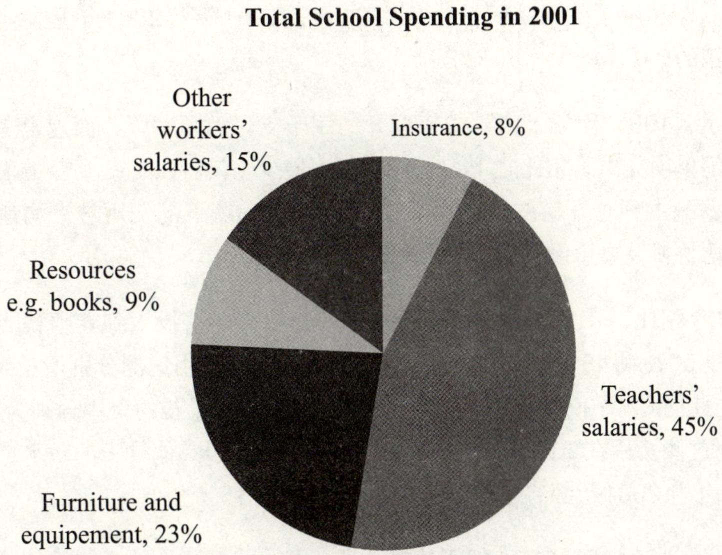

（资料来源：根据《剑桥雅思考试全真试题集8》Test 2的图表重新绘制。）

▸ 范文（206 words）

The pie charts show how a particular UK school allocated its annual spending in the years of 1981, 1991 and 2001.

As can be seen, in 1981 40% of the school's annual spending was used for teachers' salaries, which was also the largest single spending for the school. In contrast, the least money was for insurance (2% only). Other workers' salaries, on the other hand, accounted for 28% of the total annual spending. It should be noted that the remainder was equally allocated to resources and furniture with 15% for each.

Compared with in 1981, in both 1991 and 2001 higher percentages of money was spent on teachers' salaries (50% and 45% respectively). Similar situations also occurred to the insurance, and the figures rose to 3% and 8% respectively. In the meantime, while 20% and 5% of the money was used to resources and furniture separately in 1991, the figures turned into 9% and 23% respectively in 2001. As for other workers' salaries, the years of 1991 and 2001 witnessed a shrinking share to 22% and 15%.

Overall, during 1981~2001 the annual spending for the UK school was distributed in a more equal way, and the staff's salaries remained the most money-consuming sector.

【参考译文】

这些饼状图展示了英国某所学校在1981年、1991年及2001年是如何分配其年度开销的。

如图所示，1981年该校40%的年度开销用于支付教师薪资，而这也是该校最大的一笔单项支出。相比之下，保险的费用最少（仅占2%）。另一方面，其他员工的薪酬占到总开销的28%。应该注意的是，剩下的费用被平均地分配到购买书籍材料及桌椅设备上（各占15%）。

同1981年相比，在1991年和2001年该校将更多的钱投入到老师薪酬上（比例分别是50%和45%）。保险的情况与之类似，其费用比例分别增长到3%和8%。与此同时，1991年投放给购买书籍材料及桌椅设备的费用分别为20%及5%，而这些费用在2001年调整为9%及23%。至于其他员工的薪水，其比例在1991年和2001年都有所下降，分别为22%及15%。

总体而言，1981年—2001年间英国这所学校的年度开销分配得更为平均了，并且职工的薪酬始终是其最大的开销。

▷ 备注

1. 这篇文章的写作思路是：单独描述1981年的饼状图，将1991年及2001年的饼状图与1981年的进行对比。之所以这么写，是要让考生明白单个饼状图该怎么写，多个饼状图又该怎么写。

2. 很多考生在饼状图写作中都会遵循这样一个模式：A had the highest percentage with x%, followed by B, C and D which accounted for X%, X% and X% respectively, and finally E ranked the last（X%）。这个结构本身很好，不过如果动辄就将其套在所有的饼状图作文中，未免显得非常死板。而且，这种表达方式本身就像是在记流水账。因此，还是建议考生多读相关范文，从语言表达上下工夫，确保信息表达准确。

3. 第三段的写作思路为，将趋势上升的写在一起，有升有降的写在一起，最后再写一直在下降的。

4. 总结段将图表中的teachers' salaries和other workers' salaries一起归纳为staff's salaries。

（四）表格题tables

表格不像其他图表那么直观，而且数据繁多，故需要考生横纵向对比并甄选出相关数据。

同柱状图及饼状图相似，当考生逐个分析标签时，可以将表格转换成曲线图或无法将其转换成曲线图。有了前面章节的讲解，相信考生大抵都了解如何写表格题作文了。

Question 1

You should spend about 20 minutes on this task.

> The table below shows the consumer durables (mobile phones, personal computers etc.) owned in Australian families from 1989 to 2003.
>
> ***Summarise the information by selecting and reporting the main features, and make comparisons where relevant.***

Write at least 150 words.

Consumer durables	1989	1991	1993	1995	1997	1999	2001	2003
Percentage of households with:								
Television	99	99	99	99	99	99	99	99
Personal computer	5	16	24	38	48	52	80	89
Mobile phone	3	12	32	33	35	58	69	97
Refrigerator	96	96	98	99	99	99	99	99
Digital camera	0	0	4	10	12	28	35	42
Washing machine	82	83	85	85	88	94	94	94
Dishwasher	7	7	10	21	32	34	35	35
Vacuum cleaner	95	96	96	96	98	98	99	99

（资料来源：根据互联网上的数据重新绘制，原始来源不详。）

▶ 范文（210 words）

The table illustrates different types of household appliances that Australian households had over the course of 14 years from 1989 to 2003.

In general, all items except television became more and more popular among Australian families, and electronic products for personal use gained popularity much more quickly than other household appliances.

Specifically, while in 1989 only 5% and 3% of the families had personal computers and mobile phones, the figures shot up to 89% and 97% respectively over the next 14 years till 2003.

In contrast, the ownership of other household items grew relatively slowly. While the percentage of families with washing machines rose from 82% to 94%, those with refrigerators and vacuum cleaners respectively saw a growth of 3% and 4% to 99%.

It should be noted that no families had digital cameras until 1993 when 4% families bought this item, against 42% in 2003. It should also be pointed out that televisions, refrigerators and vacuum cleaners remained the most popular consumer durables in Australian families (99% after the millennium).

Overall, from 1989 to 2003, refrigerators, vacuum cleaners and televisions remained the top three common household items in Australian families while digital cameras were the least popular except in 2003 when dishwasher replaced it to be the least common item.

【参考译文】

这个表格介绍了1989年—2003年的14年间澳大利亚家庭所拥有的不同电器的情况。

总的来说，除电视机以外的其他所有产品都变得越来越普及，并且个人电子产品的普及速度远远快于其他家用电器。

具体而言，1989年时只有5%和3%的澳洲家庭拥有个人电脑和手机，而在接下来的14年间，直至2003年，该数据分别骤升到89%和97%。

相比之下，其他家用物品的拥有量则增长相对缓慢。拥有洗衣机的家庭从82%增长到94%，而拥有电冰箱和吸尘器的家庭则增长到99%，分别增长了3%和4%。

应该注意的是，直到1993年才有4%的家庭购买数码相机，到2003年增长到42%。同样也应该指出的是，电视机、电冰箱和吸尘器始终是澳洲家庭最普及的耐用消费品（千禧年后高达99%）。

总体上，1989年—2003年间电冰箱、吸尘器和电视机始终是澳洲家庭最普及的家用物品，而数码相机始终是最不普及的，除了在2003年。这一年，洗碗机取代数码相机成为了最不普及的家用电器。

▶ 备注

1. 若删掉最后一段，则本文剩下171词，也是篇很好的作文。并且，由于第二段已经做了总结，故删掉最后一段其实不会对分数造成多大影响。

2. 这篇文章在写作时要小心陷阱，考生一不小心就会写成：The percentage of personal computer increased quickly from 5% to 89%. 若此，则误解了图表的内容，因为真正的信息是The percentage of families that had personal computers increased quickly from 5% to 89%.

3. 本文的写作思路为：将普及速度迅速的归为一类来写，恰好它们属于电子数码产品；将普及速度缓慢的归到一类，恰好它们是家用电器；digital camera与television较为特殊，因此单独强调一下。

4. 当然，考生也可以逐个去写各个标签，但这种模式的挑战性很大，需要考生灵活变换句型结构，避免一直重复。例如，针对personal computer的信息，我们可以有以下几种表达方式：①The percentage of families that had personal computers increased quickly from 5% to 89%. ②Personal computers became more and more popular among Australian families, up from 5% to 89%. ③More and more Australian families had personal computers, up from 5% to 89%. ④In 1989 only 5% of the Australian households had personal computers, and the figure jumped sharply to 89% over the next 14 years till 2003. ⑤The ownership of personal computers in Australian families grew remarkably from 5% to 89%. ⑥Personal computers gained popularity quickly among Australian families, from 5% to 89%.

5. 类似表格题在《剑桥雅思考试全真试题集2》Test 1及《剑桥雅思考试全真试题集6》Test 2都出现过。

Question 2

You should spend about 20 minutes on this task.

> ***The table below gives information about changes in modes of travel in England between 1985 and 2000.***
>
> ***Summarise the information by selecting and reporting the main features, and make comparisons where relevant.***

Write at least 150 words.

Average distance in miles traveled per person per year, by various modes of travel

	1985	2000
Walking	255	237
Bicycle	51	41
Car	3,199	4,806
Local bus	429	274
Long distance bus	54	124
Train	289	366
Taxi	13	42
Other	450	585
All modes	4,740	6,475

（资料来源：根据《剑桥雅思考试全真试题集6》Test 2重新绘制。）

▶ 范文（193 words）

The table compares the average distance English people traveled by different modes of transport in the years of 1985 and 2000.

As can be seen, while people walked 255 miles on average in 1985, the figure declined to 237 in 2000. Similarly, people also traveled less by bicycle and local bus over the same period, down from 51 to 41 miles and 429 to 274 miles respectively.

In contrast, in 2000 private cars were used 1607 more miles than in 1985 (4806 against 3199 miles). Long distance bus also became more popular as people traveled 124 miles in 2000, a growth of 70 miles compared with 1985. Similar situation also occurred to train and taxi. Specifically, while 77 more miles were covered by train per person, people traveled 29 more miles by taxi compared with 13 miles in 1985. Besides all these modes of transport, "other" transport also saw an increasing trend in the distance people traveled from 450 to 585 miles.

Overall, between 1985 and 2000 English people traveled a much longer distance (from 4740 to 6475 miles). Meanwhile, private cars remained the most preferred means of travel.

【参考译文】

该表格对比了1985年与2000年英国人用不同的交通方式出行的距离。

如图所示，人们在1985年平均步行255英里，而在2000年该数据降到了237英里。同样，人们骑车及乘坐巴士的出行距离也更短了，分别从51降到41英里，从429降到274英里。

相比之下，2000年人们对私家车的使用比1985年多了1607英里（4806英里vs. 3199英里）。长途巴士也更受欢迎，体现在其出行距离比1985年多了70英里，达到124英里。火车与出租车的情况与之相类似。具体而言，平均每人乘坐火车多出行了77英里，而乘坐出租车则比1985年的13英里多出了29英里。除了上述所有出行方式外，"其他"交流方式的出行距离也呈现上升态势，从450英里增长到585英里。

总体上，1985～2000年间英国人的出行距离更长了（从4740英里增长到6475英里）。同时，乘坐私家车始终是人们最喜欢的出行方式。

▶ 备注

1. 这也是一篇极具挑战性的作文。表面上，它的数据比Question 1要少得多，但实际上它有9条线要写，对句型的多样性要求相当高。

2. 具体来说，本文的写作不能通篇都说The distance traveled by XX increased/decreased quickly from...to...。这么写的话，一是显得单调，二是会使信息的表达显得不那么地道。

3. 另外，提醒考生，表格中所有呈上升趋势的出行方式都可以归为motorized vehicles。

Question 3

You should spend about 20 minutes on this task.

> ***The table below gives information on consumer spending on different items in five different countries in 2002.***
>
> ***Summarise the information by selecting and reporting the main features, and make comparisons where relevant.***

Write at least 150 words.

Percentage of national consumer expenditure by category — 2002

Country	Food/Drink/Tobacco	Clothing/Footwear	Leisure/Education
Ireland	28.91%	6.43%	2.21%
Italy	16.36%	9.00%	3.20%
Spain	18.80%	6.51%	1.98%
Sweden	15.77%	5.40%	3.22%
Turkey	32.14%	6.63%	4.35%

（资料来源：根据《剑桥雅思考试全真试题集7》Test 1表格重新绘制。）

▶ 范文（182 words）

The table compares consumer expenditure on different items in five different

European countries in the year of 2002.

As can be seen, Turkey spent the most on Food/Drink/Tobacco among all the five countries, accounting for 32.14% of its total consumer expenditure, followed by Ireland with 28.91%. In contrast, (people in) Sweden spent the least as only 15.77% of its consumer expenditure was spent on those items, with Spain (18.80%) and Italy (16.36%) in between.

On the other hand, Italy topped the list of spending on Clothing/Footwear with 9.00% of its total expenditure, while Sweden was on the bottom with 5.40%. There were few differences among the other three countries in this category, with an average of 6.50%.

In reference to the spending on Leisure/Education, people in Turkey were the most generous as 4.35% of the country's expenditure was allocated into this category. While Sweden and Italy followed it closely with 3.22% and 3.20% respectively, Ireland and Spain only spent 2.21% and 1.98% on the same items.

Overall, among all the five countries Food/Drink/Tobacco was the most important consumer spending for people.

【参考译文】

该表格对比了2002年五个欧洲国家在不同项目上的国民开销。

如图所示，五个国家中土耳其在饮食/烟草上花费最多，占到其国民总开销的32.14%，而爱尔兰则以28.91%的比例紧随其后。相比之下，瑞典人在这上面花费最少，仅占其国民开销的15.77%。西班牙与意大利则位于中间，分别为18.80%及16.36%。

另一方面，在衣着/鞋袜方面意大利以9%的国民开销占据榜首，而瑞典则以5.40%排名最后。其他三个国家在这一类别上差别不大，平均在6.50%左右。

至于休闲/教育方面的开销，土耳其人最为大方，体现在其国民开销有4.35%用在了这个项目上。瑞典和意大利分别以3.22%及3.20%的比例紧随其后。爱尔兰与西班牙则只花费了2.21%与1.98%的费用在这上面。

总体上，对于所有这五个国家而言，饮食/烟草都是人们开销最大的项目。

▷ 备注

1. 关于土耳其是否是欧洲国家，很多人都会提出异议。考生需要注意，信息的加工才是最重要的。

2. 与前面的表格不同的是，本文没办法去写上升或下降之类的变化趋势，故需要考生认真地逐行或逐列对比信息。当然，就本文而言，逐列对比会显得更为明智。

3. 强烈建议考生在写作时不要局限于写XX's percentage上升/下降，而应采用更为通顺的表达方式进行改写。

（五）地图题maps

2015年地图题的考查频率相对比较高，总共考了8次。一般是根据地图描述某个村庄、城镇、城市、小岛、公园或是学校的发展变化。

从《剑桥雅思考试全真试题集》（1—10）所收录的地图题来看，具体分布如下：

- 《剑桥雅思考试全真试题集1》Test 4 → 一幅地图
- 《剑桥雅思考试全真试题集5》Test 3 → 两幅地图
- 《剑桥雅思考试全真试题集9》Test 1 → 两幅地图

其中考查频率最高的是《剑桥雅思考试全真试题集9》Test 1的地图题，即通过两幅地图来对比某地所经历的发展变化。

考生需要注意的是，地图题不一定要用过去时。有时，考生拿到的地图可能是对某地未来的规划，此时应该使用将来时写作。

Question 1

You should spend about 20 minutes on this task.

Chorleywood is a village near London whose population has increased steadily since the middle of the nineteenth century. The map below shows the development of the village.

Write a report for a university lecturer describing the development of the village.

Write at least 150 words.

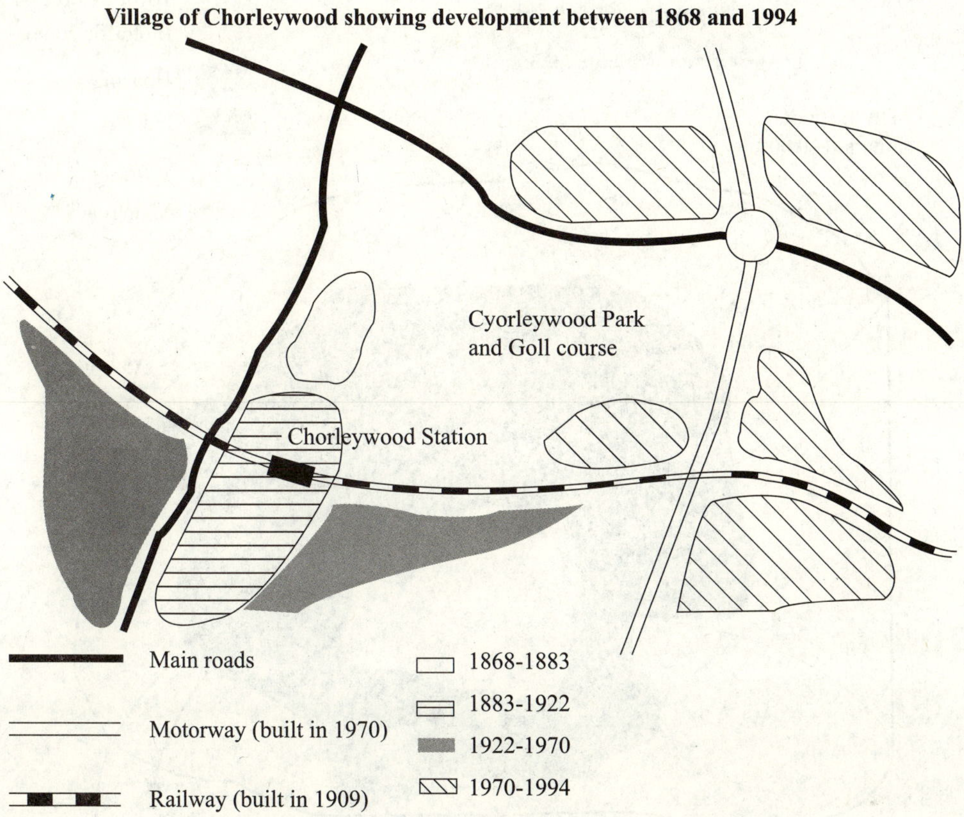

（资料来源：《剑桥雅思考试全真试题集1》Test 4。）

Question 2

You should spend about 20 minutes on this task.

> ***The map below is of the town of Garlsdon. A new supermarket (S) is planned for the town. The map shows two possible sites for the supermarket.***
>
> ***Summarise the information by selecting and reporting the main features, and make comparisons where relevant.***

Write at least 150 words.

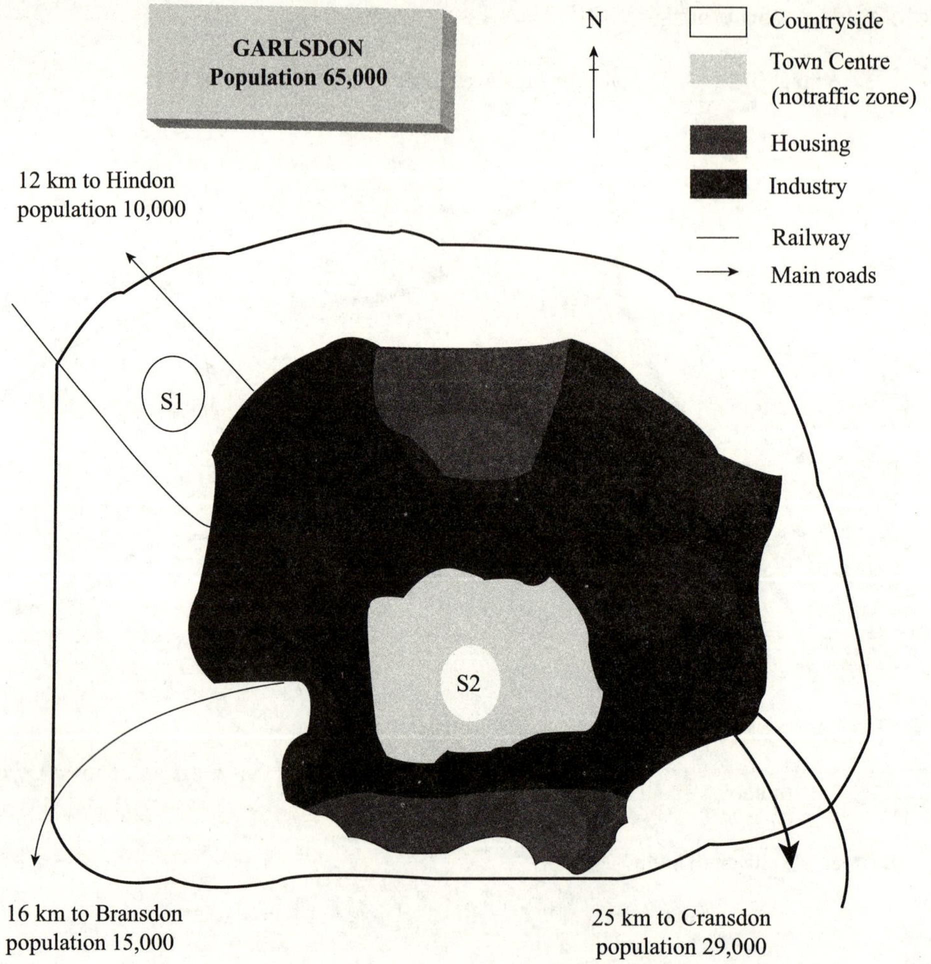

（资料来源：《剑桥雅思考试全真试题集5》Test 3。）

▸ 考官范文（193 words）

The map shows two proposed locations for a new supermarket for the town of Garlsdon.

The first potential location（S1）is outside the town itself, and is sited just off the main road to the town of Hindon, lying 12 kms to the north-west. This site is in the countryside and so would be able to accommodate a lot of car parking. This would make it accessible to shoppers from both Hindon and Bransdon who would travel by car. As it is also close to the railway line linking two towns to Garlsdon, a potentially large number of shoppers would also be able to travel by train.

In contrast, the suggested location of S2 is right in the town centre, which would be good for local residents. Theoretically the store could be accessed by road or rail from the surrounding towns, including Bransdon, but as the central area is a no-traffic zone, cars would be unable to park and access would be difficult.

Overall, neither site is appropriate for all the towns, but for customers in Bransdon, Hindon and Garlsdon, the out-of-town site（S1）would probably offer more advantages.

▷ 备注

1. 这篇考官范文中长难句比较多，尤其是包含非谓语动词和定语从句这两类结构。
2. 由于这类地图题考查频率极低，故不建议考生们花太多时间准备。

Question 3

You should spend about 20 minutes on this task.

The maps show the changes in Templeton, a coastal resort, from 1990 t0 2005.

Summarise the information by selecting and reporting the main features, and make comparisons where relevant.

Write at least 150 words.

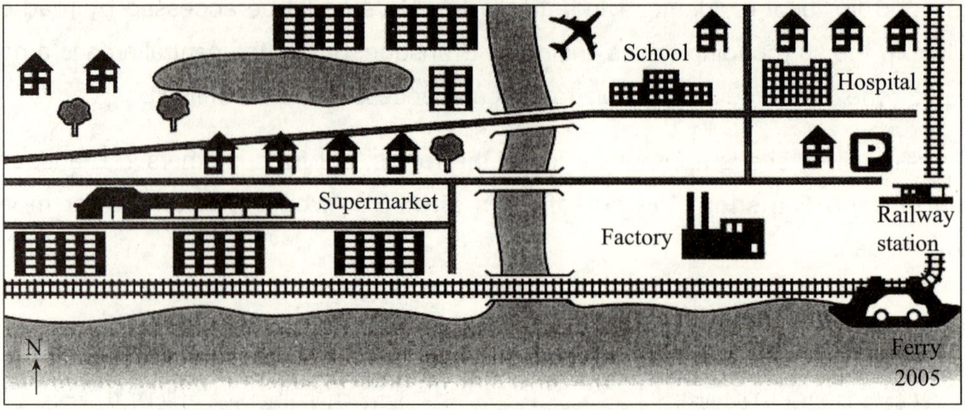

（资源来源：http://www.essayforum.com/writing-3/changes-seaside-resort-templeton-61364/，原始来源不详。）

▶ 范文（205 words）

The maps illustrate the changes (that) the coastal resort Templeton underwent over fifteen years between 1990 and 2005.

As can be seen, the town was divided into two parts by a southbound river, linked by two main roads. In 1990, houses and trees scattered in the western part of the town, whereas in the eastern part a school and a hospital could be found in the north, with a car park to the south of the latter. A railway station, meanwhile, was located in the southeast of the town, with the railway line extending to the north.

In 2005, most of the houses and trees in the western part of the town were replaced by skyscrapers, and a supermarket was also built. In the eastern part, an airport appeared to the northwest of the school. Meanwhile, a factory was built to the west of the railway station whereas a ferry appeared to its south. The railway line, on the other hand, extended along the south coastline to the very end of west, making it the third line to link the western and eastern parts of the town.

Overall, the maps show that the infrastructures in Templeton had been remarkably improved between 1990 and 2005.

【参考译文】

这些地图表明了从1990年到2005年的15年间海滨度假胜地Templeton所经历的发展变化。

如图所示，该城镇被一条南北流向的河流一分为二，由两条主干道连接在一起。1990年，住房和树木零散地分布在该镇的西区，而在东区的北部建有一所学校和一家医院，医院的南边有一个停车场。与此同时，该镇的东南部建有一个火车站，其铁路线一路向北。

2005年，该镇西区的绝大多数房子和树木都被高楼大厦所取代。并且，这里新建了一家超市。在东区，学校的西北方向兴建了一座机场。与此同时，火车站的西边修建了一座工厂，而其南边则建了一个轮渡码头。另一方面，该镇的铁路线沿着南海岸线一路向西，从而成为连接该镇东区和西区的第三条要道。

总体上，这些地图表明Templeton的基础设施在1990年到2005年期间得到了极大改善。

▶ 备注

1. 这是最典型的雅思地图题作文，请考生认真备考。
2. 本文的开头段几乎是万能的，只需调整时间及地点。
3. 同样，本文的总结段也可以灵活应用于几乎所有这类地图题作文。
4. 就正文而言，地图题的关键在于考生能够熟练表达“XX位于XX方位”、“XX的XX方位又出现/修建了XX”。考生需要掌握多样化的表达法。
5. 此外，考生还应该懂得如何表达“XX是东西/南北走向”、“XX与XX交叉，并且在十字路口出现了XX”。

（六）示意图diagrams

示意图属于非主流考题。不知为何，考生们普遍对其抱有恐惧心态。一个非常有趣的现象是，考生们经常打听并交流究竟几月份考示意图的概率最高，然后再选择考试日期时刻意避开这些月份。

这种心理恐惧可以理解，但实际上考生只要认真研究几篇范文，还是能够很好地把握示意图的写作方法的，没有必要闻之色变。

就diagrams的类别来讲，可分为：

- 流程图（flow charts/process charts/process diagrams），即有流程、有步骤。
- 示意图（diagrams），即无流程、无步骤。

就考查频率而言，流程图会相对高一些。

就《剑桥雅思考试全真试题集》（1—10）所收录的题目来看，具体分布如下：
- 《剑桥雅思考试全真试题集 1》Test 2 → 一幅流程图
- 《剑桥雅思考试全真试题集 6》Test 3 → 两幅流程图
- 《剑桥雅思考试全真试题集 8》Test 3 → 两幅流程图
- 《剑桥雅思考试全真试题集 10》Test 4 → 一幅流程图

流程图写作要点：
- 使用一般现在时。
- 使用好衔接过渡，将图表内容逐步表述清楚。
- 适当地使用非谓语动词及定语从句等高分句型。
- 尽量用图表中的标签做主语，使用被动语态。
- 务必要判断出每个步骤所发生的动作。（通常，图表中给出的单词多为名词。若是有 -er 结尾的名词，则去掉 -r 或 -er 就很可能是动词；若是出现 v-ing，则一般去掉 -ing 或者去掉 -ing 然后加上 -e 就会得到相应的动词。）
- 当步骤较多时，考生应该视情况将有些步骤合并到一起来写。
- 一幅图的总结段可以写该流程共计多少个步骤，起于何处、终于何处。
- 若不止一幅图时，则总结段可以对比其相似性及其差异。

Question 1

You should spend about 20 minutes on this task.

The diagrams below show the life cycle of the silkworm and the stages in the production of silk cloth.   ***Summarise the information by selecting and reporting the main features, and make comparisons where relevant.***

Write at least 150 words.

Life cycle of the silkworm

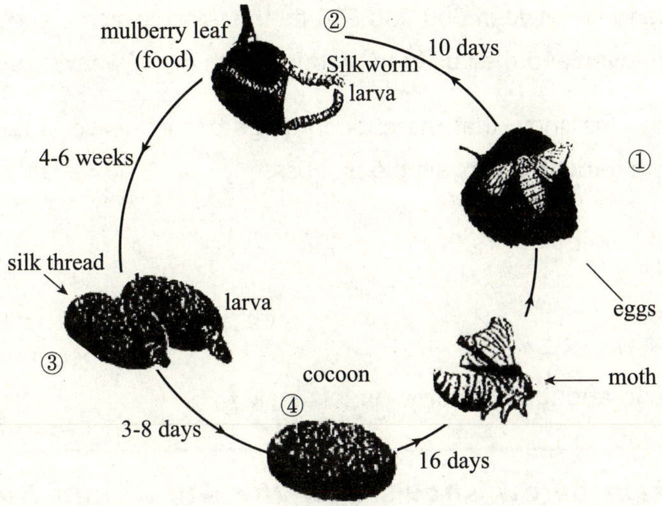

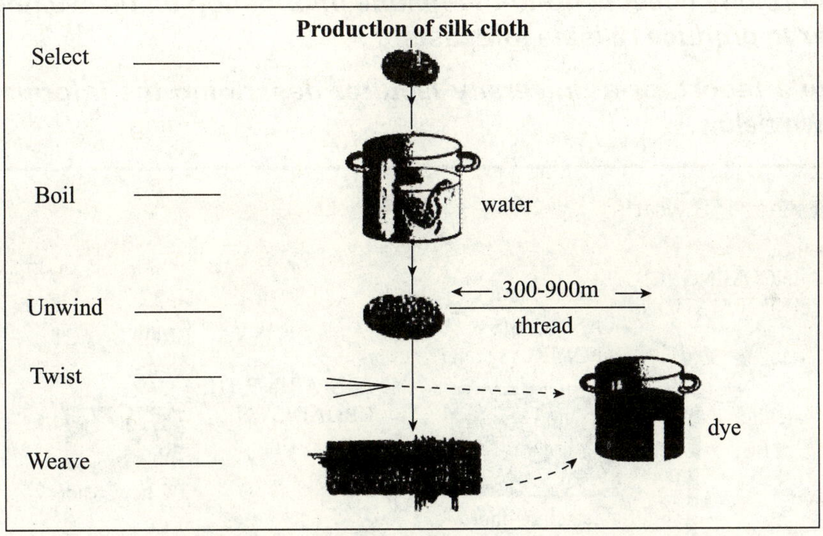

（资源来源：《剑桥雅思考试全真试题集6》Test 3。）

▶ 考官范文（163 words）

The first diagram shows that there are four main stages in the life of the silkworm. First of all, eggs are produced by the moth and it takes ten days for each egg to become a silkworm larva that feeds on mulberry leaves. This stage lasts for up to six weeks until the larva produces a cocoon of silk thread around itself. After a period of about three weeks, the adult moths eventually emerge from these cocoons and the life cycle begins again.

The cocoons are the raw material used for the production of silk cloth. Once selected, they are boiled in water and the threads can be separated in the unwinding stage. Each thread is between 300 and 900 metres long, which means they can be twisted together, dyed and then used to produce cloth in the weaving stage.

Overall, the diagrams show that the cocoon stage of the silkworm can be used to produce silk cloth through a very simple process.

Question 2

You should spend about 20 minutes on this task.

> ***The diagram below shows how the Australian Bureau of Meteorology collects up-to-the-minute information on the weather in order to produce reliable forecasts.***
>
> ***Write a report for a university lecturer describing the information shown below.***

Write at least 150 words.

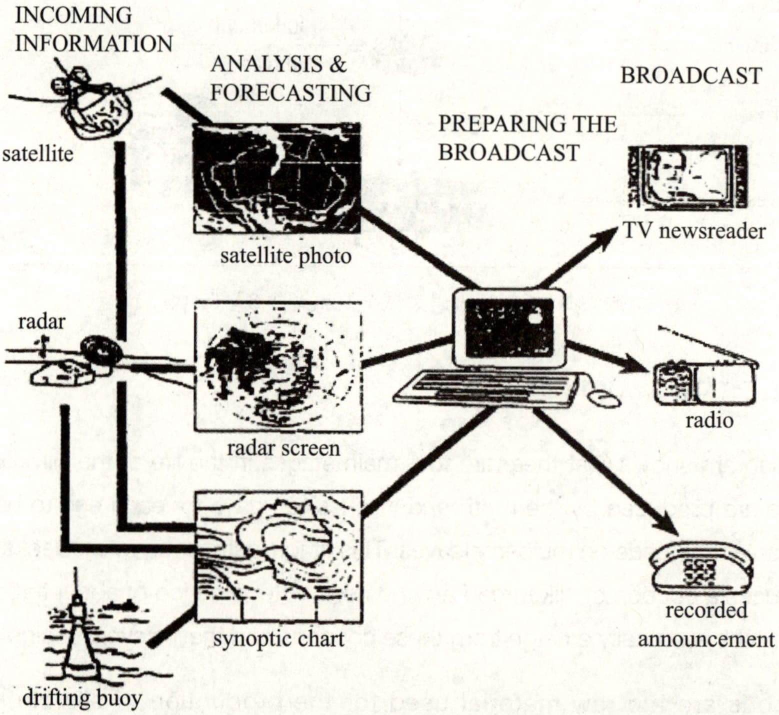

（资料来源：《剑桥雅思考试全真试题集 1》Test 2）

Question 3

You should spend about 20 minutes on this task.

The diagram shows how electricity is generated by a hydroelectric dam.

Write a report for a university lecturer describing the information shown below.

Write at least 150 words.

Hydroelectric Dam

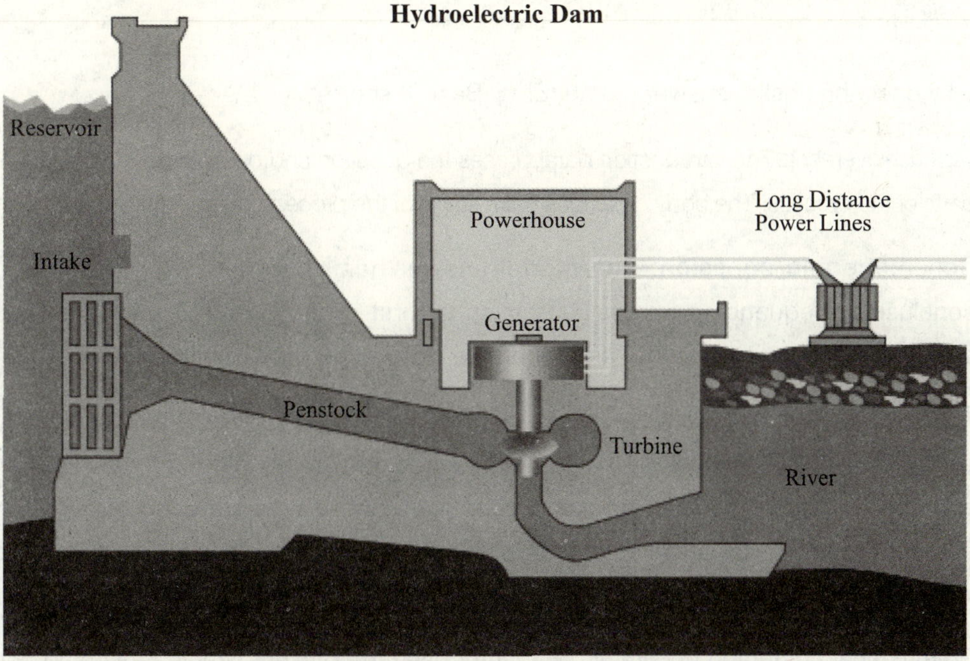

（资料来源：该图表、范文及评语均摘自 http://ielts-academic.com/2012/03/11/ielts-writing-task-1-process-diagram-with-sample-answer/。）

▶ 参考范文（163 words）

The diagram illustrates the basic principles of hydroelectric power. The process requires the construction of a large dam connected to a powerhouse. The dam creates a large reservoir and the powerhouse is where the electricity is generated.

First of all, water trapped in the reservoir behind the dam is forced through an intake.

It then flows into a narrow chamber called a penstock, where the resulting high pressure turns a turbine. The turbine is connected to a generator in the powerhouse above, and this is where the movement of the turbine is converted into electricity. The resulting electricity leaves the powerhouse via cables that carry it over long distances to where it can be used.

It is interesting to note that a hydroelectric dam creates no harmful byproducts and relies entirely on natural forces to produce electricity. After the turbine stage, water flows out through a second channel into a river. The process is renewable, thanks to the water cycle in nature.

➢ 评语：

Why does this Task 1 answer get an IELTS Band 8 score?

Task achievement: The introduction paraphrases the question and describes the constituent parts of the process. The body describes each stage of the process in sequence.

Coherence and cohesion: The model answer has an introduction, body and conclusion. Sequencing expressions such as first of all, then and after are used appropriately. The articles “a” and “the” are used effectively to introduce and refer back to different elements of the process.

Lexical resource: The labels in the diagram are well integrated into the model answer, and appropriate verbs such as converted, flows and leaves are used throughout. Less-common words such as byproducts and renewable are introduced by the writer. Spelling is always accurate.

Grammatical range and accuracy: The writer uses the present simple tense and has good control of subject-verb agreement and active/passive forms. A good balance of simple and complex sentences is used throughout.

（七）混合图 mixed types

A类小作文每年都会考到四类主流图表的混搭，即 line charts（曲线图）、bar charts（柱状图）、pie charts（饼状图）和 tables（表格题）。至于谁和谁混搭，毫无规律可言。

对于这类混搭的图表，建议考生将题目改写成一句话，正文段分别描述各图表信息，最后再综合对比进行总结。

《剑桥雅思考试全真试题集》(1—10)中收录了相关图表作文，尤其是前几套题。

Question 1

You should spend about 20 minutes on this task.

The graph and table below give information about water use worldwide and water consumption in two different countries. ①

Summarise the information by selecting and reporting the main features, and make comparisons where relevant.

Write at least 150 words.

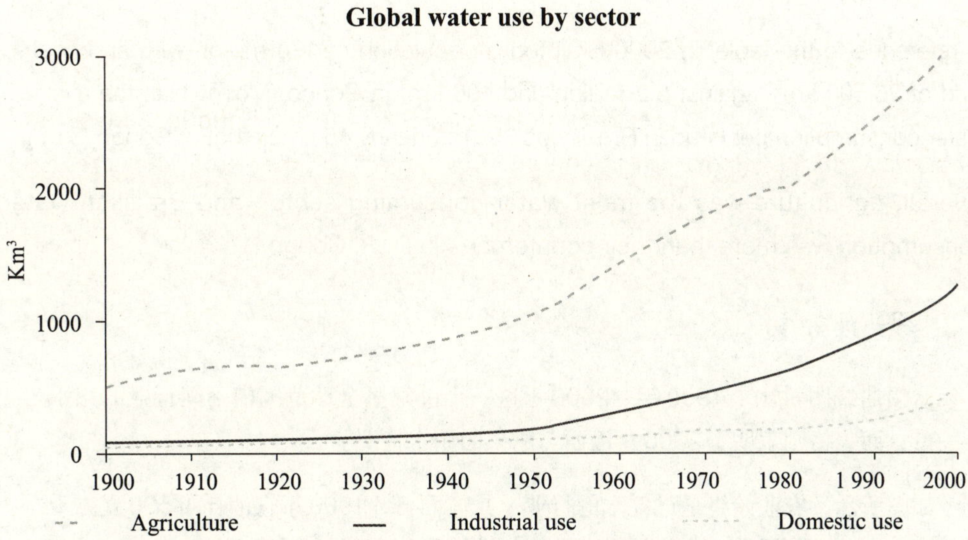

Water consumption in Brazil and Congo in 2000

Country	Population	Irrigated land	Water consumption per person
Brazil	176 million	26,500 km^2	359 m^3
Democratic Republic of Congo	5.2 million	100 km^2	8 m^3

资源来源：本图表根据《剑桥雅思考试全真试题集6》Test 1图表重新绘制。

▶ 范文（211 words）

The line chart compares the global water consumption among different sectors over the century between 1900 and 2000, while the table provides some information about the water consumption in Brazil and Congo in the year of 2000.

As can be seen, agriculture was the most water-consuming sector throughout the given time period. Specifically, while 500 km^3 of water was consumed in 1900, the next 100 years witnessed a constant and quick rise in the figure to over 3,000 km^3.

Similarly, the water consumption for industrial use and domestic use, despite at a fairly slow rate and at a low level, also had a rising trend. To be more specific, there was little water used for both industrial and domestic use over the first half century; the water consumption climbed to approximately 1,200 km^3 and 500 km^3 respectively over the second half century.

In reference to the table, in 2000 Brail fed a population of 176 million with an irrigated land of 26,500 km^2, against 5.2 million and 100 km^2 in Congo. Meanwhile, the average water consumption per head in Brazil was 359 m^3, nearly 45 times that of Congo (8 m^3).

Overall, agriculture was the most water-consuming sector, and Brazilian water consumption was more than their counterparts in D. R. Congo.

【参考译文】

这幅曲线图对比了1900年～2000年这一个世纪里全球范围内不同行业的用水量，而表格则表明了2000年巴西与刚果的用水情况。

如图所示，农业始终是最耗水的行业。具体而言，1900年它消耗了500立方千米的水，而随后的100年其用水量迅速增长到3000立方千米。

同样，工业用水和生活用水也呈现上升态势，尽管增长速度缓慢且用水量较少。具体来说，前半个世纪几乎没有多少工业用水和生活用水，但后半个世纪其用水量相应地增长到1200立方千米及500立方千米。

提及表格，2000年巴西用26500平方千米的灌溉地养活了1亿7千6百万人口，刚果则用100平方千米的灌溉地养活了520万人口。与此同时，巴西的人均用水量是359立方千米，这几乎是刚果的45倍（8立方千米）。

总体而言，农业是最耗水的行业，而巴西的用水量比刚果要多。

▷ 备注

1. 曲线图的写作思路是：将趋势比较相近的两条放在一起写。
2. 第三段写表格时所用的句型结构值得考生好好学习。例如，against可避免用完整的句子来写刚果的信息，后面的倍数比较也是如此。

Question 2

You should spend about 20 minutes on this task.

The pie chart below shows the main reasons why agricultural land becomes less productive. The table shows how these causes affected three regions of the world during the 1990s.

Summarise the information by selecting and reporting the main features, and make comparisons where relevant.

Write at least 150 words.

Causes of worldwide land degradation

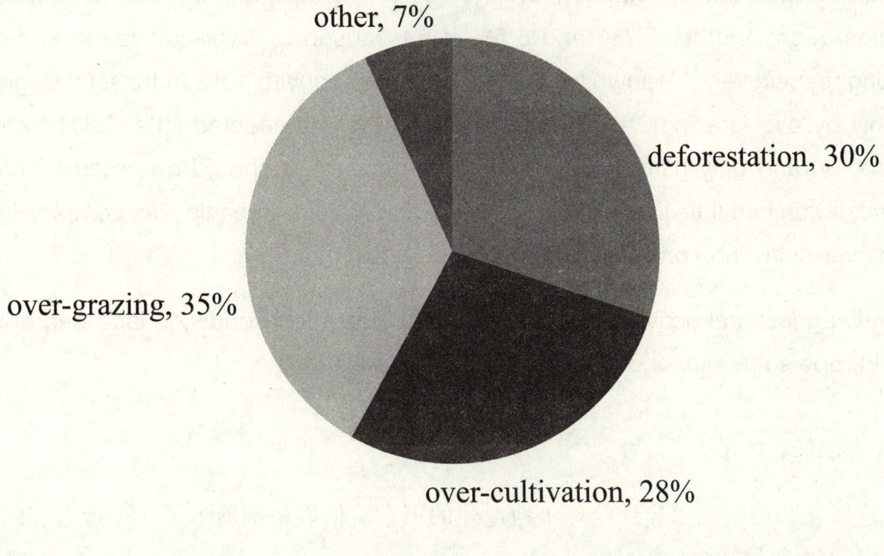

Causes of land degradation by region

Region	% land degraded by...			
	deforestation	over-cultivation	over-grazing	Total land degraded
North America	0.2	3.3	1.5	5%
Europe	9.8	7.7	5.5	23%
Oceania*	1.7	0	11.3	13%

* *A large group of islands in the South Pacific including Australia and New Zealand.*（资料来源：根据《剑桥雅思考试全真试题集8》Test 1的图表重新绘制。）

▶ 范文（178 words）

The pie chart illustrates the factors leading to global land degradation, while the table demonstrates how three different places were affected (by these factors) in the 1990s.

As can be seen, over-grazing is the most important cause for land degradation, which is responsible for 35% of the degraded land worldwide. In contrast, 30% of land degradation is blamed for deforestation, while another 28% and 7% are attributed to over-cultivation and "other reasons" respectively.

In reference to the table, in the 1990s Europe was affected the most with 23% of the land degraded. Specifically, while 9.8% of the land degradation is because of deforestation, another 7.7% and 5.5% were caused by over-cultivation and over-grazing respectively. Meanwhile, Oceania followed up with 13% of the land degraded (mainly by over-grazing). As for North America, it was affected little (3.3% for over-cultivation and only half the figure for over-grazing). It should be noted that while deforestation had little impact on North America (0.2%), Oceania was completely free from over-cultivation problems.

Overall, agricultural activities are the leading causes for worldwide land degradation and Europe suffers the most.

【参考译文】

这幅饼状图表明了导致全球土地退化的因素，而表格则展示了三个地方在20世纪90年代受影响的程度。

如图所示，过度放牧是导致土地退化最主要的原因，得为全世界35%的土地退化负责。相比之下，30%的土地退化是由于乱砍滥伐导致的，而剩下的28%及7%分别是由过度耕作和其他因素引起的。

说到表格，20世纪90年代欧洲受影响最严重，有23%的土地退化。具体而言，9.8%的土地退化是由于乱砍滥伐导致的，而过度耕作和过度放牧则分别导致了7.7%和5.5%的土地退化。同时，大洋洲以13%的土地退化排在欧洲之后（主要是过度放牧所致）。至于北美，它受到的影响很小（过度耕作造成3.3%的土地退化，而过度放牧所导致的土地退化更是减半）。应该指出的是，乱砍滥伐对北美几乎没造成什么影响（0.2%），而大洋洲则完全免受过度耕作的干扰。

总体而言，农业活动是导致全球土地退化最主要的原因，而欧洲遭受的影响最为严重。

备注

1. 题目有两个句子，而作文的开头段将其改写成一个句子，诀窍就在于while这个单词。
2. 与前面饼状图的专题一样，这里在写饼状图时也没有记流水账式地记录各个标签的数据，而是结合实际情况进行了改写。
3. 表格中有两个特殊的数据：0.2%及0%，务必要灵活转换相应信息。

CHAPTER 12
雅思写作Task 1　G类

一、G类小作文简介

G类小作文是书信写作，要求考生在20分钟左右的时间内至少写150词。

（一）书信分类

按书信类型划分，G类书信写作主要有以下几类：

- 投诉信：一般是投诉某次不愉快的经历或者是某个产品的质量，例如向酒店经理投诉房间问题，向航空公司经理投诉与空乘人员的矛盾，向房东抱怨家具问题或者是投诉其他租客太吵等等。
- 申请信：主要是求职信、申请奖学金或者是申请宿舍的信件。有时，这类信件也包括向你的前雇主或者学校教授请求一封reference letter（推荐信）。
- 推荐信：一般是应朋友之邀，给他/她写封推荐信。
- 建议信：比较常考的有给图书馆、机场建设主管单位写工作建议，又或者是给朋友写信提供建议。
- 邀请信：一般是给朋友写信，邀请朋友来你的家乡度假并将假期安排告诉对方，或是邀请朋友来参加你的聚会/婚礼并将活动安排告诉对方。
- 说明信：一般是向银行、校长、生意伙伴或者是朋友解释某件事情，而这件事情一般是存在误会或者是需要更改时间的；或者是给报社写信反映某个社会问题，等等。
- 询问信：例如给朋友写信询问某个课程，又或者是向某个单位咨询某项服务。
- 感谢信：考查频率比较高的是给朋友写信表示感谢。
- 道歉信：例如向房东或者朋友道歉。
- 寻物信：例如行李落在飞机上，写信给航空公司找回失物。

……

按收信人的身份划分，G类书信写作主要有以下几类：

- ××部门经理/主管：如酒店经理、银行经理、学校校长等。
- ××机关单位：如报社、图书馆等。
- 陌生人或是不太熟悉的人：如宿舍管理员、房东、邻居等。
- 朋友：考查频率非常高，通常是写给一位朋友，偶尔是写给一群朋友。

……

按文体划分，G类书信写作主要有以下几类：

- 正式文体：如给酒店经理写投诉信。
- 半正式文体：如给房东写信。
- 非正式文体：如给朋友写信。

▶ 样题

GENERAL WRITING TASK 1

You should spend about 20 minutes on this task.

> ***Last month you had a holiday overseas where you stayed with some friends. They have just sent you some photos of your holiday.***
>
> ***Write a letter to your friends. In your letter:***
>
> - ***thank them for the photos and for the holiday***
> - ***explain why you didn't write earlier***
> - ***invite them to come and stay with you***

You should write at least 150 words.
You do NOT need to write your own address.
Begin your letter as follows:

Dear …………… ,

（资料来源：《剑桥雅思考试全真试题集7》）

（二）评分标准

G类Task 1的评分标准包括以下四项：

- Task achievement
- Coherence and cohesion

- Lexical resource
- Grammatical range and accuracy

（详细评分标准请参照本书附录）

（三）注意事项

1. 一定要明确书信的写作目的（即purpose）。很多国内考生在写书信作文时往往一上来就写一大堆客套话或者是很多细节信息。但事实上，考生需要开门见山地指出写这封信的目的是什么。例如：

- 向上司请假：I am writing to request some unpaid leave next month.

2. 有必要的话，稍作自我介绍，但一定要简洁。例如：

- 给房东写抱怨/投诉信：I am your tenant from Flat 3 on Riverside Street. We met each other when I signed the rental agreement in your office. I have lived here for 6 months now and I am writing to complain about some of the furniture.

3. G类书信的写作文体及语调至关重要。考生在写G类书信时需要根据与收件人的关系来决定使用哪种文体，即正式文体（formal style）、半正式文体（semi-formal style）及非正式文体（informal style）。每种文体都有其相应的方式来称呼对方，正文的语言风格也需视文体风格而定，而书信最后的落笔也要与该信件的文体风格一致。广大G类考生面临的挑战是：

①如何判断某种书信的文体风格；

②如何确定文中所用的语言表达是否符合该信件所实际需要的风格；

③如何确保全文文体风格的一致性。

对于这些，考生必须确保多读考官以及native speakers的书信范文，并认真琢磨其用词。熟能生巧（Practice makes perfect），外语学习靠的就是模仿。

4. 注意时态。有些书信内容涉及到过去的事件，此时考生需要使用相应的过去时态进行写作，例如感谢信、道歉信、投诉信等。

二、G类书信写作攻略

正如前文所言，G类书信类别繁多、文体各异，考生在写作时务必规划好所要回应的内容及相应的语言。

文体风格

考生拿到题目后一定要先判断究竟该用哪种文体风格进行写作，这在评分标准中（Task Achievement）有明确要求。简言之，G类书信的文体风格特点可大致参考下表：

文体风格	对象	称呼	落款
正式文体	与对方素未谋面且不知晓其姓名	Dear Sir or Madam,	Yours faithfully,
半正式文体	未曾谋面或泛泛之交，知其姓氏	Dear Mr. Smith, Dear Ms. Thompson,	Yours sincerely,
非正式文体	朋友	Dear John,	Cheers,/Best wishes, /See you soon,

开头段的常用句型（资料来源：《剑桥雅思考试全真试题集1–10》）

G类考生最好在书信的首段就说明写信目的。针对不同的目的及文体风格，考生需要使用不同的句型表达。比较常见的有：

- 给图书馆写信解释为何借书逾期未还：I am writing this letter to explain why I have been unable to return the three books I have out on three-day loan.
- 写给上司请假：I am writing to request some unpaid leave next month.
- 给上司写信推迟入职：I am writing concerning the position of Assistant Office Manager that I am due to begin next Monday. However, a problem has arisen.
- 告知朋友搬家：I'm writing to let you know that at last we have moved into a bigger house!
- 写信卖家具给朋友：As you know, we'll be moving to a new house soon and there are a few things that I won't be able to take with me. The new house is a bit smaller so I have to sell some furniture and I was wondering if you might be interested.
- 写信告知朋友你的新工作：I hope this finds you and your family well, and I'm sorry I haven't been in touch recently. I'm writing now to let you know about my new job.
- 就噪音问题写信向邻居道歉：I was very shocked to get your letter saying that the noise from my flat has been spoiling your evenings and causing you some distress. I am really, really sorry about that. I had no idea that you would be able to hear so much, so I hope you will accept my apologies.
- 给银行经理写信解释账单有误：I am writing in reply to a letter I received from you a few days ago. In your letter you state that I am $240 overdrawn and that you will be charging me $70.

- 给房东写抱怨/投诉信：I am your tenant from Flat 3 on Riverside Street. We met each other when I signed the rental agreement in your office. I have lived here for 6 months now and I am writing to complain about some of the furniture.
- 写信给朋友请求推荐兼职工作：I was wondering if you could ask around among your friends and colleagues to see if anyone wants a house-cleaner, gardener, or nanny for their children.

结尾常用的高分句型（资料来源：《剑桥雅思考试全真试题集1–10》）

G类书信的结尾部分一般要根据写信目的再次向对方表达感谢、抱歉、静候佳音，或者是希望对方采纳建议之类，最后再落款署名。比较常见的表达法有：

- 给图书馆写信解释为何借书逾期未还：Bearing in mind the circumstances, I trust you will kindly waive any fines that may have accumulated.
- 写给上司请假：I would be very grateful if you could allow me this time. These few days are very important to my parents and the whole family, and it would be a way to thank them for all the support they have given me.
- 给上司写信推迟入职：I would like to emphasize that I remain very keen to work with you, and that I will be gaining further useful experience during this time. I look forward to hearing from you.
- 告知朋友搬家：Our new address and phone number are below, so give us a call and let us know when to expect you.
- 写信卖家具给朋友：Why don't you come around and take another look at them on Saturday? ... Give me a ring and let me know.
- 写信告知朋友你的新工作：Anyway, I have to sop now because my sister is staying with me and has brought my baby nephew to meet me. She sends you lots of love and is asking when we can all meet up. Soon, I hope.
- 就噪音问题写信向邻居道歉：Sorry to have caused these problems.
- 给房东写抱怨/投诉信：Looking forward to hearing from you.
- 写信给朋友请求推荐兼职工作：I'd be so grateful. I look forward to seeing you soon.

（一）非正式书信 Informal letters

非正式书信，顾名思义，是写给熟人，例如朋友的，故它的语言要随意。非正式文体的书信主要有以下特点：

- 称呼时直呼其名；
- 可以写缩写；

- 正文像是拉家常；
- 结尾和落款很随意。

Question 1——给朋友写信表示感谢

GENERAL WRITING TASK 1

You should spend about 20 minutes on this task.

Last month you had a holiday overseas where you stayed with some friends. They have just sent you some photos of your holiday.   ***Write a letter to your friends. In your letter:***   • ***thank them for the photos and for the holiday***   • ***explain why you didn't write earlier***   • ***invite them to come and stay with you***

You should write at least 150 words.
You do NOT need to write your own address.
Begin your letter as follows:

Dear .... ,

（资料来源：《剑桥雅思考试全真试题集7》General Training Test B）

▶ 范文（149 words）

Dear Taufik and Lina,

I'm so glad receiving your photos when we were in Singapore. The photos are so nice and bright. They remind me for my special holiday with you.

I'm sorry because I don't write a letter to you as soon as possible. After I came back to Melbourne, my boss asked me to had two weeks training in Wellington, New Zealand. I don't have any time to tell you because it happened suddenly.

My company wants to change the system of the computer into the online system. All of the staffs must have training first, before the system running.

I hope you can come and stay with me during next holiday. My address is: 888 Little Collins

Street, Melbourne, Victoria, 3000. You can contact me first if you have a plan to visit.

Thanks for your kindness and I'm looking forward for your reply.

Yours sincerely,

Victor

【参考译文】

亲爱的Taufik和Lina，

我很开心收到我们在新加坡时的照片。这些照片非常棒。它们让我想起了与你们一起度过的特殊假期。

很抱歉我没能尽早给你们写信。我回到墨尔本之后，我的老板就让我去新西兰的威灵顿参加两周的培训。我没时间告诉你们这些，因为一切发生得太突然了。

我的公司想要更换为在线的电脑系统。在这个系统运行之前，所有的员工都必须先培训。

我希望你们下次度假来我这儿。我的地址是：（澳大利亚）维多利亚州墨尔本Little Collins街888号（邮编3000）。如果你们打算来，请提前联系我。

谢谢你们的友好，敬候佳音。

您真诚的，

Victor

备注

1. 这是《剑桥雅思考试全真试题集7》中所收录的一篇考生作文。这封书信比较大的两个问题是：三个小点处理得不协调，第一点与第三点基本一笔带过，相比之下，第二点则显得比较啰唆。信件总体的文体和语调都是很随意的，符合要求，但是最后却变得比较正式，这就显得不太妥当。
2. 考官给这篇作文的评分是5.0。具体的评语为：This answer does not cover the bullets well because there are no thanks for the holiday and giving the address is not logical in the context. The second bullet is given rather too much focus, so the purpose of the letter is less clear, and the tone is inappropriate at the

end of the letter. The introduction is organized according to the ordering of the task, and although few linkers are used, there is some clear referencing. The range of vocabulary is rather restricted, but generally sufficient for the task, although inappropriacies and some word form errors occur. A mix of structures is attempted but short, simple sentences are frequent. Control of tenses and verb phrases is weak in more complex structures and this impacts on the message at time.

▶ 笔者范文（177 words）

Dear Lucy and Lily,

I've just received the photos you sent me. Thanks. Also, thanks for giving me such a wonderful holiday.

Sorry that I haven't been in touch for a while. Here is why: the second day ofter I returned, my boss sent me to a training course in New Zealand. It happened so suddenly that I didn't really have time to keep you posted. In fact, I just came back to New York yesterday and I wasn't even ready for the Halloween as it's only one week away.

Hey, you know what? Why don't you just pack up and come to New York? I know you have always wanted to see the Central Park, the Empire State Building and the Statue of Liberty. We could also go to see some Broadway shows. And oh, isn't Lily a big fan of the Brooklyn Bridge? Well, it's right here in Manhattan.

Thanks again. For your next holiday please come and stay with me. Just give me a call and I'll take care of the rest.

Cheers,

John

【参考译文】

亲爱的Lucy和Lily，

我刚刚收到了你们寄来的照片。多谢。同时，也谢谢你们给了我一个那么愉快的假期。

抱歉我这么久都没跟你们联系。情况是这样的：我回去后的第二天就被我老板派到了新西兰参加培训。一切太突然了，我都没时间告诉你们。我其实昨天刚回到纽约。还有一周就是万圣节了，我还没准备好呢。

嘿，不如你们两个打包来纽约吧？我知道你们一直想来看看中央公园、帝国大厦和自由女神像。我们还可以一起去看百老汇的表演。对了，Lily不是超级喜欢布鲁克林大桥吗？它就在曼哈顿。

再次谢谢你们。下次度假一定要来我这儿。你们只要给我打个电话就行，其他的我来搞定。

回见，

John

高分词汇精选 Word Bank

序号	词汇	意思 / 用法
1	Sorry that...	很抱歉……
2	be in touch	保持联系
3	for a while	有一阵子
4	keep someone posted	告诉某人
5	Why don't you...	何不……（表建议）
6	a big fan of	喜欢……
7	take care of	照顾；处理
8	cheers	熟人之间道别时或者表达感激时用

Question 2——给朋友写信告知近况

GENERAL WRITING TASK 1

You should spend about 20 minutes on this task.

You have recently started to work in a new company.

Write a letter to an English-speaking friend. In your letter,

- ***explain why you changed jobs***
- ***describe your new job***
- ***tell him / her your other news***

You should write at least 150 words.
You do NOT need to write your own address.
Begin your letter as follows:

Dear .... ,

（资料来源：《剑桥雅思考试全真试题集7》General Training Test A）

▶ 范文（241 words）

Dear Nigel,

I hope this letter finds you well, and sorry that I haven't been in touch for a while. I'm writing to let you know about my new job.

I quit my last job two months ago. Now you might be surprised because my last job was easy and I had two days off each week. Plus, it provided the job security that most people wanted. But you see that's the problem. I hate those nine-to-five desk jobs. Everyday back then, I was just repeating myself like a dead person, and there was no one I could talk to. It was dull and boring.

Now the new job that I got last month is awesome. The hours are great and the money is not bad. Everyday, I teach kids English and it makes me feel like being a human being. You know, you talk to them, make jokes and laugh with them. It is fun. And my workmates are very nice, no office politics at all.

There is one more thing that I'd like you to know. I'm getting married next month. I proposed last week and my girlfriend was so touched and she kept saying "yes, yes, yes". I wish you were there mate, you'd be happy for me. Now my fiancée and I are planning our wedding and we'd like to invite you to come. For more details, we'll keep you posted.

Take care and I'll see you soon.

John

【参考译文】

亲爱的Nigel，

见信好。很抱歉很久没跟你联系了。我现在要告诉你我的新工作。

我两个月前辞掉了上份工作。也许你会惊讶，毕竟我的上一份工作很轻松，每周双休。而且，工作稳定，很多人梦寐以求还来不及呢。不过这正是问题所在。我讨厌这种朝九晚五的办公室工作。上一份工作，我每天都像行尸走肉般地重复自己，也没人可以聊天，整天太无聊了。

而我现在的这份新工作非常酷。上班时间轻松而且薪水不错。每天，我教小孩子英语。我这才找回了做人的感觉。我可以每天和他们聊天，开开玩笑，同他们一起大笑，非常好玩。而且，我的同事们很好，完全没有钩心斗角这类事。

还有一件事情我想告诉你，我下个月要结婚了。我上个礼拜向我的女朋友求婚，她非常感动，不停地说"我愿意"。我真希望你当时也在，你会为我感到开心的。我未婚妻和我现在在规划我们的婚礼，我们想邀请你来参加。更多细节我会再联系你。

注意身体，我们回头见。

John

备注

1. 坦白讲，这篇作文有两点遗憾：一是字数太长，二是最后一条信息极具爆炸性以至于有可能盖过其他所有信息。不过，它仍不失为一篇好的作文供考生们参考。
2. 本文的语调十分随意，除了称呼与落款外，其他的语言也很符合非正式书信的要求，尤其是以下方面：第一段中的sorry that...，第二段中的now you might be surprised...but you see that's the problem，第三段中的now the new job I got last month is awesome...you know，第四段中的I wish you were there mate...we'll keep you posted，以及结尾处的take care and I'll see you soon。

高分词汇精选 Word Bank

序号	词汇	意思/用法
1	I hope this letter finds you well.	见信好。

序号	词汇	意思/用法
2	day off	休息日
3	job security	工作稳定性
4	nine-to-five	朝九晚五的
5	dull and boring	无聊的
6	awesome	非常棒（口语）
7	(working) hours	上班时间
8	workmate	同事
9	office politics	办公室政治/同事间的钩心斗角
10	propose	求婚
11	be touched	被感动
12	fiancée	未婚妻
13	mate	澳洲、新西兰对朋友的称呼

（二）半正式书信Semi-formal letters

半正式书信一般是写给那些见过面却又交往不深的人，如房东、学校老师或者新邻居的。一般来讲，写信人知道收信人的姓氏。半正式文体的书信用词已经开始向正式文体靠拢了。这类书信主要有以下特点：

- 称呼一般会写“尊敬的 × × 先生/女士”，如Dear Mr. Smith；
- 不可以写缩写，如I'm要写成I am；
- 正文的语调要相对正式，如不说Thanks，而说Thank you；
- 结尾和落款也要带有敬意，一般用Yours sincerely。

Question 1——给大学宿管科写信申请宿舍

GENERAL WRITING TASK 1

You should spend about 20 minutes on this task.

You are going on a short training course at a college in Sydney, Australia. You need somewhere to live while you are there.

Write a letter to the accommodation officer at the college. In your letter:

- ***explain your situation***
- ***describe the accommodation you require***
- ***say when you will need it***

You should write at least 150 words.
You do NOT need to write your own address.
Begin your letter as follows:

Dear .... ,

（资料来源：摘自 http://www.goodluckielts.com/sample-IELTS-letter-005.html，原始来源不详。）

▶ 范文（204 words）

Dear Ms. Gates,

I am a Chinese student to attend a crash course in TESOL in your college and I am writing to request for accommodation for the course duration.

As I have said, I am from China and so I would be grateful if you could arrange a room with kitchen so that I could cook myself. With due respect, but I do not think I will like the local food. I would see it as a bonus if there is a washing machine for me to do my laundry. But please do not feel any pressure because it is not a must. I do not mind sharing a room with someone else, but I would appreciate if you get me a roommate who does not smoke because I am a bit allergic to it. Now since this is my first time to visit Sydney, I was wondering if you could kindly provide me with a local map.

The course is expected to start from October 7 to October 20 and I will be arriving at the school on October 6. Therefore, if you could get the room ready before that it would help me a lot.

Thank you in advance and look forward to hearing from you.

Yours sincerely,

Michael

【参考译文】

尊敬的Gates女士，

我是到贵校参加TESOL速成课程的一名中国学生。我写信是想申请这期间的住宿。

正如我所说，我来自中国，因此如果您能够给我安排一间带厨房的房间好让我自己做饭的话，我将非常感激。我无意冒犯，但是我觉得自己不会喜欢您当地的食物。如果房间里有洗衣机洗衣服的话那就更锦上添花了。不过这不是必须的，因此请不要感到有任何压力。我不介意同他人共用一个房间，但您若能给我安排不抽烟的舍友我会非常感激，因为我对香烟有些过敏。另外，由于这是我第一次到悉尼，所以不知道您能否给我准备一张当地的地图。

该课程预计10月7日开始到10月20日结束，因此我会在10月6日到校。如果您能在此之前就将房间准备好，那会帮到我很多。

我提前向您表示感谢，敬候您的佳音。

您真诚的，

Michael

备注

1. 应该说，本文回应了题目要求写作的所有信息。
2. 文体风格偏正式，但是还能找到相对不那么正式的表达，例如称呼、落款及正文中的and so...get me a room...now since...it would help me a lot等。

高分词汇精选 Word Bank

序号	词汇	意思/用法
1	crash course	速成课程
2	accommodation	住宿

序号	词汇	意思/用法
3	be grateful	心存感激
4	with due respect	无意冒犯
5	bonus	福利
6	laundry	待洗或已经洗好的衣物
7	Don't feel any pressure.	别有什么负担。
8	must	必需品
9	I would appreciate if you could...	若您能……我会非常感激。
10	be allergic to...	对……过敏
11	in advance	提前
12	Look forward to hearing from you.	敬候佳音。

Question 2——写信给房东抱怨邻居太吵

GENERAL WRITING TASK 1

You should spend about 20 minutes on this task.

You have been living in a rental apartment for the past year. Recently a new neighbour moved in and has been making a lot of noise, which disturbs you.

Write a letter to the landlord. In your letter:

- ***explain the situation***
- ***describe why it bothers you***
- ***suggest a solution***

You should write at least 150 words.

You do NOT need to write your own address.

Begin your letter as follows:

Dear .... ,

（资料来源：《剑桥雅思考试全真试题集5》General Training Test A）

范文（181 words）

Dear Mr. Homer,

I am the Chinese tenant who has lived in your property on 10 Lakeside Road for the past year, and I am writing to complain about this new tenant and the noise he makes.

Every night my new neighbor plays loud music very late and he often throws parties till early morning. It is very noisy especially at late night. I tried to talk to him but he didn't even care.

Now the noise has turned my life and work into a nightmare. I could barely sleep at night and was diagnosed with insomnia. Every day I don't have the appetite for food and I feel dizzy at work. My supervisor said that if I kept acting like that he would have to fire me.

I would like you to reinforce house rules you have made for all tenants and I hope you can talk to this selfish guy to let him know that you do not welcome him unless he changes. Otherwise, I will have to call the police.

Thank you in advance and look forward to hearing from you.

Yours sincerely,

Allen

【参考译文】

尊敬的Homer先生，

我是您湖滨路10号的中国租户，我在这里已经住了一年了。我写信是要投诉您的新租户和他制造的噪音。

每天晚上，这位新邻居都播放喧闹的音乐直到深夜，还经常狂欢到凌晨。在深夜真的是非常吵闹。我曾试着和他沟通，但他根本不在乎。

他的噪音让我的生活和工作变成了噩梦。我晚上无法入睡，被诊断为失眠。我每天都食不下咽，工作也无精打采。我的主管说如果我再这样下去就要解雇我。

我希望您能够加强您给所有租客制定的规矩。我也希望您能够跟这个自私的家伙谈一谈，让他明白如果他再不思悔改您就不欢迎他。否则的话，我只好报警了。

提前向您表示感谢，并敬候佳音。

您真诚的，

Allen

备注

1. 给房东写信一般会采用半正式的文体。
2. 由于房东可能有好几处房产，所以最好在开头做个简要的自我介绍。
3. 一般来讲，投诉信通常会针对已经发生的事情进行描述，故要用一般过去时。不过，本文并没有太侧重使用过去时，因为这位邻居的行为一直没停止过。

高分词汇精选 Word Bank

序号	词汇	意思/用法
1	tenant	租客
2	property	房产，财产
3	complain about	抱怨
4	loud music	喧闹的音乐
5	throw parties	举办派对
6	early morning	凌晨
7	late night	深夜
8	nightmare	噩梦
9	be diagnosed with	被诊断出
10	insomnia	失眠
11	appetite	胃口
12	feel dizzy	头晕目眩
13	supervisor	主管
14	reinforce	加强，强化
15	house rules	指房主定下的规矩

（三）正式书信 Formal letters

正式书信，主要是写给某些单位的管理层，如餐厅经理等。由于写信人与收信人素未谋面，因此书信用词讲究，言简意赅。大体说来，正式文体的书信主要有以下特点：

- 称呼一般用Dear Sir or Madam；
- 绝对不可以写缩写；
- 正文的语调要正式，内容要言简意赅；
- 结尾和落款一般是感谢对方抽空查阅信件，敬候佳音，并署名Yours faithfully。

Question 1——写投诉信给酒店经理

GENERAL WRITING TASK 1

You should spend about 20 minutes on this task.

You recently stayed in a hotel in a large city. The weather was very unusual for the time of year and the heating / cooling system in the hotel was quite inadequate.

Write a letter to the manager of the hotel. In your letter:

- ***give details of what went wrong***
- ***explain what you had to do to overcome the problem at the time***
- ***say what action you would like the manager to take***

You should write at least 150 words.
You do NOT need to write your own address.
Begin your letter as follows:

Dear .... ,

（资料来源：摘自 http://testbig.com/，原始来源不详。）

▶ 范文（198 words）

Dear Sir or Madam,

I am writing to complain about an extremely unpleasant experience of the service in your Four Seasons Hotel on the 19th and 20th of December.

I was attending a conference and booked a double room for two nights in your hotel. However, the heating system in my room did not work and it was freezing at night that I caught a bad cold the first night. When I complained to the reception, they promised me to send technicians to fix it but they did not. I asked the reception to get me another room and was told that all your rooms were booked up and that there was nothing they could do about it.

To stay warm, I had to stay in my conference room all day and put on all the thick clothes I packed in my suitcase and asked for an extra quilt at night, which I think is ridiculous.

Now I would like you to pay my medical bill, give me a full refund and get me a luxury room for one night as compensation. I trust you would properly handle my request and give me an early reply before I complain to higher authority.

Yours faithfully,

Tracy McCredie

【参考译文】

尊敬的先生/女士，

我来信是要投诉我在12月19日和20日在您的四季酒店所遭遇的糟糕经历。

我当时为参加一个会议而预定了两晚的双人间。但是，我房间里的供热系统坏了。晚上房间冷得要命，我当晚就感冒了，而且很严重。当我向前台反映这个问题时，他们承诺派技术人员来维修，但是根本没人来修。我让前台给我安排另一间房间，却被告知所有房间都被订满了，他们无能为力。

为了保暖，我不得不整天待在会议室；晚上我将我带来的所有厚衣服都穿上并额外要了一条被子。这实在是太荒谬了。

我希望您支付我的医药费，给我全额退款，并安排一晚豪华间的住宿给我作为补偿。我相信在我向更高层反映这个问题之前，您会恰当地处理我的请求并尽早给我回复。

您诚挚的，

Tracy McCredie

▷ 备注

1. 写投诉信时，即使很愤怒也得把握好语气，千万不要破口大骂对方。毕竟，管理层也不希望发生这种不愉快的经历。

2. 描述不愉快的遭遇时要切换到过去时，而且内容要具体。

3. 向对方提要求时可以理直气壮甚至威胁对方，但仍要拿捏好分寸。

高分词汇精选 Word Bank

序号	词汇	意思/用法
1	attend a conference	开会
2	book	预订
3	double room	双人间
4	freezing	非常寒冷的
5	catch a cold	感冒
6	complain	抱怨，投诉
7	reception	接待处，前台
8	technician	技术人员
9	fix	维修
10	pack	打包，包装
11	suitcase	行李箱
12	quilt	被褥
13	refund	退款
14	luxury room	豪华间
15	compensation	赔偿
16	higher authority	（单位的）更高层

Question 2——写建议信给交通部门

GENERAL WRITING TASK 1

You should spend about 20 minutes on this task.

> ***There have been some problems with the public transport in your area recently.***
>
> ***Write a letter to the manager of the transport company. In your letter:***
>
> - ***describe the problems***
> - ***explain how these problems are affecting the public***
> - ***suggest some changes that could be made***

You should write at least 150 words.
You do NOT need to write your own address.
Begin your letter as follows:

Dear .... ,

（资料来源：摘自 http://vkjournal.ru/doc/1917527，原始来源不详。）

▶ 范文（187 words）

Dear Sir or Madam,

I am a local resident living near the Stadium Park and I am writing to inform you the problems with the public transport and suggest some solutions.

I have been riding with Bus Route 9 for the past few years and it has always been efficient and punctual. Recently, however, the buses have always been late, and to make matters worse the delay is unpredictable. Meanwhile, the buses are much more crowded than before. As a consequence, we the passengers have been negatively affected as we are constantly late for work recently. Some people are given oral warnings by their supervisors or even fined for that.

To improve the situation, I would suggest that you set up a team and look into it. I also recommend that you increase the number of buses running this route so that our commuting will be as easy and punctual as it used to be. I would also suggest you develop an app to provide real-time bus information online so all the passengers can better organize their time when catching a bus.

Thank you and look forward to hearing from you.

Yours faithfully,

Bruce Hanks

【参考译文】

尊敬的先生/女士，

我是家住体育场公园附近的一位居民，我来信是要告诉您公共交通存在的一些问题并提出一些解决方案。

过去几年我一直乘坐9路公交车，它非常高效准时。但是，最近这条线路的公交车经常晚点；而且更糟的是，每次晚点的时间都不固定。此外，最近的公交车也比以前更拥挤了。很多乘客因此深受影响，因为大家最近经常迟到。有些人被主管口头警告过，甚至有人因此被罚款了。

要解决这些问题，我建议您成立督察队进行调查。同时，我建议增加这条线路的公交车数量。这样的话，我们的上下班就会轻松很多。此外，我还建议你们开发app应用程序在线提供实时的公交信息。这样，赶公交的乘客就可以更好地安排出行。

谢谢！静候佳音。

您真诚的，

Bruce Hanks

备注

1. 本文简要地做了自我介绍，主要是让收信人知道具体是哪个区域的公交系统出了问题，文中提到Bus Route 9也是出于同样的目的。

2. 由于该问题已经持续了一段时间并且尚未解决，所以本文较多地使用了现在完成时。

高分词汇精选 Word Bank

序号	词汇	意思/用法
1	inform	告知
2	bus route	公交路线
3	punctual	准时的，守时的
4	delay	延误
5	unpredictable	无法预测的
6	as a consequence	因此
7	constantly	持续性地，经常
8	oral warning	口头警告
9	fine	罚款
10	to improve the situation	改善局面
11	set up	成立
12	look into	调查
13	recommend	推荐
14	commuting	通勤
15	app	手机应用程序
16	real-time	实时的
17	organize one's time	安排时间

附录1
最新雅思写作考试近十年完整题库

（一）雅思议论文

▶ 教育篇

1. Some people think university education should prepare students for employment. Other people think university has other functions. Discuss both views and what you think the function of university education should be.

2. Many people believe that the main aim for university education is to help graduates to find better jobs, while some people believe that university education has wider benefits for individual and society. Discuss both views and give your opinion.

3. Some people think the main purpose of schools is to turn children into good citizens and workers, rather than to benefit them as individuals. To what extent do you agree or disagree with this opinion?

4. Some people think that universities should provide graduates with knowledge and skills needed in the workplace, while others argue that the main function of a university is to teach students theoretical knowledge. What's your opinion?

5. Some people think universities should provide graduates with the knowledge and skills needed in the workplace in the future. Others think the true function of the university is to give access to knowledge for its own sake. What do you think are the main functions of a university?

6. It is generally believed that education is vital for the development of individuals

and the well-being of society. How can education fulfill both of these functions?

7. Some people think that teachers should be responsible for teaching students how to judge right and wrong and how to behave well. Some say that teachers should only teach students academic subjects. Discuss both views and give your opinion.

8. In some countries, secondary schools aim to provide a general education across a range of subjects. In others, children focus on a narrow range of subjects related to a particular career. For today's world, which system is more appropriate?

9. It is often said that the subjects taught in schools are too academic in orientation and that it would be more useful for children to learn about practical matters such as home management, work and interpersonal skills. To what extent do you agree or disagree?

10. Nowadays, more university students choose to study some practical subjects (such as marketing, computer programming, etc.) instead of theoretical subjects (such as economics, math, and chemistry). Some people suggest that universities should focus on practical subjects, but not theoretical subjects. What's your opinion?

11. Some people think secondary students should study international news as a school subject, but others argue that it is a waste of their valuable school time. What's your opinion?

12. Some people believe history has little or nothing to tell people. Others believe people must study history to understand the present. What's your opinion?

13. Children who find the subjects such as maths and philosophy difficult should not be made to study these. These subjects should be optional rather than compulsory. To what extent do you agree with the statement?

14. Schools should teach children some academic subjects which will be beneficial to their future careers. Therefore, other subjects such as music and sports are not important. To what extent do you agree or disagree with this opinion?

15. The qualities of being successful can not be learnt in university. To what extent do you agree or disagree?

16. Some people think that school should put students in different classes according to their academic ability, while some others believe that students of different abilities should be educated together. Discuss both views and give your own opinion.

17. Some people think that schools should select pupils according to their academic abilities, while others believe that it is better to have pupils with different abilities study together. Discuss both views and give your own opinion.

18. Some people think it is better for children to attend boarding schools while others believe day schools are better. Discuss both views and give your own opinion. (OR, Boarding schools are becoming popular. Why is the case? Do you think it is a positive or negative trend? OR, Is it better for students to live at home with their parents or in school accommodations?)

19. Some people think that it is beneficial for students to go to the private secondary school, but other people think that it can have a negative effect. Discuss the two points and give your own opinion.

20. In the past, lectures were used as a way of teaching large numbers of students, but now with the development of technology for education, many people think there is no justification for attending lectures. To what extent do you agree or disagree?

21. Computers are increasingly used in education. In which areas do you think computers are more important and in which areas are teachers more important?

22. Some people believe that computers and the Internet can take the place of schools, while others contend that teachers play an important role in schools. Discuss both views and give your opinion.

23. Many people use distance-learning programs (study material post, TV, the Internet, etc.) to study at home, but some people think that it cannot bring the benefit as much as attending college or university. To what extent do you agree or disagree with this opinion?

24. School teachers used to be the source of information; however, some people argue that teachers are not as important as before with the increasing variety of information resources. What is your opinion?

25. Some people think students learn far more from class with teachers than other resources, such as the Internet and television. Do you agree or disagree?

26. Some people believe that the teaching method with a teacher and students in a classroom will not exist by the year 2050. To what extent do you agree or disagree?

27. Once children start school, teachers have more influence than parents on their intellectual and social development. To what extent do you agree or disagree?

28. Some people believe that a country benefits greatly from a high percentage of young people who go to university, while others argue that it only leads to graduate unemployment. Discuss both views and give your opinion.

29. Some people think that studying in college or university is the best way for students to prepare for their future career. But others think they should leave school as soon as possible to develop their career through work experience. Discuss both views and give your own opinion.

30. Students from poor background such as rural areas often find it difficult to access to university education, so people think universities should make it especially easy for them to study at. To what extent do you agree or disagree?

31. Some people think students should take the subjects which are decided by the government in the university. Others think that students can apply for the subjects they prefer. Discuss the two situations and give your opinion.

32. More and more students choose to go to another country to finish their higher education. Do you think the advantages outweigh the disadvantages?

33. In some countries, some high school leavers are choosing to work or travel for a period of time before going to university. Do the advantages outweigh the disadvantages? Give your own opinion and reasons using your own experience.

34. In some countries parents expect their children to spend long time studying in school and after school. What are the positive or negative effects on children and the society they live in?

▶ 环境篇

1. Many people think cheap air travel should be encouraged because it gives ordinary people freedom to travel further. However, others think this leads to environmental problems, so air travel should be more expensive in order to discourage people from having it. Discuss both views and give your own opinion.

2. Some people believe that air travel should be restricted because it causes serious pollution and uses up the world's fuel resources. To what extent do you agree or disagree?

3. Long distance flight uses more fuel than car and brings pollution to the environment. We should discourage non-essential flight (such as tourist travel) rather than limit the use of car. To what extent do you agree or disagree?

4. Some people think it is beneficial that traveling by air is becoming cheaper and cheaper, while other people think it has drawbacks to environment and the recourses of the world. Discuss both views and give your own opinion.

5. Many people think it is very important to protect the environment, but they make no effort to do it themselves. Why does it happen? How to solve this problem?

6. Many people realize the importance of protecting the environment. But they still make no effort to do it. Why is the case? What can individuals do to improve the situation?

7. Individuals can do nothing to improve the environment. Only governments and large companies can make a difference. To what extent do you agree or disagree with this opinion?

8. Some people believe that environmental problems are too big for individuals to deal with, while others think that individuals should take some actions. Discuss both views and give your opinion.

9. Environmental problems are too big for individual countries and individual people to address; we have reached the stage where the only way to protect the environment is at an international level. To what extent do you agree or disagree with this opinion?

10. An increase in production of consumer goods results in the damage of the

natural environment. What are the causes and possible solutions?

11. An increase in the production of popular consumer goods can damage the natural environment. To what extent do you agree or disagree?

12. Pollution and other environmental problems are resulting from a country's developing and becoming richer. Some think this cannot be avoided. To what extent do you agree or disagree?

13. Some people think the international cooperation has brought benefits to the world environment protection, while some people think more benefits have been brought to the international business. Discuss both views and give your own opinion.

14. Many people say that we have developed a "throw-away" culture, because we are filling up our environment with so many plastic bags and rubbish that we cannot fully dispose of. To what extent do you agree or disagree with this opinion and what measures can be taken to reduce this problem?

15. We have entered a throw-away society and fill the environment with rubbish. What are the causes and what are your solutions?

16. Now the increased demand of fresh water has became a global problem. Discuss the causes of the increased demand and what measures the government and individuals should do to solve this problem.

17. The consumption of the resources on the earth such as oil, forests and fresh water is increasing at an alarming rate and above a dangerous level. What are the causes of this? What can be done to solve the problem?

18. Fossil fuels (coal, oil, natural gas) are the main sources in many countries, but in some countries the use of alternative sources of energy (wind energy and solar energy) are encouraged. To what extent do you think it is a positive or negative development?

19. The increasing level of noise pollution has affected people's life significantly. What factors caused this problem? How to solve this problem?

20. The best way to solve the world's environmental problems is to increase the price of fuel. To what extent do you agree or disagree? Use your own experience and give an example to support your idea.

21. The development in technology causes environmental problems. Some people believe the solution to these problems is everyone accepts a simpler way of life, while others say that technology can solve these problems. Discuss both views and give your own opinion.

22. Many tourist attractions such as mountains, rivers and beaches are heavily polluted by visitors. Why is the case? What can be done to change it?

▶ 科技篇

1. The development of technology changes the way people connect with each other. In which way does the development of technology change the types of relationships among people? Does it have positive or negative effects on the relationships?

2. Some people think technology such as mobile phones are destroying the social interaction. Do you disagree or not? Give your reasons and relevant examples.

3. Someone believes that modern telecommunication devices have many benefits to human, while others think otherwise. What is your opinion? Please discuss and use examples to support your own ideas.

4. It is now possible to perform everyday tasks, such as bank transaction, shopping or even office work, without meeting people face to face. What are the effects it may have on individuals and the society as a whole?

5. There are social, medical, and technical problems associated with the use of mobile phones. What forms do they take? Do you agree that the problems outweigh the benefits of the mobile phone?

6. More and more work is done by machines. Do you think the positive impact on the development outweighs the negative impact on individuals or the society?

7. Anyone can use a mobile phone to answer the work call and home call at any place, 7 days a week. Some people think this development has negative effects on both individuals and the society. Do you agree or disagree?

8. There are more workers who work from home and more students who study from home. This is because the computer technology is more and more easily accessible and cheaper. Do you think it is a positive or negative development?

9. Many employees may work at home with modern technology. Some people claim that it can benefit only the workers, not the employers. Do you agree or disagree?

10. The speeding up of life in many areas such as travel and communication has negative effects on society at all levels—individual, national and global. To what extent do you agree or disagree?

11. Food can be produced cheaper if we use improved fertilizers and better machinery. However, some of the methods may be dangerous for human health, and have negative effects on local communities. What is your opinion?

12. The range and quality of the food have been improved by the advancement of science and technology. Discuss the advantages and disadvantages about this and present your view.

13. Some people support the developments in agriculture such as factory farming and creations of new types of fruits and vegetables, while others oppose this view. Discuss both views and give your opinion.

14. Many people believe that the increasing use of modern technology at work and in leisure is reducing people's creativity. To what extent do you agree or disagree?

15. Leisure is a growing industry. Nowadays, more modern technology is used in entertainment, which may lead people to be less creative. Do you agree or disagree?

16. Some people believe that computers and the Internet can take the place of schools, while others contend that teachers play an important role in schools. Discuss both views and give your opinion.

17. Some people claim that public museums and art galleries will not be needed because people can see historical objects and works of art by using a computer. Do you agree or disagree with this opinion?

18. Maintaining public libraries is a waste of money since the computer technology is now replacing their functions. To what extent do you agree or disagree?

19. It is inevitable that as technology develops traditional cultures must be lost. Technology and tradition are incompatible—you cannot have them both

together. To what extent do you agree or disagree?

20. With the increasing use of mobile phones and computers, less people tend to write letters. Some people even think the skill of writing letters will disappear completely. To what extent do you agree or disagree? How important do you think letter writing is?

21. It is not necessary to travel to other places to learn about other cultures. We can learn just as much from books, films and the Internet. To what extent do you agree or disagree?

22. Children spend much time on TV, video and PC games. Some people believe it is good for them while others believe that is bad. Discuss these two views and give your own opinion.

23. Mobile phones and the Internet are very useful. However, it is rare for old people to use them. In what ways could mobile phones and the Internet be useful to old people? How to encourage the old people to uss this new technology?

24. Some people believe that robots will play an important role in future society, while others argue that robots might have negative effects on society. Discuss both views and give your opinion. (OR, Some people think that robots are very important for human's future developments, while others argue that they are dangerous and have negative effects on society. Discuss the advantages and disadvantages brought by intelligent robots.)

25. Lately, more and more work has to be done by machines. To what extent do you think the positive effects of this development outweigh the negative effects on individuals and society?

▸ 政府篇

1. Some people think the government should pay for those who go to university while others believe students should pay themselves. Discuss both views and give your own opinion.

2. Some people say that governments should pay for the public health care and education, while others say that it is not the government's responsibility. Please discuss both views and give your own opinion.

3. As the number of cars increases, more money has to be spent on road systems. Some people think the government should pay for these. Others, however, think that the user should pay for the cost. Discuss both views and give your own opinion.

4. In some countries, when someone gets old they often go to live in a home with other old people where there are nurses to look after them. Sometimes the government has to pay for this care. Who should pay for this care, the government or old people themselves?

5. Some people argue that the companies and private individuals should pay the bill of cleaning up the pollution they produced, while others believe that it is the government's responsibility. What is your opinion?

6. Some people believe that people who work for arts, such as painting, theatre or music should be supported financially by the government. Some people believe that they should find other financial support resources instead. Discuss both views and give your opinion.

7. Some people think it is wrong for the government to spend much money on artistic projects such as sculptures and art galleries. Do you agree or disagree?

8. Some people say the government shouldn't put money on art such as music and painting; they should spend more money on the construction of public facilities. Do you agree or disagree?

9. Some people say the government shouldn't put money on building theaters and sports stadiums; they should spend more money on medical care and education. Do you agree or disagree?

10. Some people believe governments should spend money on saving languages of few speakers from dying out completely. Others think this is a waste of financial resources. Discuss both views and give your position.

11. Maintaining public libraries is a waste of money since the computer technology is so advanced that the Internet and computer can replace them. To what extend do you agree or disagree?

12. Most countries spend a large amount of money in weapons to defend themselves though they are not at war. To the countries it should spend money to help the citizens who are poor and disadvantaged. Do you agree or disagree?

13. The first time when man arrived on Moon, he said: "It's a big step for mankind". But some people think it only made a little impact on our daily life. Millions of dollars has been spent on space research. But somebody says space research wastes money; they suppose money should be used to improve life consumption. To what extent do you agree or disagree?

14. It is more important for the government to spend money on promoting healthy lifestyle to prevent the illness rather than on the treatment for people who are already ill. Do you agree or disagree?

15. Money for postgraduate research is limited. Therefore some people think financial support from governments should be provided only for scientific research rather than research for less useful subjects. Do you agree or disagree?

16. Some people believe that national sports teams and individual men and women who represent their countries should be financially supported by the government. Others think they should be funded by non-government organizations (business, scholarship). Discuss both views and give your position.

17. Many people think that we are spending too much time and money on protecting animals. The money should be spent on human. Do you agree or disagree?

18. The restoration of old buildings in major cities in the world spends numerous government expenditures. This money should be used in new housing and road development. To what extent do you agree or disagree?

19. Some people think the government should encourage a healthy lifestyle while others believe that people can choose to live the way they like. Discuss both views and give your own opinion.

20. Violence in TV programs and movies results in juvenile delinquency. Therefore, the government should impose censorship on the violence in TV programs and movies. To what extent do you agree or disagree?

21. Some people think students should take the subjects which are decided by the government in the university. Others think that students can choose the subjects they prefer. Discuss the two situations and give your opinion.

22. Creative artists should always be given the freedom to express their own ideas

(in words, pictures, music or film) in whichever way they wish. There should be no government restrictions on what they do. To what extent do you agree or disagree?

23. Some countries have introduced a law to limit working hours for employees. Why is the law introduced? Do you think it is a positive or negative development?

24. Nowadays many people enjoy dangerous sports such as mountain climbing or parachuting. Governments should ban these sports to protect the safety of people. To what extent do you agree or disagree with this opinion?

25. In some countries, governments are encouraging industries and businesses to move out of large cities and into regional areas. Do you think the advantages of this development outweigh its disadvantages? Give reasons for you answer and include examples from your knowledge or experiences.

26. In many cities, planners locate schools, homes, offices, shops in specific areas which are widely separate from each other. Do you agree the advantages of this policy outweigh the disadvantages?

27. Some people believe that environmental problems are too big for individuals. Only governments and big companies can make a difference. To what extend do you agree or disagree?

28. The shortage of housing in big cities can cause severe consequences and only governmental actions can solve the problem. Do you agree or disagree?

29. Some people think that good health is very important to every person, so medical services should only be run by the government, not profit-making companies. Do you agree or disagree? (OR, Some people think that good health is a basic human need, so the medical service should not be run by profit-making companies. Do you think the disadvantages of the private health care outweigh the advantages?)

30. Some people think scientific research should be controlled by governments rather than private companies. Do you agree or disagree? (OR, Governments should be responsible for funding and controlling the scientific research rather than private organizations. To what extent do you agree or disagree?)

31. Many governments in developing countries are expanding tourism. Do the

problems outweigh the advantages?

32. Some people say that giving aid to poor countries has more negative effects than positive effects. To what extent do you agree or disagree?

33. Some people think that the way to judge the success of a nation is the quality of average person's life, while some others insist a promising economy should be most essential. What is your opinion?

34. More and more young people hold important positions in government. Some people think it is not suitable but others think otherwise. Discuss both views and give your own opinion.

文化篇

1. Some people think that traditional culture can be destroyed by using it as money-making attractions to tourists. However, others believe that it is the only way to save traditions. Discuss both views and give your opinion.

2. Some people suggest when people move to a new country, they should accept the new culture as their own. To what extent do you agree or disagree?

3. As mass communication and transport continue to grow, societies are becoming more and more alike, leading to a phenomenon known as globalization. Some people fear that globalization will inevitably lead to the total loss of cultural identity. To what extent do you agree or disagree with this statement?

4. Some people say that the increasing business and cultural contact between countries is a positive development, while others think that many countries will lose their national identities. Discuss both views and give your opinion.

5. Some people think that increasing business and cultural contacts have positive influences on development; others think that it has negative effects on national identities. Discuss both views and give your opinion.

6. Exposure to international media, e.g. films, TV and magazines, has an impact on the local culture. Please discuss whether the advantages outweigh the disadvantages.

7. Multi-cultural societies, which are a mixture of different ethnic groups, bring more benefits than drawbacks to a country. To what extent do you agree or disagree

with this conclusion?

8. It is inevitable that as technology develops traditional cultures must be lost. Technology and tradition are incompatible—you cannot have them both together. To what extent do you agree or disagree?

9. Modern buildings have greatly changed the appearance of the city. Yet some people think that buildings should be built in traditional styles to protect the traditional culture. To what extent do you agree or disagree with this opinion?

10. Government should protect the culture; some people believe new buildings should be built in traditional styles. Do you agree or disagree?

11. To learn a language well, we should also learn about the country as well as the cultures and lifestyles of the people who speak the language. To what extent do you agree or disagree?

12. Some people think it is wrong for the government to spend much money on artistic projects such as sculptures and art galleries. Do you agree or disagree?

13. Several languages are in danger of extinction because they are spoken by very small numbers of people. Some people say that governments should spend public money on saving these languages, while others believe that it would be a waste of money. Discuss both views and give your opinion.

14. Some people think that a common language should be adopted globally to improve international communication and understanding. Others, however, think it would lead to the loss of cultural identity. Discuss both views and give your own opinion.

15. Some people think that a new language should be invented for people from different countries to use for international communication. To what extent do you think its advantages far outweigh disadvantages?

▶ 犯罪篇

1. Crime is a problem all over the world and there is nothing that can be done to prevent it. To what extent do you agree or disagree?

2. Many people are afraid to leave home because of crime. Some believe that more actions should be taken to prevent crime, but others feel little can be done.

What's your view?

3. Some people think the best way of reducing crime is to give longer prison sentences. Others, however, think there are other better ways to reduce crime. Discuss both views and give your own opinion.

4. Some people think that all the lawbreakers should be sent into the jail, while others believe that they should also be made to do some work or learn some skills in the community. What is your opinion?

5. Putting criminals into prison is not so effective in dealing with them. Instead, education and job training should be offered to them. To what extent do you agree or disagree?

6. Some people think the only purpose of prison is to punish crime. Others think it has other functions. Discuss the two views and give your opinions.

7. More and more measures to improve the security in the urban area have been introduced because of the increased crime. Do the benefits of the measures outweigh the drawbacks?

8. It is reported that most/many criminals commit crime again when they are released from prison. What are the causes and how can we solve this problem?

9. Some people think the media should not report details of crimes to the public. To what extent do you agree or disagree? (OR, Detailed reporting on crime in the mass media can have bad effects on society. To what extent do you agree or disagree?)

10. In some countries, young criminals are not put in to prison; instead, they are required to do unpaid work in community. Do you think it has more advantages or disadvantages?

11. Statistics suggest that nowadays an increasing number of crimes are committed by the young people. What are its causes and how can we solve this problem? (OR, In some countries, the rate of teenagers' criminal acts is increasing. What are the reasons? Give your measures to reduce it. OR, What are the possible causes for, and solutions to, juvenile delinquency?)

12. Violence in TV programs and movies results in juvenile delinquency. Therefore, the government should impose censorship on the violence in TV programs and

movies. To what extent do you agree or disagree?

13. Today there is a general increase in anti-social behaviors. What might have caused this situation? How to improve it?

14. Many scientists believe that now we can study the behavior of a three-year-old child to see whether they will grow up to be criminals. To what extent do you think the human nature produces crime? And how can we prevent children from growing up to be criminals?

15. Young people who commit serious crimes should be punished in the same way as adults. Do you agree or disagree?

16. Society is based on rules and laws. It could not function if individuals were free to do whatever they want. To what extent do you agree or disagree?

17. Some people think there should be fixed punishments for each type of crime while others think the motivation and the effects of the crime should be considered while deciding on the punishment. What's your opinion?

18. Some people believe that the police force carrying guns would cause a high level of violence. Do you agree or disagree?

▶ 社会生活篇

1. Today, the high sales of popular goods reflect the power of advertising and not the real needs of the society in which they are sold. To what extent do you agree or disagree?

2. If a product is good or it meets people's needs, people will buy it. So advertising is unnecessary and no more than an entertainment. To what extent do you agree or disagree?

3. Advertising encourages consumers to buy in quantity rather than promoting quality. To what extent do you agree or disagree?

4. Consumers are faced with increasing numbers of advertisements from competing companies. To what extent do you think consumers are influenced by advertisements? What measures can be taken to protect them?

5. The society would benefit from a ban on all forms of advertising because it serves

no useful purpose, and can even be damaging. To what extent do you agree or disagree with this opinion?

6. Advertising discourages people from becoming different individuals and makes them look the same. Do you agree or disagree?

7. There is an increasing amount of advertising directed at children which encourages them to buy goods such as toys and snacks. Many parents are worried that these advertisements put too much pressure on children, while some advertisers claim that they provide useful information to children. Discuss both views and give your opinion.

8. Every day people are presented with different news reports. Some people think we should not trust these reports. To what extent do you agree or disagree with it? What qualities should journalists have?

9. News media is more influential nowadays. Some people think it is a negative development. To what extent do you agree or disagree?

10. News media are important in modern society. Why are they important? Are their influences generally positive or negative?

11. Newspapers have become an enormous influence on people's ideas and opinions. Why is this case? Is it a positive or negative situation?

12. Today, there are more and more reports on violence and disasters in the media. Why is the case? What effects can this have?

13. Some people think that the use of animal for experimentation is cruel. Others think it is good for the development of science. Discuss the two sides and give your opinion.

14. It is no longer necessary that animals should be slaughtered and made into either human foodstuffs or non-foodstuffs, such as fur and medicine. Do you agree or disagree?

15. In many countries, the proportion of older people is steadily increasing. Does this trend have more positive or negative effects on the society?

16. Some people say that workers over 55 must retire while some disagree. What's your opinion?

17. Some people believe that personal happiness is directly related to one's material wealth. Others believe there are other factors. Discuss the two sides and give your opinion.

18. In modern society, fashion is becoming more and more popular in people's choice of clothes. Why? Do you think it is a positive development or a negative development?

19. An increasing number of people change their career and place of residence several times during their lives. Is this a positive or negative development?

20. Some people say job satisfaction is more important than job security, while others think people cannot always expect to enjoy their work so finding a permanent job is more important. Discuss both views and give your own opinion.

21. In some countries, small town-centre shops are out of business because people are driving to large out-of-town stores. As a result, people without cars have limited access to shops, so more and more people buy cars. Do you think the disadvantages of this development outweigh the advantages?

22. Some people say that it brings more negative effects when rich countries help poor countries. To what extent do you agree or disagree?

23. Many people are optimistic about the 21st century and see it as an opportunity to make positive changes to the world. To what extent do you agree or disagree with their optimism? What changes would you like to see in the new century?

24. Modern lifestyles make many people hard to lead active and healthy lives. What are the factors contributing to that? How to suggest the governments and other large companies helping them do more exercise?

25. In recent years, traffic jam has become a headache problem around the world. In order to solve this problem, some people think governments have to build wider roads to satisfy and solve the traffic jam. Do you agree or disagree?

26. The quality of life in the city is getting worse and worse. What are the possible reasons and what can be done to improve the situation?

（二）cause + solution 雅思大作文

▶ 青少年篇

1. In some countries, the rate of teenagers' criminal acts is increasing. What are the reasons? Give your measures to reduce it.

2. The incidence of violence/crimes for young people is increasing. Give possible reasons and recommendations of punishment and measures to the situation.

3. Recent research shows that the majority of the criminals who are sent into the prison continue to commit crimes after they are set free. What do you think about the case? What should be done to solve this problem?

4. Many schools have problems with student behavior. What are the possible causes? What measures can be taken to improve the situation?

5. Young people are now less respectful and polite than before. What are its causes and what solutions can be taken to solve this problem?

6. Teenagers have problems at both home and school. What difficulties are they facing now? What should parents and schools do to help them?

7. In some countries young people have little leisure time and are under a lot of pressure to work hard at their studies. What do you think are the causes of this? What solutions can you suggest?

8. Many young people nowadays leave school with negative attitudes towards learning. Why does this happen? What do you think would encourage young people to have a positive attitude?

9. Many children spend much time on watching TV and seldom do active and creative activities. Why do you think this is a case? What measures will be helpful to change this situation?

10. In many countries, after young people graduate, they still have little chance to find a job. What do you think are the reasons for this from individual and social angles? What solutions would you suggest?

11. Nowadays children are becoming lazier and lazier while in the meantime they are getting fatter and unsociable. Give reasons and solutions.

12. Today, fewer and fewer young people pursue a career in teaching. Why is the case? What can be done to change the situation?

▶ 环境篇

13. Many people say that we have developed a "throw-away" culture, because we are filling up our environment with so many plastic bags and rubbish that we cannot fully dispose of. To what extent do you agree or disagree with this opinion and what measures can be taken to solve this problem?

14. We have entered a throw-away society and fill the environment with rubbish. What are the causes and what are your solutions?

15. Many people think it is very important to protect the environment, but they make no effort to do it themselves. Why does it happen? How to solve this problem?

16. In many tourist attractions such as lakes, mountains and beaches, the environment is polluted because of the rubbish and litters produced by tourists. Why is this? How can we solve the problem?

17. The level of noise around us is constantly increasing, and is affecting the quality of our lives. What causes the noise? What should be done about it?

18. The increasing level of noise pollution has affected people's life significantly. What factors caused this problem? How to solve this problem?

19. Now, more and more people want to buy cars. However, cars cause many problems. What are these problems? How can we encourage people to take public transportation?

20. Traffic is developing rapidly all round the world at present. What are the traffic problems in your country? What causes these problems? Give some recommendations of solution.

21. Some people think building more roads can reduce the traffic problems. What do you think of this solution?

22. The unlimited use of cars may cause many problems. What are those problems? In order to solve the problems, should we discourage people to use cars?

23. The natural resources such as oil, forests and fresh water are being consumed

at an alarming rate. What problems does it cause? How can we solve these problems?

24. In many countries around the world, there is a serious shortage of water. What are the causes of and the possible solutions to the scarcity of water resources?

▷ 社会生活篇

25. Many people have unhealthy diet and do not do enough exercises. What are the reasons for this? How can we encourage people to have a healthier lifestyle?

26. Doctors say that in many countries, people do not have enough physical exercise. What are the causes for this problem? What can be done to solve it?

27. Modern lifestyles make many people hard to lead active and healthy lives. Why? How to suggest the governments and other large companies helping them do more exercise?

28. International travel sometimes makes people more prejudiced rather than board-minded. Give out reasons why it cannot bring benefits to those visitors. Do you have ways to improve people's understanding of the countries they visit?

29. People's attitude towards international travel turns to be more prejudiced instead of open-minded. Why is the case? What can be done to improve the situation?

30. Nowadays, many people have to work longer time, and they feel more stressed than before. What are the reasons? What can the employers do to make the employees' life easier?

31. There is too much stress in the workplace. What can employees and employers do about it?

32. Many people change their jobs often. Why is the case? What can the employers do to make the employees stay?

33. Many people want to have both a successful career and a happy family life. What problems are involved in combining a career and the family life? How to overcome such problems?

34. Many people believe that today there is a general increase in anti-social

behaviors and lack of respect for others. What might have caused this situation? How to improve it?

35. Today there is a great increase in anti-social behaviors and lack of respect for others. What are the causes of this? Who should take responsibility for dealing with it?

36. Some people say that it is impossible to live comfortably in big cities. What problems are faced by the people living in big cities? What solutions can be taken to solve those problems?

37. Today, the quality of life in some big cities is getting worse. What are the causes for this problem? What measures should be taken to deal with the problem?

38. What problems for the young people living in major cities are caused by the development of the cities? How to solve those problems?

39. The movement of people from agricultural areas to cities to work can cause serious problems in both places. What are the serious problems and what measures can be taken to solve those problems?

40. The gap between the rich and the poor is widening. Why is the case? What can be done to improve the situation?

41. It is generally acknowledged that families are now not so close as they used to be. What are the possible reasons and what can be done to reverse the trend?

附录 2
雅思评分标准

雅思听力与阅读（A&G）评分标准

Number of correct Listening answers	IELTS band score	Number of correct Reading answers（A）	IELTS band score	Number of correct Reading answers（G）	IELTS band score
39-40	9.0	39-40	9.0	40	9.0
37-38	8.5	37-38	8.5	39	8.5
35-36	8.0	35-36	8.0	38	8.0
33-34	7.5	33-34	7.5	36-37	7.5
30-32	7.0	30-32	7.0	34-35	7.0
27-29	6.5	27-29	6.5	32-33	6.5
23-26	6.0	23-26	6.0	30-31	6.0
20-22	5.5	20-22	5.5	26-29	5.5
16-19	5.0	16-19	5.0	23-25	5.0
13-15	4.5	13-15	4.5	19-22	4.5
10-12	4.0	10-12	4.0	15-18	4.0
6-9	3.5	6-9	3.5	12-14	3.5
4-5	3.0	4-5	3.0	8-11	3.0
3	2.5	3	2.5	5-7	2.5
2	2.0	2	2.0	2-4	2.0
1	1.0	1	1.0	1	1.0
absent	0.0	absent	0.0	absent	0.0

（资料来源：以上表格来自互联网，原始来源不详。）

➢ Task 1 评分标准

Band	Task Achievement	Coherence and Cohesion	Lexical Resource	Grammatical Range and Accuracy
9	◆ fully satisfies all the requirements of the task ◆ clearly presents a fully developed response	◆ uses cohesion in such a way that it attracts no attention ◆ skilfully manages paragraphing	◆ uses a wide range of vocabulary with very natural and sophisticated control of lexical features; rare minor errors occur only as 'slips'	◆ uses a wide range of structures with full flexibility and accuracy; rare minor errors occur only as 'slips'
8	◆ covers all requirements of the task sufficiently ◆ presents, highlights and illustrates key features / bullet points clearly and appropriately	◆ sequences information and ideas logically ◆ manages all aspects of cohesion well ◆ uses paragraphing sufficiently and appropriately	◆ uses a wide range of vocabulary fluently and flexibly to convey precise meanings ◆ skilfully uses uncommon lexical items but there may be occasional inaccuracies in word choice and collocation ◆ produces rare errors in spelling and/or word formation	◆ uses a wide range of structures ◆ the majority of sentences are error-free ◆ makes only very occasional errors or inappropriacies
7	◆ covers the requirements of the task ◆ (Academic) presents a clear overview of main trends, differences or stages ◆ (General Training) presents a clear purpose, with the tone consistent and appropriate ◆ clearly presents and highlights key features / bullet points but could be more fully extended	◆ logically organises information and ideas; there is clear progression throughout ◆ uses a range of cohesive devices appropriately although there may be some under-/over-use	◆ uses a sufficient range of vocabulary to allow some flexibility and precision ◆ uses less common lexical items with some awareness of style and collocation ◆ may produce occasional errors in word choice, spelling and/or word formation	◆ uses a variety of complex structures ◆ produces frequent error-free sentences ◆ has good control of grammar and punctuation but may make a few errors

Band	Task Achievement	Coherence and Cohesion	Lexical Resource	Grammatical Range and Accuracy
6	◆ addresses the requirements of the task ◆ (Academic) presents an overview with information appropriately selected ◆ (General Training) presents a purpose that is generally clear; there may be inconsistencies in tone ◆ presents and adequately highlights key features / bullet points but details may be irrelevant, inappropriate or inaccurate	◆ arranges information and ideas coherently and there is a clear overall progression ◆ uses cohesive devices effectively, but cohesion within and/or between sentences may be faulty or mechanical ◆ may not always use referencing clearly or appropriately	◆ uses an adequate range of vocabulary for the task ◆ attempts to use less common vocabulary but with some inaccuracy ◆ makes some errors in spelling and/or word formation, but they do not impede communication	◆ uses a mix of simple and complex sentence forms ◆ makes some errors in grammar and punctuation but they rarely reduce communication
5	◆ generally addresses the task; the format may be inappropriate in places ◆ (Academic) recounts detail mechanically with no clear overview; there may be no data to support the description ◆ (General Training) may present a purpose for the letter that is unclear at times; the tone may be variable and sometimes inappropriate ◆ presents, but inadequately covers, key features / bullet points; there may be a tendency to focus on details	◆ presents information with some organisation but there may be a lack of overall progression ◆ makes inadequate, inaccurate or over-use of cohesive devices ◆ may be repetitive because of lack of referencing and substitution	◆ uses a limited range of vocabulary, but this is minimally adequate for the task ◆ may make noticeable errors in spelling and/or word formation that may cause some difficulty for the reader	◆ uses only a limited range of structures ◆ attempts complex sentences but these tend to be less accurate than simple sentences ◆ may make frequent grammatical errors and punctuation may be faulty; errors can cause some difficulty for the reader

Band	Task Achievement	Coherence and Cohesion	Lexical Resource	Grammatical Range and Accuracy
4	◆ attempts to address the task but does not cover all key features / bullet points; the format may be inappropriate ◆ (General Training) fails to clearly explain the purpose of the letter; the tone may be inappropriate ◆ may confuse key features / bullet points with detail; parts may be unclear, irrelevant, repetitive or inaccurate	◆ presents information and ideas but these are not arranged coherently and there is no clear progression in the response ◆ uses some basic cohesive devices but these may be inaccurate or repetitive	◆ uses only basic vocabulary which may be used repetitively or which may be inappropriate for the task ◆ has limited control of word formation and/or spelling ◆ errors may cause strain for the reader	◆ uses only a very limited range of structures with only rare use of subordinate clauses ◆ some structures are accurate but errors predominate, and punctuation is often faulty
3	◆ fails to address the task, which may have been completely misunderstood ◆ presents limited ideas which may be largely irrelevant/repetitive	◆ does not organise ideas logically ◆ may use a very limited range of cohesive devices, and those used may not indicate a logical relationship between ideas	◆ uses only a very limited range of words and expressions with very limited control of word formation and/or spelling ◆ errors may severely distort the message	◆ attempts sentence forms but errors in grammar and punctuation predominate and distort the meaning
2	◆ answer is barely related to the task	◆ has very little control of organisational features	◆ uses an extremely limited range of vocabulary; essentially no control of word formation and/or spelling	◆ cannot use sentence forms except in memorised phrases
1	◆ answer is completely unrelated to the task	◆ fails to communicate any message	◆ can only use a few isolated words	◆ cannot use sentence forms at all
0	◆ does not attend ◆ does not attempt the task in any way ◆ writes a totally memorised response			

写作任务1评分标准（* 评分标准以英文版为准，中文翻译仅供参考。）

分数	写作任务完成情况	连贯与衔接	词汇丰富程度	语法多样性及准确性
9	◆ 完全满足所有的写作任务要求 ◆ 清晰地呈现充分展开的写作内容	◆ 衔接手段运用自如，行文连贯 ◆ 熟练地运用分段	◆ 使用丰富的词汇，能自然地使用并掌握复杂的词汇特征；极少出现轻微错误，且仅属笔误	◆ 完全灵活且准确地运用丰富多样的语法结构；极少出现轻微错误，且仅属笔误
8	◆ 写作内容充分地涵盖了所有的写作任务要求 ◆ 就主要内容 / 要点进行清晰和恰当的呈现、强调以及阐述	◆ 将信息与观点进行有逻辑的排序 ◆ 各种衔接手段运用得当 ◆ 充分且合理地使用分段	◆ 流畅和灵活地使用丰富的词汇，达意准确 ◆ 熟练地使用不常用词汇，但在词语选择及搭配方面有时偶尔出现错误 ◆ 拼写及 / 或构词方面错误极少	◆ 运用丰富多样的语法结构 ◆ 大多数句子准确无误 ◆ 只在极偶然情况下出现错误或存在不当之处
7	◆ 写作内容涵盖写作任务的要求 ◆（学术类）清晰地呈现关于主要趋势、区别或不同阶段的概述 ◆（培训类）清晰地呈现写作目的，行文语气一致且恰当 ◆ 能就主要内容 / 要点进行清晰的呈现与强调，但未能更为充分地展开	◆ 符合逻辑地组织信息及观点；清晰的行文推进贯穿全文 ◆ 恰当地使用一系列衔接手段，尽管有时使用不足或过多	◆ 使用足够的词汇，体现一定的灵活性及准确性 ◆ 使用不常见词汇，对语体及搭配有一定认识 ◆ 在选择用词、拼写及 / 或构词方面可能偶尔出现错误	◆ 运用各种复杂的语法结构 ◆ 多数句子准确无误 ◆ 对语法及标点符号掌握较好，但有时出现少许错误

分数	写作任务完成情况	连贯与衔接	词汇丰富程度	语法多样性及准确性
6	◆根据写作任务要求行文 ◆（学术类）选择恰当的信息进行概述 ◆（培训类）写作目的基本清晰；行文语气有时未能保持前后一致 ◆呈现并充分强调了主要内容 / 要点，但有时含有不相关、不恰当或不准确的细节信息	◆连贯地组织信息及观点，总体来说，能清晰地推进行文发展 ◆有效地使用衔接手段，但句内及 / 或句间的衔接有时有误或过于机械 ◆有时无法一贯清晰或恰当地使用指代	◆使用足够的词汇开展写作任务 ◆试图使用不常用词汇，但有时使用不准确 ◆在拼写及 / 或构词方面有错误，但不影响交流	◆综合使用简单句式与复杂句式 ◆在语法及标点符号方面有一些错误，但这些错误很少影响交流
5	◆基本上能就写作任务行文，但某些地方写作格式有时存在不当之处 ◆（学术类）机械地描述细节，缺乏清晰的概述；有时未能提供数据支持所描述的内容 ◆（培训类）信函有时能体现特定的写作目的，但有时目的不清晰；行文语气变化不定，且有时不得体 ◆呈现但不能充分地涵盖主要内容 / 要点；有时出现着重表述细节的倾向	◆有一定组织性地呈现信息，但总体来说有时缺乏清晰的行文推进 ◆衔接手段不足、不准确或过度使用 ◆由于指代和替换不足显得行文重复	◆使用词汇范围有限，但能达到进行写作任务的最低限度 ◆在拼写及 / 或构词方面可能出现明显的错误，且可能会给读者造成一定的阅读困难	◆仅能使用有限的语法结构 ◆试图使用复杂句，但复杂句的准确性常不及简单句的准确性 ◆可能经常出现语法及标点符号使用的错误；这些错误会给读者造成一定的阅读困难

分数	写作任务完成情况	连贯与衔接	词汇丰富程度	语法多样性及准确性
4	◆ 试图就写作任务要求行文，但未能包含所有主要信息 / 要点；写作格式有时不恰当 ◆（培训类）未能清晰地说明信件的写作目的；行文语气有时不恰当 ◆ 有时混淆主要信息 / 要点与细节信息；部分写作内容有时不清晰、不相关、重复或不准确	◆ 呈现了信息及观点，但未能连贯地组织这些信息及观点，且未能清晰地推进行文发展 ◆ 使用了一些基本的衔接手段，但有时不准确或重复使用	◆ 只使用基本词汇，且有时重复使用这些词汇或使用之于写作任务不恰当的词汇 ◆ 对构词及 / 或拼写掌握有限； ◆ 错误可能给读者造成阅读困难	◆ 仅能使用非常有限的语法结构，只能偶尔使用从句 ◆ 一些语法结构使用正确，但错误占多数，且标点符号经常出错
3	◆ 可能因完全曲解写作任务而未能根据写作任务行文 ◆ 所表达的观点有限，可能大部分并不相关或重复	◆ 不能有逻辑地组织观点 ◆ 所用衔接手段有时非常有限，且有时未能体现观点之间的逻辑关系	◆ 只使用非常有限的词汇及表达方式，对构词及 / 或拼写掌握也非常有限 ◆ 错误可能严重影响信息的传达	◆ 尝试造句，但语法及标点符号错误占多数，意思被扭曲
2	◆ 写作内容与写作任务几乎无关	◆ 在内容组织方面能力非常有限	◆ 词汇的使用极其有限；基本上未能掌握构词及 / 或拼写	◆ 除了使用预先背诵的短语外，无法造句
1	◆ 写作内容与写作任务完全无关	◆ 未能传达任何信息	◆ 仅能孤立地使用少数单词	◆ 完全无法造句
0	◆ 缺考 ◆ 未以任何方式尝试写作 ◆ 写作内容完全是预先背诵的内容			

➢ Task 2评分标准

Band	Task Response	Coherence and Cohesion	Lexical Resource	Grammatical Range and Accuracy
9	◆ fully addresses all parts of the task ◆ presents a fully developed position in answer to the question with relevant, fully extended and well supported ideas	◆ uses cohesion in such a way that it attracts no attention ◆ skilfully manages paragraphing	◆ uses a wide range of vocabulary with very natural and sophisticated control of lexical features; rare minor errors occur only as 'slips'	◆ uses a wide range of structures with full flexibility and accuracy; rare minor errors occur only as 'slips'
8	◆ sufficiently addresses all parts of the task ◆ presents a well-developed response to the question with relevant, extended and supported ideas	◆ sequences information and ideas logically ◆ manages all aspects of cohesion well ◆ uses paragraphing sufficiently and appropriately	◆ uses a wide range of vocabulary fluently and flexibly to convey precise meanings ◆ skilfully uses uncommon lexical items but there may be occasional inaccuracies in word choice and collocation ◆ produces rare errors in spelling and/or word formation	◆ uses a wide range of structures ◆ the majority of sentences are error- free ◆ makes only very occasional errors or inappropriacies
7	◆ addresses all parts of the task ◆ presents a clear position throughout the response ◆ presents, extends and supports main ideas, but there may be a tendency to overgeneralise and/or supporting ideas may lack focus	◆ logically organises information and ideas; there is clear progression throughout ◆ uses a range of cohesive devices appropriately although there may be some under-/over-use ◆ presents a clear central topic within each paragraph	◆ uses a sufficient range of vocabulary to allow some flexibility and precision ◆ uses less common lexical items with some awareness of style and collocation ◆ may produce occasional errors in word choice, spelling and/or word formation	◆ uses a variety of complex structures ◆ produces frequent error-free sentences ◆ has good control of grammar and punctuation but may make a few errors

Band	Task Response	Coherence and Cohesion	Lexical Resource	Grammatical Range and Accuracy
6	◆ addresses all parts of the task although some parts may be more fully covered than others ◆ presents a relevant position although the conclusions may become unclear or repetitive ◆ presents relevant main ideas but some may be inadequately developed/unclear	◆ arranges information and ideas coherently and there is a clear overall progression ◆ uses cohesive devices effectively, but cohesion within and/or between sentences may be faulty or mechanical ◆ may not always use referencing clearly or appropriately ◆ uses paragraphing, but not always logically	◆ uses an adequate range of vocabulary for the task ◆ attempts to use less common vocabulary but with some inaccuracy ◆ makes some errors in spelling and/or word formation, but they do not impede communication	◆ uses a mix of simple and complex sentence forms ◆ makes some errors in grammar and punctuation but they rarely reduce communication
5	◆ addresses the task only partially; the format may be inappropriate in places ◆ expresses a position but the development is not always clear and there may be no conclusions drawn ◆ presents some main ideas but these are limited and not sufficiently developed; there may be irrelevant detail	◆ presents information with some organisation but there may be a lack of overall progression ◆ makes inadequate, inaccurate or over-use of cohesive devices ◆ may be repetitive because of lack of referencing and substitution ◆ may not write in paragraphs, or paragraphing may be inadequate	◆ uses a limited range of vocabulary, but this is minimally adequate for the task ◆ may make noticeable errors in spelling and/or word formation that may cause some difficulty for the reader	◆ uses only a limited range of structures ◆ attempts complex sentences but these tend to be less accurate than simple sentences ◆ may make frequent grammatical errors and punctuation may be faulty; errors can cause some difficulty for the reader

Band	Task Response	Coherence and Cohesion	Lexical Resource	Grammatical Range and Accuracy
4	◆ responds to the task only in a minimal way or the answer is tangential; the format may be inappropriate ◆ presents a position but this is unclear ◆ presents some main ideas but these are difficult to identify and may be repetitive, irrelevant or not well supported	◆ presents information and ideas but these are not arranged coherently and there is no clear progression in the response ◆ uses some basic cohesive devices but these may be inaccurate or repetitive ◆ may not write in paragraphs or their use may be confusing	◆ uses only basic vocabulary which may be used repetitively or which may be inappropriate for the task ◆ has limited control of word formation and/or spelling; errors may cause strain for the reader	◆ uses only a very limited range of structures with only rare use of subordinate clauses ◆ some structures are accurate but errors predominate, and punctuation is often faulty
3	◆ does not adequately address any part of the task ◆ does not express a clear position ◆ presents few ideas, which are largely undeveloped or irrelevant	◆ does not organise ideas logically ◆ may use a very limited range of cohesive devices, and those used may not indicate a logical relationship between ideas	◆ uses only a very limited range of words and expressions with very limited control of word formation and/or spelling ◆ errors may severely distort the message	◆ attempts sentence forms but errors in grammar and punctuation predominate and distort the meaning
2	◆ barely responds to the task ◆ does not express a position ◆ may attempt to present one or two ideas but there is no development	◆ has very little control of organisational features	◆ uses an extremely limited range of vocabulary; essentially no control of word formation and/or spelling	◆ cannot use sentence forms except in memorised phrases
1	◆ answer is completely unrelated to the task	◆ fails to communicate any message	◆ can only use a few isolated words	◆ cannot use sentence forms at all
0	◆ does not attend ◆ does not attempt the task in any way ◆ writes a totally memorised response			

写作任务2评分标准（* 评分标准以英文版为准，中文翻译仅供参考。）

分数	写作任务回应情况	连贯与衔接	词汇丰富程度	语法多样性及准确性
9	◆ 全面地回应各部分写作任务 ◆ 就写作任务中的问题提出充分展开的观点，并提出相关的、得以充分延伸的以及论据充分的论点	◆ 衔接手段运用自如，行文连贯 ◆ 熟练地运用分段	◆ 使用丰富的词汇，能自然地使用并掌握复杂的词汇特征；极少出现轻微错误，且仅属笔误	◆ 完全灵活且准确地运用丰富多样的语法结构；极少出现轻微错误，且仅属笔误
8	◆ 充分地回应各部分写作任务 ◆ 就写作任务中的问题进行较为充分展开的回应，并提出相关的、得以延伸的以及含有论据的论点	◆ 将信息与论点进行有逻辑的排序 ◆ 各种衔接手段运用得当 ◆ 充分且合理地使用分段	◆ 流畅和灵活地使用丰富的词汇，达意准确 ◆ 熟练地使用不常用词汇，但在词语选择及搭配方面有时偶尔出现错误 ◆ 拼写及/或构词方面错误极少	◆ 运用丰富多样的语法结构 ◆ 大多数句子准确无误 ◆ 只在极偶然的情况下出现错误或存在不当之处
7	◆ 回应各部分写作任务 ◆ 回应写作任务过程中始终呈现一个清晰的观点 ◆ 呈现、发展主要论点并就其进行论证，但有时出现过于一概而论的倾向及/或论点缺乏重点的倾向	◆ 符合逻辑地组织信息及论点；清晰的行文推进发展贯穿全文 ◆ 恰当地使用一系列衔接手段，尽管有时使用不足或过多 ◆ 每个段落均有一个清晰的中心主题	◆ 使用足够的词汇，体现一定的灵活性及准确性 ◆ 使用不常见词汇，对语体及搭配有一定认识 ◆ 在选择用词、拼写及/或构词方面可能偶尔出现错误	◆ 运用各种复杂的语法结构 ◆ 多数句子准确无误 ◆ 对语法及标点符号掌握较好，但有时出现少许错误

分数	写作任务回应情况	连贯与衔接	词汇丰富程度	语法多样性及准确性
6	◆回应了各部分写作任务，但某些部分的论证可能比其他部分更为充分 ◆提出了一个切题的观点，尽管各种结论有时不甚清晰或重复 ◆提出了多个相关的主要论点，但某些论点可能未能充分展开进行论证或不甚清晰	◆连贯地组织信息及论点，总体来说，能清晰地推进行文发展 ◆有效地使用衔接手段，但句内及/或句间的衔接有时有误或过于机械 ◆有时无法一贯清晰或恰当地使用指代 ◆使用段落写作，但未能保持段落间的逻辑	◆使用足够的词汇开展写作任务 ◆试图使用不常用词汇，但有时使用不准确 ◆在拼写及/或构词方面有错误，但不影响交流	◆综合使用简单句式与复杂句式 ◆在语法及标点符号方面有一些错误，但这些错误很少影响交流
5	◆仅回应了部分写作任务；写作格式有时在某些地方不甚恰当 ◆表述了一个观点，但展开论证过程未能保持一贯清晰，且可能缺乏结论 ◆提出一些主要论点，但十分有限，且未能充分展开论证；有时出现无关细节	◆有一定组织性地呈现信息，但总体来说有时缺乏清晰的行文推进 ◆衔接手段不足、不准确或过度使用 ◆由于指代和替换不足显得行文重复 ◆没有使用段落写作，或者分段不足	◆使用词汇范围有限，但能达到进行写作任务的最低限度 ◆在拼写及/或构词方面可能出现明显的错误，且可能会给读者造成一定的阅读困难	◆仅能使用有限的语法结构 ◆试图使用复杂句，但复杂句的准确性常不及简单句的准确性 ◆可能经常出现语法及标点符号使用的错误；这些错误会给读者造成一定的阅读困难

分数	写作任务回应情况	连贯与衔接	词汇丰富程度	语法多样性及准确性
4	◆仅最低限度地回应了写作任务，或所答相关性不大；写作格式有时不甚恰当 ◆提出了一个观点但并不清晰 ◆提出了一些主要论点但难以在文中确认，且这些观点可能重复、不相关或缺乏论据支持	◆呈现了信息及论点，但未能连贯地组织这些信息及论点，且未能清晰地推进行文发展 ◆使用了一些基本的衔接手段，但有时不准确或重复使用 ◆没有使用段落写作，或段落使用造成疑惑	◆只使用基本词汇，且有时重复使用这些词汇或使用之于写作任务不恰当的词汇 ◆对构词及/或拼写掌握有限；错误可能给读者造成阅读困难	◆仅能使用非常有限的语法结构，只能偶尔使用从句 ◆一些语法结构使用正确，但错误占多数，且标点符号经常出错
3	◆未能足以回应任一部分的写作任务 ◆未能表达一个清晰的论点 ◆提出甚少论点，且基本上未能就其展开论证或观点不切题	◆不能有逻辑地组织论点 ◆所用衔接手段有时非常有限，且有时未能体现论点之间的逻辑关系	◆只使用非常有限的词汇及表达方式，对构词及/或拼写掌握也非常有限 ◆错误可能严重地影响信息的传达	◆尝试造句，但语法及标点符号错误占多数，意思被扭曲
2	◆几乎未回应写作任务 ◆未能表达一个观点 ◆可能试图提出一两个论点，但未能展开论证	◆在内容组织方面能力非常有限	◆词汇的使用极其有限；基本上未能掌握构词及/或拼写	◆除了使用预先背诵的短语外，无法造句
1	◆写作内容与写作任务完全无关	◆未能传达任何信息	◆仅能孤立地使用少数单词	◆完全无法造句
0	◆缺考 ◆未以任何方式尝试写作 ◆写作内容完全是预先背诵的内容			

附录3
雅思写作答题纸

2014年，雅思写作的答题纸有所变化。具体如下：

1. 答题纸改为Task 1和Task 2分开，有两份答题纸。
2. Task 1答题纸为黄色，Task 2答题纸为白色。
3. Task 1及Task 2都需要填写考生信息。
4. Task 1正面有15行，背面有24行。行间距缩小30%至0.8CM。
5. 新加入了条形码。
6. 写作是由两位考官批改，一位打分，一位复核。

（资料来源：http://edu.163.com/14/0821/11/A45UHF1L00293L7F.html）

BRITISH COUNCIL　idp IELTS AUSTRALIA　CAMBRIDGE ENGLISH Language Assessment Part of the University of Cambridge

IELTS Writing Answer Sheet – TASK 1

Candidate Name

Centre Number　　Candidate Number

Module (shade one box):　Academic　General Training

Test date　D D　M M　Y Y Y Y

新版增加了二维码 **TASK 1**

Task1正面有15行

Do not write below this line

Task 1答题纸为黄色

总共有24行，行间距缩小30%至0.8CM

Do not write below this line

OFFICIAL USE ONLY

写作是由两位考官批改，一位打分，一位复核

Candidate Number:		TA		CC		LR		GRA
Examiner 2 Number:		Underlength	No. of words	Penalty		Off-topic	Memorised	Illegible

Candidate Number:		TA		CC		LR		GRA
Examiner 1 Number:		Underlength	No. of words	Penalty		Off-topic	Memorised	Illegible

BRITISH COUNCIL   idp IELTS AUSTRALIA   CAMBRIDGE ENGLISH Language Assessment Part of the University of Cambridge

IELTS Writing Answer Sheet – TASK 2

Candidate Name

Centre Number　　Candidate Number

Module (shade one box):　Academic　General Training

Test date　D D　M M　Y Y Y Y

TASK 2

Task 2也需要填考生信息

SAMPLE

Do not write below this line

Task 2答题纸为白色

100896/2

SAMPLE

6项低分项目位置为一排，请大家注意规避

Do not write below this line

OFFICIAL USE ONLY

Candidate Number:		TR		CC		LR		GRA
Examiner 2 Number:		Underlength	No. of words	Penalty		Off-topic	Memorised	Illegible
Candidate Number:		TR		CC		LR		GRA
Examiner 1 Number:		Underlength	No. of words	Penalty		Off-topic	Memorised	Illegible

IELTS
IELTS
IELTS
IELTS
IELTS
IELTS
IELTS
IELTS
IELTS
IELTS
IELTS
IELTS
IELTS
IELTS
IELTS
IELTS
IELTS

我们的真诚回报

亲爱的读者朋友，首先感谢您阅读我社图书，请您在阅读完本书后填写以下信息。我社将长期开展『读石油版书，获亲情馈赠』活动，凡是关注我社图书并认真填写读者信息反馈卡的朋友都有机会获得亲情馈赠，我们将定期从信息反馈卡中评选出有价值的意见和建议，并为填写这些信息的读者朋友免费赠送一本好书。

您的资料

您的姓名：__________ 性别：__________ 出生年月：__________ 电话：__________

文化程度：__________ 单位名称：__________

通信地址：__________ 邮编__________

E-mail：__________ 特别提示新老读者：您的资料是我们与您取得联系、反馈信息最重要的途径，请务必填写工整。如果您的联络方式发生了变化，请再次填写此卡并及时邮寄或传真到我社。

您的意见《雅思写作题库全攻略》

您填写本卡的时间是：________年____月____日

是什么促使您决定购买本书的？

○封面○书名○内容○版式○亲朋好友推荐○索引及目录

如果是报纸或杂志的书评，请写明具体报刊名称：__________

您在何处购买到本书（请写明具体书店的名称）：

○新华书店__________ ○民营书店__________

○大型书城__________ ○其他__________

您希望通过什么渠道获得我社新书的消息：

○信函○传真○书店○网络○其他__________

您愿意成为我们的会员吗？○愿意○不愿意

您会推荐本书给您的亲朋好友吗？__________

您对本书的综合评价和建议：__________

____

您最喜欢的一本书是什么？__________

您最喜欢的作者是谁？__________

别忘了保持联系

联系地址：北京安定门外安华西里三区 18 号楼 1001 室 石油工业出版社 大众图书出版公司 朱世元

邮编：100011 E-mail：shiyuan zhu@263.net